Micro-ISV
From Vision to Reality

Bob Walsh

Micro-ISV: From Vision to Reality

Copyright © 2006 by Bob Walsh

ISBN-13 (pbk): 978-1-59059-601-2
ISBN-10 (pbk): 1-59059-601-3

Printed and bound in the United States of America 9 8 7 6 5 4 3 2

Lead Editor: Jonathan Hassell
Technical Reviewers: Craig Snyder, Thomas Rushton
Editorial Board: Steve Anglin, Dan Appleman, Ewan Buckingham, Gary Cornell, Tony Davis, Jason Gilmore, Jonathan Hassell, Chris Mills, Dominic Shakeshaft, Jim Sumser
Project Manager: Kylie Johnston
Copy Edit Manager: Nicole LeClerc
Copy Editor: Kim Wimpsett
Assistant Production Director: Kari Brooks-Copony
Production Editor: Lori Bring
Compositor: Susan Glinert
Proofreader: Linda Seifert
Indexer: Carol Burbo
Cover Designer: Kurt Krames
Manufacturing Director: Tom Debolski

Distributed to the book trade worldwide by Springer-Verlag New York, Inc., 233 Spring Street, 6th Floor, New York, NY 10013. Phone 1-800-SPRINGER, fax 201-348-4505, e-mail orders-ny@springer-sbm.com, or visit http://www.springeronline.com.

For information on translations, please contact Apress directly at 2560 Ninth Street, Suite 219, Berkeley, CA 94710. Phone 510-549-5930, fax 510-549-5939, e-mail info@apress.com, or visit http://www.apress.com.

The source code for this book is available to readers at http://www.apress.com in the Source Code section.

This book is for the woman I love and my partner in life, love, and work: Tina Marie Rossi.

Contents at a Glance

Contents

Foreword

How the heck did *I* become the poster child for the micro-ISV movement?

Of all people. Sheesh.

When I started Fog Creek Software, there was gonna be nothing "micro" about it. The plan was to build a big, multinational software company with offices in 120 countries and a skyscraper headquarters in Manhattan, complete with a heliport on the roof for quick access to the Hamptons. It might be a few decades—after all, we were going to be bootstrapped, and we always planned to grow slowly and carefully—but our ambitions were anything but small.

Heck, I don't even *like* the term *micro-ISV*. The *ISV* part stands for Independent Software Vendor. It's a made-up word, made up by Microsoft, to mean "software company that is not Microsoft," or, more specifically, "software company that for some reason we have not yet bought or eliminated, probably because they are in some charming, twee line of business, like wedding table arrangements, the quaintness of which we are just *way* too cool to stoop down to, but you little people feel free to enjoy yourselves. Just remember to use .NET!"

It's like that other term, *legacy*, that Microsoft uses to refer to all non-Microsoft software. So when they refer to Google, say, as a *legacy search engine*, they are trying to imply that Google is merely "an old, crappy search engine that you're still using by historical accident, until you bow to the inevitable and switch to MSN." What*ever*.

I prefer *software company*, and there's nothing wrong with being a start-up. *Start-up software company*, that's how we describe ourselves, and we don't see any need to define ourselves in relation to Microsoft.

I suppose you're reading this book because you want to start a small software company, and it's a good book to read for that purpose, so let me use my pulpit here to provide you with my personal checklist of three things you should have before you start your micro...*ahem*, start-up software company. You should also do some other things—Bob covers them pretty well in the rest of the book—but before you get started, here's my contribution.

Number One: Don't start a business if you can't explain what pain it solves, for whom, why your product will eliminate this pain, and how the customer will pay to solve this pain. The other day I went to a presentation of six high-tech start-ups and not *one* of them had a clear idea for what pain they were proposing to solve. For example, I saw a start-up that was building a way to set a time to meet your friends for coffee, a start-up that wanted you to install a plug-in in your browser to track your every movement online in exchange for being able to delete things from that history, and a start-up that wanted you to be able to leave text messages for your friend who was tied to a particular location (so if they ever walked past the same bar they could get a message you had left for them there). What they all had in common was that none of them solved a problem, and all of them were as doomed as a long-tailed cat in a room full of rocking chairs.

Number Two: Don't start a business by yourself. I know, there are lots of successful one-person start-ups, but there are even more failed one-person start-ups. If you can't even convince *one friend* that your idea has merit...um...maybe it doesn't. Besides, it's lonely and depressing, and you won't have anyone to bounce ideas off of. And when the going gets tough, which it will, as a one-person operation, you'll just fold up shop. With two people, you'll feel an obligation to your partner to push on through. (P.S. Cats do not count.)

Number Three: Don't expect much at first. People never know how much money they're going to make in the first month when their product goes on sale. I remember five years ago, when we started selling FogBugz, we had no idea if the first month of sales would be $0 or $50,000. Both figures seemed just as likely to me. I have talked to enough entrepreneurs and have enough data now to give you a definitive answer for *your* start-up.

That's right, I have a crystal ball and can now tell you the one fact you need to know more than anything else: exactly how much money you're going to make during the first month after your product goes live.

Ready?

OK.

In the first month, you are going to make…

about…

$364, *if you do everything right*. If you charge too little, you're going to make $40. If you charge too much, you're going to make $0. If you expect to make any more than that, you're going to be really disappointed and you're going to give up and get a job working for The Man and referring to us people in start-up-land as *legacy micro-ISVs*.

That $364 sounds depressing, but it's not, because you'll soon discover the one fatal flaw that's keeping 50 percent of your potential customers from whipping out their wallets, and then *tada!* you'll be making $728 a month. And then you'll work really hard, and you'll get some publicity, and you'll figure out how to use AdWords effectively, and there will be a story about your company in the local wedding planner newsletter, and *tada!* You'll be making $1,456 a month. And you'll ship version 2.0, with spam filtering and a Common Lisp interpreter built in, and your customers will chat amongst themselves, and *tada!* You'll be making $2,912 a month. And you'll tweak the pricing, add support contracts, ship version 3.0, and get mentioned by Jon Stewart on *The Daily Show* and *tada!* $5,824 a month.

Now we're cooking with fire. Project out a few years, and if you plug away at it, there's no reason you can't double your revenues every 12 to 18 months. So, no matter how small you start (detailed math formula omitted—*Ed.*), you'll soon be building your own skyscraper in Manhattan with a heliport so you can get to that 20-acre Southampton spread in 30 minutes flat.

And that, I think, is the real joy of starting a company: creating something all by yourself, nurturing it, working on it, investing in it, watching it grow, and watching the investments pay off. It's a hell of a journey, and I wouldn't miss it for the world.

Joel Spolsky
Cofounder, Fog Creek Software

About the Author

 **BOB WALSH** has been a contract software developer in the San Francisco Bay Area for the past 22 years, specializing in desktop information systems. His company, Safari Software, has for the past decade amazingly focused on the same thing, albeit at a higher hourly rate.

In 2003, as outsourcing finished what the dot-com bust started, he developed MasterList Standard Version, an Excel-based project and task management application. Two years and 40,000 users later, Safari Software became a real, live, rootin'-tootin' micro-ISV by releasing MasterList Professional, a Windows personal project and task management application that, unlike traditional time management tools, gives you total control over your business and personal life while improving how you spend your time.

Before joining the ranks of the computer industry, Bob was a reporter for several news organizations, most worth bragging about being United Press International (UPI).

About the Technical Reviewers

CRAIG SNYDER is currently the chief software architect for Inclue, the publisher of a new RSS/Web feed reader for Microsoft Outlook.

Craig has a bachelor's degree in computer science from a local university in San Diego and and has more than 25 years of experience in all facets of engineering and engineering management, including software development, quality assurance, and technical publications for start-ups and established organizations. Craig has a diverse background in several vertical markets spanning entertainment, financial, Internet security, homeland security, industrial controls, customer management, real estate, and communications.

THOMAS RUSHTON has been programming since his first computer, a Sinclair ZX80. He has since progressed through creating complex workflow and document management systems for financial and legal organizations and now works as the IT technical development manager for a U.K.-based law firm. He has a bachelor's degree in computer science from Durham University and spent some research time in the field of software quality before moving into the more financially rewarding IT career roles of programmer, DBA, and consultant.

When not slaving away over a hot keyboard, he enjoys spending time with his wife, Sarah; their young son, William; and his double bass.

Acknowledgments

Acknowledgement sections of books tend to get skipped by readers eager to get to the good stuff, and that's a shame because without these people this book would not have happened.

First off to my Apress editor, Jonathan Hassell, and project manager, Kylie Johnston: thanks guys for your help and support and for holding my feet to the fire when deadlines loomed! Also thanks to Kim Wimpsett for whacking my poor prose into proper copyedited shape, Kurt Krames for the cover, and to Susan Glinert and Lori Bring for getting everything to actually fit on a printed page.

Next off, Joel Spolsky, who helped sell Apress on the idea of this book, let me badger him with questions and has helped hundreds of developers with Joel on Software: thanks, Joel!

A great many people were interviewed for this book, and to each and every one of them I say, thanks for taking the time out of your busy lives to answer my questions about what you do.

Introduction

In February 2005, after releasing my first commercial application, I went looking for all sorts of information that would help me market, support, and improve my product. I wasn't especially happy with what I found.

There were books aplenty on starting retail businesses, restaurants, inns—you name it—except a self-funded software company. There were a few pre-Internet books, now mostly out of print, about how to start a shareware company, and there were a few books out about how to write the killer business plan that would woo venture capitalists to fund your start-up but nothing about how to define a product, develop it, support it, market it, and do all this 100 percent on the Web.

I did find one really good Web site, the Business of Software forum at Joel on Software (`http://discuss.joelonsoftware.com/?biz`), where a whole bunch of developers starting or running companies would offer suggestions and advice to anyone politely asking.

As plentiful as the advice was at Joel on Software, it tended to be uneven and fragmentary. I decided that if there wasn't a single good book on how to start an Internet-based software company, then I should go out there and research and write one. This is that book.

A very long time ago, before becoming a programmer, then a developer, I was a reporter. I figured that if I dusted off my old journalism habits and went looking for the information I and lots of other developers needed, I could find people out there with the answers.

What I did not figure on when I started this book was that there is real *news* going on here: from Boise to Bulgaria, developers are starting their own companies to bring to market their own solutions in record numbers.

For every Internet software vendor you read about who just got funded by one or another venture capital funds, there are hundreds of micro–Internet software vendors successfully building desktop applications and Web-based products, distributing their software exclusively on the Net, and building companies that start with one person and often scale up to 20, 50, and 100 employees in a few short years.

Who This Book Is For

This book is for that one developer who starts the whole thing off. One day, after yet another mind-numbing meeting at Big Company, Inc., when they've had a bellyful of working for clueless people, I want that developer to go searching with Google or browsing Amazon, find this book, and see how the pieces can come together for them to start their own, wildly successful micro-ISV.

I'm assuming you already know how to code: in fact, this is one of those rare Apress books without a single line of code! What I'm guessing you're looking for is really current, Internet-centric information about how to go from the desire to be your own boss, how to define what you want to work on, and exactly how best to code a solution through all the facets of running an online software business all the way to seeing the money roll in.

How This Book Is Structured

In a lot of ways, this book is a process book. You start at the beginning with a desire and then work through in roughly chronological order all the moving parts you need to connect to get to the point where your micro-ISV is up, running, and making money.

Here's the chapter-by-chapter rundown:

Chapter 1, "Having the Vision": The two big take-aways from this chapter are how we got to a place where micro-ISVs can be successful and how you can find a problem worth solving as your micro-ISV's first product. I'll also cover who thought up this mouthful of a term, *micro-ISV*, and seven rules for avoiding much micro-ISV pain.

Chapter 2, "Developing the Micro-ISV Way": Once you've found the right idea, it's time to get into developing. But not so fast—developing your micro-ISV's product is unlike working at Big Company, Inc., or being a contract developer.

In this chapter, I cover those differences and look at designing your first commercial product, setting up a development environment that leverages your limited time and money to produce high-quality, customer-focused software, and finding and managing beta testers.

Chapter 3, "Presenting the Product": While you're developing away, it's time to look at your product. Your application is not your product. Your application plus your Web site, blog, documentation, installer, license, graphics, collaterals, payment processing, customer experience, and Unique Selling Proposition is your product.

Everything from finding the right domain name to how easy it is to buy your software is going to affect your sales, and in this chapter, I cover a slew of things that go into how potential customers experience your software.

You will especially take a look, bit by bit, at what makes a good micro-ISV Web site good. And I'll talk with Mena Trott, cofounder of Six Apart (makers of TypePad and Movable Type), about how to build a blog that makes friends, builds credibility, and influences potential customers.

Chapter 4, "Business Is Business": This chapter focuses on the business aspects of creating a micro-ISV business: finding the right legal structure for your fledgling firm (in the United States, in the United Kingdom, or in Australia). Once you get the paperwork out of the way, you need to focus on Getting Things Done (GTD), so I'll review the GTD approach many micro-ISVs use and talk with its creator, David Allen, about applying GTD to building and running a micro-ISV.

Chapter 5, "Focusing on the Customer": Now we get to the start of your micro-ISV show—your customers. In this chapter, I cover a systematic way of defining, finding, and marketing to your customers. I'll also cover some of the other ways you interface with your customers: email (wholesale and retail), customer support (a micro-ISV must get right), and how to set up and run a robust discussion forum about your company and its products.

You'll also look at how customers find you on the Net: Search Engine Optimization techniques, download sites, and Google AdWords. And you'll see how you can and should get the attention of reporters and editors in the mainstream media.

Chapter 6, "Welcome to Your Industry": In this chapter you'll broaden your micro-ISV horizons and take a look at what developer and ISV resources are out there that you can benefit from. Interestingly enough, several of those resources come from Microsoft, and whether you love or loath Microsoft, you can't afford to ignore them.

Chapter 7, "What Happens Next?": That's going to be largely up to you. But in this chapter you'll hear from 25 micro and not-so-micro ISVs about how their stories have turned out so far and what advice they'd like to pass on to you.

Appendix: Don't look for 200 pages of error codes and API syntax in this appendix—you won't find it. Instead, I'll recap all the links you've seen in Chapters 1–7 and recommend books for those who want to dig deeper into specific aspects of business, law, productivity, developer best practices, and online marketing.

And yes, the links in this chapter are online! (See the next section.)

Downloading the Code

You'll find all the checklists, templates, and other files for this book, as well as a page of links chapter by chapter, at this book's page at Apress (http://www.apress.com) and at my micro-ISV, Safari Software, at http://safarisoftware.com.

Contacting the Author

Got a question, or want to learn more? Please visit my blog, http://www.todoorelse.com; stop by my micro-ISV's Web site at http://safarisoftware.com; or drop me an email at bobw@safarisoftware.com.

CHAPTER 1

■ ■ ■

Having a Vision

We are told that talent creates its opportunities. But it sometimes seems that intense desire creates not only its own opportunities, but its own talents.

—Eric Hoffer, author and philosopher[1]

This chapter introduces what this book is all about: building a successful micro-ISV. But before getting into all the plans and practices of creating an Internet-based, self-funded, start-up company to sell software, a service, or a product (and make a nice pile of change in the process), I'll discuss a few issues. For example, is it really possible you can—from scratch—build a real, live company in today's global, interconnected, multinational marketplace? And if you can in theory do that, how do you in practice decide on and define an application, a Web service, or a product for which people will pay good money?

The short answer to both questions is the Internet. Ten years ago, when Netscape blew away the collective wisdom of the financial establishment, people wondered, "Where is this Internet thing going?" Now, after a dot-com boom and a bust, as well as tens of thousands of new companies—large and small—selling applications, services, and products not possible ten years ago, you can see where at least some of this is heading:

- The Internet makes possible a different kind of business model than what has worked in the past.

- The Internet means even a one-person company can connect to the right people in a billion-person market instantaneously if that person has something of value to offer.

I could bore you to death right now by citing all the little one-person start-ups that are now 60-person businesses valued in the millions or by citing all the cool apps and products popping up all over the Net being produced by other little companies, but I won't. Well, I'll mention just one: Niklas Zennström and Janus Friis started a company called Skype in Europe late in 2003. It was their fourth start-up, so they had some experience and access to capital and had weathered some legal troubles, but the bottom line was that these two guys built and sold an Internet-based company that delivered a new service to 54 million people in 24 months for $4.1 billion to eBay.

That's $4.1 billion—with a *b*. In 24 months.

---

1. http://quotations.about.com/cs/inspirationquotes/a/Ability12.htm

Still doubt that conventional business wisdom isn't worth the paper it's not written on? Look at your Start menu or your favorite Web sites. Besides Microsoft (or Apple) products, how many of the apps or Web services you use are sold by obviously big companies, and how many are brought to you by inconspicuously small start-ups?

Game, set, and match.

In this chapter, I'll cover four topics: how we got here, what *here* looks like, how you can join the micro-ISV party, and what the cover charge is for getting in the door.

How We Got Here

To understand just how you can make a bigger pile of money than you'd make in a hundred years of working in a corporation's cubicle, you'll have to jump in your handy time machine and go back in history—back before the Internet was public, back before Microsoft had more money than Norway, back when Osborne was a type of computer, back when laptops were bigger than suitcases, and back when coffee came in two flavors: Folgers and Maxwell House.

Let's say your time machine deposited you in San Francisco, California, in 1983. Ignoring the boring politics, economics, and all the rest, what was going on with software and personal computers?

- IBM had made the idea of Personal Computers (PCs) safe for businesses with its IBM PC two years before. PCs were springing up in offices all over the place.

- Hundreds of programs were available for PCs—either running CP/M or the newfangled MS-DOS operating system. But they weren't cheap; you had to buy them to try them, and most were saddled with copy protection schemes heavier than a 20-pound bicycle lock.

- Three programmers—one an IBMer in Bellevue, Washington; one an attorney and computer magazine editor based near San Francisco; and one a programmer who was one of the first programmers to leave Microsoft—each decided to buck this trend of expensive, shrink-wrapped software with a different approach. Jim Knopf (known as Jim Button), Andrew Fluegelman, and Bob Wallace were selling, respectively, a flat-file database, a modem application, and a word processor by giving the software away and requesting a small payment. All three programs, despite distributions limited to fledgling computer clubs, disk duplicators, and word of mouth, did extremely well financially. "I could not have predicted what would happen next," says Jim, in a piece he posted years later on the Internet.[2]

> *My wife said I was "a foolish old man" if I thought even one person would voluntarily send me money for the program. I was more optimistic. I suspected that enough voluntary payments would come to help pay for expansions to my personal computer hobby—perhaps several hundred dollars. Maybe even a thousand dollars (in my wildest dreams!). But my tiny post office box was too small to receive the responses from a wildly enthusiastic public.*

> *I had always said I would never consider leaving my secure job with IBM until I was receiving at least twice as much money from another source. I was wrong. By the summer of 1984 I was making ten times as much with my little software business.*

---

2. http://www.freewarehof.org/sstory.html

In another interview,[3] Jim reiterates the point:

Question: Do you believe being a shareware programmer will make you rich someday?

Answer: Well, it already has. My shareware program PC-File netted many millions of dollars in sales. If I had spent the money more wisely in my business, I would be a gazillionaire today. But as it is, I'm merely comfortably retired.

If you put your time machine in fast-forward mode, you'd see throughout the 1980s the rise and fall of shareware-centric little companies all over the world, filling specific niches in business in the United States and other countries. You'd see little tiny ads in the back of computer magazines and hear the squeal of modems dialing into Bulletin Board Systems (BBSs) at the blazing speed of 9,600 baud.

As you move into the 1990s, click Pause on your time machine in 1994. Marc Andreessen (whose University of Illinois–Champaign's undergraduate project had, through his strong tech support efforts, gotten a lot of attention) hooked up with one of the Silicon Valley start-up legends, Jim Clark. They started a company, and after a quick name change pressed on them by Andreessen's alma mater, Netscape Communications started giving away the first commercial Internet browser, as shown in Figure 1-1.

Over the next five years, Netscape went from the third largest initial public offering ever on the NASDAQ stock exchange to Microsoft roadkill. While the "browser wars" and "search engine wars" were being fought on the Internet, the number of people and businesses using the Internet continued to grow like some sort of mad scientist's dream project. Meanwhile, venture capital–funded start-ups intent on becoming first movers of *something* were having nightly bonfires of greenbacks in the City by the Bay, and Internet Millionaires were roaming Ferrari dealerships looking for new toys to buy. The dot-com boom was in full swing.

As you get to 2000–2001, you can speed up the ol' time machine and zip past the dot-com bust when the Other People's Money (OPM) ran out. It wasn't pretty. The mainstream media declared the Internet age officially dead, and September 11, 2001 changed everything in the real world.

While the dot-com party was coming to a screeching halt, another movement was gathering strength. It was a movement programmers in developed nations found deeply troubling: the jobs started going to India. Seemingly overnight, the party was over for programmers in the United States, the United Kingdom, Europe, and Australia, and the good times were rolling in Bangalore, Beijing, Romania, and elsewhere.

■**Note** Since our hypothetical time machine doesn't cover side trips, I'll reluctantly skip over outsourcing and its tangible goods' twin, offshoring—not because they aren't important (they are) and not because I don't have strong feelings about them (I do) but because three other writers[4] have already done a better job than I could, and this trip down memory lane is for your benefit, not mine.

---

3. http://www.sharewarejunkies.com/invjikn.htm
4. *Offshoring IT: The Good, The Bad, and The Ugly* by Bill Blunden (Apress, 2004); *The World Is Flat: A Brief History of the Twenty-first Century* by Thomas L. Friedman (Farrar, Straus, and Giroux, 2005); and *Exporting America: Why Corporate Greed Is Shipping American Jobs Overseas* by Lou Dobbs (Warner Business Books, 2004)

Welcome to Netscape

You have just embarked on a journey across the Internet, and Netscape is your vehicle. This welcome page will help you get started on your use of Netscape and your exploration of the Internet.

To get around, just single-click on any blue or purple word or phrase (here's an example). These are "hyperlinks" to other pages. Also, images with blue or purple borders are hyperlinks and can be single-clicked as well. You can always return to this page by choosing *Welcome* from your *Directory* menu.

Getting Started...

If you're just getting started and want some help on how to use Netscape, start by single-clicking on the following hyperlink: Guided Tour. Also, check out the Netscape Handbook for a more in depth view of Netscape.

Should you have any other questions while you are using Netscape, please check out our Frequently Asked Questions page.

Exploring the Internet

If you are ready to get on with exploring, you'll find some good Internet starting points under the *Directory* menu. They are:

Welcome
>   That's this page -- your initial home page.

What's New!
>   Want to discover the newest interesting places and events on the Internet? The net is growing every day, and the What's New page will provide you with links to the newest pages and services that you can visit.

What's Cool!
>   Tired of slogging through the What's New page looking at every new Internet site under the sun? The What's Cool page highlights some of the most interesting and compelling resources on the Internet. It changes regularly, so stop back often.

Go to Newsgroups
>   There are thousands of newsgroups on the Internet where users get together to discuss a wide variety of topics. With Netscape, you can participate in these groups, follow along and get involved in conversations, and post your own replies.

Internet Directory
>   This is your Directory of Directories: each of these directories is a catalog of available information on the Internet.

Internet Search

Figure 1-1. *Netscape's home page in 1994*

If your time machine had a micro-ISV meter, you'd be wondering if it's broken right now. As venture capital–funded start-ups were popping like balloons, little one- and two-person software companies were springing up all over the Internet, at an increasing rate. It's almost as if as the Internet grew, the shareware companies that started with Jim and Andrew and Bob in 1983 and continued through the 1980s and 1990s were starting to draw all seven lucky numbers in the evolutionary lottery. This could be interesting!

Well, the time machine has stopped, and you're now back to where you started, the here and now. What does *here* look like, though?

What *Here* Looks Like

Here looks very different from 1983. While the first Internet age died when the dot-com boom went bust, someone forgot to tell the Internet. Each year more people with faster connections are spending more time and buying more products via the Internet while interacting with more people in more ways.

First, something like *one billion people* now use the Internet,[5] with more people all over the world getting online. One billion is such a nice round number; the cynic in you might distrust it. That's fine—it may only be 995 million, or perhaps by the time you read this it's 1.1 billion. Either way, it's the largest number of potential customers for anything—ever.

Second, e-commerce continues to grow, even faster than the number of Internet users. In the United States in 2004, online sales were estimated at $69 billion+, with predictions for 2005 heading north of $80 billion.[6]

Third, although no one has a handle on the hard numbers, something is changing:

- In CorpTech's (http://www.corptech.com/) database of 95,111 high-tech companies, 20,823 have fewer than 10 employees, 12,575 have 5 or fewer employees, and 3,846 have just 1 employee. And traditionally, such databases underreport these numbers.

- CNET Download.com "serves over 27,000 publishers representing 35,000 products and 132 countries around the world, [with more than] 2.3 million downloads each day." Somewhere around 85 percent of these publishers are in fact micro-ISVs.

- Several leading companies in their market segments are actually micro-ISVs: Fog Creek Software (FogBugz), Webroot Software (Spy Sweeper), and Sunbelt Software (CounterSpy) come to mind.

Although the number of small, self-funded companies is growing like wild, how they describe themselves and how they see themselves vary. Some call themselves *shareware companies*, others call themselves *ISVs*, and most don't know what to call themselves. And then along comes Eric Sink.

ERIC SINK, SOFTWARE CRAFTSMAN, SOURCEGEAR

In September 2004, Eric Sink was running his successful source control software company and writing a column for Microsoft's MSDN site about the business of software. Eleven columns in, Eric's "Exploring Micro-ISVs" column hit a nerve with me and many other developers looking for a way to describe our as-yet-unnamed business model.

Eric is also the moderator for the Business of Software forum at Joel on Software (http://discuss.joelonsoftware.com/?biz), a longtime haunt and great information source for people starting micro-ISVs.

Q. Tell me about SourceGear—did it start as a micro-ISV?

A. First of all, I would have to confess that calling us a micro-ISV was not quite accurate—although I coined that term, I've never succeeded at running a micro-ISV.

---

5. http://www.Internetworldstats.com/stats.htm and http://www.c-i-a.com/pr0904.htm
6. http://answers.google.com/answers/threadview?id=555501 and http://www.census.gov/mrts/www/data/html/05Q1.html

Q. OK....

A. The real stars are people like Thomas Warfield, with the [Pretty Good] Solitaire game (`http://www.asharewarelife.com/`); he's made millions off that game, I think. When I started out, it was as a one-person company but purely with the intention of doing consulting. I had no intention of building something or a product, and I ended up doing both.

Q. When was that?

A. SourceGear started in early '97.

Q. When you started and you were basically a one-man company, what type of consulting were you doing?

A. Just kind of rent-a-brain type of work, I guess you'd say—hiring myself out to do contract development, advice on development, things like that. Primarily, I was just writing code as a hired gun.

Q. Been there, done that, and have the T-shirts. So, how did you go from "I'm a happy contractor" to doing a product?

A. Well, the first thing that changed was that about two months after I got started, the company I previously worked for laid off all my former co-workers. So, all of a sudden, there's 40 people I know well out of a job. So I started talking with them, and the idea of hiring one or two of them started to get some airtime. Anyway, by the end of that year, I'd hired seven of them. And we were doing contracting.

Along the way, our first product was not my idea; it was somebody else's. In fact, I tried to shoot it down because I did not think it was a good idea. But to make a long story short, we're still shipping it today.

Q. Was that the application you sell that lets you do Microsoft Visual SourceSafe remotely (SourceOffSite)?

A. That's right. It really all started because we used SourceSafe as our source control tool and one of our guys commutes from an hour away, and he wanted to work from home sometimes and couldn't. So, he wrote this tool, and people started talking about shipping it as a product, and before you know it, we did.

Q. So, basically, it started out solving a problem you had, and then you realized that you had a really good solution here and other people had the same problem?

A. That's right.

Q. That explains how SourceOffSite came to be, but how did Vault come to be?

A. Vault happened because from the day we built SourceOffSite, we understood that Microsoft could kill it by simply adding remote access to SourceSafe. We have always believed that SourceOffSite is, say, one year away from being stopped by Microsoft, but the thing is, they kept not doing it. After three or four years of SourceOffSite shipping, we had accumulated a pretty large number of SourceSafe customers who were also our customers.

Microsoft was just not doing much with SourceSafe, and some of our customers started planting the idea in our heads, "You know, you guys ought to just create a replacement for SourceSafe, because Microsoft clearly isn't doing anything decent with it." And we had thought about it ourselves, plus being prodded by our customers; we decided to just go ahead and do it.

Q. So, you developed Vault and started selling it in February 2003. Were your first customers the people you'd already been selling to?

A. Yep.

Q. I never ask people how much they've made because I never get an answer. But has Vault met your sales expectations?

A. It has—significantly—exceeded our sales expectations. We went into this thinking this might be a decent idea, but the response from customers has been quite a bit larger than we ever expected.

Q. So, how did you come up with this micro-ISV thing?

A. I was writing a column for Chris Sells at Microsoft. After writing my first few columns, I somehow got it into my head I wanted to write about the notion of a one-person company, partly because I had talked to several guys doing this one-person company thing, and some of them were a lot more successful than anyone thinks they are.

So, partly, I wanted to shine a light on their success and kind of spread the word that a one-person company can accomplish more than you might think even if they never grow more, and if they do, it's a great way to get started.

So, I sat down to write this article after I dealt with the research; one of the things I wanted to tell you in this phone call, and I cannot find it, is that I am quite confident from memory that the article was changed at the last minute—I had another term for *micro-ISV*. The day before I submitted it to my editors, I decided I didn't like the term and changed it to *micro-ISV* instead. But I don't remember what the other term was!

Q. What has been the response to that article?

A. The overwhelming response has been positive. I get mail almost every day from somebody telling me about their micro-ISV [or] their product idea; I get requests to review business plans. I mean, I get a steady stream of enthusiasm from people who say, "You know, I like this idea. I want to do a product of my own!" That aspect has resonated with people. Now Winnable Solitaire, that's a whole different story. That was my little stunt to basically give me an excuse to write an article.

Q. Halfway between that article and your Winnable Solitaire experiment, you started moderating the Business of Software forum at Joel on Software. How did that happen?

A. No big story there. Joel asked me to do it one day, and I said, "Sure." I would consider Joel a friend, and I've known him at somewhat arm's length for several years. It was the kind of thing where we knew each other fairly well, so I did [it].

Q. I'm curious—how long does it take you to moderate this forum?

A. Oh, not very long; I pop into it once or twice a day. The forum is to some extent self-moderating because he's got this Bayesian filtering thing that actually filters out a lot of the spam. So most of what I do is just confirm that the system has properly identified something as spam.

Q. Sounds like a no-brainer, or at least a lot easier to moderate than some of the forum software out there....

A. Yeah. The real issue for moderating the forum is not administration but to actually be a valued contributor to the forum by posting my thoughts and opinions. And that takes more time. And frankly, I don't necessarily do a very good job of it, but I try to chime in on questions every now and then.

Q. Let's go back to Winnable Solitaire for a moment. There's a question on the forum right now: whatever happened to it?

A. [laughs] Well, it still sells!

Q. That's good! Would you be willing to say how many a day?

A. Oh, it doesn't sell a copy a day. The revenue from it has been insignificant. I spent more on a dinner last week than I've made with Winnable Solitaire in total.

Q. So, was it just to illustrate the article?

A. To be honest, I thought it might sell more than it has, but it really was just a stunt to write an article. When I talked to Chris Sells about the article, I said, "Hey, everyone else has sample code on MSDN. I write about the business of software—what do I use for a sample?" A sample product, so I did one. I was able to justify the time spent developing it because for totally unrelated reasons I needed to learn the wxWindows API anyway.

Q. There was one other thing I wanted to ask you. A couple of your articles talked about business transparency— the idea of letting the world in on how your business is run. What has been the reaction to that, and do you still think transparency is the right way to go for micro-ISVs?

A. I don't think a blanket statement like that makes sense. I can say a couple of things I do think make sense as blanket statements.

Q. Please do!

A. Every micro-ISV needs to figure out what level of transparency makes sense to them and not treat transparency as a bool or a checkbox. What I do think makes sense in general is if you are not willing to trust your customers, your customers will figure it out and they won't trust you.

> Now, does that mean trusting your customers means the same thing for every company? No. But it's an attitude that has to be thought about. In our case, since we are software developers and our market is also software developers, transparency has a bigger advantage for us. It's like trying to sell car repairs to people who know how to repair cars—they want to know.
>
> Q. OK, by the way, how big is SourceGear now?
>
> A. A little under 20 employees.
>
> Q. Any advice for anyone starting a micro-ISV now?
>
> A. One thing I would say is that it's worth the journey.

Eric's article gave this new type of business a name: *micro-ISV*. A micro-ISV is the following:

Self-funded: This means maybe you max your credit cards and maybe Uncle Jim helps you out, but your business is going to be largely self-funded and way below the radar of venture capitalists looking for the next billion-dollar hit.

Small: This means your company is one person the majority of the time or has maybe a couple of partners. If it's larger than that, other dynamics such as what you're using for salaries come into play.

Internet: Although Eric was talking about small, independent software vendors, *independent software vendors* was a term coined at Microsoft to cover everyone else in the software industry it had not acquired, partnered with, or driven out of business.[7] In actuality, the *I* in micro-ISV really means Internet, since it's the Internet that makes micro-ISVs possible, not Microsoft.

I'll have a lot more to say about micro-ISVs, a whole book in fact, but the last point I want to make before getting to the part of this chapter you really want to read (how to start your micro-ISV) is that a few years ago, we hit a point of discontinuity.

Although today's micro-ISV can trace its roots back to when shareware was born more than 20 years ago, micro-ISVs are more than that. For starters, with the laudable exception of people and companies under the open source banner, self-funded start-ups don't merely hope to get paid—they do get paid, or the software stops or the account is canceled.

On the Internet, no one knows or cares how big your company is, how many people work there, or whether you're sitting in a cubicle or sitting on your redwood deck with one of your cats in your lap. The only thing they care about is whether your software, Web service, or emerging tangible product *gets the job done*.

The Internet, the billion people using it every day, the hundreds of billions of dollars of commerce taking place via it, and the sheer near-instantaneous speed and connectivity of all things Internet have made micro-ISVs not just a viable way to start a company but the real next killer app.

---

7. You'll find out more about how to stop worrying and love Microsoft (or Apple or whatever firm is big in your programming world) in Chapter 6.

Joining the Party

So, you've decided to trade in your seat and oar in some corporation's galley and start your own micro-ISV. After all, you bought this book! So, where's the party with all the attractive people, great food, cool music, and adult beverages?[8] In other words, where do you start?

You start with a vision.

This isn't just an idea, a concept, a marketing niche, or a business plan. You'll need a true-blue vision to sustain you when you start working longer and harder than you ever thought humanly (or inhumanly) possible. You'll need a burning bush's worth of ambition to make it. Of the nearly 200 founders of micro-ISVs I've talked to, interviewed, emailed, or read about, the single trait that comes across in each of them is a strong desire to be their own bosses and run their own lives.

Since California strongly frowns on dispensing visions without at least a medical license, you'll have to find your own. Sorry, you won't find any easy answers here.

But what I can do in the following sections of this chapter is show you three approaches for creating the vision of what your micro-ISV could be. If you've found your muse or your muse has found you, by all means skip ahead. If not, the following sections offer you some takes on getting into the right space to find your vision.

The Systematic Approach

The following sections are a "I haven't a clue what application to write to start my micro-ISV" guide for your consideration. Your experience may vary, but these sections will at least get you going.

Step 1: Find at Least Three Interesting Industries or Marketplaces

The goal here is not to find three industries where you think your micro-ISV can make money but three areas of human endeavor you find interesting. I'll get to the money part next (in the "Paying the Cover Charge" section).

If you're not sure what you find interesting, you need to do some remedial work. Read *What Color Is Your Parachute? 2005: A Practical Manual for Job-Hunters and Career-Changers* by Richard Nelson Bolles (Ten Speed Press, 2004), which is an excellent guide for dissecting not just how to find a job working for someone else but what sort of topics, people, and businesses you find interesting.

And like many good books, you'll find that this classic is supplemented by a Web site (http://www.jobhuntersbible.com/), as shown in Figure 1-2.

---

8. Er...not quite. See the "Paying the Cover Charge" section.

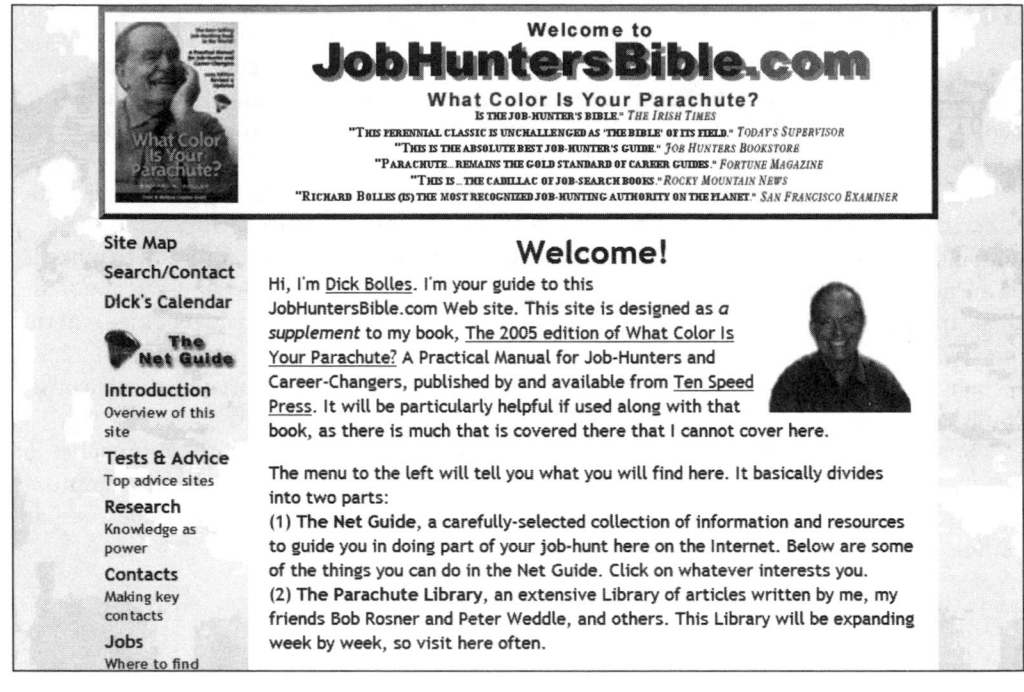

Figure 1-2. *Finding your interests*

Another way to find interesting parts of the economy is to refer to the more than 300 California Occupational Guides (http://www.labormarketinfo.edd.ca.gov/cgi/career/ ?PageID=3&SubID=139), as shown in Figure 1-3.

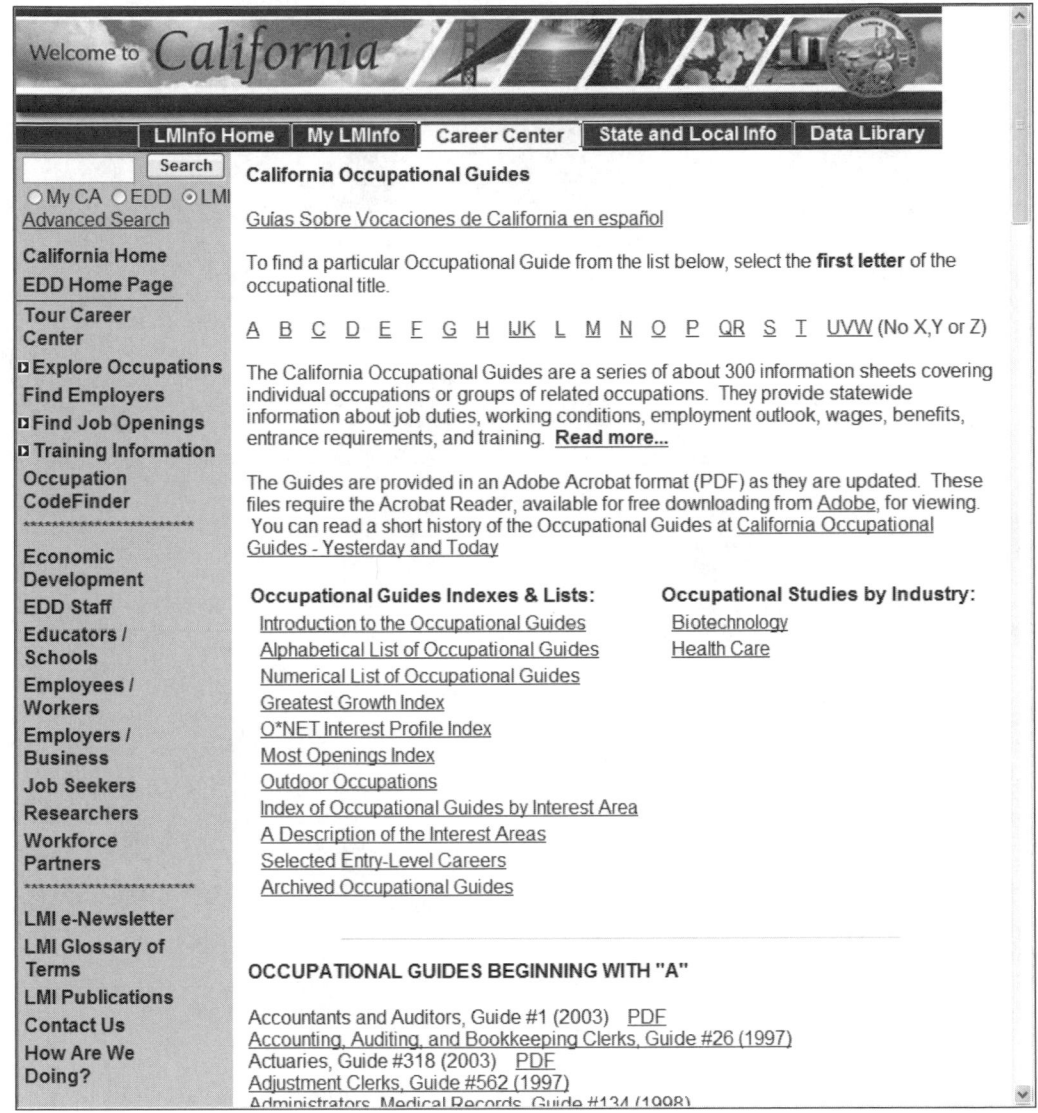

Figure 1-3. *Starting your career goals with* A

Of course, you can always research industries by...researching industries. Visit the excellent research portal hosted by market research firm Polson Enterprises at `http://www.virtualpet.com/industry/howto/search.htm#identify`, as shown in Figure 1-4. Don't let the dull appearance and lack of pretty pictures fool you; you can spend the next year or so just working through half of the Web sites listed at this site.

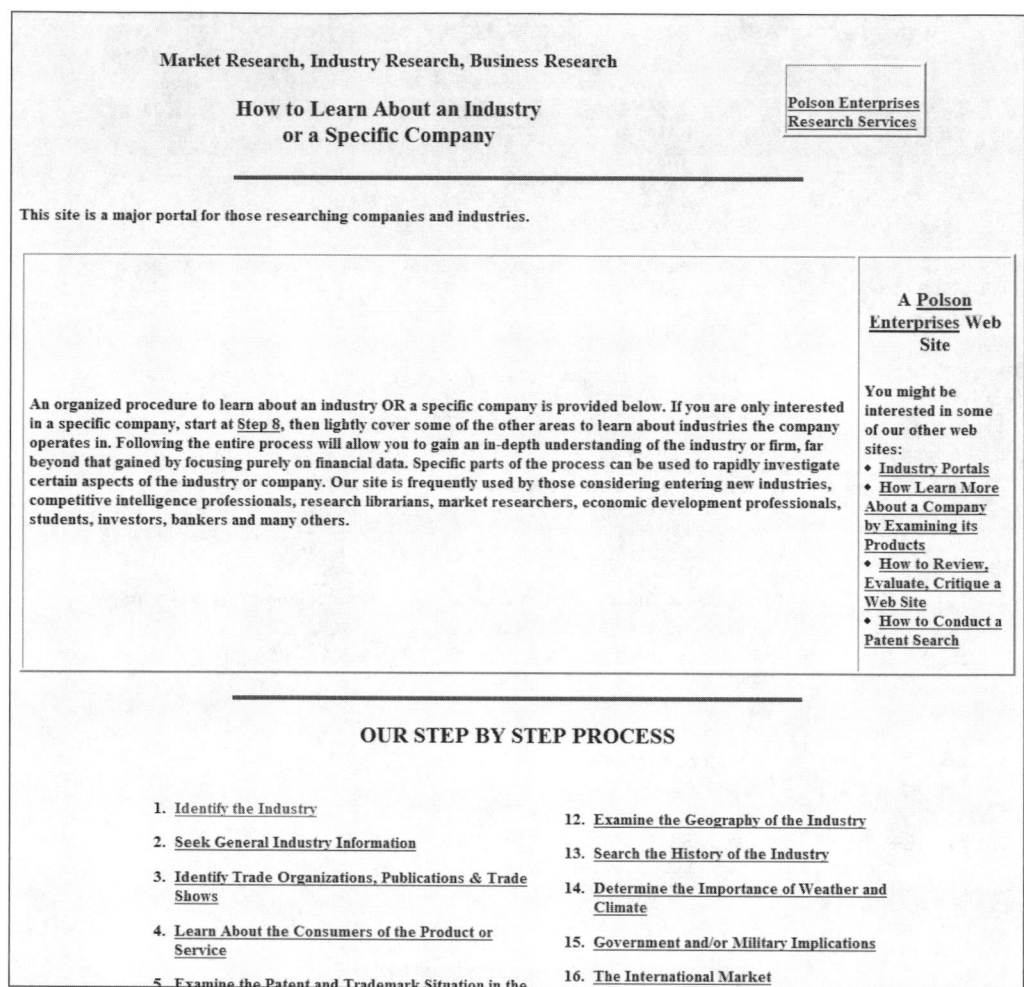

Figure 1-4. *Researching industries step by step*

OK, so you want pictures. Check out Hoovers, one of the early Internet-based business research companies that's now a Dun & Bradstreet company. The breakdown of industries at http://www.hoovers.com/free/ind/dir.xhtml, as shown in Figure 1-5, leads to a helpful list of major players, which in turn leads to a free dossier about each company, as shown in Figure 1-6.

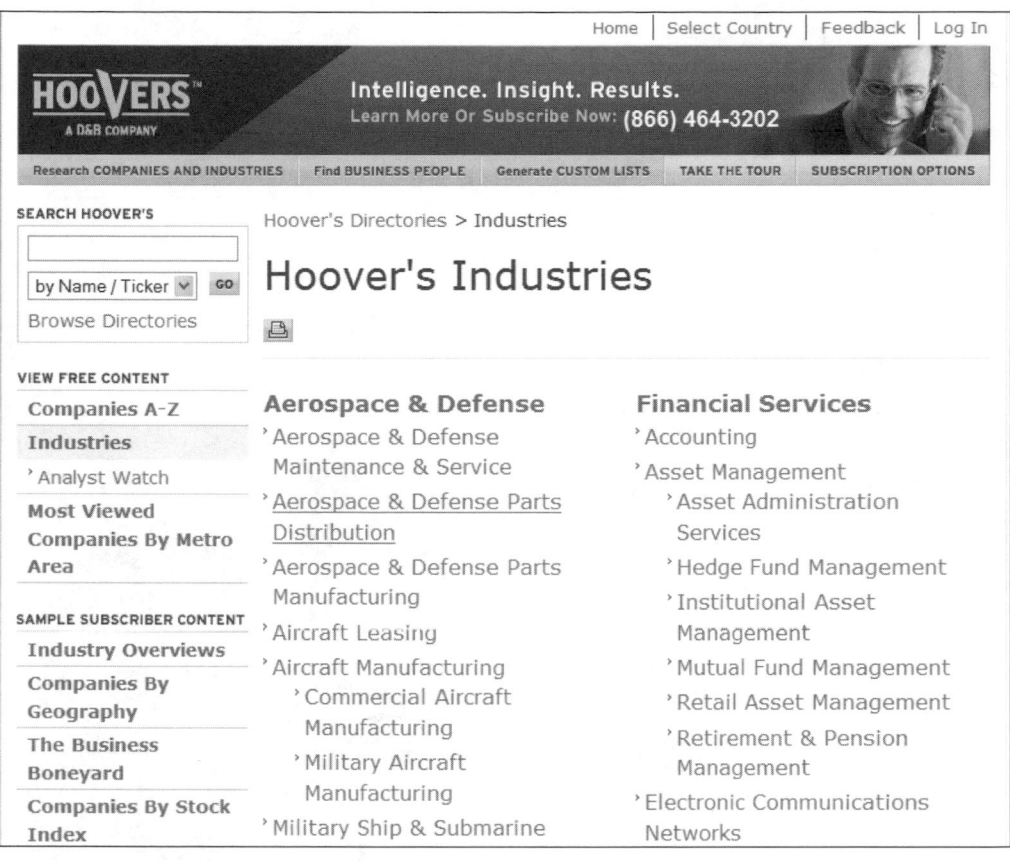

Figure 1-5. *Exploring Hoovers*

Figure 1-6. *Viewing a company snapshot at Hoovers*

Prefer a more academic approach? The State University of New York at Geneseo has a good list at `http://library.geneseo.edu/info/sirind.shtml`, as shown in Figure 1-7.

Now, the tough part of step 1 isn't finding information, and it isn't getting your head rearranged by the plethora of information available. Don't try to do this in one sitting or be overly serious about it. You haven't made any emotional investment yet, and you can go wherever you like. Just start a new bookmarks folder in your favorite browser, stick it at the start of your bookmarks toolbar so you can actually find it again, and let your fingers do the clicking for you.

When the list is feeling long enough, you're ready for step 2.

Selected Information Resources:
Researching Industries

ONLINE CATALOGS

RESEARCH RESOURCES

ABOUT THE LIBRARY

LIBRARY SERVICES

Contents

Searching Government Web Pages
Industry Descriptions
Industry Statistics
Industry Financial Data and Operating Ratios
Directories
Finding Magazines and Newspaper Articles
Finding Books
Finding Additional Information

NOTE: This guide includes books in Milne Library as well as electronic computer indexes and Internet web sites. Most of the sources are general. That is, they provide information on a variety of industries. Instructions on finding books or articles on specific industries are provided at the end of this guide. When searching the web for specific industries, either use the general links provided and find the industry needed, or type "aerospace industry" or "restaurant industry" or any industry you are studying.

Contents

Searching Government Web Pages

Government web sites are good sources for industry information. Some sites of interest have been highlighted in this pathfinder, but for a more exhaustive search, use Govbot for key word searching of Government web pages. (http://cobar.cs.umass.edu/ciirdemo/Govbot/)

Industry Classification Systems

Figure 1-7. *Taking a more academic approach*

Step 2: Research Computer-Related Topics in Your Three Markets

Here's a nice bit of pseudocode for you: for each interesting industry/marketplace, find three interesting segments, and research who and how people/organizations use computers and are making money.

Take, for example, agriculture: this is a big industry, with lots of needs. But am I talking about small farmers, agribusiness, food transport companies, distributors, large retail chains, or the corner neighborhood store?

Dig deeper with the tools you liked in step 1.

And as you look at your favorite segments, figure out who uses computers and who is making money and therefore has money to spend. If your potential market targets don't have money and don't use computers, it's unlikely they'll connect with and buy from your micro-ISV.

Step 3: Talk with People Working in Each Market

Pick up the phone, and call them. Ask them, "Hi, I'm [insert name here]. I'm thinking about writing a [desktop application][Web-based service] to help people who do what you do. What problems do you have you wish were solved?"

It may sound weird to call up people you've never met, and some may take offense and hang up on you. But if you make it clear you're not looking for a job or a donation, some of these people will start getting excited and start telling you about issues you never knew about the industry market segment you're interested in; before you know it, you might find a really good problem that you can solve in a totally cool way and make money for doing so!

This is called *defining the problem domain*. Write a one-page, top-level description about how you'd apply your technical know-how to solve the problem you just heard about and got excited about. Keep it to one page, if you can. (If you just can't, that's a good sign.)

You might be tempted to stop after the first person you connect with, but resist that temptation. You're still in the exploration stage, and the next person you talk to might have an even more interesting problem that you could solve in an even cooler way while making even more money! Do some due diligence here, and corral a set of possibilities; you'll need them for the gloomy step 4.

Step 4: Determine Whether Someone Already Solved the Same Problem in the Same Way

Your goal in this step is to winnow your list to just those possible apps on which you can build a successful micro-ISV. For each of your possible apps for a potential market segment, pretend you get a $10,000 check if you can find on Google the same solution to that problem. If you find that solution, put that choice out of its misery, and cross it off your list now. Congratulations— you just saved substantially more than $10,000!

Micro-ISVs have the advantages of being fast, nimble, and flexible, but they're roadkill when going up against an established, large company already selling the same solution. Don't go there; it will hurt.

This step does have some wiggle room: what does *in the same way* mean? If you have a potential app that solves a problem that existing companies solve but does it much better, or much more cheaply or much more deeply, you may still have a chance.

Having competitors is a good thing—they give you legitimacy, potential customers, price points, and all sorts of good things, if, and only if, you can do a better job of solving some or all of the problems they solve for their customers in a new way and those potential customers aren't locked in tighter than the occupants of the penitentiary at Leavenworth, Kansas.

Step 5: Listen to Yourself

By this point in this process, you've most likely found two or three market segments that have computers and money to spend with problems you can solve that aren't currently being solved. Now it's decision time: which one do you pick?

Put another way, you're about to trade a couple of years of your life and more hard work than you ever imagined for the chance to maybe, just maybe, make some serious money while living and breathing the challenges, concerns, and worldview of your selected market segment. Are you really comfortable with that idea? Do you like these people and feel good when their lives improve? If not, move to the next item on your list. If so, welcome to your new life.

The Joel Approach

So, perhaps a smarter way exists for finding the right application to build. Joel Spolsky, founder of Fog Creek Software and a "graduated" micro-ISV, has a different approach.

JOEL SPOLSKY, CEO, FOG CREEK SOFTWARE

After researching my five-step approach to finding the right application, I decided to ask someone who had been there and done that. Joel Spolsky's Fog Creek Software currently sells three very different products: CityDesk, a Windows desktop Web site content management tool; FogBugz, a Web-based defect-tracking application; and Fog Creek Copilot, a new remote PC control service.

Q. How did you get the idea of starting Fog Creek Software with CityDesk?

A. Well, we really didn't start Fog Creek Software with CityDesk—we started with FogBugz, and the product we really wanted to launch never launched, and that was probably a good thing. We really didn't have a commitment then to any particular product; we didn't start the company because there was some particular product we wanted to make.

Q. So the first product didn't come out?

A. We had three ideas. There was CityDesk, FogBugz, and this thing we called TinTin. It was going to be an application server basically. And we already had code for most of these things.

FogBugz was the closest to being ready, and a bunch of people kept asking me if they could have the code. And we had to say, "Yeah, but it's kind of hard to install and set up and get running on your system, and we'd have to make a bunch of changes to customize it for you, so it would take a few days—and in those days we were set up as a consulting business—so we'd say three days of consulting and the license, maybe $10,000, and it just wasn't a product worth $10,000 to people then.

Q. When was that?

A. Fall of 2000. So, given how many people were asking for it and that it just was not selling as consultingware, we thought if we could make it shrink-wrap and lower the price to a tenth, we could actually sell some copies. So we put a bunch of effort into an easy setup and cleaning out all the dependencies on the particular server it had been installed on and started selling it, sort of as an experiment. And it did quite well, and we did start getting sales right away.

At first it was a few thousand dollars a month, but it built up pretty quickly, and now that's the bulk of our business.

Q. So basically, you started with three ideas, and the one that ran is the one you're running with?

A. And that was the one we expected.

Q. If there were a couple of guys like you and Michael Pryor [Fog Creek Software's cofounder] and they were casting about for an idea to build their micro-ISV on, what would you advise them?

A. It's a little hard to say, but you have to know where the pain is. My rule of thumb is, tell me what pain you are eliminating with this product. If you're not eliminating some piece of pain, nobody is going to break out the checkbook. You have to tell me what's not working, what one thing is painful.

If it's Skype, it's long-distance phone bills that's the pain. If it's FogBugz, it's that you just can't get a handle on what it's going to take to ship your software. If it's CityDesk, you have to change 27 different things in 28 different steps every time you want to make a small change in your Web site.

So, if there isn't a piece of pain you can explain, then I don't feel you have a product. And I see a lot of products that are spiffy, cool doodads, but they're not going to make you money unless you can explain what problem they solve really.

There's a small market for things that just make people happy, like Konfabulator, where you can put a little analog clock on your desktop, but it's really hard to make a living that way. You really have to identify the pain and solve it.

Now, other people will come up with other criteria that I don't agree with for the micro-ISV. For example, a venture capitalist will say, "Does this have the potential to be a multibillion-dollar business?" For a micro-ISV, it doesn't matter. You're not taking venture capital; you're bootstrapping. If it's a three-million-dollar business, you're going to be the richest guy in Chattanooga, Tennessee.

An Even Shorter Approach

"What's your 'dammit'?" says Mike Johnson, chief executive officer (CEO) of BigAtticHouse Software (`http://www.bigattichouse.com/whaddidoo.html`), as shown in Figure 1-8. He add this:

> When you find a customer's "dammit" (the part about their current process or software that eats up their day and makes them say "Dammit!"), then you have found something you can build. You just found a project.
>
> Immersed in a domain/field for a year or more, and you can find "dammit" for a whole industry. You just found a product.
>
> In case you're wondering about the history, it's just that I noticed when speaking with secretaries and managers that they tend to have something they must "fight with" every day on their systems...hence "dammit." I just try to help find their "dammit" and make it go away.

Whatever approach you take to finding the right problem you can solve and people are willing and able to pay you to solve, take heart. Every technological, social, and business advance; invention; or labor-saving innovation has a whole new slew of problems, hassles, and annoyances just waiting.

Damn it!

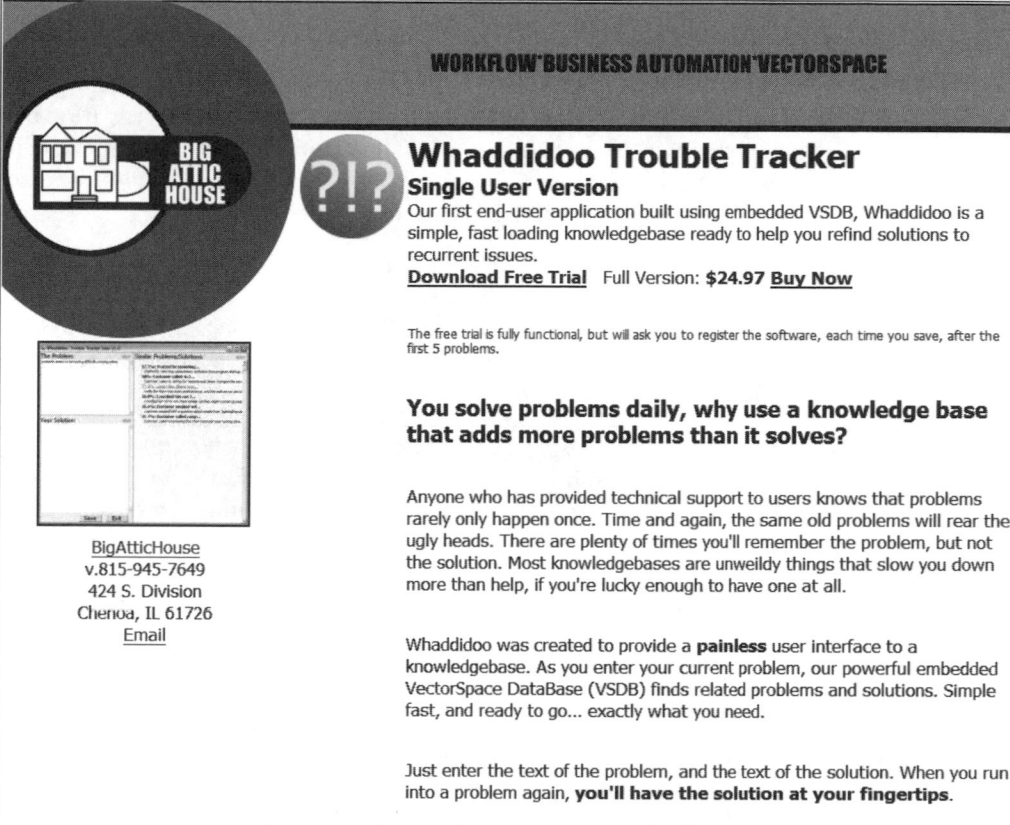

Figure 1-8. *Exploring BigAtticHouse.com*

Paying the Cover Charge

Before you head to the following chapters, which cover the nuts and bolts of building your micro-ISV and your first commercial application, I'll discuss a rather large charge on your account in life that this little venture is going to cost you.

Make no mistake—writing a commercial-grade application and defining and building your micro-ISV are going to take a *large* bite out of your life for at least months, probably years, and there's always the chance that all your blood, sweat, toil, and tears will get you exactly nothing.

All the parts of starting a micro-ISV are (except for writing the actual code) pretty simple. In other words, the tasks are simple like moving the ball down the field in soccer, or American football, or sometimes more like rugby or Australian rules (what rules?) football—and sometimes just as painful. Simple doesn't—emphatically—mean the same as painless.

If you'd like to avoid some of this pain, the following are eight opinionated rules for you to consider before taking the plunge:

Rule 1: Be prepared to work more and longer hours than you ever thought possible: If you thought working in today's Internet-speed IT world was grueling, wait until you try to both work in IT in some fashion *and* start your micro-ISV. Remember the self-funded part of the micro-ISV definition? This means odds are good you'll be working days, nights, weekends, and your birthday to get your micro-ISV off the ground.

Rule 2: The only thing you get for free is failure: While the direct costs of starting a micro-ISV are potentially as little as zero, using certain tools and services will significantly improve your chances of producing a successful micro-ISV. These tools will cost money, and you'll have to finance your regular monthly expenses.[9] Yes, you can get away with financing your micro-ISV on credit, but you'll pay for it in stress.

Rule 3: If you have a wife, husband, spouse, significant other, or combination thereof, fully disclose what you're going to do, and get their buy-in before you start: Do this, or don't even start. Some things money can't buy, and if you lose sight of that, you'll bitterly regret it. On the plus side, having a supportive person—not to mention a steady second income coming in—can make all the difference between success and failure. For me, without Tina's support, love, and help, I wouldn't have gotten my micro-ISV off the ground, let alone written this book.

Rule 4: You'll need a plan: Actually, you'll need a bunch of them—an application development plan with milestones, a software development plan, a code backup plan so your code base doesn't disappear one fine day, a Web site development plan, a payment processing plan, a tech support plan, a marketing plan, and so on.

Now, you could spend, say, six months or so defining and detailing each part of each plan. *Don't*. Planning is good, and you'll need to do some, but all the plans in the world aren't going to earn you a single dollar. Also, you don't yet know what you don't know that you need to know. Plan in broad strokes, and fill in as needs and circumstances dictate, but paralysis by analysis has been the downfall of many too obsessive IT people.

Rule 5: Law 1440 doesn't take a day off: Just like gravity, you can't ignore that you get 1,440 minutes to the day and no more. If you haven't gotten good at managing your time and tasks at your day job, you need to find the time and task management procedures that work for you. You'll find more about living with Law 1440 in Chapter 4.

Rule 6: Focus on revenue: This is a simple but profound rule. How do you decide whether to add a feature to your first application? *Focus on revenue*. Don't know what to do next today among half a dozen different tasks? *Focus on revenue*. Building a micro-ISV is all about making money: other programming efforts may be noble, but a micro-ISV is all about the money, and you need to prioritize your time on what is going to maximize your revenue.

Sometimes you can overdo applying this rule; it's not just about today's revenue but also this week's and month's and year's revenue. Don't forget that your customers expect to see a better product over time, including more useful features and less obnoxious bugs.

---

9. Good news! I can confidently predict you'll save a pile on vacations. You won't have one for the first three years.

Rule 7: Listen: Listen to your beta testers, your market, your customers, and your potential customers. You don't already know everything; otherwise, you'd be so rich you wouldn't need to build a micro-ISV. A little considered listening can go a long way to finding the tipping point from a struggling to a soaring micro-ISV.

Rule 8: Rock on: Don't spend your days in a cubicle wondering if you can turn that burning desire in your guts into something real—go for it!

CHAPTER 2

■■■

Developing the Micro-ISV Way

You were probably tempted to skip this chapter. The first chapter was helpful for finding what to write, and the following chapters on the business and marketing stuff look useful—but you already know how to program, you've done it for a living, and you've found what works for classes, for clients, or in your IT shop, right?

If only that were so!

Writing software from scratch to solve a problem you've picked, especially software you're going to turn around and actually sell to some (you hope!) measurable part of the human race, is incredibly different from what you're most likely used to doing in a class or a job. That's why this chapter is a must read: you need to understand the realities of micro-ISV design and development.

When you're working for a company, a good grade, or a client, someone else defines at least initially what you're developing. In other words, when you get a requirements document, meet with the users, get a class syllabus, or sit down with someone who is going to pay you, someone else defines the problem you need to solve.

When you're a micro-ISV, there is no *someone else*. It's all up to you, whether the *you* at your micro-ISV means one programmer or a set of partners.

In this chapter, you'll move from vision to beta product. Along the way, you'll see some of the tools and methods that work for micro-ISV development and look at some of the features of the code base about which you need to be concerned.

In this chapter, however, you won't find a whole lot about software development methodologies you may have used or at least read about: no Extreme Programming (XP) or Agile Software Development (ASD) and no Scrum, Rational Unified Process (RUP), Common Object Request Broker Architecture (CORBA), or Structured Systems Analysis and Design Methodology (SSADM). All these methodologies focus on how groups of programmers can work together—which isn't much help when your programming team consists of just you.

While I'm still wearing my flame-proof shorts, let me throw a bit more lighter fluid around: I won't cover how embracing open source will make your micro-ISV a success, because I don't think it will. Now, please, before every open source zealot flames me and my copy of Firefox stops working, hear me out. Open source may just be the greatest way to create anything, but it's a lousy way to start a small profit-making business, which is the focus of this book.

Instead, I'll first cover a few techniques that have worked in my micro-ISV and have worked for other micro-ISVs for getting to beta—that wonderful point when you actually have something to show for all your hard work and something that may, just may, replace that regular paycheck you gave up. Then, again from a profit-making perspective, you'll learn some of the "production values" that will make your micro-ISV ready for the big time.

Designing Your Application

Before you can start coding your micro-ISV application or manufacturing your micro-product, you need to design it. At the start of the process (see Chapter 1), you identified a problem a bunch of people have that you want to solve in a better or different way from the existing solutions.

By the end of the design phase, you want a coherent and realistic definition of what your product looks like, acts like, and feels like for the people who are going to buy it. Once you have the design, although plenty of technical challenges are still ahead, you've accomplished the first goal and can see where you have to go from there.

Now, one fine day some bright young thing is going to build something that is half–crystal ball and half–neural net that will read your innermost design thoughts, pass them through the collective unconsciousness, and spit out a 300-page specification detailing every function, screen, dialog box, and button your application will need. In the meantime, there's use cases and paper prototyping.

Creating Use Cases

Way back when, in 1986, Ivar Jacobson formalized the idea of writing down how users interact with a software application, instead of leaving that to the tech writers who would write the documentation a few weeks before the app shipped. At the time, it was a fairly heretical idea that a programmer would actually leave the MIS department (the old buzzword for IT), sit down with a bunch of users, and actually work out what those users would see an application doing.

The funny thing about heretical ideas is that given enough time, more than a few of them become conventional wisdom: whether you do XP, ASD, RUP, or some flavor of Unified Modeling Language (UML), use cases have become the accepted way of defining the interaction between people and software for design purposes.

Use cases are the natural bridge between the overall concept of your micro-ISV application and the stuff on the screen that performs actions when clicked; working through how your customers will use your software is a surefire technique for getting the scope of your application down on paper.

Generally, a use case will have the following sections:

A name: For example, Print Reports, Subscribe to New Service, or Add Task to Task Catalog.

A date stamp, version number, and IDs of related use cases: Use cases are meant to be iterative; keeping track of what version you're looking at is a must.

A summary: For example, "The user has decided to add an existing task to the Task Catalog. They select the task, click Add, and immediately see a copy of the task listed in the Task Catalog."

Precondition(s): This is where you cover what has to already be true before this use case will work. For example, "A task exists."

Trigger(s): This is how the use case starts. For example, a trigger could be "The user selects a task displayed in the section grid."

Main path: This is the play-by-play description of what the user does, how the system responds, and the back-and-forth through the main path of what the user case is about. Usually this is the successful path, and it doesn't describe at all what the application is doing internally.

Alternatives: This is a polite way of saying what happens when either the user or the application (or both) does something wrong in the main path. This can also cover alternative ways of performing actions.

Postconditions: Postconditions describe the effects of the use case and cover what has been accomplished.

Business rules: Here's where you make sure you capture whatever rules and restrictions your program needs to correctly mirror what people expect. For example, a business rule could be that "A checking account contains debits and credits."

Notes: Sometimes this is the best part of a use case; this is where you stick protoclass structure ideas, features to check, and open issues.

One of the nice parts of starting a micro-ISV (besides burning most of your ties) is that you get to decide how much or how little of any given structure or formalism you want to use. For me, as I work through a major chunk of a program, I first write a bunch of use case headlines, as shown in Figure 2-1. Then, once I have good coverage of everything, I flesh out the preconditions, triggers, main path, and postconditions.

When I started working on my micro-ISV's first commercial product, a task and project management application called MasterList Professional, I defined what problems MasterList Professional would solve by creating use cases. By doing this, I could start thinking about how best to solve those problems.

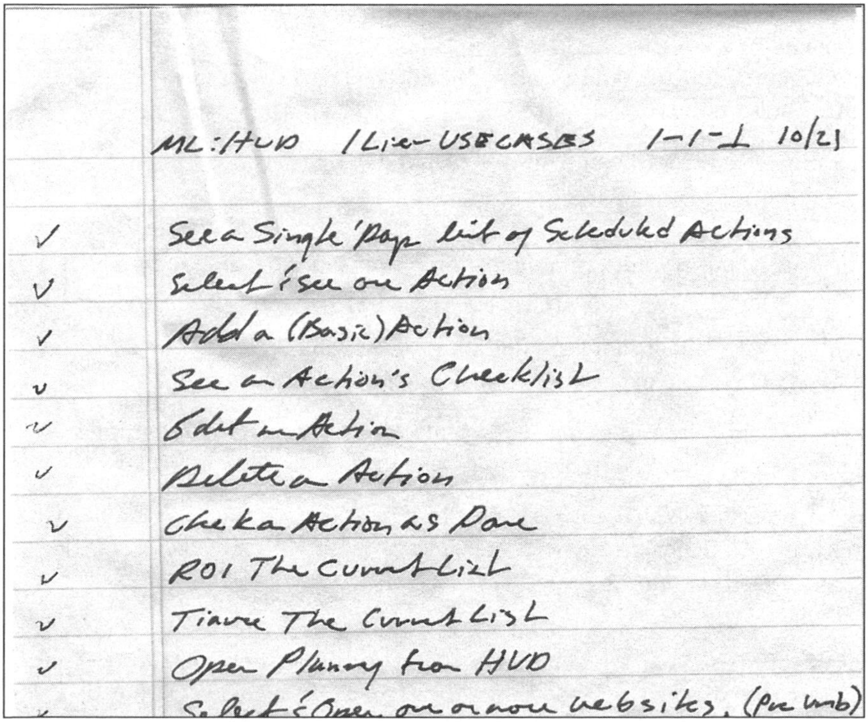

Figure 2-1. *Jotting down use case headlines for MasterList Professional*

Use cases are the logical, deterministic, word-processed half of the design story. They don't really describe the application—just the interaction between your potential customers and your application. As helpful as use cases are for identifying what your application will do, they are by no means the only tool you need to develop a design you can start architecting.

Creating Paper Prototypes

Most programmers, once they've gotten their use cases together, will either jump right in and start defining classes and objects or, worse, fire up their Integrated Development Environment (IDE) and start creating code—anything to avoid that messy, gooey human interface stuff.

Big mistake.

Pick any category of software you want at http://www.download.com. Take a quick look at any eight of the apps from what sound like small companies. Write down your gut reaction to the screen shot for each app, ranking it from a low of 1 ("Yuck!") to a high of 5 ("Ooh, shiny!").

Now look at their number of downloads. Notice the correlation?

The bottom-line reality of selling software is, Ugly doesn't cut it. As indifferent as you might be to how a program or a Web service looks because you have an educated idea about how a given function works, the other 99.9 percent of people will pick pretty over ugly every time.

This has some pretty serious implications for micro-ISV development: it's not enough for your application, Web service, or product to work right; it needs to make it past the customer's ugly filter if you're going to have the chance to sell it. Instead of slapping a Windows Explorer–like tree view on top of your application, you need to take a user interface–centric approach to both design and development.

The specifics of good user interface design are beyond the scope of this book, but you'll find a slew of books and Web sites listed in this book's appendix to get you started. I also can summarize the general principles of good user interface design, particularly for micro-ISV applications, in three bullet points:

- Do what people expect. (And if you're not sure what that is, ask.)

- Be nice to your users.

- Create *prototypes on paper* until your application makes sense to someone who has never seen it.

Paper prototyping is the tool of choice for defining the user interface for your micro-ISV's software, Web service, or product for several reasons:

Paper prototypes are fast: No matter how many years you've programmed, you can still draw a screen faster on paper than programming one in Flash, Delphi, or Visual Basic 6.

Paper prototypes let you focus on one aspect of the interface: Say, for example, you're trying to decide the layout of a dialog box for your app. You can start with how the user makes their initial selections and "squiggle" out the rest.

Paper prototypes keep you focused on the interface: If you use, say, Visual Basic 6 to work out the design of your app's interface, you'll have to constantly fight the temptation to think about the programming that will be needed, not the interface that defines what's needed.

Paper prototypes keep expectations low: No one expects a paper prototype to work, and for every drawing you save, you'll toss four.

While paper prototyping MasterList Professional, and about 50 custom applications for corporate customers, I've found that not all paper is created equal. When it comes time to start defining a new part of an application's interface, I take three or four 5×8-inch legal pads, a large cup of strong coffee, and a cat and then go sit away from all computers and start sketching the user interface.

Now, these sketches are terrible—they're just little squiggly lines in something like a box, as shown in Figure 2-2.

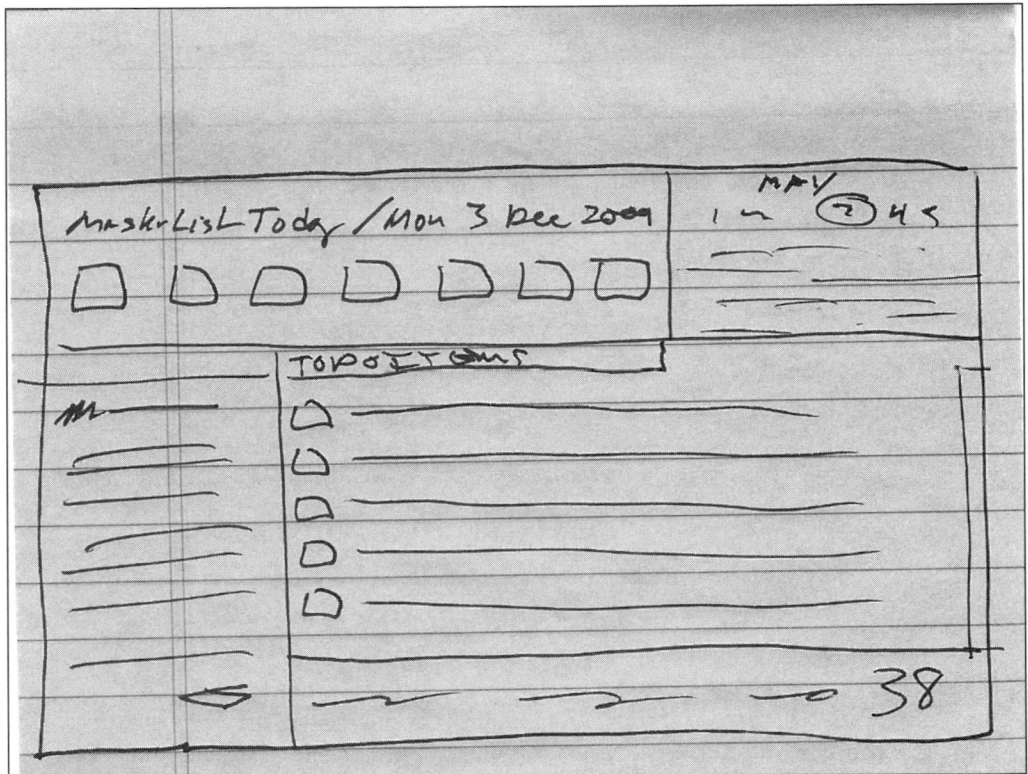

Figure 2-2. *Creating MasterList Professional's small paper prototype*

The nice feature of paper prototypes is that I can whip out five or six in the time it takes for the cat to get fidgety and decide he has better things to do. With the rough cuts and the relevant use cases, I can sit down, finish my coffee, and draw a full paper version of the screen I'm working on (as shown in Figure 2-3) and then move on to the next thing.

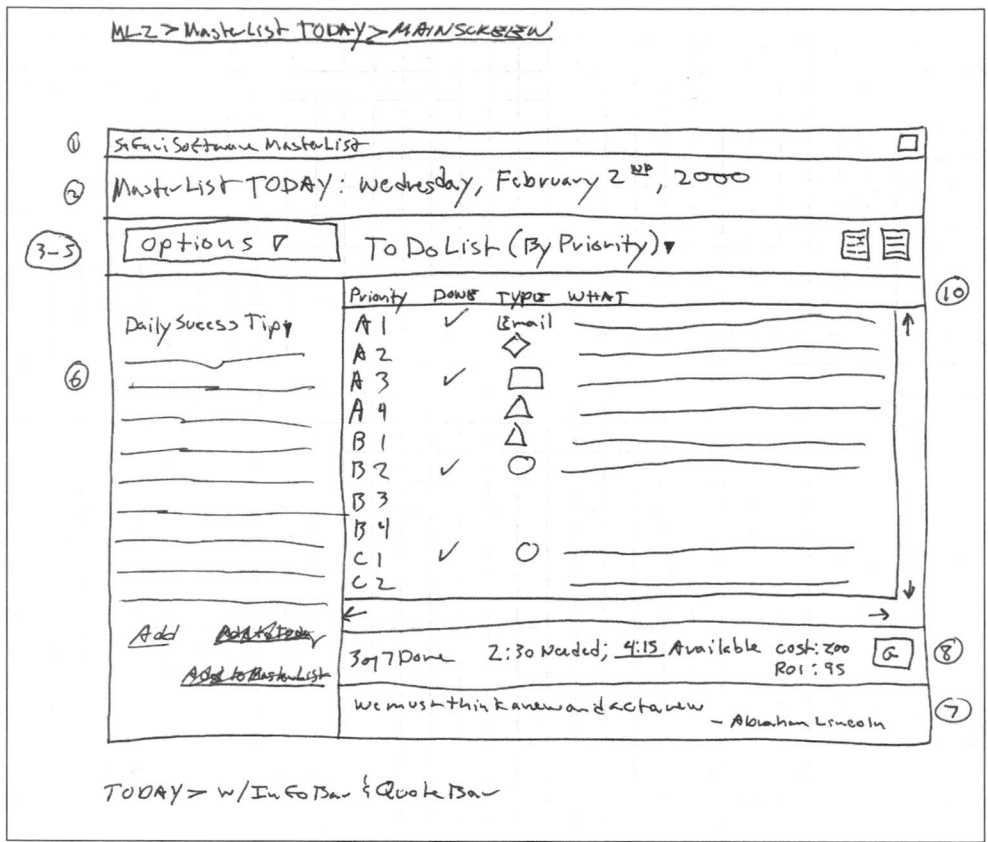

Figure 2-3. *Creating an early paper prototype for MasterList Professional's Home tab*

Paper prototypes aren't just about static screens. Another technique I've found that works is *storyboarding*. A storyboard is nothing more than a successive set of drawings or sketches showing how features progress; creative types in film, television, and advertising have been using storyboards for decades, as shown in Figure 2-4.

The reason I'm showing you some of the 70,000 or so images of storyboards Google has indexed is to drive home two points about storyboarding: there's no one right way to create storyboards, and storyboards can be extremely flexible to suit your needs.

Now, I'll be the first to admit that if I had to make my living drawing, I'd be living under an overpass in short order. Your drawing ability isn't the point. All you want to do when you initially create paper prototypes is create something that's a useful approximation of what your customers will ultimately see.

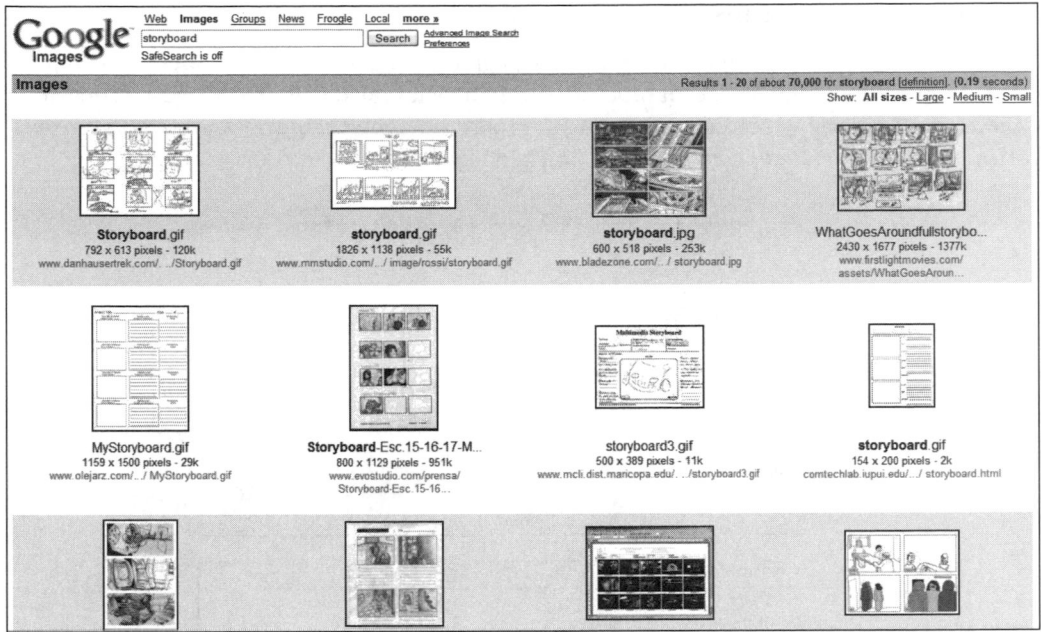

Figure 2-4. *Viewing storyboards in Google Images*

If you want to dig further into paper prototyping, I strongly recommend *Paper Prototyping: The Fast and Easy Way to Design and Refine User Interfaces* by Carolyn Snyder (Morgan Kaufmann, 2003). In the meantime, Table 2-1 describes some of the finer points to keep in mind when paper prototyping your micro-ISV application.

Table 2-1. *Dos and Don'ts for Paper Prototyping*

Do	Don't
Do draw first, critique later.	Don't get hung up on making features exactly to scale.
Do use big pads, little pads, and paper stolen from your printer.	Don't redo entire drawings because one part is wrong. (Instead, draw it on another sheet, cut it out, and paste over it.)
Do try to find a methodology for paper prototyping that yields the same level of detail each time.	Don't ignore times when you find too many interface elements on one paper "screen shot." This is a warning you're expecting too much from your customer!
Do write as many notes as you need on the same sheet as the drawing.	Don't forget to process these notes into your decisions document (see the next section) and your schedule (see the "Developing the Schedule" section).
Do refer to your use cases to make sure your interface delivers.	Don't try to draw every possible variation of a process.

Decisions, Decisions

One of the less frequently mentioned parts of designing is that it isn't just about what you put into an application, Web service, or product; it's about what you decide to omit. As you develop your micro-ISV flagship product, keep a log or project notebook of the decisions you make as you go along in a *decisions document,* as shown in Figure 2-5.

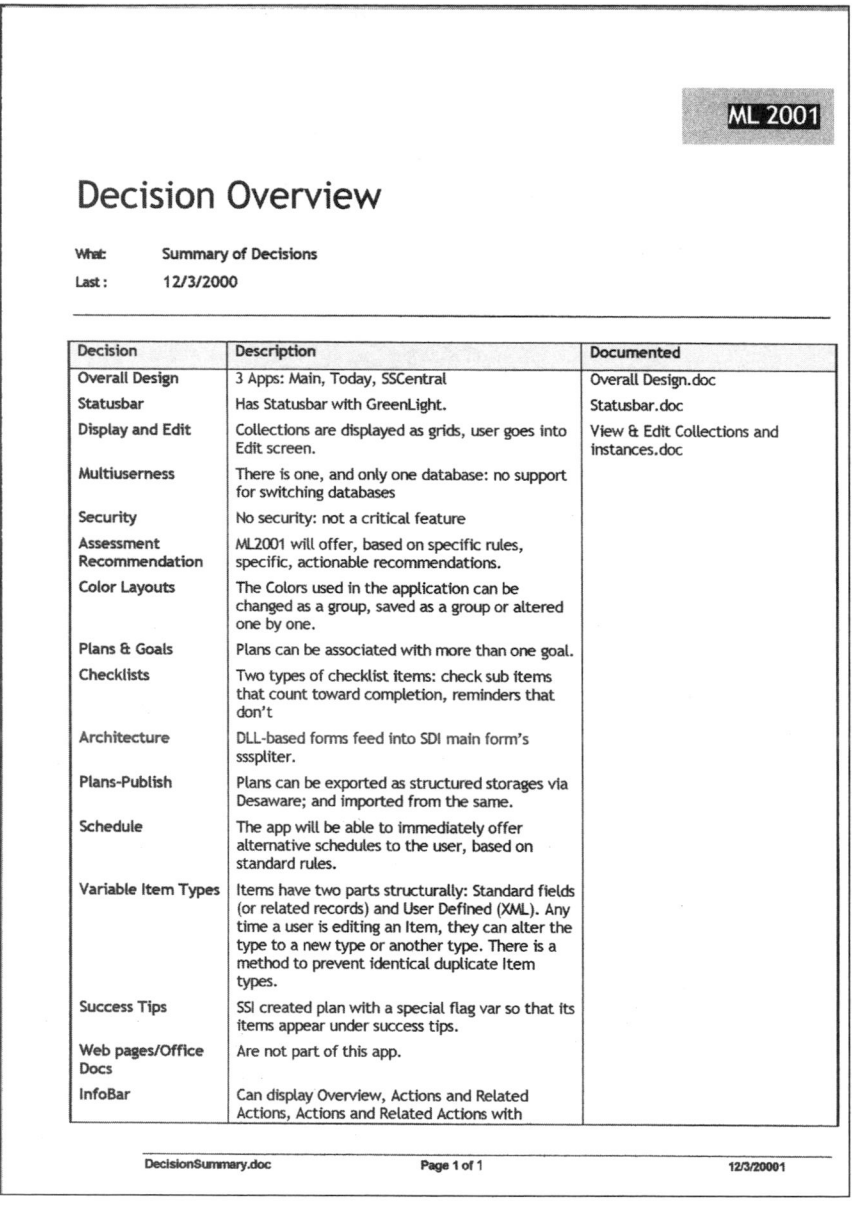

Figure 2-5. *Creating a decisions document for MasterList Professional*

Few tasks are more frustrating than working through how one part of your program should work and then revisiting the design weeks or months later and wondering why you decided on that design.

A good decisions document helps you set the scope of your product, records the fruits of your research efforts, and identifies potential enhancements. Whether you create the document in a word processor, a spreadsheet, a database, as Web pages, or a wiki is up to you. Just keep in mind that like a lot of design issues, you want to keep it simple enough so you never need to worry about how to record your decisions.

Instead, you can worry about something everybody just loves: the schedule.

Developing the Schedule

A man is known by the company he organizes.

—Ambrose Bierce (1842–1914), American author, editor, journalist[1]

Ambrose didn't have to deal with milestones, deadlines, or the dreaded schedule; otherwise, his dictionary would have been about three times longer. But you do, even if the only resource you have to level is you, and every critical path runs from your fingers to your keyboard.

When you're a team of one programmer (or even two or three people), you can narrow the process of creating, revising, updating, and completing the dreaded schedule to the core essentials:

- What has to be done?

- How long do you think it will take to do each task?

- How long did it take in reality?

Reread that last bullet—it's a killer. Estimating software tasks is somewhere between a best guess and throwing darts blindfolded in a high wind. Results are going to vary widely. That may be OK if you're working for someone else (even if you're working 18-hour days, your paycheck is hitting your account as scheduled); it's Definitely Not OK if you're in a race between getting your micro-ISV up and running and making money before the last of yours runs out.

Make no mistake: if you're going to make it to the Promised Land of milk, honey, and revenue, you'll have to find some way to keep and maintain your development schedule.

In the following sections, I'll cover the two methods that I know work: a method based on Joe Spolsky's Painless Software Schedules and MasterList Professional.

Using Painless Software Schedules

If you search for the term *software schedule* on Google, the first entry you're likely to find is the "Painless Software Schedules" article Joel Spolsky wrote on his Web site in 2000.[2] Now, Joel is a genuinely Smart Guy, and this article lays out a simple way to use Microsoft Excel to create software schedules worth the paper they're printed on.

Here's the gist of Joel's approach:

---

1. *The Devil's Dictionary* (Bloomsbury, 2004)
2. http://www.joelonsoftware.com/articles/fog0000000245.html

1. Use Microsoft Excel.

2. Keep it simple. Seven columns will do, as shown in Figure 2-6.

Schedule.xls							
1		**2**	**3**	**4**	**5**	**6**	**7**
1	Feature	Task	Priority	Orig Est	Curr Est	Elapsed	Remain
2	Spell Checker	Add Menu Item	1	12	8	8	0
3	Spell Checker	Main Dialog	1	8	12	8	4
4	Spell Checker	Dictionary	2	4	4	4	0
5	Grammar Checker	Add Menu Item	1	16	16	0	16
6							
7							
8							
◄ ◄ ► ►◄ Sheet1 ⟨ Sheet2 ⟨ Sheet3 ⟩				◄			►

Figure 2-6. *Doing Painless Software Schedules the Joel way*

3. Divide features into tasks.

4. Only the programmer who is going to write the code can schedule it.

5. Define tasks as hours so you describe real blocks of programming effort, not wishful thinking.

6. Keep your schedule working by keeping track of both the original estimate and current estimate for each task. The difference between the two is important and useful.

7. Update your elapsed time daily.

8. Include debugging, integration, and other tasks such as updating your documentation and performing unit test cases.

9. The schedule works if it's telling you the truth. You may not like the truth, you may have to decide to cut features, but that's not the schedule's fault.

The beauty of Joel's method is that as long as you stick to it, the method will tell you the truth about your development schedule; I know of several micro-ISVs that have used Joel's method to develop their software. And, in 2002 and 2003, I used Joel's method to plan and execute my first foray into noncustom software, MasterList-XL.

MasterList-XL (http://www.safarisoftware.com/mlxlDownload.htm) took Joel's ideas and ran. Specifically, I tracked my tasks in Microsoft Excel, made them real tasks and not wishes, and added two points I thought were missing from Joel's original equation: some tasks have to be done by a certain date, and the more time you spend on less important tasks, the less time you can spend on more important tasks.

Something like 40,000 people have downloaded MasterList-XL since I first made it available, and I've heard from enough people over the years who still use it to manage all sorts of projects, including micro-ISV projects, to know it works.

But although I still give MasterList-XL away for free, I've developed what I think is a better tool for managing projects: MasterList Professional.

Using MasterList Professional

I'll keep this section of this book ultrashort for a couple of reasons. First, the software itself, my company's Web site, and my blog do a good job of making the case for using MasterList Professional to manage not just the design and development of a micro-ISV's product but all the other projects you need to complete. You can read about it, watch movies of it, and try it for free for 45 days at `http://www.safarisoftware.com`.

The second reason is to demonstrate a little applied earnestness of intent here: the main message I hope you take away from this section of the book is that whatever has been your business experience with scheduling projects, scheduling your micro-ISV product's development is both doable and necessary.

Examining Your Development Infrastructure

Source Control Management (SCM) is one of those "infrastructure" things you usually get to take for granted when you get paid on a regular schedule to program and get a steady supply of electricity, phones that work, and office supplies. Entire chunks of IT departments spend their time worrying about repository backups and the like; aren't you glad you don't have to do this?

That was then, this is now, and now the IT department is just you. Just as there's a programmer's heaven where you can buy fun, interesting things, there's a programmer's hell where you go if you don't build a safety net for your development efforts. You don't want to go there—it's a painful place, with lots of unhappy people, and it takes a long time to leave.

Been there, done that.

Let me tell you a quick story of why SCM for a micro-ISV isn't like shoes for fish: In the first half of 2005 when I was still doing contract development, the latest version of an application I wrote for a good client of mine who provides specialized management consulting to certain portions of the U.S. government developed a wee problem. The app stopped working.

Build 79 worked fine on my dev machine, my test boxes, and the client's test boxes, and it locked up tight when installed using a special installer that had worked fine for the past 78 builds.

Now, the usual solution would be to rebuild the install script or, if necessary, change installers. No can-do: we had to use the existing installer, because it manages to let you install a Windows app through some parallel dimension that never touches the actual operating system, letting people install the app and run it from a CD—something my client's client, those certain portions of the federal government, is quite fond of nowadays.

Did I mention the installer stopped running the new build five days before a key presentation to one of my client's clients? Did I mention that some features in the new build absolutely had to be demonstrated? Did I mention that the makers of this installer had decided to take a collective trip to some small Pacific island and weren't answering their phones or emails? Did I mention that the man whom this presentation was going to be made to was at the top of a chain of command with more firepower than all the bombs dropped during World War II?

Now, I wish I could say that with a quick flip of the SCM's diffing software I was able to move the key features back into a build that this transdimensional installer liked, but I can't.

You see, about five years ago when the SCM system that came with a certain IDE I used for most of my work died for no apparent reason, I did what a lot of small developers do and swore off SCM as something just not worth the bother. Oops!

Well, after spending 36 hours straight programming the new features back into a build that could be installed, the presentation went off without a hitch. And after the install vendor's staff came back from wherever they were and revved their installer, the mysterious problem disappeared. And after I had ended up with two differing code bases because some of my client's clients control weapons of mass destruction and others don't, I was able to easily merge the two code bases into one using one of the two SCMs I'll cover next.

What's more, by some fluke in the free market system, both these SCM tools offer a free license to solo developers.

Using SourceGear Vault

Remember Eric Sink from Chapter 1, the guy who coined the term *micro-ISV*? Eric's company, SourceGear, makes one of the best ways micro-ISVs can protect their code: Vault.

Vault (http://www.sourcegear.com, $199 USD per license without support) is a source control client-server application for Windows environments built as a seamless replacement for Microsoft's moribund Visual SourceSafe. Figure 2-7 shows Vault at work.

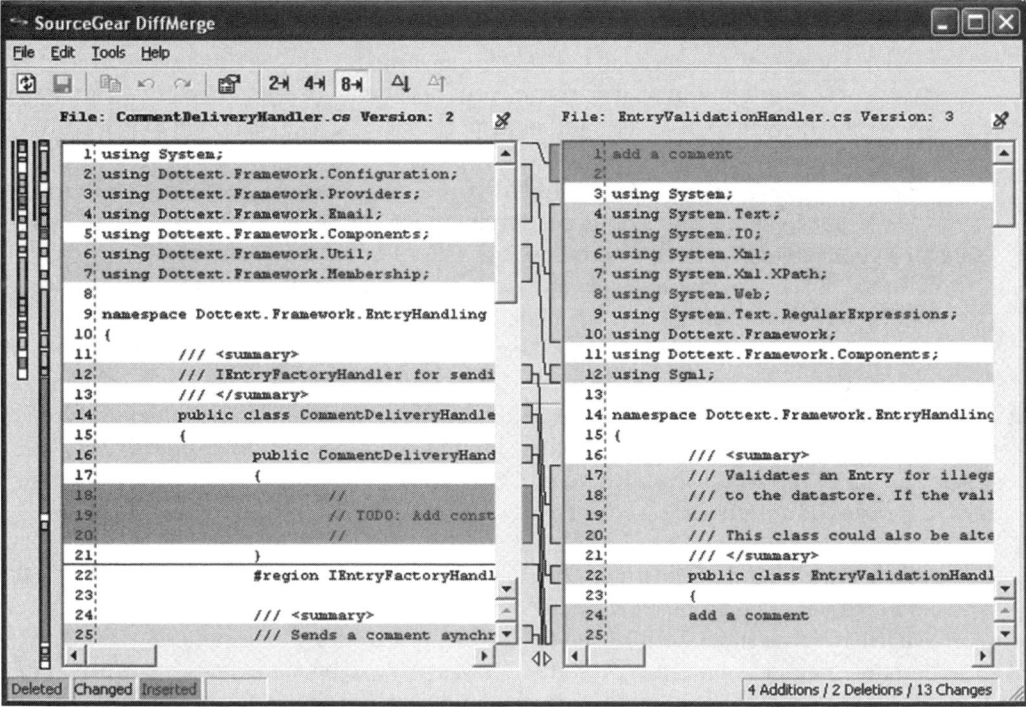

Figure 2-7. *A tale of two code bases: Vault at work*

SourceGear's main market is all those development shops and IT departments that are fed up with Microsoft Visual SourceSafe's limitations and arthritis and are comfortable adding another SQL Server–driven application to their production mix.

Although SourceGear's main market is enterprise, Sink makes the following points about why SCM should be part of every programmer's development infrastructure in his blog:

When I use a source control tool all by myself, here are the benefits that I find still apply:

It's an undo mechanism. Whenever I get to a good stopping point in my code, I check in my changes to the repository. From that point on, I can be less careful. I can try coding some crazy new idea, and when it doesn't work, I just revert my working folder to my last check-in point.

It's a historical archive. Sometimes I want to undo much further back. My repository history contains a full copy of every version I have ever checked in. If I ever need to go back and find something I once had, it's there.

It's a reference point for diff. A source control tool can easily show a diff of all the changes I've made since my last check-in.

It's a backup. When I regularly check in my work, I always know that there are two copies of it. If my *&^%#@! laptop hard drive dies again, my code is still safe in the repository.

It's a journal of my progress. When I do my regular check-ins, I write a comment explaining what I was doing. These comments serve as a log or a journal, explaining the motivation behind every change I have ever made.

It's a server. Sometimes I'm coding on different computers. The repository becomes my central server. I can go anywhere I want, and I can still get to my code.

When I interviewed Sink for this book, I asked him if he had any other points to add:

People who don't think source control is helpful for one person are usually the same people who think they can live without it for a team of two or three. So they try to "just get by," storing their files on a public file server. Anyone who has experienced the pain of this situation has realized that source control is always worth the trouble for any plurality of developers and has vowed never to repeat the mistake.

Those who have not experienced this pain would be wise to learn from those who have.

Another interesting aspect of Vault is that it's free for a single developer. Why? "The main reason is that it allows Vault to be used by a whole bunch of solo consultants, many of whom go on to recommend Vault to their clients," Sink explains.

Using Perforce Software

With more than 160,000 developers at 3,500+ organizations worldwide, Perforce is based in Alameda, California, and is a major player in the SCM world. The Perforce SCM system (http://www.perforce.com/perforce/products.html, $800 USD per single annual license) has clients for Windows, Mac OS X, Linux, Solaris, and FreeBSD. Figure 2-8 shows Perforce's Windows client, and Figure 2-9 shows Perforce's WinMerge program.

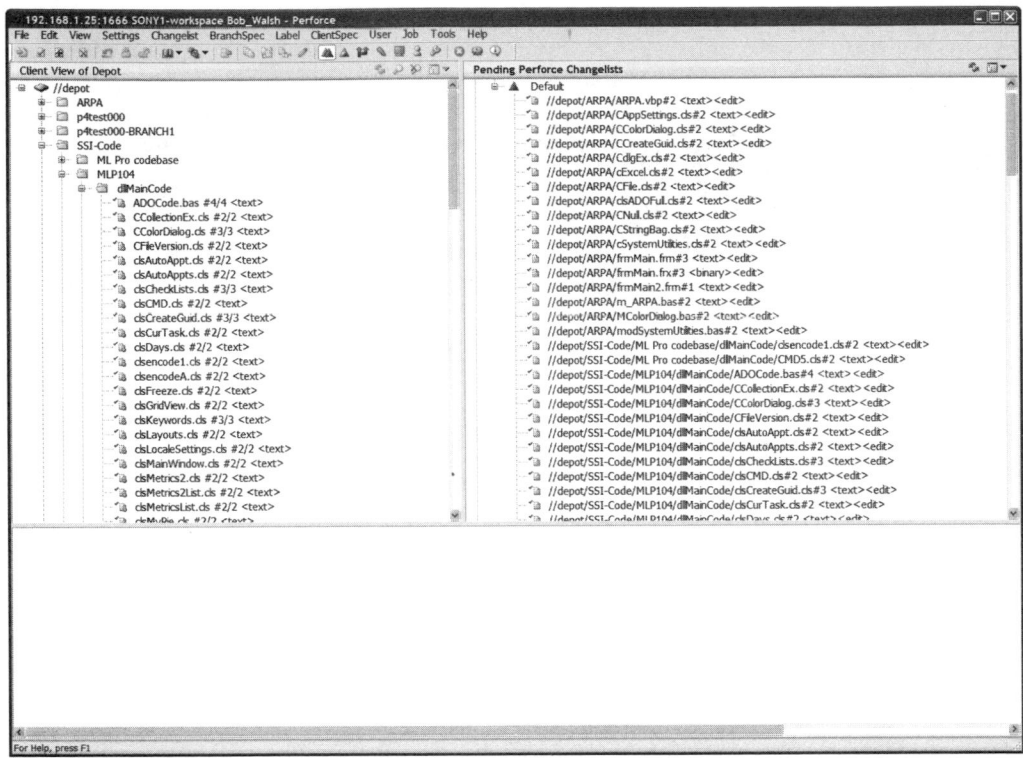

Figure 2-8. *Perforce's Windows client*

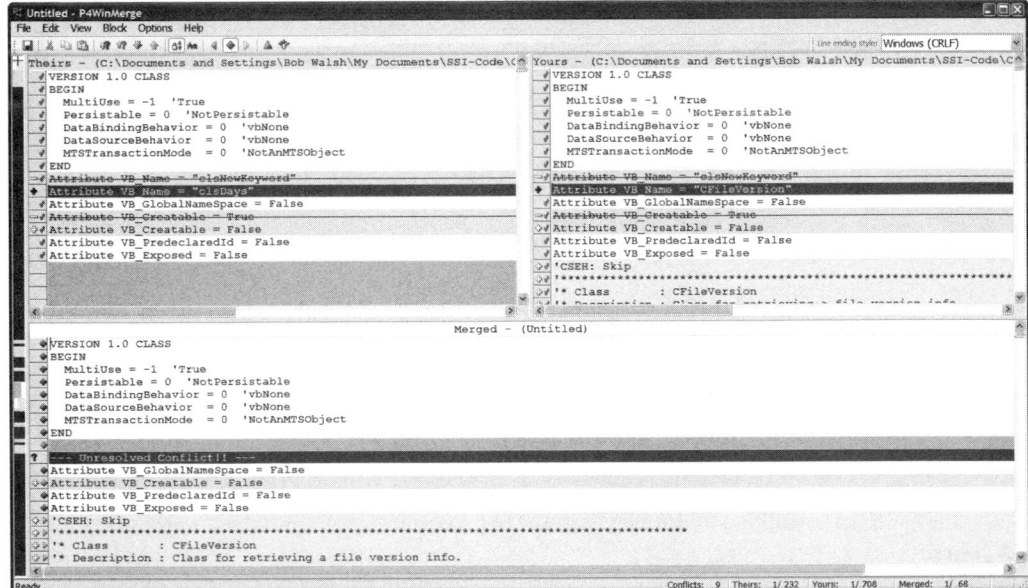

Figure 2-9. *Perforce's WinMerge program*

Perforce may look like massive overkill for a micro-ISV. This isn't so, says Nigel Chanter, Perforce's chief operating officer (COO):

> *Programming teams of any size need Source Control. Without it, releases go out the door with uncertain contents. Bug fixes get lost, and engineers see their development efforts wasted in a blundered process.*
>
> *What could be more frustrating than debugging a block of code only to discover that someone else debugged that same block of code the day before? Imagine hunting for the most recent revision of a software module, completed three weeks ago by a team that has since been reassigned.... Finally, picture the amount of time wasted if you had to re-create a specific version of a piece of software shipped to a customer six months ago, and the customer is now calling you because there are bugs that need fixing.*
>
> *All of these problems could be avoided by employing Source Control.*
>
> *Source Control tools are the means by which the evolution of a software product can be tracked and managed. As a subject, Source Control has often been accused of lacking excitement. That is, in fact, the point of SCM: some excitement can be done without. All these examples apply to teams of two or two thousand, and some apply to that lone developer.*

Also, interestingly enough, Perforce is free for up to two developers: "Perforce does indeed offer a free two-user version (five client workspaces); however, we offer technical support only to paying customers or prospects evaluating the product for purchase," Chanter adds.

When the Going Gets Tough, the Tough Get Virtual

One of the hardest parts of being a micro-ISV is dealing with the god-awful configuration mess. Regardless of whether you're developing a desktop, server-based, or hybrid application, the endless permutations of operating systems, browsers, and core components can drive you crazy. Then, just for fun, add the need to support at least a modicum of international audiences, and you have a major risk factor to becoming a successful micro-ISV.

For example, MasterList Professional is a relatively simple Visual Basic 6 application storing its data in a single Microsoft Access (.mdb) file, incorporating ten third-party controls (.ocx files). Or at least I thought it was simple until I found myself dealing with about ten flavors of ActiveX Data Objects (ADO), screen resolutions that ran from 640×800 to dual 1600×1200 monitors, and the joys of Hungarian date formats.

If you want your application to succeed (make money and not drive you crazy), you want to manage this risk from the start of your development process. And unless you happen to own a couple dozen computers, you need to think about how to create and manage virtual test environments.

In the following sections, I'll cover three strategies that use different toolsets and give you a way to define your own. These strategies are by no means equal, but they're all better than not having any strategy at all.

Strategy 1: Back Up Images

Until a few years ago, creating hard disk images was the best available way of "provisioning" your testing environment. You can still use a product such as Symantec Norton Ghost 10.0

(http://www.symantec.com, $69.95 USD) to create images of a working base machine and then restore your test machine as needed by overwriting it with an image when you need to do so.

Although creating a test machine from an image works, it's at best only a partial solution. It's slow, taking anywhere from 10 to 20 minutes to reapply an image stored on the testing computer's hard drive and longer—much longer—if you have to go across the network.

Many a developer cried out for a better tool, and unsurprisingly, the call was answered.

Strategy 2: Use Microsoft Virtual PC (Connectix)

In the last decade, Connectix started selling a nifty application that could somehow create a Windows PC running inside a Windows PC. This Virtual PC for Windows solution could do just about everything a real PC could do: install and test software, run Microsoft Office, talk to the network, and talk to the Internet. If you crashed the *virtual machine*, no big deal: just restart the app, and try again.

This development didn't go unnoticed in Redmond, Washington. In August 2003, Microsoft acquired Connectix for a large, undisclosed sum, promising to continue to develop and support these *virtualization* products.

As of this writing, not much has happened with Microsoft Virtual PC. It still lets you run as a guest operating system every operating system Microsoft has released back to MS-DOS 6.22; the software comes free as part of the MSDN Universal Subscription via the Empower Program, which is very good. Or, you can buy it as a stand-alone product (https://partner.microsoft.com/global/40010429, $129 USD).

Strategy 3: Use VMware and VMTN

Then there's VMware. Where Virtual PC ends, VMware Workstation 5 (http://www.vmware.com/, $189 USD per developer), Physical to Virtual (P2V) Assistant, and virtualization servers take off.

Take, for instance, the Snapshot Manager, as shown in Figure 2-10. With snapshots, you can incrementally save your virtual machine like you would a document or spreadsheet. With the Snapshot Manager, you get a clear, simple interface for managing those snapshots that shows how each virtual machine you created relates to its predecessor and successors.

VMware performs all the features Microsoft Virtual PC does but does them so much better that you end up with another level of functionality. Figure 2-11 and Figure 2-12 show running Windows XP in a virtual PC in VMware on a Windows XP notebook, complete with antispyware and antivirus programs running. Figure 2-13 and Figure 2-14 show MasterList Professional being downloaded and installed, and Figure 2-15 shows it running.

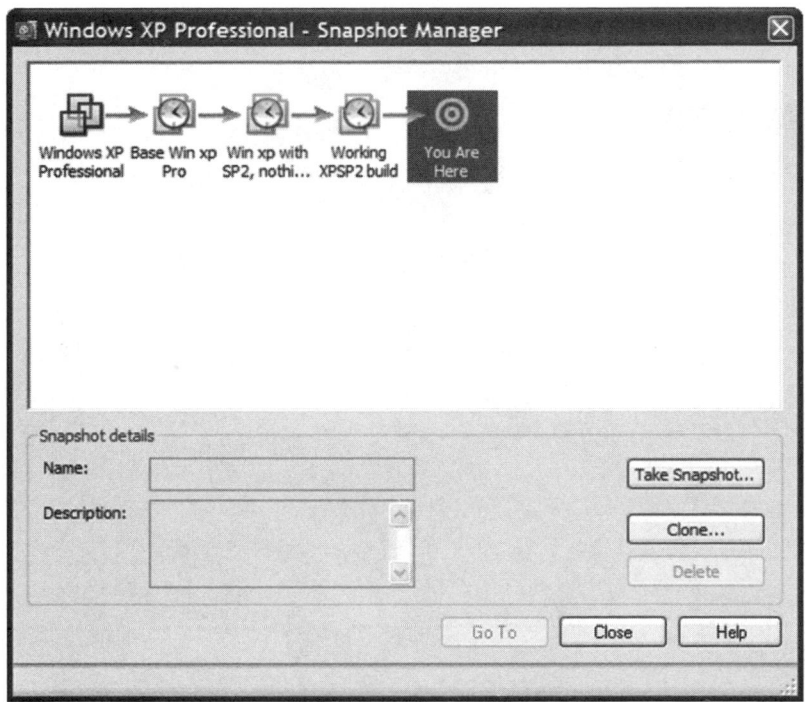

Figure 2-10. *I'm in love: the Snapshot Manager.*

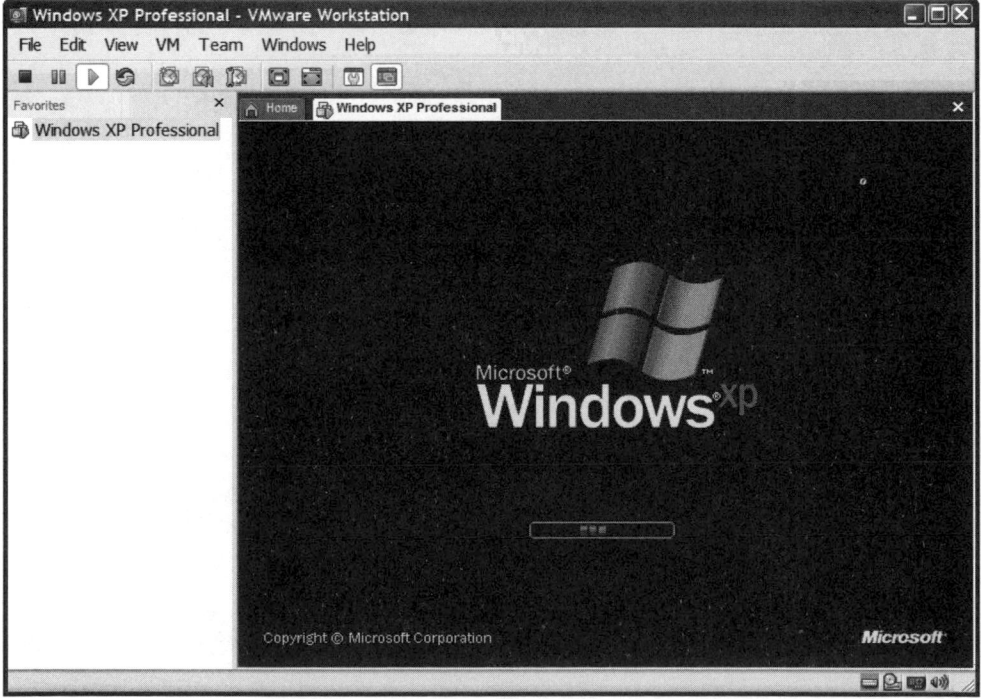

Figure 2-11. *Running Windows XP in VMware*

Figure 2-12. *Viewing a too real virtual machine*

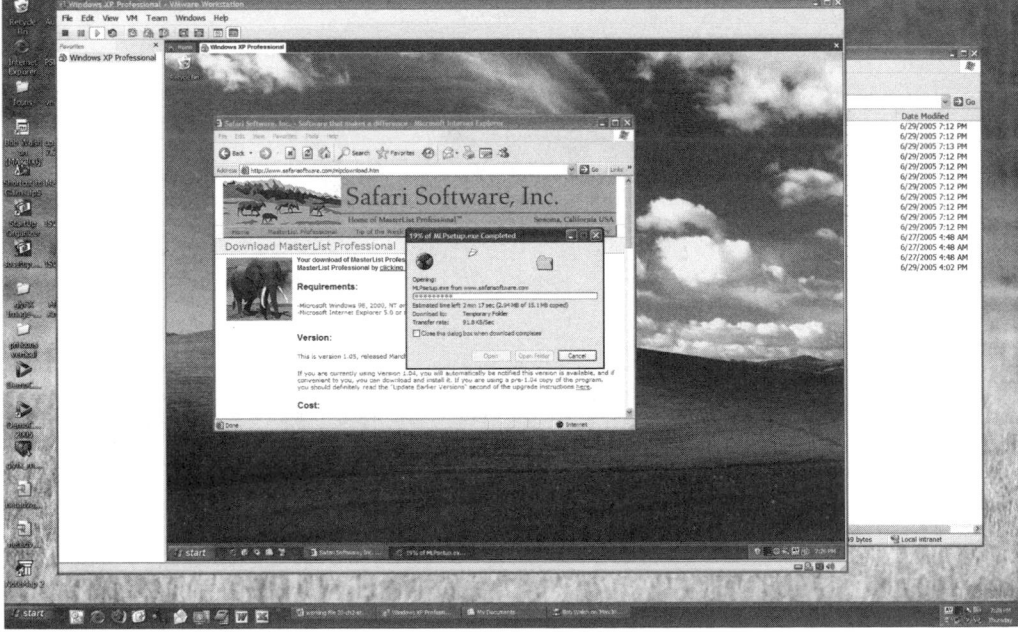

Figure 2-13. *Downloading MasterList Professional*

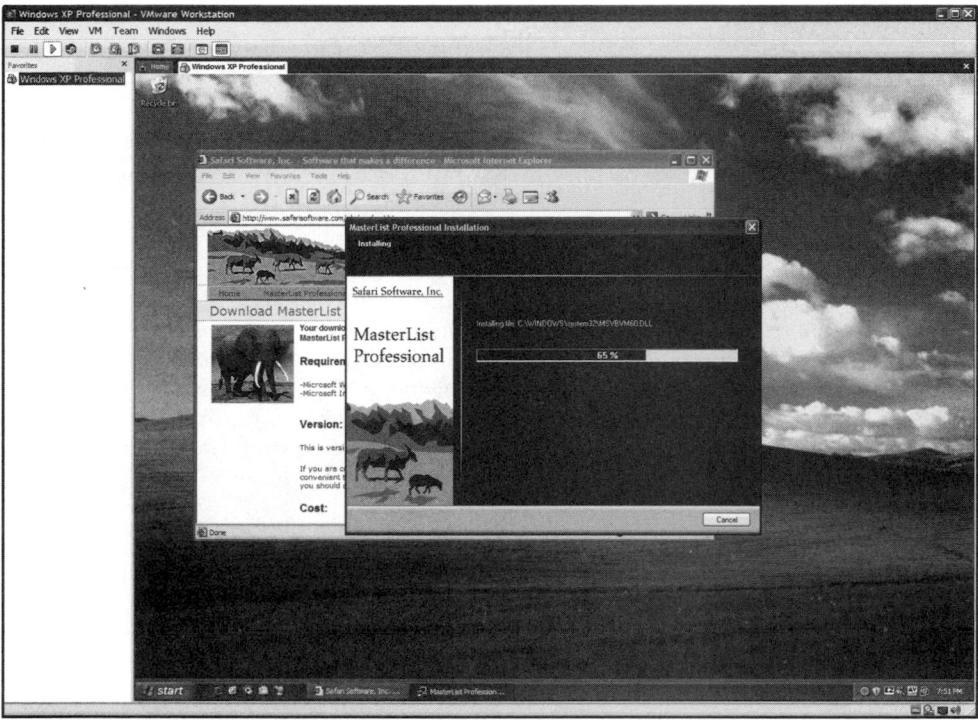

Figure 2-14. *Installing MasterList Professional*

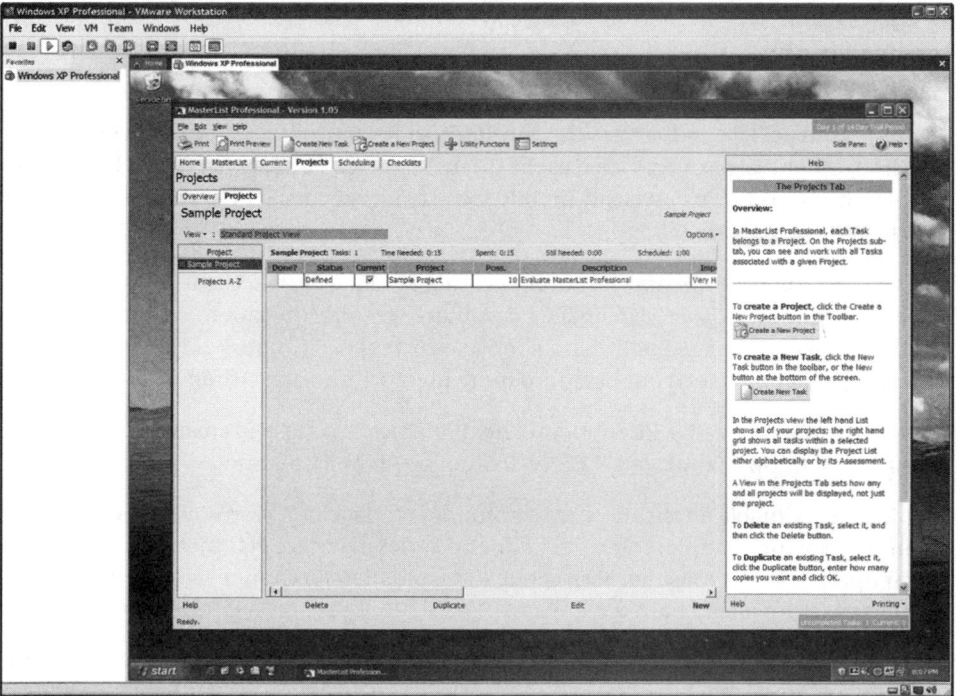

Figure 2-15. *Running MasterList Professional in its own VM*

Although aimed squarely at enterprise-sized companies that want to save on development and deployment costs, a VMware solution means micro-ISVs can create and manage entire virtual testing centers for a pittance.

"I would argue that VMware is one of those critical pieces of software for a start-up, precisely because it allows you to use the resources of a much larger company without actually deploying those physical resources," says Kevin Epstein, VMware's vice president for marketing. He adds the following:

> *If I'm a single guy in a garage with two solid server machines, and I'm trying to develop a multitier app and test it against ten clients, I don't have the physical resources to do that. But if I choose to deploy all those resources within a set of virtual machines, I could create that infrastructure within the confines of a single physical machine and still have leftover workspace—instead of developing something, testing something, and finding it doesn't work and having to wipe the entire system and start over [on a test PC]. Even if I backed it up, it's still several hours' time. With VMware, I just hit reset, and I'm back to a clean state.*

Like Virtual PC, VMware lets you create a virtual PC, install your operating system and app, and then test. But it's the "deeper-thinking" features of VMware that make it a compelling micro-ISV tool:

- You can quickly take snapshots while deep in your application and then quickly reset to exactly where you were (no more virtual reboots).

- The built-in movie recorder lets you capture the steps leading to a bug's appearance.

- You can set how much random access memory (RAM), disk space, and bandwidth your virtual PC will have. Besides meaning you no longer need to keep old PCs around for testing, you can test other features such as how your Web site looks to a visitor accessing the Internet via dial-up access.

- Multiple virtual PCs and servers can run at the same time, talking with each other and, if desired, other real resources such as the Internet. You can box sets of virtual PCs, controlling them as a set. You can easily modify these teams of virtual PCs, adding or dropping virtual PCs as needed.

- It offers extremely good optimization. A virtual PC typically runs faster than a real PC, you can clone a virtual PC as a linked clone that saves only the difference between states, and memory is managed and shared between virtual PCs running at the same time, meaning you don't need about a third more memory for each virtual PC.

- You can run VMware on a PC running either Windows or Linux and create virtual machines running Windows, Linux, or a variety of other x86-based operating systems.

- It offers a scriptable application programming interface (API) for VMware's virtualization servers; for example, you could launch a series of virtual PCs that each launches your application or a test harness application and then takes snapshots of the results while you sleep after a hard day's work.

- It gives you the ability to import a Microsoft Virtual PC or a Norton Ghost image file into a VMware virtual machine file.

So, what does your testing or development PC need to run VMware well? From my experience, a virtual Windows XP PC runs as fast or faster than a physical computer on a notebook computer with an Intel Pentium M processor 750 and 1GB of PC2700 DDR RAM. The key factor is memory; you need "good, high-speed RAM and lots of it," according to Epstein. "With a lot of RAM, you can build things that will work faster and better in virtual space than in physical space. He adds the following:

> *It's the same thing as if you had a room full of physical machines, with someone walking around, turning one on, starting tests, waiting for results to compile, and stopping tests. But instead of physically turning them on, the API is doing all the work for you.*

In June 2005, VMware went one large step further and started offering its entire set of applications and servers on a subscription basis for $299 USD per developer per year for development and testing.

Addressing the Quality Issue

Although it may seem strange to talk about quality here, ensuring that your development process delivers a product with as few bugs as possible is an infrastructure issue. You can't add quality to a code base; you need to have a process that makes quality code.

The quality issue is especially important for micro-ISVs. Customers tend to take bugs more personally when they're in an application from a small company than from, say, Microsoft. Also, the more bugs in your product, the more of your limited time will have to go to tech support and be stolen from marketing; remember, you get only 1,440 minutes a day.

A robust beta program with at least the second phase of it public will reveal bugs (see the next section), but you want to give some serious thought about how to make quality improvements part of your development infrastructure. And that means testing.

By and by, programmers hate to test their code. For some, this is because they came up the ranks from testing. For others, this is because that's what testers do. For most, this is because after spending two or six or sixteen hours coding, all the little gray cells are limp. However, as bad as testing is, not testing is worse. At the very least, you need to reread the code you write.

Let me tell you a little story about what not reading your code can cost you: In the early 1980s, I got one of my first contract programming jobs at AT&T when the big, nasty monopoly was being subdivided into a bunch of mini-monopolies, and somebody had to do the programming to tally for the first time whether a customer was going to defect from Ma Bell. Since AT&T's MIS division said it would take five years to develop a polling system, but the federal judge said it would take one year, each region got to work out—somehow—how to process this data.

I got to be, along with a few others, a junior part of the *somehow*.

The processing had to be done using a statistics package called SAS and JCL—that's Statistical Analysis System and Job Control Language—because that was all we could run on AT&T's mainframes. Think of the scene in Mel Brooks' *Young Frankenstein* when the creature is brought to life, and you have the right idea.

Anyway, one day when I got to work I found the rest of the team huddled around a desk looking fairly nauseous, pouring over the job results of the run I'd coded and submitted the day before. Roy, my boss, looked up, and asked me the following:

"Bob, did you remember to check your JCL code before submitting it last night?"

"Yeah, I think I did…uhh…why?"

"Well, if you'd checked line 144, you would have found the statement where you incremented by zero."

"Incremented by zero?"

"Right. And that means this entire data run is junk. Expensive junk. Very, very expensive junk."

"Uhh…how expensive, Roy?"

"Oh, about a quarter million dollars. But don't worry, we won't take it out of your pay this time."

Needless to say, the lesson stuck in my mind.

The following are three methods you can use to avoid the mistakes that might cost your micro-ISV a great deal of potential revenue. These are by no means the only ways of ensuring quality code, but they should get you started.

Method 1: Use a Code Checklist

Using a code checklist is the easiest method of the lot. Go into Microsoft Word, write the half-dozen coding mistakes you've last made, print the document, and look at the list as you review the code you wrote today. See any familiar faces? Write down other ways you miss the mark as they crop up, and revise your code's checklist.doc periodically.

What you'll notice over time is coding is just like spelling. You make certain coding mistakes repeatedly, but if you focus on them, you'll make them less often.

Just the process of checking my code against my private coding checklist identifies about half of the coding mistakes I make, especially those nasty increment-by-zero blunders and other simple errors. Give it a try!

Strategy 2: Use Unit Testing and Test Driven Development

Depending on what you're using to code your micro-ISV's application, you may be able to sufficiently modularize your code to test each unit independently from the rest of your code base. Visual Basic 6, ASP Classic, and JavaScript don't lend themselves to class-by-class or unit-by-unit testing; Visual Basic .NET, C#, .NET, ASP.NET, Java, and other modern languages do.

The concept of unit testing is simple: build a test harness that exercises each unit of code for correctness and can be repeated as often as that code changes. One of the shining success stories of the open source movement has been a family of tools by different teams, starting with Erick Gamma and Kent Beck, for automating creating and running unit tests for Java.

In the Windows development community, NUnit (http://www.nunit.org) is by far the most popular tool and has spawned a constellation of alternative interfaces and add-ons. With Microsoft Visual Studio 2005, NUnit has been "embraced and expanded" as a standard best practice for enterprise programming. Figure 2-16 shows you NUnit in action.

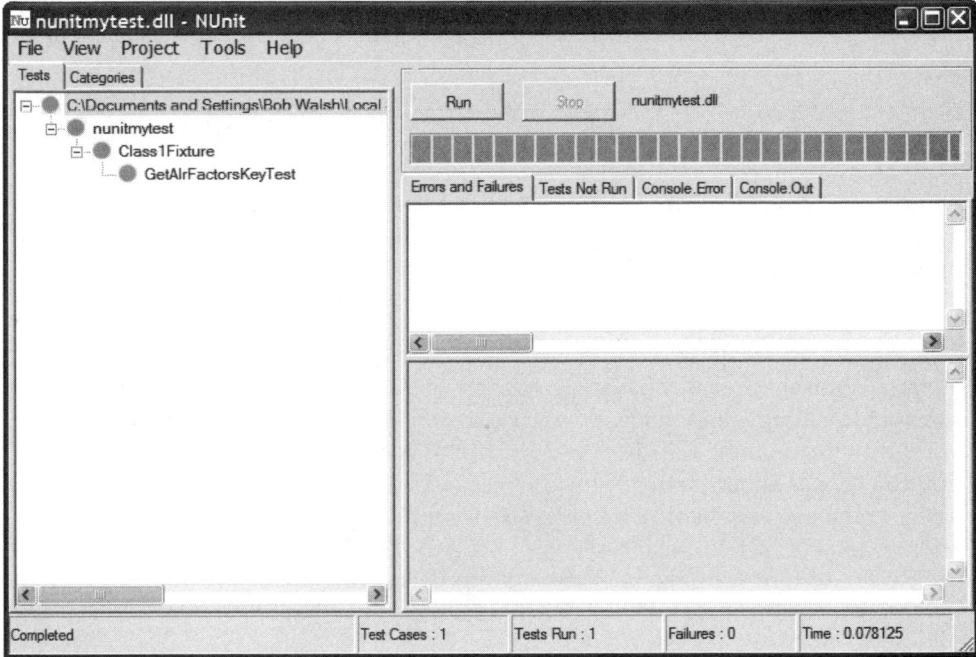

Figure 2-16. *Running NUnit 2.2 tests*

How to use NUnit as part of your testing and development infrastructure is beyond the scope of this book; you'll find a set of resources to get you started in the appendix. The point I'm making here is one of the emerging core best practices of professional programmers (bugs = less money): you should strongly consider incorporating at least some unit testing in your micro-ISV development process.

In fact, a growing school (swarm? flock?) of developers say not only should developers create and manage their own unit tests but they should create the unit tests *before* they code.

Pioneered by XP proponents, Test Driven Development (TDD) is unit testing squared and cubed:

1. Quickly add a test.

2. Run all tests to see the new one fail (there's no code there yet!).

3. Code just enough so the new test might work.

4. Run all the tests, and see them all work, including the new test.

5. Refactor your code.

By iteratively writing your tests first, several good things happen: you're forced to think about what each module or class is supposed to do, your code has far fewer bugs, and your refactored code tends to be of a higher quality.

TDD has its disadvantages too: much of your time is going to go to writing tests, not production code. And, although TDD works great on the internal aspects of an application, it isn't well suited to testing the user interface. Although you'll find a list of TDD resources in the appendix, here are two thoughts to consider before dismissing TDD as too "out there" for practical use:

- Would you rather spend x amount of time writing tests or at least 2x debugging code downstream?

- Software tools exist that are explicitly designed for testing applications from the user interface in; in fact, one of them is the third method for building quality into your development infrastructure.

Strategy 3: Use AutomatedQA's Test Complete

As thoroughly as you check your code against your list and unit test your classes, there's still the little matter of something going wrong as your customers actually use your application. Actually, it's not a little matter; nothing will kill a potential sale as fast as when a potential customer clicks a button in your application only to have it crash.

In the past, most companies' IT shops had dedicated testers who spent their days (and nights sometimes) clicking through test scripts and black-box testing your apps. Or, if an IT department was well funded (or has been recently embarrassed), the testers would work within an expensive automated testing suite such as IBM Rational Functional Tester or Mercury TestDirector.

Like your company ID card, those resources have gone away. So, what's a micro-ISV to do? In short, get AutomatedQA's TestComplete (http://www.automatedqa.com/products/testcomplete/; $349.99 USD for the standard version, $799.99 USD for the web application testing enterprise version, 30-day trial version available). TestComplete is a remarkable product for various forms of testing but shines for its ability to test on Windows platform desktop applications.

Learning, let alone mastering, TestComplete isn't something you can do over a lunch break, so let me run quickly through how this tool works so you can see whether it will work for your micro-ISV.

Let's say you're planning to make a million bucks with your micro-ISV's first Windows desktop application, Orders.[3] After you download, install, and start TestComplete, you start your application and click the Record Script button in TestComplete. You'll then see TestComplete's Recording toolbar, as shown in Figure 2-17.

Next, you exercise a function, such as creating a new order while TestComplete is recording your mouse and keyboard's events. (You can opt for recording at an even lower level, but most times that just gets in the way, since TestComplete can find most controls in most programming environments.) Along the way, you can save what your app or the screen looks like and the internal state of most variables in your application for later automated comparison.

So, you've created your order, stopped recording, and returned to TestComplete. TestComplete has written the test for you, as shown in Figure 2-18.

---

3. Yes, some micro-ISVs have made more than $1 million over the course of a few years; no, they didn't do so with this example application.

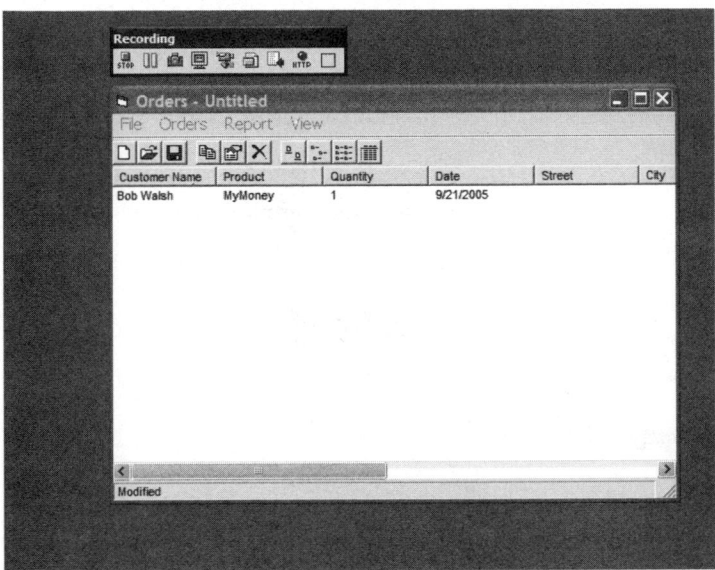

Figure 2-17. *Recording your application with TestComplete*

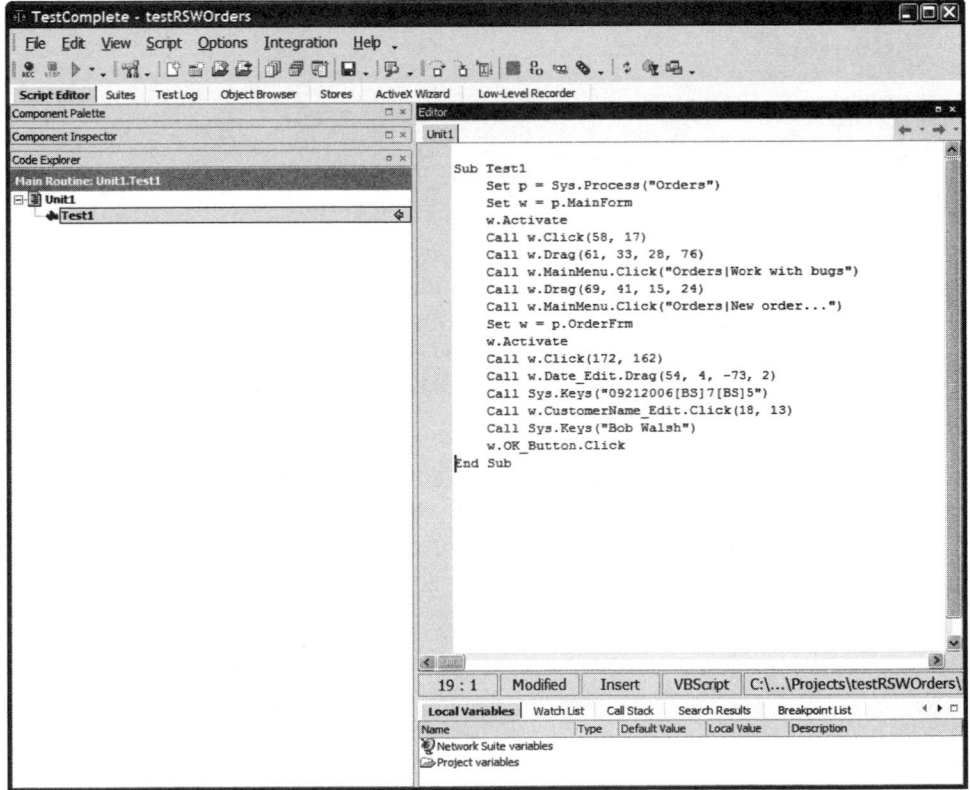

Figure 2-18. *Viewing the recorded script*

Now, TestComplete could have written this test in any of five programming languages (VBScript, JScript, Delphi, C++, and C#). Also, this could have been an app written in any .NET language, Visual Basic 6, Visual C++, MFC, ATL, Java, or Borland VCL, or it could have been a Web-based application (PHP or Ruby on Rails). In any of these cases, TestComplete could have handled it with aplomb.

By the way, if this looks more like an IDE than a simple editor, it is. TestComplete supports breakpoints, call stacks, watchpoints, and the ever-popular autocompletion feature when you're editing or writing tests, as shown in Figure 2-19.

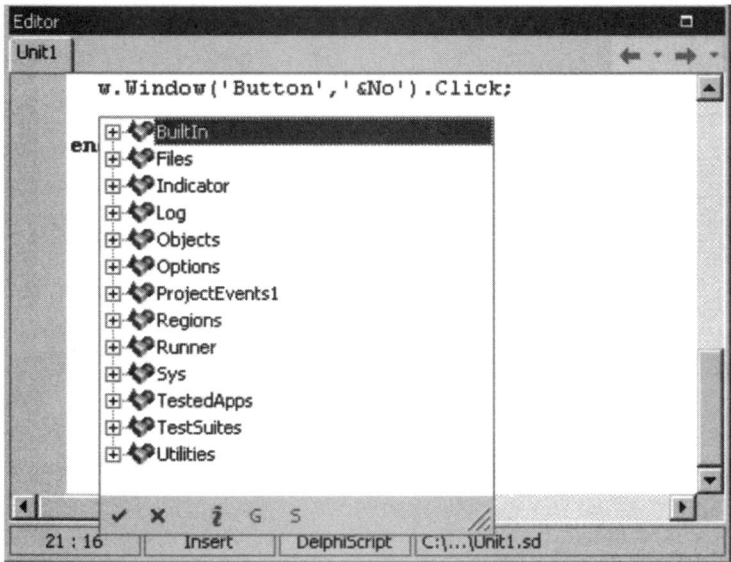

Figure 2-19. *Using TestComplete autocompletion*

Now that you have a test, you can run it. TestComplete saves detailed information on each test run inside itself or externally as Extensible Markup Language (XML), XML Style Language (XSL), and Hypertext Markup Language (HTML) that you can peruse in a browser, and you can build a whole set of structured and conditional tests as part of your test project, as shown in Figure 2-20.

TestComplete has been around since 1999 and has won numerous industry awards. The bottom line is the time, effort, and money it will cost you to implement TestComplete are all paid back when you release, and it pays back even more with each subsequent release.

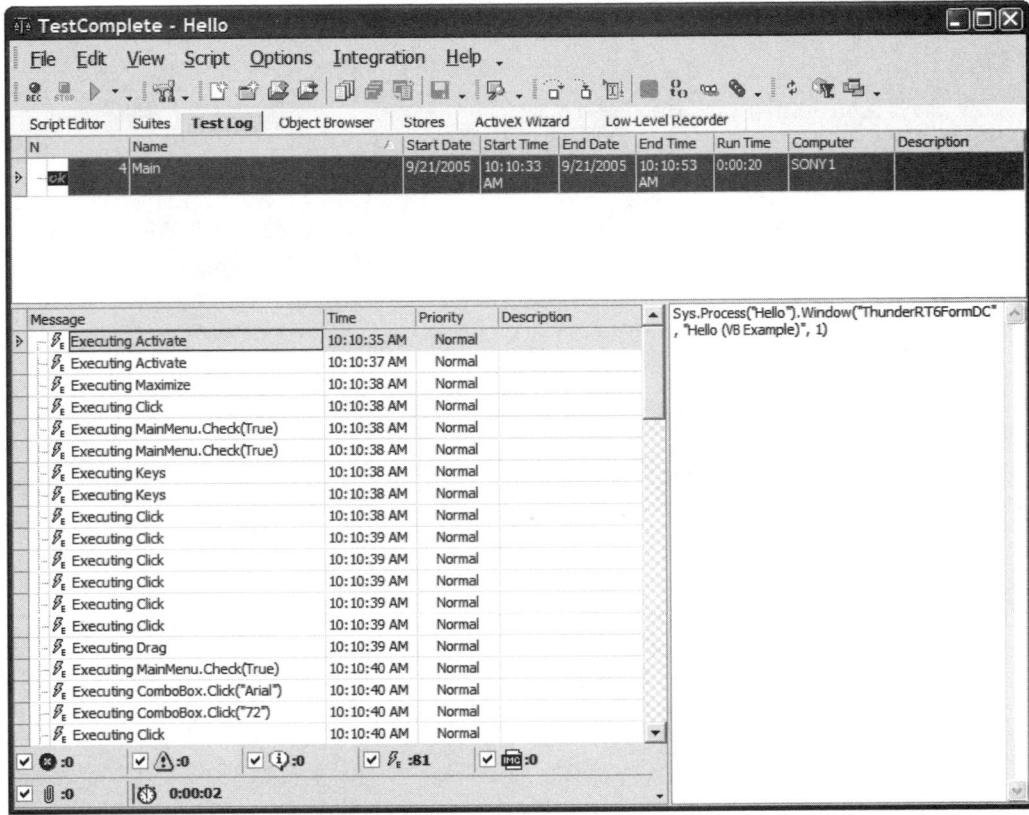

Figure 2-20. *Viewing the results of this test*

ATANAS STOYANOV, CHIEF SCIENTIST AND CEO, AUTOMATEDQA

It doesn't hurt that AutomatedQA, the company that makes, supports, and sells TestComplete (and several other useful products), was started by one man.

Q. For starters, why should a start-up company care about Quality Assurance (QA)?

A. Well, for background, AutomatedQA started out pretty much as a micro-ISV. I myself created the first product for the company between two jobs, so technically it was a single-man company.

Q. So, you were a micro-ISV as well.

A. Well, let's say yes, but we were lucky and able to grow very fast. In retrospect, there have been a couple things that have been very valuable. From the beginning, as I was designing the product and creating it, I had in mind that quality would be one of the top factors for our growth. As a small company, we relied heavily on customer satisfaction—we did not have money to advertise at all or go to shows, so definitely word of mouth has been the biggest factor in our growth.

Q. So, would you say the quality of the product can substitute for a marketing budget?

A. I would definitely say so, yes. At the initial phase, you don't have funds to advertise, and you don't have funds to market to other companies. In this respect, I can't say enough good things about the power of word-of-mouth advertising and how much of a driving force it has been.

Second, even when you are starting on your own, you are setting the company's culture. So, whatever you do when you are one, two, or five people, those things will be repeated when you grow. So, if you don't implement a proper setting by yourself of tracking issues, doing automated builds, and doing regression testing, and so on, those will be things that when you start having employees will get worse. So, if the founder doesn't really care about quality, obviously that will pass on to your company's culture.

Another thing I would say, especially about regression tests, is they really allow you to go very fast and be very flexible in the marketplace. Again, when you are a small company, that is one of the deciding factors when you are competing against huge companies with R&D budgets in the millions. Being fast and able to satisfy customers needs to be a driving force; you don't have the luxury of being able to send them a sales-person or invite them onto a golf course. Instead, you satisfy their wish list. Again, if you don't have the regression tests, you start adding features, but you'll be breaking something else.

Q. By the way, where are you from?

A. Bulgaria.

Q. And you came to California when?

A. About nine years ago—AutomatedQA started seven years ago.

Q. That counts as hitting the ground running where I'm from!

A. Developer tools for quality assurance and the development process has always been an area I have had personal interest. So, when I had an opportunity to create some products, that was the area I focused on. Before creating AutomatedQA, I created a freeware tool for mainly the Borland market, which gained a lot of popularity, and it was a driving factor for the commercial product as well.

Q. When you start developing for yourself, and you're not part of a company, how do you get into the mind-set of developing quality code?

A. Well, you're a developer yourself. When you worked at a company, didn't you have the feeling that 'If I were able to make the decisions, that's how I would have done it'? Not just coding but application structure—the whole development process. Then, once you are working for yourself, isn't it a little bit like the dream came true? At least for me, that's how it has been. Finally, the possibility of actually working on those things and concentrating on the quality of the product instead of more on, let's say, management issues.

Q. There's various industry benchmarks of how many defects are acceptable per x lines of code. Where do you think most developers are, and where can they go with tools like those your company sells?

A. Well, I would rather say that most developers are quality conscious. But the problem is, they are not aware of those defects. If they knew there were bugs in the code, if nothing else than as a matter of professional pride, they would fix them. So, probably tools like TestComplete, our profiling tools, and so on, help them become aware that these problems exist.

As a profession, especially these last years, it has been pretty clear that features are nice, but without quality, software just doesn't sell. Especially nowadays with the Internet, if you release a bad version, pretty much everyone will know it very soon. There's a lot more communication going on, and customers are more aware that they can get this type of information.

Q. So, you see that since the Internet is becoming the predominant means of getting information, let alone information about software, that that's upping the ante as far as the level of quality?

A. I would say so, yes. You know, blogs, forums…all those tools have a huge impact today. It's a lot more transparent today. About 20 years ago, I was working in the United Kingdom, in Africa, and in Tunisia, and I do remember years when you were pretty much on your own about a product; be it a good product or a bad product, you had to try it on your own. Nowadays, if you need a tool or a component, in about an hour you can see a lot of information from a lot of people about it, and you don't have to waste your time.

Q. What do you think of TDD?

A. Pretty much as a company that's how we develop. If not completely developing the tests first, then tests are always developed at the same time as code, in the same way we develop the documentation, the installation…all of those things at the same time. But we are not a test-driven shop in the sense that developers develop all tests. We have a separate testing department from the development department.

Q. What would you say to a single programmer, however you define it, who is going to be the tester and the developer for much of what they do. Would you say TDD is an avenue worth perusing?

A. Yes, definitely. The biggest problem is not writing good code but forgetting your code—forgetting what you wrote a month ago. So, if you consider TDD as writing the documentation of what you had in mind when you wrote the code, definitely.

Q. One thing I've had problems doing and I know other developers have too is testing the interface. It's all fine to build unit tests for various classes, but when it comes time to test the interface, the idea has a tendency to break down. Any advice there?

A. Well, I can give you the sales pitch for TestComplete….

Q. Please do.

A. Basically, TestComplete is mostly a Graphical User Interface (GUI) testing tool. For unit testing, there are a lot of free tools, like NUnit and NMock, and with Visual Studio 2005 they have their own variation. Unit tests—I would say petty much everyone has them available. GUI tests have been more difficult.

Q But it's the GUI that customers see.

A. Yes, and basically TestComplete automates the manual testing of the GUI. In a big organization, you have testers who are testing the product, and if they find anything they will see it as the customers would see it. For a small developer, they will see it the way developers see it. But it is a little bit different; it's disconnected from what the customer actually sees.

Again, as a single developer, you don't really have manual testers until you do the beta, and an automated GUI testing tool can save on those resources.

Q. Well, what about the objection to automated testing that the testing can get more complicated than the application? And if the application is already complicated, you can end up with ten times the code, but only 1/ 10 the code actually ships. Based on what you've heard from your customers, what's the most complex project you've heard TestComplete and/or AQTime [a profiler tool] being used on successfully? How big can it scale?

A. One of our customers I am intimately involved with is McDonald's Worldwide. They standardized worldwide on TestComplete. They have several different user interfaces for their points of sale. They are testing from the customer ordering a hamburger to the order going to the kitchen to the order going the front desk where they are using barcode readers. The project is also in multiple languages because they have franchises all over the world and sometimes with slightly different systems in different countries.

We've worked with them on a one-on-one basis, so it is a fairly large deployment. Worldwide, it has all the complexities you can imagine. They have tests in the thousands in their test suite. I have another customer who sells ticketing software. They will have for their daily test—or their nightly test—about a half an hour of testing. For their weekly test that runs over the weekend, they have 23 hours of regression testing.

Q. Twenty-three hours of tests for a single application?

A. Yes, because they sell worldwide, and they have to rewrite their taxation modules. So, the developers were all happy; they developed a new taxation module that was so much better, and so on, and they ran the regression tests for the first time and found more than 1,000 bugs compared to the old system. And again, this happens fairly frequently. The new code works much better, and it's much better refactored, but it introduced issues the old code did not have. Overall, the developers were really happy about having the bugs get found.

Q. Should you start creating tests as soon as you have a GUI? Even if it's one form with one button and you know it's going to change? Should GUI testing run concurrently with unit testing? Maybe that's the way to ask this question.

A. GUI testing should be at the level of, let's say, acceptance testing. Once you feel you are reaching the functionality acceptance level for a form, then that's the best time to actually write the tests for that form.

Q. I want to make sure I've got this point. With unit testing, especially TDD, you are constantly refactoring as you develop from the very first line of code. I think what you are telling me is at the point where the code starts to manifest a GUI of some sort, that's when you should start using a GUI test application?

A. Yes, I would say that's the most effective way.

Q. And if you develop out from your classes, you should be doing more and more GUI testing and less and less unit testing.

A. Yes. And that's how it works in our company.

Q. Now that Microsoft has gotten the testing religion, at least as far as Visual Studio 2005 Team System, do you think it has sort of taken over your space? Or do you think there's still room for you and other people like you?

A. They haven't really taken on our space, especially for the testing part. In the Team System they will have unit testing, and they will have a little bit of user interface to manage tests, manual tests, and unit tests, but they do not have GUI tests. So, they are not really encroaching into our market. On the other hand, there are sometimes opportunities also. They have an integration SDK for Team System, and we have already integrated into it.

Q. I notice that you have a blog at your company's site. How have people responded to that?

A. To be honest, we started it fairly recently. I don't have hard data about it. But overall, I did some measurements on our return on printed advertisements, our return on shows, and our return on Google advertising. And basically, the Internet is the number-one sales-driving venue for us. If we increase by 20 percent the number of people coming to our Web site, we have about 20 percent more business as well.

Q. Have Google Adwords worked for you?

A. Yes, consistently. We don't really go into a price war for keywords. Some of our competitors are spending ten times our expenses. Obviously, for them to pay $4 or $5 a lead it's worthwhile; for us, it's not. But it has been consistently very good for us.

Q. Anything you care to mention that has not turned out to be good?

A. Probably printed advertisements haven't really worked. We've tracked ads in different magazines, and pretty much across the board results have been very poor.

We also ask on our order form why our customers are purchasing. The number-one reason is referrals from friends and associates. That's what the data suggests. It might be skewed because people don't want to admit they are influenced by ads, but we included discount codes in the ads as an incentive, and to be honest I wouldn't do that again.

Q. Just not worthwhile for you?

A. It's one of those things you start doing; it's a little hard. You think, "Oh, maybe if I stop my advertising, maybe my revenue might go down." It's a little bit like drugs.

Q. I promise I won't share that with anyone I know who sells print advertising! How many people now work at AutomatedQA?

A. About 50.

Q. I guess you're out of the leagues of micro-ISVs now. Any advice you would give to a micro-ISV about testing or anything else?

A. Again, on testing, sometimes their budgets are so small they can't afford to purchase anything. But definitely have the quality of the application during the development process in mind.

They can also use some of the open source solutions to unit test and then use some issue tracking—again, there are some open source; it doesn't matter really which specific tool. Later on, when they get some revenue, they can upgrade or not.

But again, they can start the culture of the company so that quality is important and it's one of the main features of the product. When they are designing version 1 of their product, put as a main feature quality. It is a major selling point—a major marketing point.

Getting the Beta Advantage

Up to now I've been talking about your micro-ISV as if it were a one-person show and its success were up to you (and your partners, if you have them). But you should be working with a whole other crew of people during the design and development phase: your beta testers.

At some point between when the last major feature is working and before you expect to actually make money, it's time to find as many people as you can who, in exchange for your undying gratitude and a free license, will put your software or Web service through various kinds of tests, tortures, and tribulations.

I say *various* because beta testers will range from a bunch of people who say they will try your software to a precious few who will stay up nights coming up with suggestions to improve your product.

Over the years, more and more micro-ISVs have come to realize the power, value, and necessity of getting lots of beta testers to try their product, so you actually have two problems as a start-up: how do you get enough beta testers to give your product a thorough whacking, and how do get good enough beta testers who will like your product so much that they start that all-important word of mouth?

Quantity Has a Quality All Its Own

How hard it will be to solve the first problem—getting enough active beta testers—will depend on two considerations primarily: the type of product you're developing and the size of your market. A nearly infinite number of people seem to exist who are willing to play…er…test game software, and exactly zero exist who are willing to work the bugs out of your electrical power grid optimization software.

Although no one solution exists for every micro-ISV, here are five strategies you can try:

- Ask everyone for whom you have an email address.

- Announce it on your Web site, if you have one.

- Post short announcements at any forum you regularly contribute to and that allows such notices.

- Post short announcements at forums concerned with the problem you're going to solve, if that forum, mailing list, or discussion group allows such postings.

- Blog about your micro-ISV, and let people find you.

- Email bloggers who are writing about the problem, and invite them to try your application, Web service, or product before it goes public.

This last tactic is a definite win-win: bloggers get more grist for their mills, an opportunity to "discover" something neat, and at the least a new take on something they care about. You get a beta tester who, if they like your product, can pull in a whole bunch more beta testers and perhaps get a buzz about your product going.

The tactics that work for your micro-ISV and how hard you have to work to attract beta testers will give you a changeable prediction of how your product is likely to fare once you release it: if no one is interested in beta testing it, the outlook isn't good.

Organizing Your Beta Program

However you find beta testers, you'll want at least three features in place before you launch your beta test:

- A mailing list program or service that will let you easily communicate with just your beta testers. I've used both Infacta's GroupMail (http://www.infacta.com/asp/common/groupmail.asp, starting at $99 USD) and MailerMailer (http://www.mailermailer.com/; see also Chapter 5) and recommend both. They make it easy to send semipersonalized emails to the people who raised their hand when you asked for volunteers.

- Some form of a beta tester agreement each person agrees to before they get access. At a minimum, the agreement should spell out what you want (frequent bug reports), what they get (something valuable for free), that they don't get what they want unless you get what you want, and that they shouldn't attempt to share, sell, or otherwise distribute access to your product without your prior consent.

- A way for beta testers to be able to talk to other testers without giving up their privacy—in short, some form of discussion forum. Forums are a great way to let your beta testers know you know what they know.

Once you have your initial batch of beta testers (you'll need more later when half your beta testers find better uses of their time, believe me), how do you get the quality of information out of them you want? First, your software or Web service needs to report beta problems to you automatically. Second, talk to them—not just about bugs that surface but about what they like or dislike about your app.

The more you talk to them and listen to what they have to say, the more likely they are to help you by pointing out missing features, suggesting improvements, and asking questions you haven't thought of asking.

CHAPTER 3

■■■

Presenting the Product

Remember the last time you bought software online? Maybe it was a utility, blog reader, or whatever, but I bet if you think about it, you'll get a warm, cozy feeling, and you'll remember the Web site you bought the app at but not the payment process, because it was easy and normal. In fact, you might be tempted right now to put this book down and take a quick look at the site to see what's new. Even if you don't remember the name of the company exactly, you probably remember what it looked like, and you're not about to mistake it for some other site.

That's positive *brand identity* at work and the customer experience you want your customers to have, which are the reasons for this chapter.

Your product—be it desktop software, a Web service, or an actual entity that comes in a box—isn't going to make you enough to buy a small Caribbean island let alone quit your day job if it's not firmly embedded in an identity your customers can understand, remember, relate to, and like.

Your application alone isn't your product. Your application plus your Web site, blog, graphics, payment processing, and overall customer experience is your product. This fundamental shift in mind-set—from developer to brand manager of a three-dimensional, multilayered, message-consistent way of describing how you help people solve some of their problems—is what I'll cover in this chapter.

One topic I won't cover is advertising. This isn't because it doesn't work—it does. In fact, it works very, very well. That's why every person reading this book goes through life being pummeled with product messages about how they can be younger, sexier, wealthier, or thinner if they just buy Product X. Traditional mainstream advertising—whether it be TV commercials, newspaper ads, or Web site banner ads—works on the proposition that if you smack 1,000 people in the face, two of them are going listen to you. It's weird but true: a typical advertising campaign is considered successful if a tiny percent[1] of the people who see it buy the product.

But advertising has a problem: it takes money and time you don't have.

Instead, you have (you hope) an original and fresh way to make the lives of some people easier, and if you can hitch your micro-ISV to the back of the roaring juggernaut called the Internet, you have a good chance at an exhilarating and rewarding ride on something called the *cluetrain*.

---

1. http://www.morganstanley.com/institutional/techresearch/pdfs/iadc0222.pdf, http://www.agora-business-center.com/0805postcards.htm, and http://www.forbes.com/fdc/mediaresourcecenter/documents/gertner.pdf

Getting on the Cluetrain

In 1999, four early "Internet sages," for lack of a better term, created a Web site (http://www.cluetrain.com) and authored a best-selling book[2] about how the Internet was changing the relationship between companies, markets, and people. This public call for change—*The Cluetrain Manifesto*—was adopted by hundreds of people, many of them influential in how the Internet grows and evolves.

In a nutshell, the *cluetrain* is the idea that in the Internet age, the old way of doing marketing—advertisers interrupt and consumers listen—would be overtaken by the concept and practice of markets as conversations in which both parties speak and listen.

For micro-ISVs, the idea of *not* being a faceless corporation working to your advantage is sweet indeed, since micro-ISVs have no chance of doing business the old way. *The Cluetrain Manifesto* of 95 theses was meant to stir up trouble, and it did: it's anticorporate tone rubbed more than a few people the wrong way. Yet, you can't deny that many of the Web's hottest areas—blogs, social networking, and podcasting, to name three—are in sync with the manifesto.

As I cover all the moving parts you need to assemble correctly to coherently bring your micro-ISV's product to market, keep in mind I'm talking more about how you present *you* than anything else.

Beginning at the Beginning: Who Are You?

When you're starting a micro-ISV, even before you name your company or product or search for a domain name, you need to figure out a few issues. Different people describe these issues in different ways: your brand, your market position, your corporate identity, your logo, your name…in a word: you.

Danny Altman, Chief Executive Officer (CEO) and founder of the naming and branding consulting company A Hundred Monkeys (http://www.ahundredmonkeys.com), suggests—whether you're a one-person start-up or a major corporate effort—that the place to start is figuring out the answers to what he calls his list of primal questions:

- Who are you?

- Why are you here?

- What do you believe in?

- What territory do you want to own?

- Who do you want to connect with?

- And, what kind of relationship do you want to have with them?

"Basically, our view is that these are questions that you have to answer, whether you're a large company or a small company," Danny says. "Those answers will provide the foundation, because these are the foundational questions that define how are we different from everyone else, what's the kind of soul of our brand, [and] what are the things that are compelling to us."

---

2. The book, *The Cluetrain Manifesto* (Perseus Book Group, 2001), is available for free at http://www.cluetrain.com.

Answering these questions might not be easy:

These are things that people have a really hard time grappling with. But if you kind of force them to go through this process, or you force yourself to go through this process, you'll actually find yourself with a lot of material that shows you how unique you really are.

We tell people it's really important to be committed to doing something different—don't build a brand that makes you one of the trees in the forest and then spend the rest of your marketing budget trying to stand out—because that's what most companies do, and it's an appalling waste.

When should a micro-ISV tackle these questions or seek help if "you lack the marketing instinct," as Danny puts it?

All of this stuff can happen pretty early in the process, and what happens is that it becomes a kind of a template or a guide for a lot of other decisions that this company has to make. That's the whole reason you do all this foundational stuff because it keeps you from reinventing the wheel every time you have to do something.

Because, if I know who I am, and I know what the problem is, then a lot of times the answer is, like, right in front of me. But if I don't know who I am, then I've got to figure out who I am right now, which is different [from] who I am tomorrow. And that's the trap I think a lot of companies get into.

Having a company is about building equity in your identity.

Danny's ten-year-old company, based in the San Francisco Bay Area, uses the same approach of working through these questions when consulting with large multinational companies or small businesses. A Hundred Monkeys has two divisions, and one works exclusively with small companies through a process that can take place both face to face and remotely.

The time and cost for expert help in defining who you are from your company's name on up isn't cheap. Danny says that a typical small company brand definition project can take two-and-a-half months and cost from $5,000 to $10,000.

On the other hand, the only thing more expensive than knowledge is ignorance!

If you decide to come up with your own name (or if the cost for one of the leading professionals in the business is a bit out of your budget), refer to A Hundred Monkeys' client profiles to get a feel for how this works, and then download the Igor Naming Guide (`http://www.igorinternational.com/process/naming-guide-product-company-names.php`). The Igor naming and branding agency's great guide demystifies the naming process.

Good Looks Matter

A long time ago, I happened to end up on a stage in Monte Carlo, Monaco, with Michael Spindler, then CEO of Apple Computer. This wasn't by choice—I would have preferred being dead. I had been awake for about 40 hours straight after flying to Monaco from California, redoing the redos of the redone speaker support slides I'd been contracted by Apple to do.

And he couldn't decide whether he wanted thin, blue lines on his slides or thick, red lines, so he had me up there changing them as fast as my fatigued, shaking hands could since the sales conference was ten minutes from starting. Five minutes. Two minutes. Thirty seconds. I finished changing the last slide to bold, red, ten-point lines as the walk-in music faded, and as I scampered off the stage, I could hear the CEO say, "Now it will make the right impression!"

Whatever "the Diesel's" shortcomings as a CEO, he was absolutely right: you get only one chance to make a first impression, and looks matter.

While you may have built an absolutely killer app or the best Web service since Google came along, it will die a miserable, slow death in the market if it's ugly or introduced to the world via an ugly Web site. As the head honcho of your own micro-ISV, you're not only the head developer but the artistic director, in charge of getting the visuals right.

This may not come naturally to you. You may not be able to draw a straight line or tell teal from aquamarine to save your life. That's OK: you have a computer and the Internet. But you've got to start from the point of view that visual impressions matter, and like the ferret in a popular online cartoon strip,[3] you want your prospective customers to exclaim, "Oooh, shiny!" rather than feel physical discomfort when they see your graphics.

You can use a couple of straightforward strategies to give your graphics a professional, attractive feel, and I'll cover them in a moment. But first, Mike Rohde, the design director at MakaluMedia, talks about the first bit of artwork you'll need: your micro-ISV's and product's logos.

MIKE ROHDE, DESIGN DIRECTOR, MAKALUMEDIA

In early 2005, Ian Landsman, who is starting a micro-ISV called UserScape to sell a Web-based application called HelpSpot, hooked up with a professional graphic artist to create logos for UserScape and HelpSpot. Ian created a great blog well worth reading (`http://www.userscape.com/blog/2005/01/31/creating-a-business-logo/`) on his experience working with Mike Rohde, a graphic artist based in Milwaukee, Wisconsin, who is the design director of the distributed company MakaluMedia (`http://www.makalumedia.com/`). You can read Ian's blog to see how the process went for him; I followed up with Mike to see what he thought of working with a micro-ISV.

Q. Why should a micro-ISV hire a professional to do their logo?

A. There are certainly ways of doing it yourself or buying an off-the-shelf stock logo for 50 bucks, with exclusive rights in the $200 range. One of the problems with that approach is if you have a very specific company and you are looking to suggest an idea of what your company means, the problem is you are already adapting to a logo that already exists that doesn't necessarily fit what it is you do. You are already starting off on the foot of compromising in some way.

It's subtle, but it becomes an issue because if it's important to you to get the idea of your company or product over quickly. If it's confusing in any way or disjointed or not clear, that can be a problem because design is becoming more and more a critical thing for businesses on the Internet.

In a nutshell, the reason to hire a design professional is it's not your specialty; and if you are a micro-ISV, you are trying to be very effective with your time and your energy, and by doing it yourself you can spend a lot more time on it and may not be as happy with the results.

Q. When you work with a micro-ISV, what kind of money are we talking about?

A. We charge usually between $400 and $600, and [this] includes lots of back and forth [and] lots of collaboration with the client, which may be different from other places. One of the differences is I'm sort of old-school and start by making a lot of sketches. And one of the advantages of this is that I can produce a lot of ideas on paper very quickly, and it also involves the client because they can see the process going forward, instead of waiting two to three weeks and being presented with a color logo and being told that's your logo.

---

3. `http://www.sluggy.com/`

Q. It sounds like that collaborative process between yourself who is a professional at this and the client is the meat of what you're selling.

A. Yes, I think it is. The more I've sat back and thought about why do people come to me—and obviously some people are going to choose other ways for various reasons such as budget—the people who have chosen me like the fact that I sketch, and they feel like they can be involved in the process and have a say in where things are going.

Q. So how long does the process take?

A. Generally a couple of weeks, from sketch to final. Sometimes as short as a week, sometimes three to four weeks. It varies.

Q. Do you get involved before they have a name or after?

A. Up to this point we get involved after the naming. And I think in a way that works well because the client generally thought about what they are going to do, what is the idea behind the thing they are going to do, what separates them from others—and they've usually got a name down before they come to us.

Q. Are you finding your micro-ISV customers want one logo for both the company and the product or two different logos?

A. Generally they're separate. In the case of Ian, he wanted a product logo and a company logo and came to us to do both because he wanted them to be consistent and complementary to each other and work as a unit. But it varies; generally it's the company logo and one product.

Q. What mistakes do you see start-up companies making when it comes to graphic design?

A. I think a lot of times they don't consider it at all or think of it as an afterthought. If they don't have those skills, they tend to put up something very rudimentary. They don't consider design to be important, and I think that is something that they are missing in the world going forward.

Design, whether it's complex or simple, needs to be thought about. It needs to be considered.

Q. Why?

A. It's the identity of your company. We're raising a very visual generation who's coming up now, and they identify with visual things. I think it is becoming more of an accepted or assumed thing that you're going to have some kind of identity—whether it's complex or simple. I think it's important with a company, especially a micro-ISV, that the more professional it can look, the more comfortable people are with it.

Q. What should a micro-ISV look for in a graphic designer?

A. Nowadays everything is done remotely, so you need a designer who can design visually and can communicate in writing and by telephone as well to be able to understand what a client wants. It's not always easy to put in writing what a design should be. Reliability is another issue. And I think the way to do that is to request references from that person.

I think reliability, a good eye for design, and the ability to communicate pretty much covers everything.

Icons for You

Once you've sorted out your company's and product's logos, and before releasing your software or Web service, take a look at another way potential customers will judge your product: your icons. Are you using the same old, crappy images that came with Visual Basic 4, circa 1995? Do they look professional and snappy or haphazard and last-century?

In 2004 I was prepping MasterList Professional for release, and I asked Nick Bradbury—founder of the micro-ISV Bradbury Software (now "graduated" to a subsidiary of NewsGator) and creator of the RSS aggregator FeedDemon—for the name of his graphic artist. "Glad to hear you like FeedDemon," Nick said in an email. "I hired GlyFX (http://www.glyfx.com/) to

design the graphics for both TopStyle and FeedDemon, and I recommend them highly."
Figure 3-1 shows the GlyFX site.

Figure 3-1. *Visiting GlyFX*

The $150 or so I spent on GlyFX's tool icon sets for using in MasterList Professional was money incredibly well spent. Not only did I pick up a well-written explanation of dos and don'ts for Windows icons (at http://www.glyfx.com/article_application_icons.html), but I got hundreds of immediately recognizable, professionally rendered icons.

GlyFX, based in Perth, Australia, creates both icon sets for sale and custom development. GlyFX is part of a larger Web design firm based in Perth, PerthWeb, and is headed up by David Ridgway.

DAVID RIDGWAY, MANAGER, GLYFX

Having seen way too many good Micro-ISV applications ruined by bad graphics, I thought I'd seek out the advice of someone who spends most of his waking moments creating great icons for applications. You can find David's GlyFX icons and artwork in numerous applications.

Q. Any advice for nonartistic programmers on using icons, making their app look good, or working with companies such as yours?

A. Number-one rule—don't reinvent the wheel. Stick to accepted standards when designing your interface. I am not discouraging innovation, of course, because if I did, we would still be using the Windows 3.1 interface. However, I would very much recommend doing research and user testing before implementing a "never seen before" feature of the interface. You have to ask yourself, "Why have I not seen this feature before? Is there something about it that I am overlooking?" Doing this can save you a lot of time and support issues.

The other thing being—if you know that you are not good at interface design (or if your users tell you that, and you cannot see where you went wrong)—get some help from a professional. The interface is what sells your product; feature lists are important, of course, but if your application is hard to use or unappealing, the potential user may not even download it to test. Don't underestimate the value that a polished, slick interface plays on the sale of your products.

There is a huge amount of software on the market and in any particular category you are up against some major competition. Make your product shine.

We do a lot of UI recommendations for developers; one of our services is a full range of GUI design/redesign. You need to calculate the cost of designing an effective interface vs. having it done (or evaluated after being done). Has everything been considered—fonts, control layout, tab stops, menu layout, colors, choice of control, etc.?

The last point to make of course would be icons—if you are on a tight budget and can only afford to have some of your icons in a high-color style, *don't*. There is nothing worse than a toolbar displaying a mish-mash of 16-color and high-color icons. You are better off keeping the older style, until you can convert the whole thing. If you are unsure about what to do with an icon, ask your friendly local icon developer. :) As a shameless plug, we package our icons into affordable sets, so you can buy what you need at the time.

It is also important to know the technical implications/limitations of icons: color depths, sizes, and where to use them. There are many documents available describing this. I have written an article [that] gives a rundown on the basics, which can be found here: http://www.glyfx.com/article_application_icons.html.

Also, when updating your interface, don't just stop at the toolbar icons.

Make sure your application icon is also done with a matching style and quality, along with your splash screen. The app icon is the first thing your users see, so give them something really great to look at.

Finally, don't be afraid to ask about the cost of custom work—you may be pleasantly surprised. While I can't comment about other companies, we are always happy to speak to developers and not just quote a job as outlined but try to find something that will fit their budget. Even if you are not sure what you actually want and need, please ask—I am more than happy to talk and run over concepts/ideas and to give feedback on products.

Happy People Being Happy

I'll now cover a few more visual topics before getting down to the nuts and bolts of your Web site. Have you noticed when visiting Web sites that sell products that there seems to be an endless supply of photos of businesspeople looking businesslike and consumers just like you looking happy? This is for good reason—showing happy people being happy is a proven advertising technique.

Despite rumors that some hidden cloning machine is turning out these scenes, for decades a niche industry has provided stock images to print advertisers who need just the right image of people looking happy, concerned, or businesslike.

The Google Directory lists 207 stock image companies on the Web under Business > Arts and Entertainment > Photography > Stock > Royalty Free.[4] (The royalty-free part refers to not having to pay a fee based on the number of magazines printed, instead paying a flat fee for the specified use.)

In addition to the big names in stock photography such as Comstock and iStockPhoto,[5] hundreds if not thousands of professional photographers all over the world are selling their images directly via the Web, as shown in Figure 3-2; I buy images through CafePress.com from a photographer who lives and works in Mozambique, Africa.

Figure 3-2. *Exploring iStockPhoto.com*

The ascendancy of the Web has not been kind to stock image companies; many have consolidated or been bought. That trend will probably only accelerate as more and more

---

4. http://www.google.com/Top/Business/Arts_and_Entertainment/Photography/Stock/Royalty_Free/
5. http://www.comstock.com/Web/default.asp and http://www.istockphoto.com/

people share their visual point of view via sites such as Flickr (`http://www.flickr.com/`), as shown in Figure 3-3.

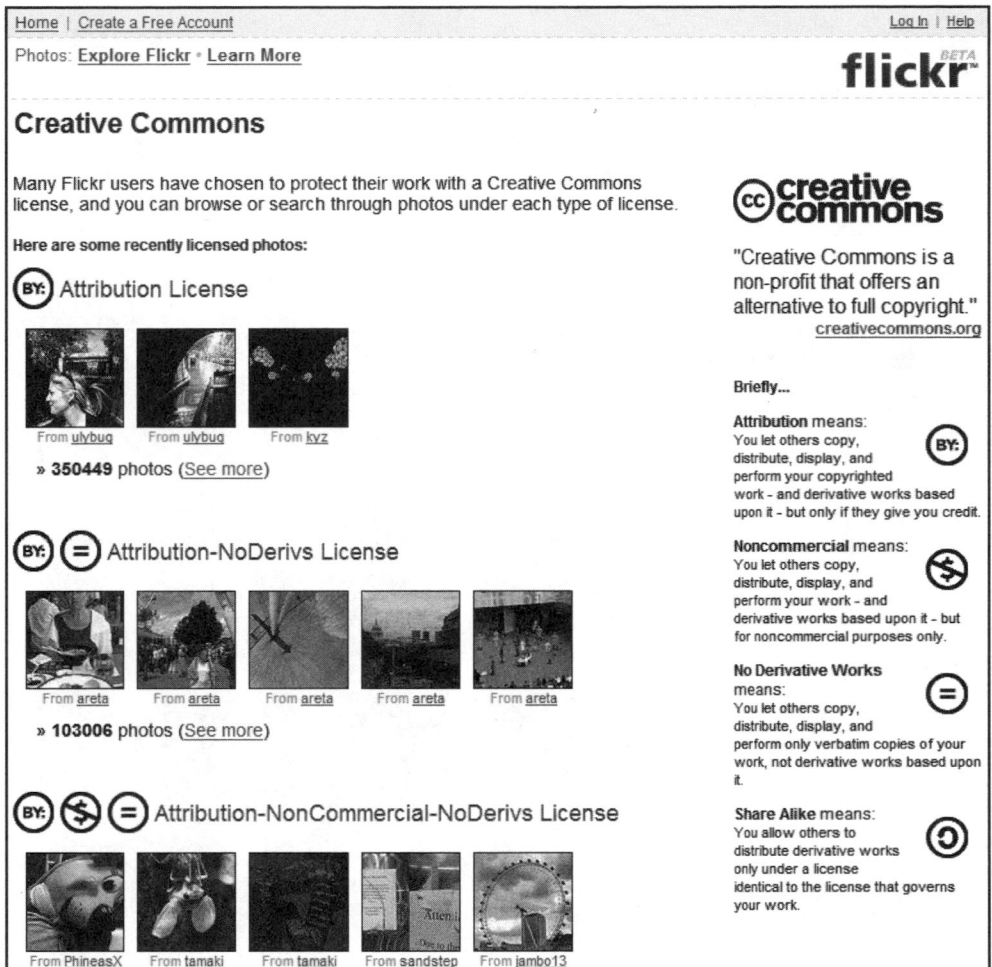

Figure 3-3. *Exploring the photos at Flickr*

Now, before you start commandeering images right and left, keep in mind that it's illegal to use copyrighted images without prior permission, and there's no faster way to kill your micro-ISV than to get an online reputation as someone who steals other people's work.

That's why Flickr's adoption of the Creative Commons copyright process is extremely cool. Simply put, people who want you to use their photos have already granted you a clear means to do so, as shown in Figure 3-4. As of this writing there are more than 350,000 photos with a Creative Commons Attribution License, meaning you're free to use them as artwork on your site as long as you provide a photo credit. And new ones are being added at the rate of several thousand a day. (For more information about the license, see Flickr's Creative Commons page at `http://www.flickr.com/creativecommons/`, or visit Creative Commons at `http://creativecommons.org/`.)

These people may put the stock agencies out of business!

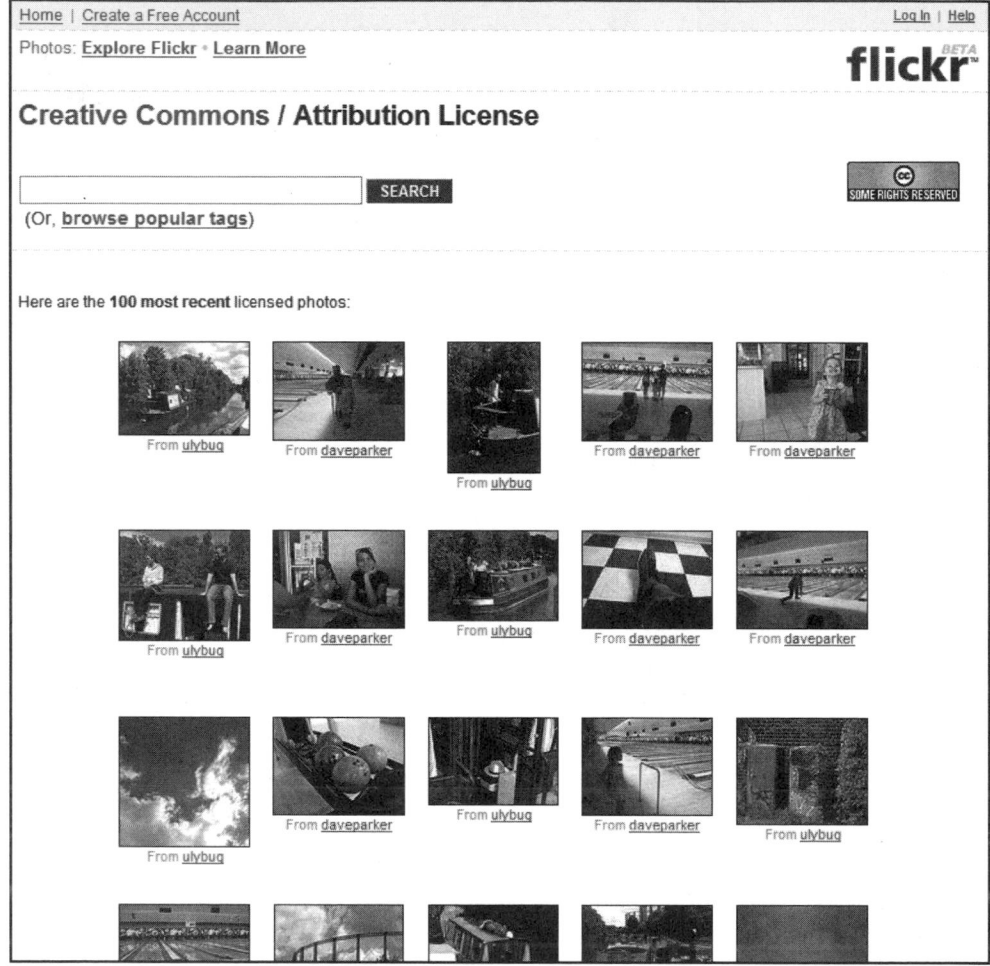

Figure 3-4. *Viewing recent photos under the Creative Commons Attribution License at Flickr*

Show, Don't Tell

As nice as it is to have pictures of happy people being happy, it's not as important as communicating a clear message of what your application, Web service, or product is all about. One of the first tasks potential customers do when evaluating software is to look at your screen shots.

Producing good software screen shots is fairly easy. You start with a screen-capture program that lets you annotate and add short annotations that don't get in the way of the pretty picture you're providing would-be downloaders. You'll want to keep the file size small but the image large enough to tell the story.

One strong recommendation: spend the time to annotate your screen shots and narrate them. Many good applications have been crippled by a page of itsy-bitsy screen shots with uncaptivating titles such as "main input screen." Blah! Step back from your software, show off the most exciting features, and explain their benefits to the person looking at them.

An excellent screen-capture tool I've used for several years is TechSmith's SnagIt (http://www.techsmith.com/products/snagit/default.asp, $39.95 USD, 30-day trial), as shown in Figure 3-5. SnagIt's ability to scroll browser windows and to capture menus, as well as its excellent free technical support, make this an easy recommendation.

Figure 3-5. *Checking out SnagIt*

Moving Pictures

Although making sure you have good screen shots of your software on your Web site is important, static images in and by themselves aren't enough. Potential customers want to see their problems being solved right before their eyes—screen shots are necessary but not sufficient.

Whether you call them *animated demos, interactive video tutorials*, or *Macromedia Flash movies*, few offerings beat a well-done three-minute product demo showing your software hard at work making the viewer's life easy.

One product that does a great job of this is DemoCharge 2005 from YesSoftware (http://www.yessoftware.com/products/product.php?product_id=19, starting at $49.95 USD, 20-day trial version), as shown in Figure 3-6.

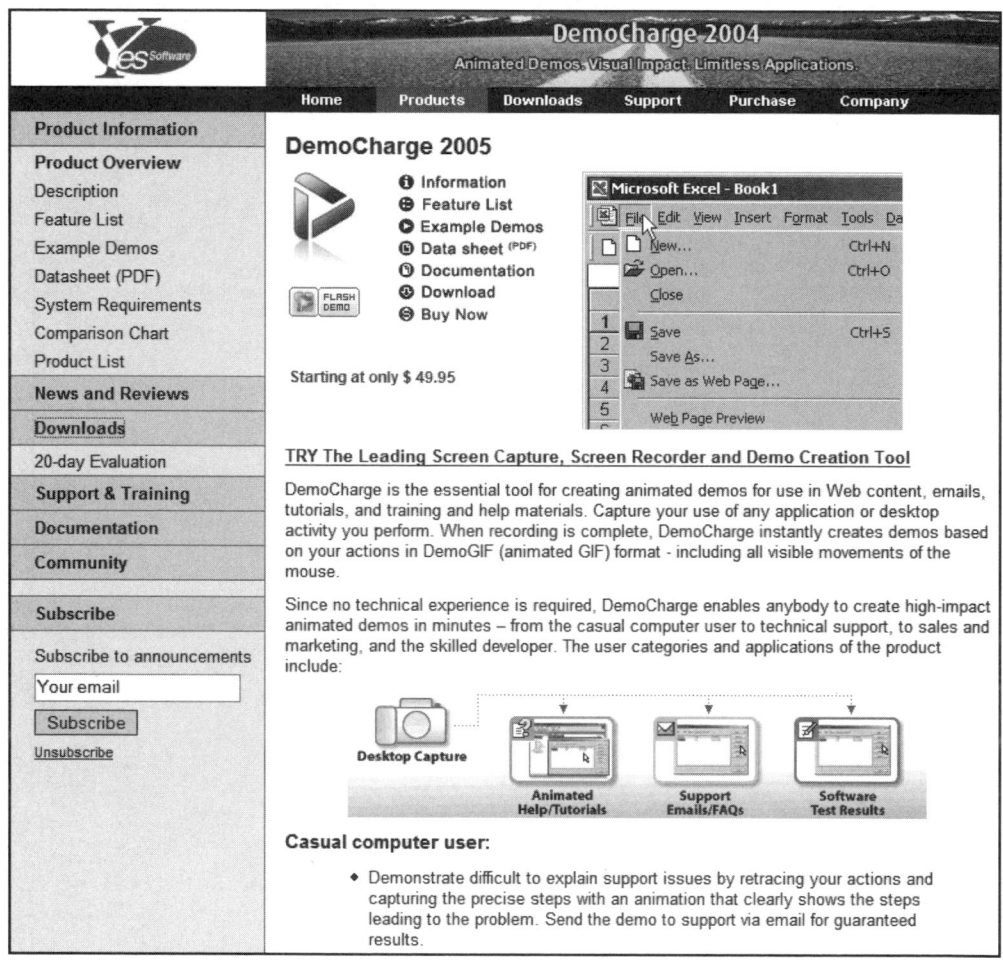

Figure 3-6. *Seeing DemoCharge 2005 solve your customers' problems right before their eyes*

I first came across DemoCharge at Mike Gunderloy's site (http://www.larkware.com/) where he uses it to create animated movies to illustrate some of his excellent software reviews.

Using DemoCharge to make a movie of your app is deceptively simple, as shown in Figure 3-7: start DemoCharge, run through what you want to demo, and then save and output it as a Flash movie or animated GIF file.

It turns out that the makers of this tool, YesSoftware, started a few years ago as a micro-ISV; their story and advice makes for interesting reading (see the following sidebar).

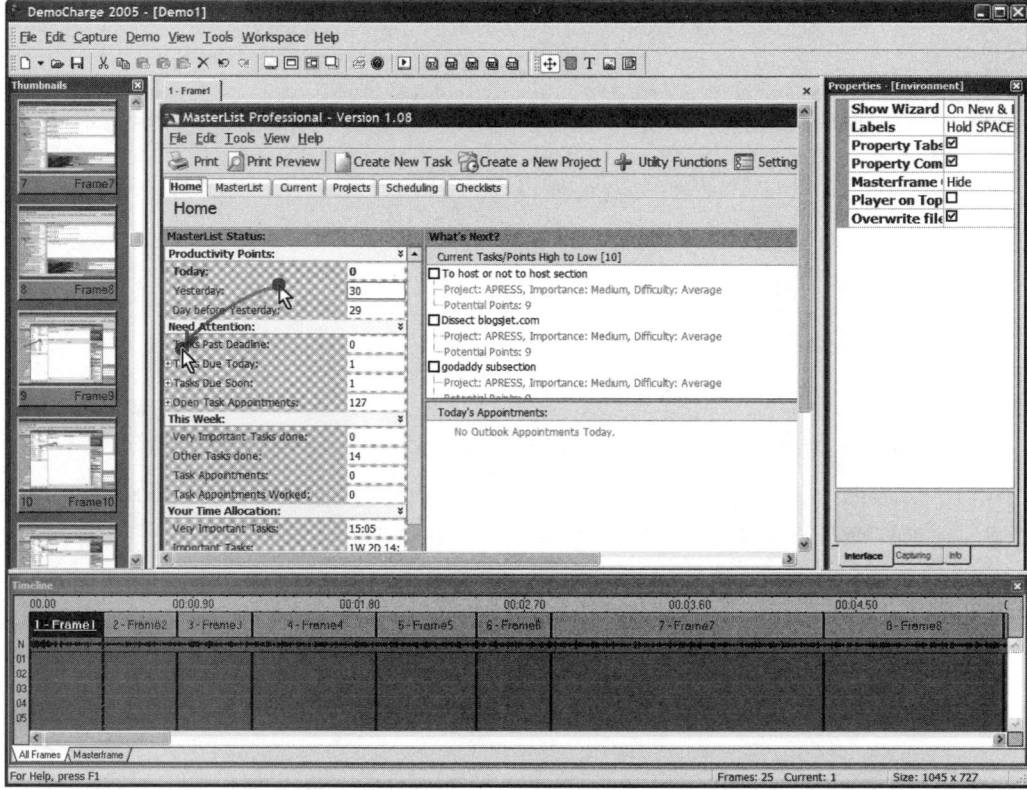

Figure 3-7. *Going to the movies with DemoCharge 2005*

Of course, a world of difference exists between making good movies and bad movies, whether you're talking Hollywood, Bollywood, or your laptop. Here are a few pointers:

Have a script: Like any good movie, your software demos need a script. Take the time to plan what you want to demo.

Rehearsals are cheaper than takes: Before saying "Action!" walk your application through your script several times to ensure it works, it's easy to follow, and you're ready.

Don't try to imitate Orson Wells: A movie needs a soundtrack, and that means planning the voice narration that you add in DemoCharge. Use your normal speaking voice, keep it simple, don't chatter, and let the movie tell the story.

Postproduction matters: After you've recorded your movie, you can in DemoCharge change how long things take, delete dead time, and generally clean it up.

Welcome to multimedia: Keep in mind that you can spend hours, days, and even weeks tweaking your movie, fiddling with fonts for adding pop-up annotations, and generally getting lost in multimedia hell. Good is often good enough, and no one expects you to be the next Hitchcock, so set limits. Besides, you'll need to do it again when the next version of your app or Web service ships.

KONRAD MUSIAL, CEO AND FOUNDER, YESSOFTWARE

YesSoftware is a good example of a micro-ISV that turned an in-house solution into a profitable second product. In this interview, Konrad Musial, CEO of YesSoftware, talks about how that happened.

Q. So Konrad, what are some ways that a micro-ISV could use DemoCharge 2005?

A. DemoCharge demos have many applications that a micro-ISV could benefit from. It can be used to

- Create online and offline presentations that demonstrate their product's capabilities,

- Create walk-through demos for the press and users,

- Create animated tutorials,

- Create animated documentation (help), [and]

- Provide support for case resolution in visual format, as step-by-step instructions.

As you know, the product requires no programming skills and can literally be used by anybody. According to customers this is one of its main strengths—simplicity. It is a tool that can help any company add significant value to their Web site and product(s).

Q. Are your micro-ISV customers finding Flash/Java/GIF demos are easier to create, more interesting to their customers, or both?

A. This really depends on the demo's final use. All resulting demos are similar, while the selection of the format usually depends on the benefits of the format itself. Flash is always a popular format for Web-based demos and was widely requested by our customers. GIF is a great format to use in documentation or for a simple online demo to show product features. EXE is great for emailing demos internally, for example, within [the] QA department. AVI might be best for including on tutorial CDs. Basically it comes down to preference, but I would say Flash is the most widely accepted format.

Q. How did you get the idea for DemoCharge?

A. The idea came from an internal need and desire to offer better documentation to our customers for our main product, CodeCharge Studio. We decided that screen shots are not sufficient to explain the complexities of the product, and the animated images would help us transfer our knowledge to the users. At the same time, many users asked for more tutorials; therefore, we thought that it would be best to combine animated documentation that uses GIFs with online demos in Flash.

Q. I notice you have an "affiliate" version besides the professional and standard. What's the idea there?

A. The idea is twofold. First, we wanted to create a viral marketing campaign for DemoCharge. Users of the DemoCharge copromoted version get a heavily discount product in exchange for doing viral marketing for us. All demos created with the copromoted version have a logo at the bottom of the page that reads "Created with DemoCharge."

Second, it was a way for us to offer the product at a price point that just about anybody can afford.

Q. Can you tell me how YesSoftware got started and when? How many people = YesSoftware?

A. YesSoftware got started in 2000 with two partners who funded the company and about ten employees, and we currently have approximately forty people.

We started the company and the development of our first product, CodeCharge, after realizing that there were no software development tools for Web developers, except high-end Java IDEs. Like most Web developers at that time, we were programming our applications using text editors and other unsophisticated tools. We were basically manually coding entire Web applications, which later would need to be modified or sometimes rewritten [because of] changing requirements and the lack of prototyping. It was clear to me that there was a need for a tool that would maximize a developer's skills to quickly create everything from a prototype to a complete, multiplatform application—and YesSoftware was started.

CodeCharge has since evolved into CodeCharge Studio (now in version 3), we've released DemoCharge, and we have a road map in place to support our long-term goal of providing multiple solutions for software developers and Webmasters.

Q. Can you tell me a bit about yourself?

A. Here's a brief bio of my experience: I've worked in the software industry for over 15 years in product development and marketing. Before YesSoftware, I was involved with several Silicon Valley technology incubators and Internet companies. I spent the first part of my career as a developer and technology consultant to manufacturing companies in the United States, including Cott Corporation where I received Cott's corporate award for "Excellence in Innovation" for the creation of an enterprise, neutral-language processing and reporting system. I have a bachelor's of science degree in computer science from Silesian Polytechnic in Poland.

Q. Any advice for other micro-ISVs? Any lessons to pass on?

A. In today's highly competitive technology environment we differentiate by originality, ease of use, and overall customer experience. All these are keys to any successful company. This means that you need good, smart people working with you; you need to make a product that customers need and want; and [you need to] offer them better technology than they currently have available to them.

Templates for Success

More than a decade ago, I had fun creating an early Web site to promote New Zealand to American tourists for the New Zealand consulate in Los Angeles. I learned three valuable lessons:

- Creating a Web site from scratch can be a daunting task.

- It's easy to get lost in the tiny details of building a good-looking Web site.

- Clients who are prepared to fly you from San Francisco to Los Angeles may not be willing to fly from San Francisco to New Zealand themselves, no matter how good a case you make for on-site research.

Time and redoing my own Web site have reinforced the first two lessons: unless you're a Web designer by trade or you plan to sell a Web design tool, use templates to give your Web site a solid, professional look.

Over the years, I've bought and deployed several Microsoft FrontPage templates from PixelMill (`http://www.pixelmill.com`), as shown in Figure 3-8, where they have about 3,000 FrontPage, Dreamweaver, and generic HTML templates, from $20 to $100 USD. Although plenty of template vendors exist (115 are currently listed in the Google Directory[6]), a lot of really good Web designers sell their wares through PixelMill.

---

6. `http://www.google.com/Top/Computers/Graphics/Web/Templates/`

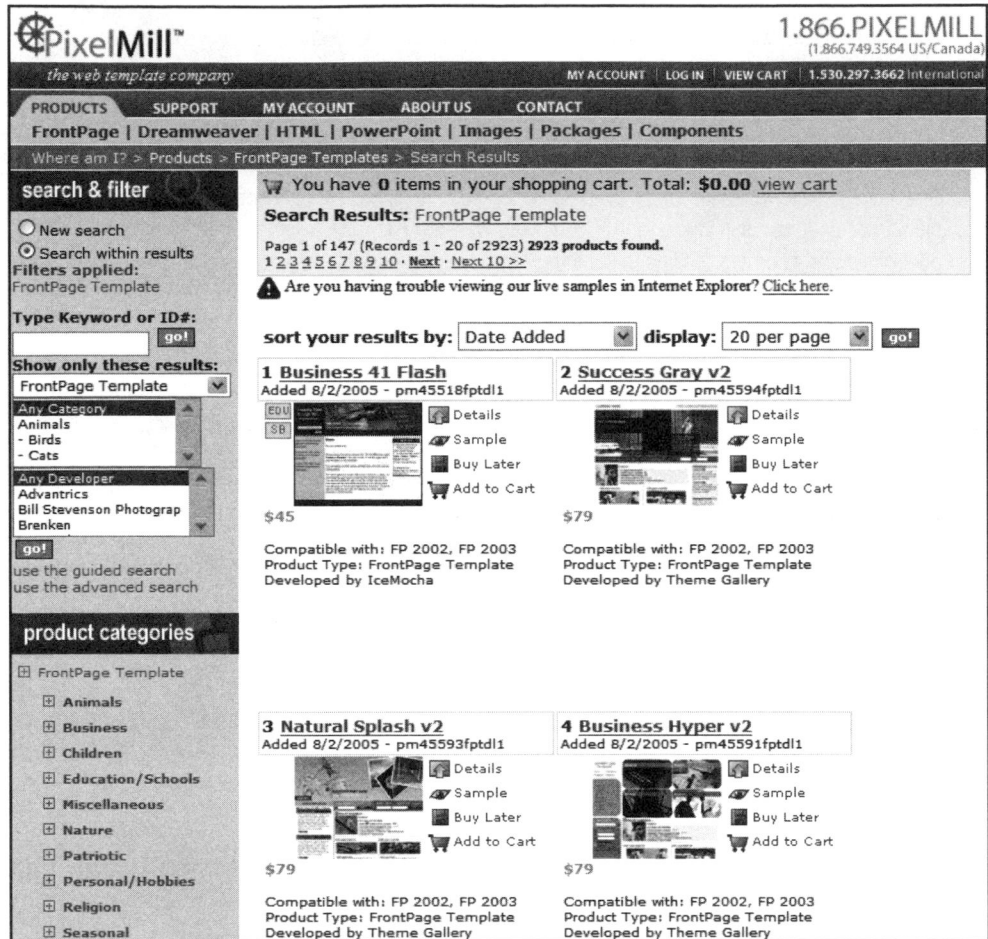

Figure 3-8. *PixelMill: nearly 3,000 FrontPage templates and counting*

Another source for good templates is Open Source Web Design at http://oswd.org/, as shown in Figure 3-9. You'll find more than 1,000 for-fee templates and a great range of good free templates by designers who want to give something back, promote their services, and make the Web a prettier place (or all three).

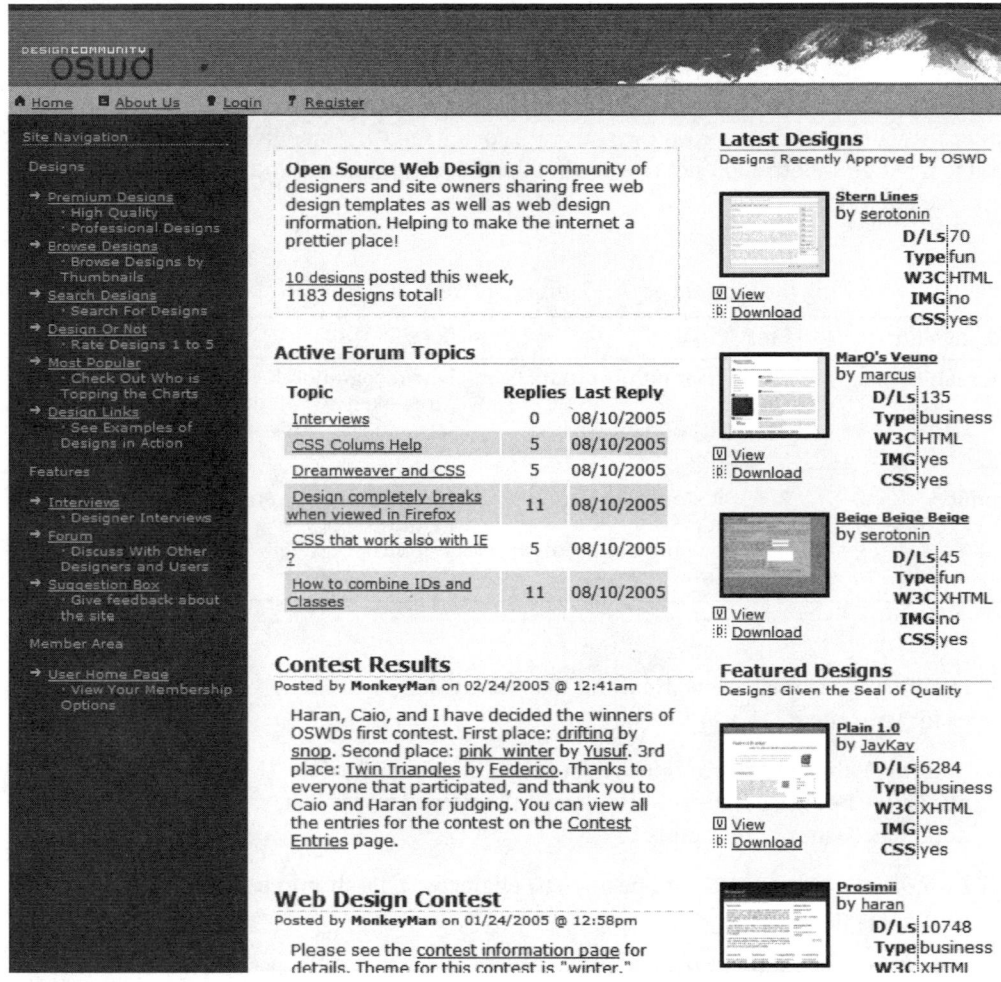

Figure 3-9. *Giving back and showing off at Open Source Web Design*

Mastering Your Domain

A lot of the moving parts covered in this chapter will come together as your Web site, so now I'll cover the core nuts and bolts of Web site building, visit with a micro-ISV whose site is well worth emulating, and consider one of the most perplexing issues for micro-ISVs—getting paid. Keep in mind that although some of these topics may be kindergarten-type technological information for you, you'll find more than a few marketing/branding/positioning nuggets mixed in; even if you've been running your own site on your own server for a decade, read on!

Creating a Good Domain Name

It's always good to start at the beginning, and the beginning of the beginning of your micro-ISV's presence on the Internet is securing a good domain name for either your micro-ISV or your product. Notice how I said that? Even before you start checking possible Uniform Resource

Locators (URLs) in your favorite WHOIS interface, you need to make a marketing decision: will you promote the product or promote your new company's identity?

The key question isn't about the general advantages and disadvantages of linking your URL to either your company or your product; it's about what you want to be. Are you building a micro-ISV in order to start your own business, or are focusing on a Really Good Idea that you want to make real? Both approaches work, but they have implications you'll be wise to consider now (see Table 3-1).

Table 3-1. *Promoting the Product or the Company: Pros vs. Cons*

URL Identifies	Pros	Cons
Company	Supports multiple products or services Generally easier to define Less gimmicky	Less recognition for your first product More likely to collide with other companies Less effective for your first product
Product	Keeps it simple for your customer Requires only one set of logos/ graphics	Makes it hard to rename your product Requires one very good set of logos/ graphics

In either case, here are few tried-and-true rules to keep in mind as you start kicking around names for your site:

Be clear: This is the first and foremost rule of creating a "good" URL; violators will be punished. Being clear means you shouldn't misspell words just to get the domain. And don't use dashes or numerals.

Be short: While your URL can be up to 67 characters, the shorter it is, the less likely it will be mistyped.

Be different: Be different from your potential competitors in your market; large existing companies take brand identity seriously and will sue you to death.

Be dot-com: The .com domain remains the most prestigious, the default for most browsers, and the first choice most people will make when trying to remember your name.

Be national, if national makes sense: The one major exception to the previous rule is if your company/product focuses on a particular national market. For example, if you focus your micro-ISV on a new business translation application between British English and French, either or both `http://bettertrans.co.uk` and `http://bettertrans.fr` makes sense.

"But All the Good Names Are Taken!"

If you visit any online marketing forum, you'll find post after post along the lines of "I've tried 214 different names, and every one of them is taken! Help!" Just about all of these people are making the mistake of trying to get a domain name that either uses some common hot term or is a variation on some other company's name. This is the wrong approach.

Instead, if you're going to promote your product in your URL, think about what your product does for its user.

Here's one approach: Let's say I decide after looking at all the other Internet bookmark managers available that I can create a much better one, and it will be the first product my new micro-ISV releases. Now, there's no shortage of competing micro-ISVs for this type of product, and just about every imaginable use of the word *bookmark* or *favorite* is already in use. In fact, as of this writing, Google finds 77 Web-based bookmark managers, 26 non-Web-based bookmark products, and 16 shareware applications.

What to do? Well, let's say the most important feature of my hypothetical product is its ability to take all my bookmarks and reorganize them for me. How do I know what my product's most important feature is? It's the point you make first in your "elevator pitch"—your 60-second explanation of what your product is good for.[7]

Now I have a verb—*reorganize*. And a noun—*bookmark*. And a URL: *reorgbookmarks.com*. One of the least used—and therefore powerful—ways of creating a URL is to combine the one verb and the one noun that describes your product best, as shown in Figure 3-10.

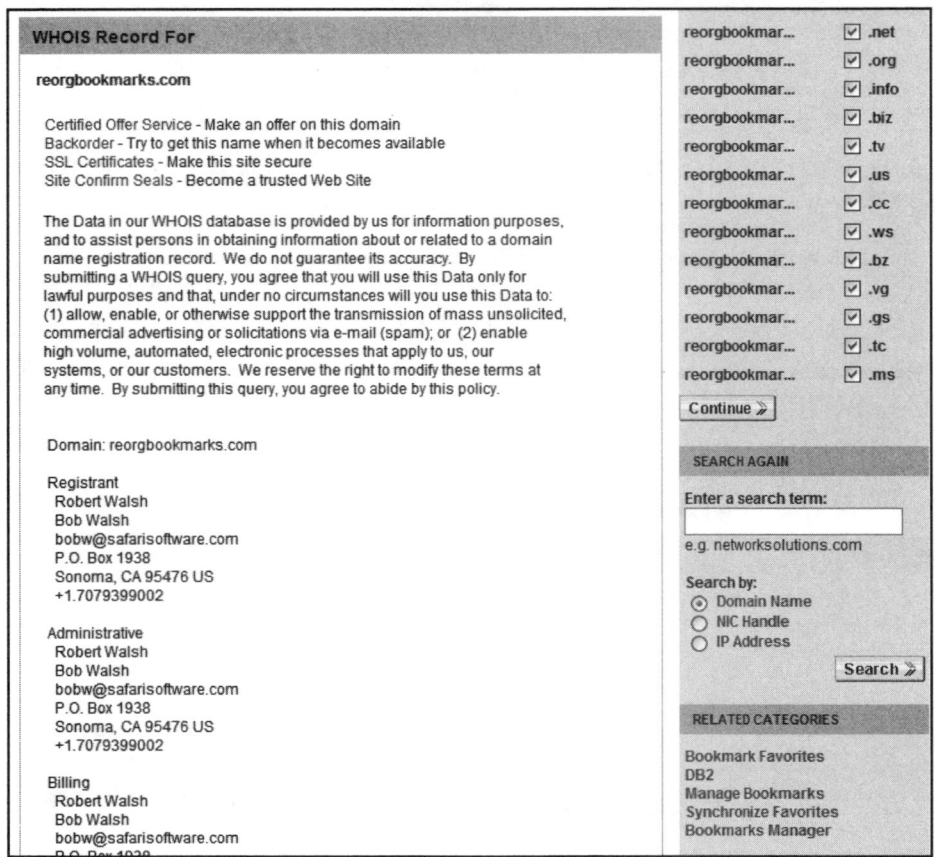

Figure 3-10. *Viewing reorgbookmarks.com's WHOIS record*

---

7. For an excellent summary of what to include in an elevator pitch, see `http://www.fastcompany.com/articles/archive/act_joos1.html`. Hint: assume a short building!

Naming the business after the URL can be trickier. I'll cover the mechanics of naming your business for all the world to see in Chapter 4; for now, all you need to be concerned with is devising a means to come up with that all-important URL.

If you'd like to see an expert name maker at work, refer to A Hundred Monkeys (http://ahundredmonkeys.com). This site can give you a bunch of ideas, but the best advice can be summed up in five words: every name tells a story.

Buying Your Domain: Go Daddy, Go!

Worth a special mention because of its fanatical customer service, GoDaddy.com (http://godaddy.com) is a cheap, fast, and easy way to register domains, as shown in Figure 3-11.

Figure 3-11. *Buying your name via GoDaddy.com*

Also, GoDaddy.com lets you get deep into your domain record: a necessity if you decide to set up a blog through a hosting service and want to give it your unique domain name.

In an age of outsourced and offshored technical support, it's nice to find a company that understands that great tech support equals raving customers, as shown in Figure 3-12.

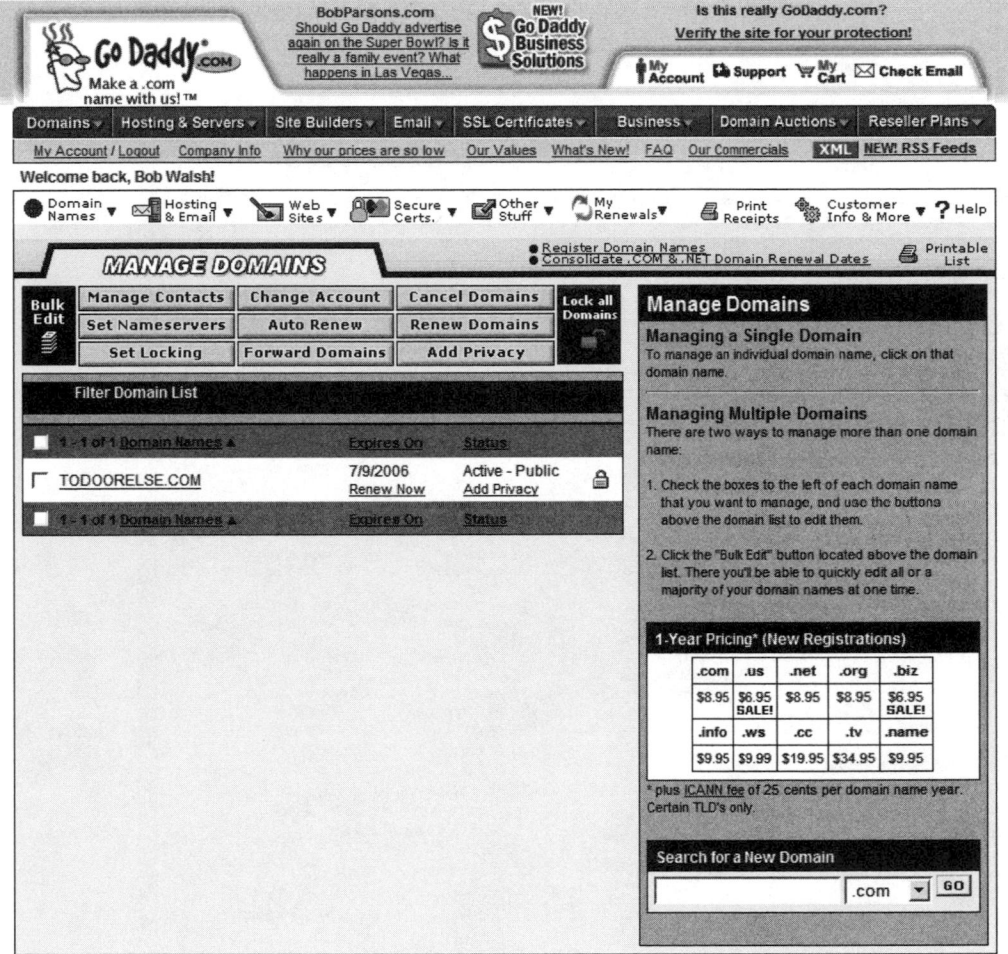

Figure 3-12. *Controlling your domains at GoDaddy.com*

Covering the Nuts and Bolts

And now, I'll cover the star of this chapter: your Web site. Actually, since your Web site may not yet exist, I'll pick apart an existing micro-ISV's Web site: BlogJet at `http://blogjet.com`. When I started researching this chapter, I expected to have to pull bits and pieces from several sites to illustrate the right way to do a micro-ISV Web site. Happily, this site, as shown in Figure 3-13, covers all the features a good micro-ISV should include.

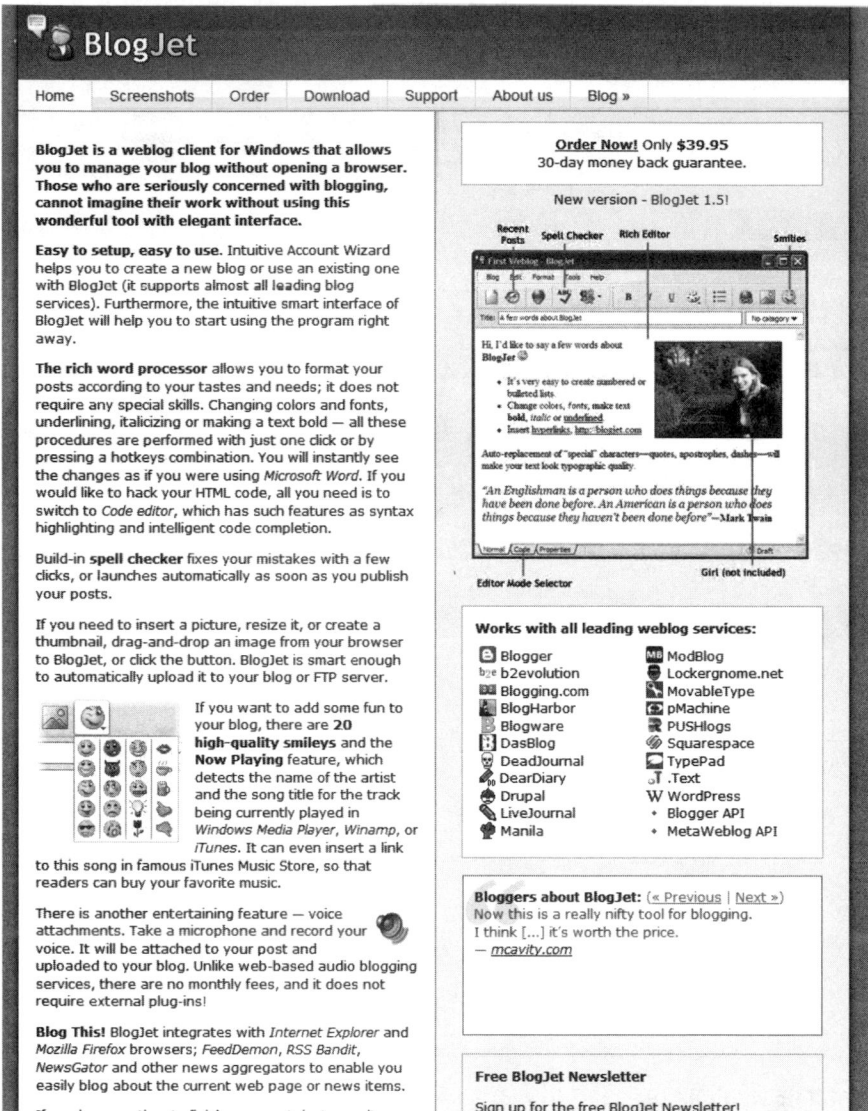

Figure 3-13. *Viewing all the right parts for a micro-ISV Web site at BlogJet*

Let's start dissecting this page starting with the menu. Complexity isn't what you want on your micro-ISV Web site's home page. BlogJet's menu contains seven straightforward choices, as shown in Figure 3-14. On a general note, people handle situations where they have about a maximum of nine options, be it your site's menu or your Web or desktop application.

Next, look at what you see first on the site. The first text you probably read is what BlogJet is and why should you care, as shown in Figure 3-15. Furthermore, the site gives you a specific idea of the main differentiator ("without opening a browser"), its main market ("serious bloggers"), and its main selling point ("elegant interface").

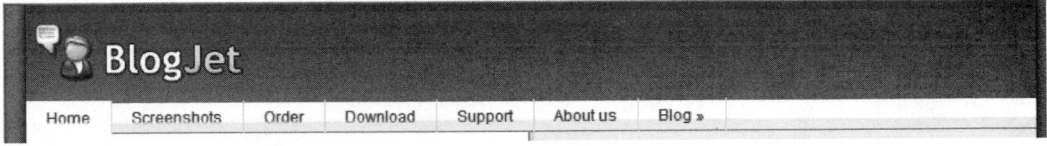

Figure 3-14. *Keeping menus simple and easy to read*

Home	Screenshots	Order	Download	Support

BlogJet is a weblog client for Windows that allows
you to manage your blog without opening a browser.
Those who are seriously concerned with blogging,
cannot imagine their work without using this
wonderful tool with elegant interface.

Figure 3-15. *Placing the important information up front*

This is BlogJet's Unique Selling Proposition (USP). If you don't have a USP, neither you nor your customers know what you're selling. These are the five parts of a complete USP:

- The name of your micro-ISV product ("BlogJet")

- The type of category of product ("blog client")

- The main market segment of your product ("those who are seriously concerned with blogging")

- Its key benefit to that market ("wonderful tool with elegant interface")

- The key thing that differentiates you from your competitors ("manage your blog without opening a browser")

Take the time to define your USP—it's a key tool in defining and selling your product. (For more information about creating USPs, see http://en.wikipedia.org/wiki/ Unique_selling_proposition and the appendix.)

BlogJet's USP: but is it true or spin? You don't know yet, but if you consider yourself a serious blogger and want some other way of posting than via the interface you get in your browser, you'll probably read more.

Next—and it should be close to the USP—the makers of BlogJet start backing up their USP with benefits, as shown in Figure 3-16. The site doesn't say "Account Wizard is used to create a blog or use one," which would be a feature or function but says the following (the emphasis is mine):

> **Easy to setup, easy to use.** *Intuitive Account Wizard* helps you *to create a new blog or use an existing one with BlogJet (it supports almost all leading blog services). Furthermore, the intuitive smart interface of BlogJet* will help you to start using the program right away.

> **Easy to setup, easy to use.** Intuitive Account Wizard helps you to create a new blog or use an existing one with BlogJet (it supports almost all leading blog services). Furthermore, the intuitive smart interface of BlogJet will help you to start using the program right away.
>
> **The rich word processor** allows you to format your posts according to your tastes and needs; it does not require any special skills. Changing colors and fonts, underlining, italicizing or making a text bold — all these procedures are performed with just one click or by pressing a hotkeys combination. You will instantly see the changes as if you were using *Microsoft Word*. If you would like to hack your HTML code, all you need is to switch to *Code editor*, which has such features as syntax highlighting and intelligent code completion.
>
> Build-in **spell checker** fixes your mistakes with a few clicks, or launches automatically as soon as you publish your posts.
>
> If you need to insert a picture, resize it, or create a thumbnail, drag-and-drop an image from your browser to BlogJet, or click the button. BlogJet is smart enough to automatically upload it to your blog or FTP server.

Figure 3-16. *Layering the message*

People buy products for their perceived benefits, not for their actual functions. If I want to buy a new lawn mower, for example, I spend a couple hundred dollars to get a self-propelled mower because it makes it *easier and faster,* not because it has a little metal box that transfers some of the engine's power to the back wheels.

Also note that by having the really key point in bold, BlogJet layers the message. If your eyes are zipping past the "blah blah" text, you'll still probably read the 11 bold words out of 197. Also worth noting is the drawing of an analogy to a product the prospective BlogJet customer probably knows: Microsoft Word.

Now, if someone reads those 197 words, they probably took about 42 seconds to do so. They're tired. They need a rest. In Internet Time, 42 seconds is a long time. So, it's time for a little visual change of pace and the first graphic you encounter, as shown in Figure 3-17. This visual change of pace is a good thing and continues the next four paragraphs that further buttress the USP.

Next comes a two-word link—nicely set off by whitespace above and below that leads to an animated walk-through of BlogJet, as shown in Figure 3-18.

If you want to add some fun to your blog, there are **20 high-quality smileys** and the **Now Playing** feature, which detects the name of the artist and the song title for the track being currently played in *Windows Media Player, Winamp*, or *iTunes*. It can even insert a link to this song in famous iTunes Music Store, so that readers can buy your favorite music.

There is another entertaining feature — voice attachments. Take a microphone and record your voice. It will be attached to your post and uploaded to your blog. Unlike web-based audio blogging services, there are no monthly fees, and it does not require external plug-ins!

Blog This! BlogJet integrates with *Internet Explorer* and *Mozilla Firefox* browsers; *FeedDemon, RSS Bandit, NewsGator* and other news aggregators to enable you easily blog about the current web page or news items.

If you have no time to finish your post, just save it as a *draft file* on your computer, so that you would be able to continue writing at any time you like.

In addition, you can not only create new posts in BlogJet. The program also allows you to **view and edit** your previous posts.

Finally, support for **secure data transmission** based on the *OpenSSL* industry standard guarantees that the data you send by BlogJet is encrypted.

Watch demo »

Figure 3-17. *I've been reading for 42 whole seconds. Time for a break!*

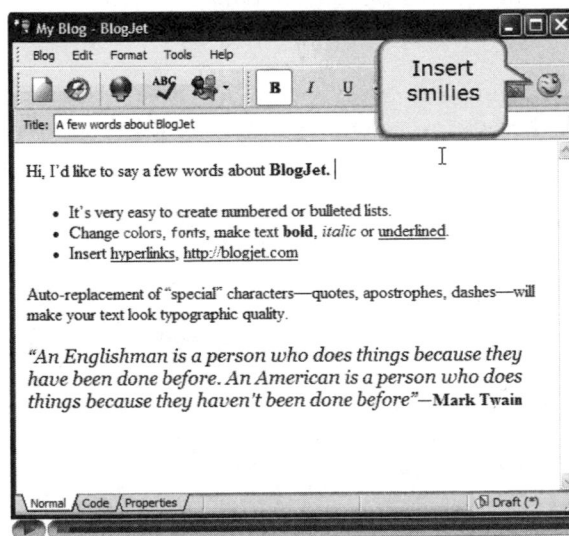

Figure 3-18. *It's movie time!*

This 45-second walk-through of creating a blog posting in BlogJet is a gem: slow enough to follow and have a sense of what's being done but fast enough not to be boring. When various dialog boxes open, you see them being used and you see them long enough to get the sense of them, but they are not explained in mind-numbing detail (see Figure 3-19).

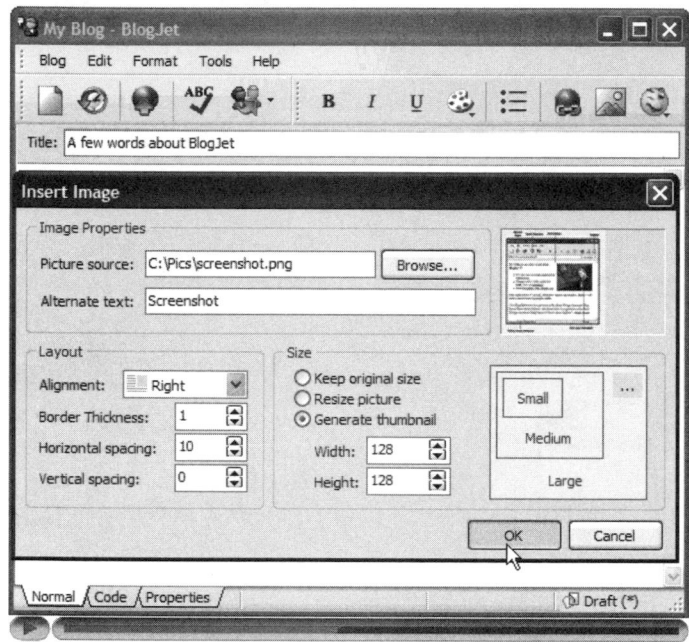

Figure 3-19. *Viewing the nine-second Insert Image dialog box*

A lot is potentially going on in this Insert Image dialog box, but it doesn't matter yet; BlogJet stays on message, and the message is this tool makes blogging easier for serious bloggers.

By now, some of BlogJet's prospective customers are ready, willing, and eager to buy. So, let them, and deal with a concern they have because everybody has, as shown in Figure 3-20: can they get their money back?

Figure 3-20. *Ask for the order—it never hurts.*

However you plan to get paid (see the next section), odds are good your customers are going to use a credit card, and that credit card company expects you to let their customers "unbuy" from you for at least 30 days. So, say so, and mean it. And if they aren't ready to spend an as yet unknown amount of money, give them the application or service for 30 days so they get hooked on it.

The bottom line is that if you're a micro-ISV, plan from the start to offer a free 30-day trial and a 30-day money-back guarantee. Shortening or skipping either of these expectations will cost you sales.

Let's return to the BlogJet site. Oh, look, here's the name of the company! Other than the About Us menu item, Figure 3-21 shows the only mention of who sells BlogJet. Every micro-ISV has to decide where the balance point is between promoting their company vs. a product or products for their Web site. DiFolders Software goes about as far as it can to focus on the product.

Figure 3-21. *Deemphasizing the company and playing up the product*

You'll also see something else here that you definitely need: a privacy policy, as shown in Figure 3-22.

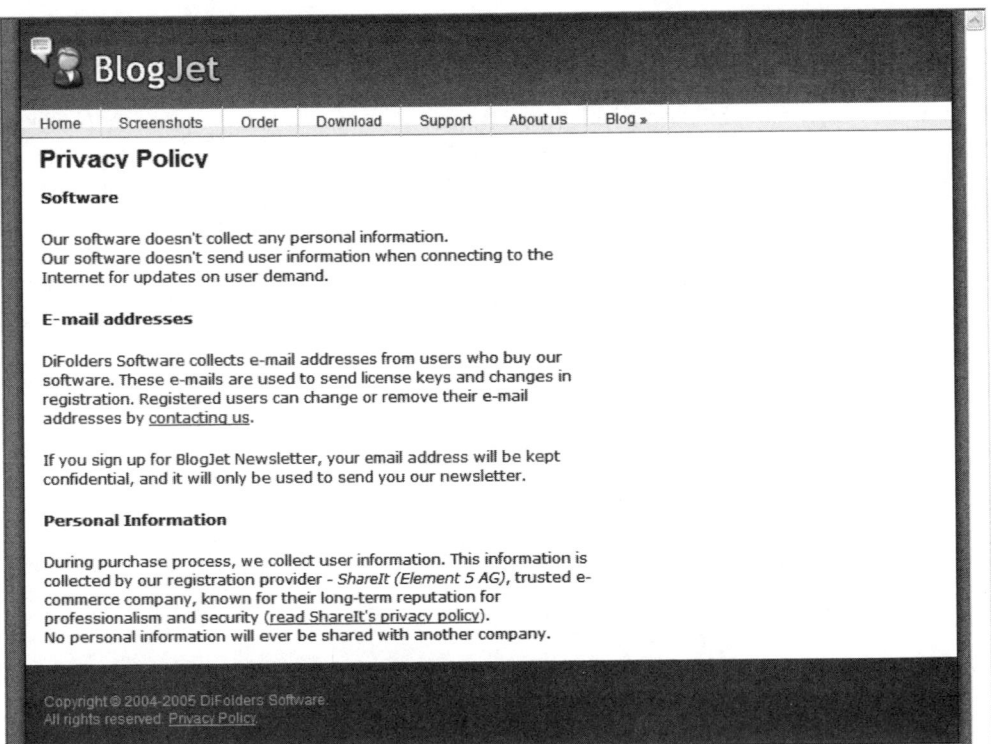

Figure 3-22. *Privacy policy: no lawyers, please!*

Besides a 30-day free demo and a 30-day money-back guarantee, you better have a privacy policy and better still have one that can easily be understood.

That's the end of the left column. It's time to continue this digital dissection from the top of the right column, as shown in Figure 3-23.

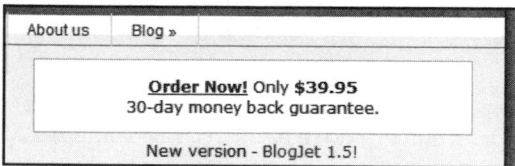

Figure 3-23. *Getting four messages in one*

A couple things are happening here: First, you learn BlogJet's price, $39.95. Next, you're reminded that there's a 30-day money-back guarantee, and you get a third way to order the product. Finally, you see that a new version of BlogJet is out, and you can go to a page where the company covers what's new.

But not really. You can click the release notes link and see a lot of information, but since you don't have BlogJet, that information conveys only that DiFolders Software is serious about making BlogJet a great product.

And that is the point. No one expects software or Web services to be perfect when they're first released; conventional wisdom says *avoid* 1.0 products. Apparently knowing this—or just doing the right thing anyway—DiFolders Software shows you it's serious about improving BlogJet and moves you over to the Download tab, as shown in Figure 3-24. Figure 3-25 shows a good example of what a screen shot should look like: fewer than nine callouts and maybe a little humor too. A screen shot doesn't explain; it entices, it reassures, and it gets your prospective customer to do something that moves along this process.

But let's say you're not quite ready to download, so you hit the back button to return to the Home tab. Maybe it's time to take another tack to convince you to buy: show a screen shot.

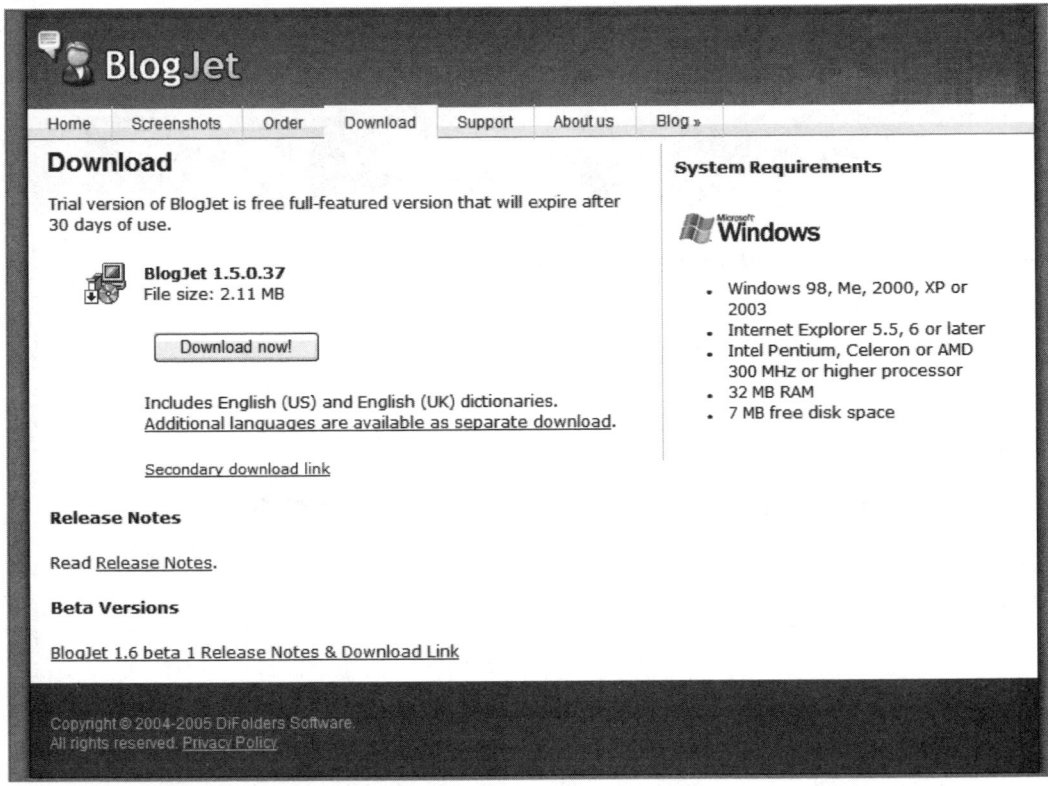

Figure 3-24. *Viewing the release notes, requirements, and, for the brave, a beta version*

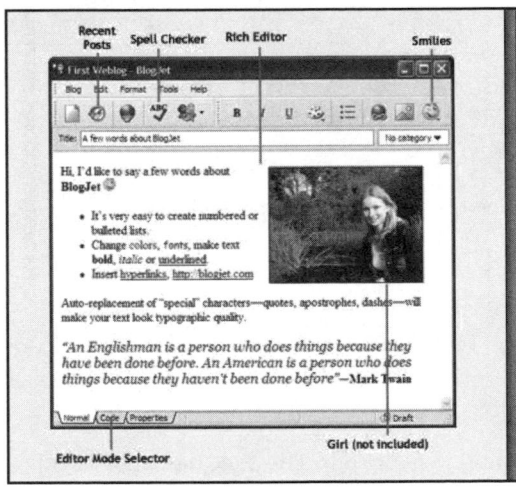

Figure 3-25. *Making six points (girl not included)*

If you happen to want to see more screen shots, clicking this one opens the Screenshots tab, as shown in Figure 3-26.

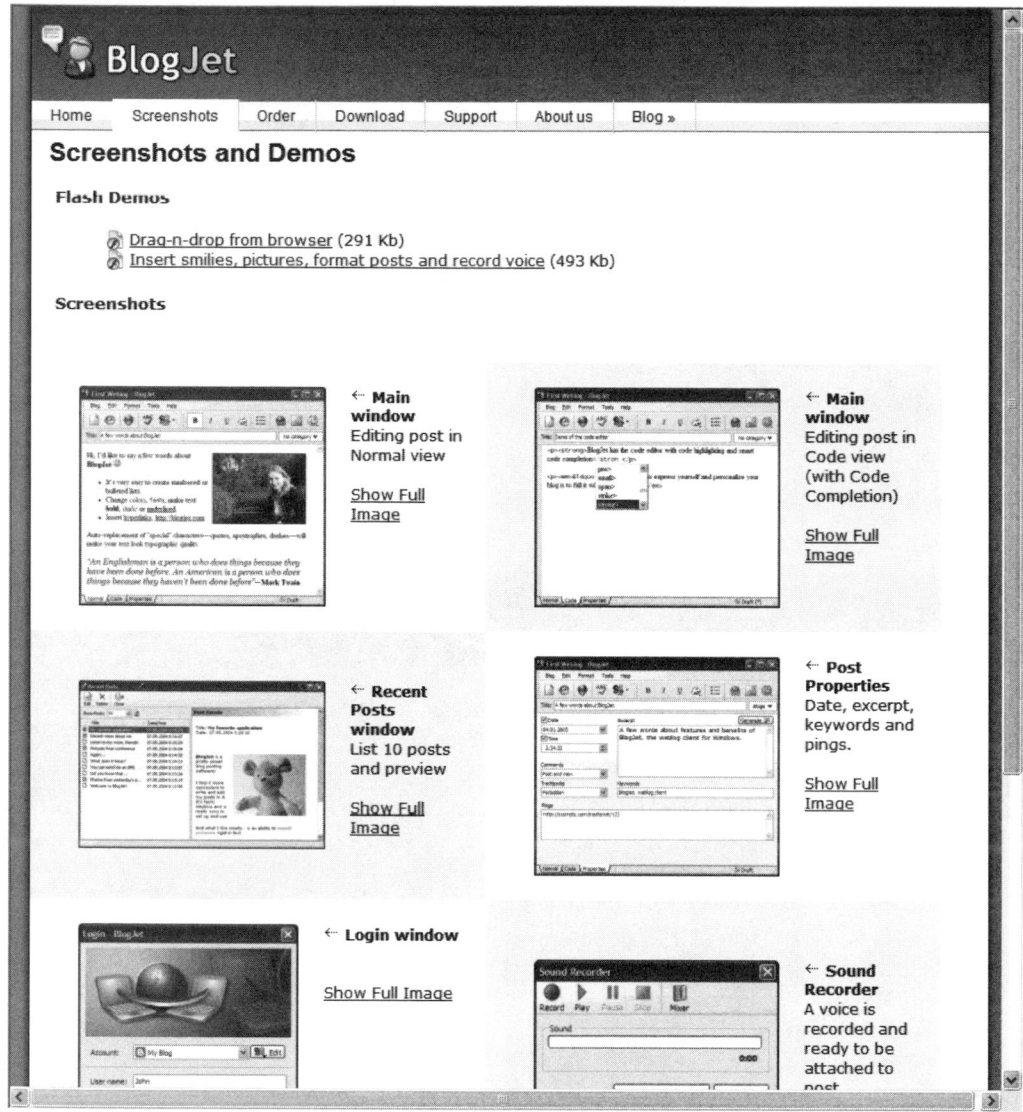

Figure 3-26. *Explaining screen shots*

Again, this is nothing fancy; nothing is too hard to figure out. The page has eight screen shots, two Flash movies, and a link to take you to more detail for each screen shot, if you so desire. If you click Post Properties, you get a bigger image.

Now, since I've been talking up BlogJet's site, I should point out it's far from perfect. For example, clicking the Show Full Image link takes you to a completely unrelated image. No one is perfect, especially micro-ISVs!

Let's return to the home page. So far, DiFolders Software has done a good job of selling BlogJet. But what is the most likely question customers are going to have? It's this: BlogJet might be great and all that, but does it work with my way of blogging? Figure 3-27 answers this question.

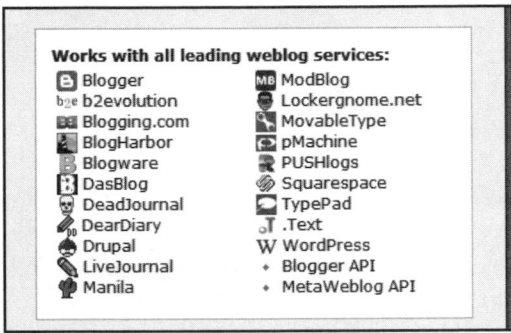

Figure 3-27. *Finding 22 ways to be happy*

Well, so much for that question. OK—you've read it, watched it, and looked at it. Any other ways to convince you to at least try this app? How about having someone else tell you about BlogJet? Figure 3-28 shows that DiFolders Software covers that too.

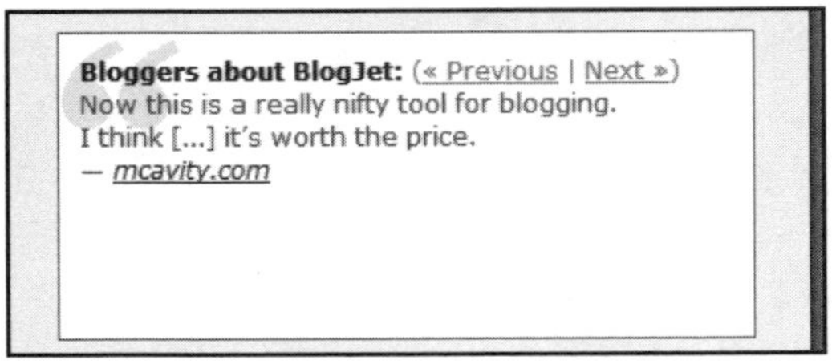

Bloggers about BlogJet: (« Previous | Next »)
Now this is a really nifty tool for blogging.
I think [...] it's worth the price.
— *mcavity.com*

Figure 3-28. *People listen to testimonials.*

Every 15 seconds or so, you'll see a new testimonial with attribution. And, these testimonials aren't by football players or movie stars; they're by bloggers just like you.

Good testimonials are priceless for micro-ISVs. Gather them when you can from your beta testers and customers and even by giving your product away to people you want to influence. The only golden rule is make sure you have their explicit permission to quote them.

Speaking of permission, DiFolders Software asks you whether you'd like to subscribe to its free newsletter; fortunately, the micro-ISV promises to keep your email confidential and use it only to send you its free newsletter, as shown in Figure 3-29.

> **Free BlogJet Newsletter**
>
> Sign up for the free BlogJet Newsletter!
> You will be receiving information about *new
> releases* of BlogJet, *tips & hints* on how to
> improve your weblog and how to *spread a word
> out* about it.
>
> E-mail: [_____]   [Subscribe]
>
> Your email address will be kept confidential, and it will
> only be used to send you our free newsletter.

Figure 3-29. *Everybody wants to do better.*

Repeating the word *free* is good, and so is being clear about why you want people's email addresses and why it's worth their time to sign up.

Email newsletters work, but only if the people who receive them gave their permission and feel the time they spend reading them is worth it. (See Chapter 5 for more about permissions and email.)

By now, if this Web site were a salesperson, they would be collapsed on the ground and be ready to call it quits. They've done everything to get you to buy or at least try this product, and you're still here! It's time for one more go, as shown in Figure 3-30.

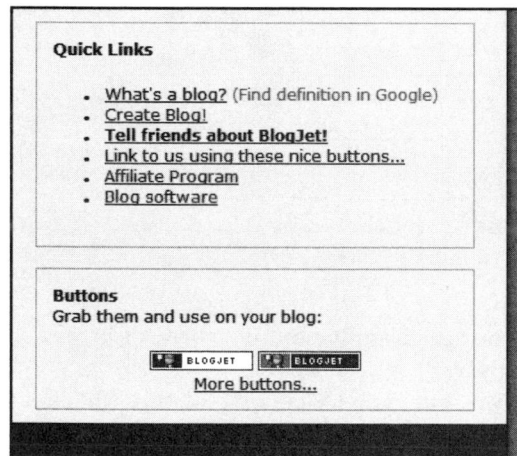

Figure 3-30. *When all else fails, give people helpful links.*

You can take a few last shots at selling: maybe potential customers aren't sure what a blog is (see the "Blogging for Fun and Profit" section). Or maybe someone isn't sure how to create one. Maybe they're actually a returning customer, and you can get them to email their friends or link to your Web site.

When all else fails, you can try money, as shown in Figure 3-31.

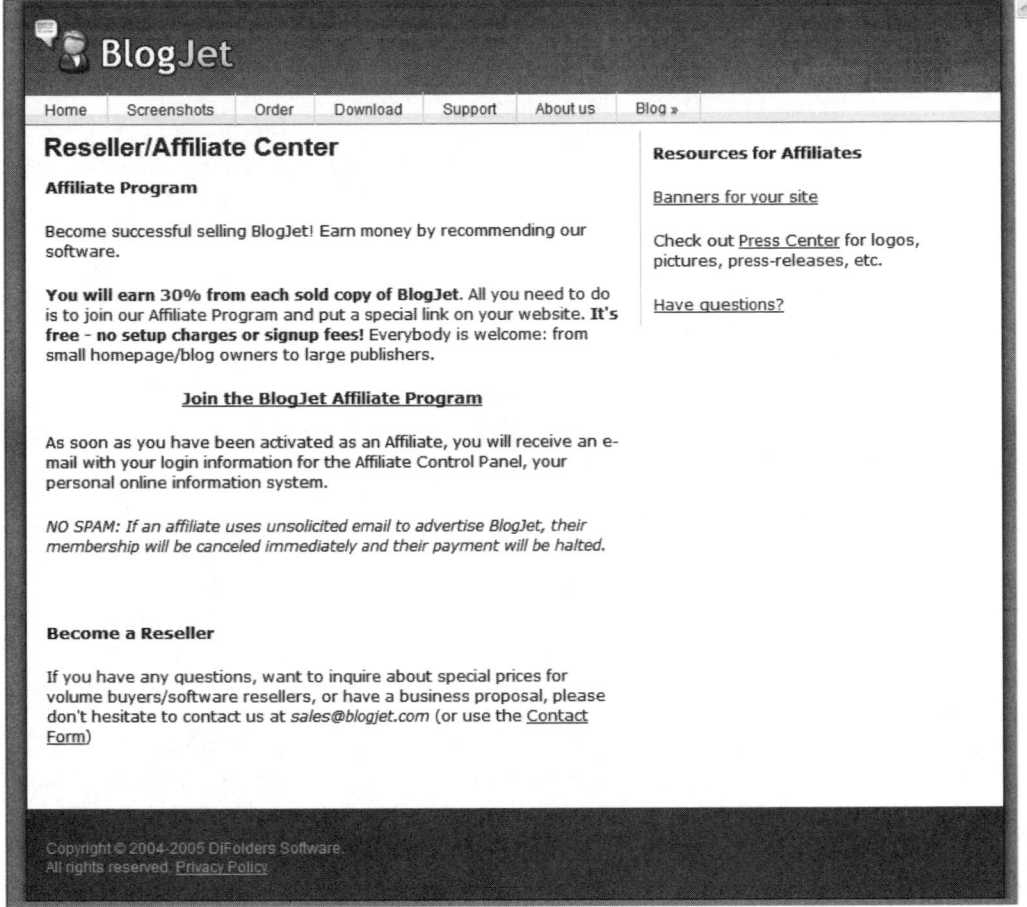

Figure 3-31. *We* really *want you!*

All and all, this site does a masterful job of marketing without heavy-handed selling. Of course, no two visitors to this site are going to read all the text or read it in the order I've covered it. They're going to pick and choose their preferred way of getting information about a product for the purposes of deciding whether to spend their hard-earned dollars on it. Or rubles, as in this case!

DMITRY CHESTNYKH, FOUNDER AND CEO, DIFOLDERS SOFTWARE

Just before starting this book, I went looking on the Internet for a better way to blog. When I found BlogJet, it took me about 30 seconds to be convinced this was an excellent product presented professionally. Here's Dmitry's story of how BlogJet came to be.

Q. Can you tell me a bit about yourself and why you started DiFolders?

A. When I was young (something about 13), I developed my first shareware product; that's because I thought it was cool to have a nag screen [and] write all those license.txt and readme.txt [files]. It was a text-mode game for DOS called Dome. Though, I was the only user of this software....

I released my first product, DiFolders, in 2002. I always wanted to be financially independent, and I thought that was the real path for this. The first sale was in the next month after releasing it. The second sale came in the next few hours. But…I had only two sales per month or so.

Then I decided to write another application called Active Cleaner. With it I began to earn about $300–$400 per month—not so successful but enough to tell my friends and my mom that I earn money in the Internet selling my own software. (My mom earns less working here in Russia as a nurse.)

Then I created BlogJet, and it was a success. Now I'm 22, still working alone for myself, [and] still have big plans.

I live near Moscow, Russia. I graduated from the Moscow Institute of Physics and Technology in 2005. My email is dmitry@blogjet.com. :)

Q. Why did you create BlogJet?

A. [I was] blogging since 2000 or 2001 and never liked [the] Web interface. My first blog was on DeadJournal (which was based on LiveJournal sources), and they had a simple client for posting from [the] desktop. I liked it, but I wanted more. Then I found a few freeware tools, which offered basically the same features but were compatible with other blog services (such as Blogger [and] Movable Type). I never used them, though—they had ugly interfaces, and I had to write HTML code. Then I thought that I wanted to write my posts using a WYSIWYG editor—something like Microsoft Word. I wanted to easily include pictures in my posts without having to upload them to server. Finally, I came to conclusion that it must be me who would write this application. :) Also, I read in Thomas Warfield's blog A Shareware Life (`http://www.asharewarelife.com`) that if he didn't make games, he would create something connected with blogs. Good enough for marketing research. :)

Q. I noticed your Web site does a lot of things right—did you design it, or did you/do you have someone you work with?

A. I design my Web sites myself (excluding the BlogJet icon; it was designed by Alexandra Pavlova). Like all things in my micro-ISV business (programming, marketing, etc.), I learned how to design Web sites myself. Of course, I could outsource this work, but—hey—I like to do things! I just enjoy creating software, creating sites, [and] selling and marketing products. I always try to do only what I love to do.

Q. What advice would you give to other people starting their own micro-ISVs?

A. My advice:

- Learn marketing.

- Don't stop on one product if it's not successful.

- Stop copying. Start creating "wow!" products.

- Look for a growing but empty niche.

- Release your first beta for free.

- Try to get a lot of buzz.

- Don't bother if you have free competitors—people like to spend money!

- Forget about cracks, hacks, keygen, etc. (at least for the first version); you'll never win this fight. Don't care about piracy too much.

- Be remarkable; make your products remarkable.

- Believe that you *can* do it!

- Don't worry—be happy!

- Enjoy your life. Enjoy what you do.

Q. [Dmitry also had some good advice pertaining to another section later in this chapter, "Blogging for Fun and Profit."] What should be a micro-ISV's "blogging strategy"?

A. I wrote a small article about blogging strategy for micro-ISVs at SharewareBlogs.com, so you can count it as my answer: "Having a Blog Is Critical for Your Shareware Business" (`http://sharewareblogs.com/node/35`). See especially the "What Should I Write About?" section.

Q. Can you share any instances when your blog has led to increased sales of your software or product reviews?

A. Well, since I'm totally blog-related, and just so close to blogosphere with my application, I can't depict some special statistics about increased sales: I must have a blog, and I have it. I didn't make any testing of how it helps, but I know it does. :)

I know a lot of examples of how blogs help sell software (Nick Bradbury, Joel Spolsky, Delicious Monster, etc.). Anyway, micro-ISVs should test themselves for what is good for their business. Do you have a money-back guarantee? Why not? Try it, and then decide. Does your Order button look like button, or is it just a link? Try different things, and then decide.

Just set up a blog (it's so easy), and write. Then see how your sales increase/buzz. If not, perhaps, stop doing it. Test!

As for product reviews, yes, it's very easy to track such things with blogs: someone who reviews your product on their blog just left a trackback on your blog. This helps not only track reviews but respond to their writings.

I call blogs *word of mouth on steroids*. They help create a lot of buzz about your products and your company (or personality).

Q. I notice that you are interviewing people (Jack Trout) on your blog; what's your strategy for getting/doing these interviews?

A. I learned a great lesson from my software business. It can be expressed in only two words: just ask. Most people like to be asked. When you ask someone for help or advice, they are most likely to help you because they feel comfortable doing this. So, again, just ask. If a person does not answer, don't annoy her. But most likely you'll get a response.

Getting Paid: Nuts, Bolts, and Bucks

Few tasks are as enjoyable for a micro-ISV as seeing the money start coming in. I still remember when two days after starting to sell MasterList Professional I saw my first sales email notification that someone I'd never heard of liked my product well enough to part with their $24.95 USD.

Of course, getting paid means you have a reliable, hack-proof mechanism that moves real, live customers through the purchase process in absolutely the least amount of clicks, fill-ins, and minutes as possible.

■**Note** Usability study after study has shown that the more steps in the process, the fewer people finish making an online purchase. See, for example, Webcredible at `http://www.webcredible.co.uk/user-friendly-resources/web-usability/ecommerce-usability.shtml`.

Getting paid isn't hard, but it's not simple either. You'll need to bring three worldviews together to see the money: the technical world of online processing, the financial world of payment transactions, and the customer's world of online shopping experiences. Complicating matters is a decade's worth of e-commerce evolution, mutation, and innovation. The problem isn't too few options—it's too many.

You'll take a cursory look at two ways of getting paid that I think time has passed by before getting down to business: the shareware approach and the shareware author's payment processors.

Once long ago (before the commercial Internet), programmers who wanted to sell applications outside retail channels would make their software available via electronic BBSs such as CompuServe and America Online in the hope that passersby who liked their software would throw a few coins in their hats. This was the pure expression of the shareware model, where users would pay what they thought the application was worth.

If this approach sounds a lot like *buskers*—starving musicians who play for money in public places—it is (especially the starving part)! Few people could make this work pre-Internet, but you'll still find good and steward programmers who take this approach.

Starting with the rise of the Internet in the early 1990s, a host of companies sprang into existence to make it possible for shareware authors to actually sell their wares. These shareware author payment processors offered a good deal at the time: for about 10 percent of the retail price, they would send you a regular check and provide shareware buyers with a reliable, trustworthy, real company to do business with.

Some of these companies did more than just collect payments; they would help promote your product, issue keys to registered users, find paying customers, and track sales. These companies prospered at a time when buying something on the Internet was akin to jumping through flaming hoops—new, exciting, and a bit dangerous. However, by this decade, online shopping had gone from something amazing to something mundane, and more than a few of these shareware payment processors went under, merged, or were acquired by Digital River (http://www.digitalriver.com/corporate/solutions03.shtml), as shown in Figure 3-32.

Although many existing micro-ISVs swear by shareware payment processors, the industry has moved on in two ways: it's altogether possible to build a robust payment processing system for your micro-ISV yourself, and more than a few companies now exist to do this for you for a lot less than 10 percent of your sales price. You'll take an in-depth look at three of these, but before I get into the technical details of all this, I'm going to steal from you.

That's right, steal.

Here's how it's done: I go to your Web site where I buy your product, and like 93 percent of the online transactions, I pay with a credit card.[8] Only it's not my card—it's someone else's. I "bought" this card and a few dozen other identities for a pittance online from a Web site you won't find in Google, and besides a bunch of other goodies, I'm going to pick up a copy of your latest and greatest. But what do I care? It's not like it costs you anything, right?

Wrong. Let's say you decide to build your own custom online processing system—you take transactions through your shopping cart and fire them off to your merchant account at your bank, just like you would cash a check. While the bank may initially process it and you see another $19.95 or $199.95 in your account, sooner or later that transaction is going to be discovered as fraudulent and transform from a credit in your merchant account to a debit for the same amount called a *chargeback* and a nice fat bank processing fee ($20–$30 is common in the United States). If this happens enough, you'll get a little letter from your friendly bank informing you your account has been closed and you're in deep doo-doo.

---

8. "The Truth About Internet Fraud," *Ziff Davis Smart Business*, April 2001. See also http://www.findarticles.com/p/articles/mi_zdzsb/is_200104/ai_ziff8442.

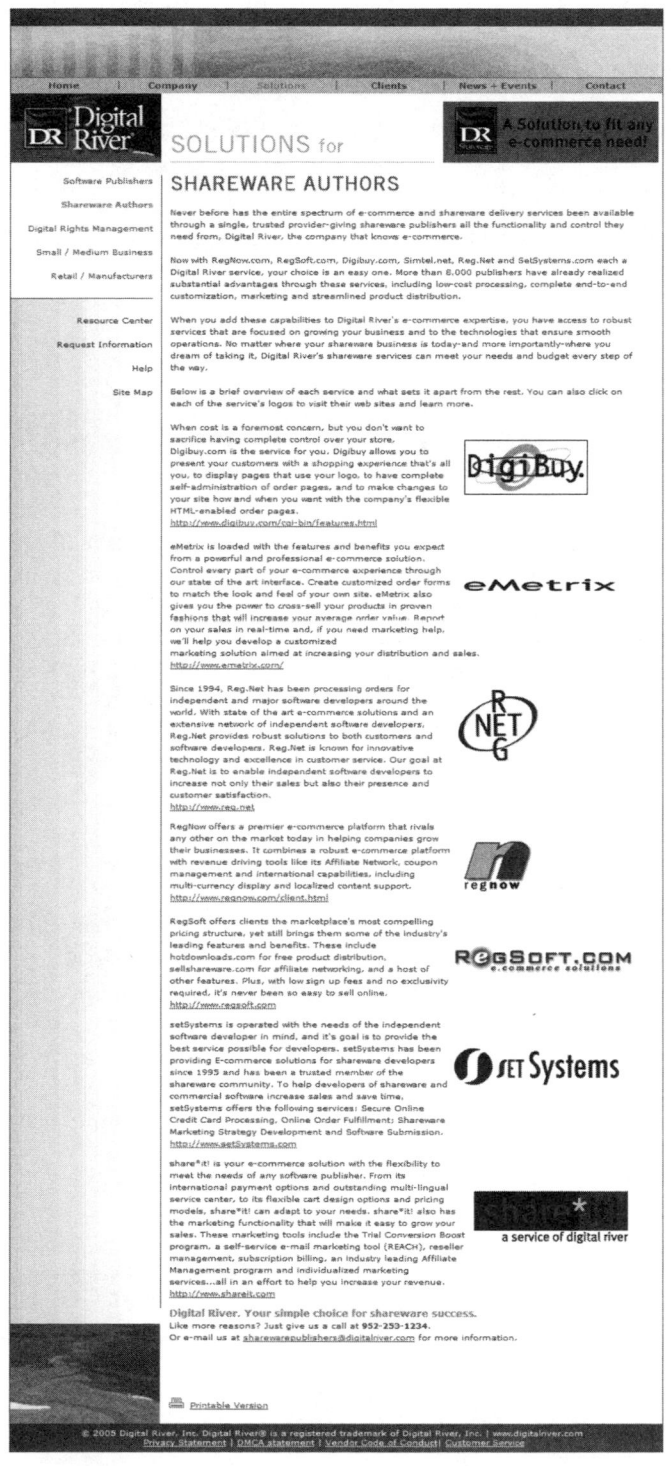

Figure 3-32. *Exploring Digital River's flock of shareware payment processors*

This isn't what you want to be doing, but online fraud is a reality that every micro-ISV has to face; and the smaller your company, the bigger the problem is for you.

Unless your micro-ISV is about an e-commerce solution, it's time to think like a business-person, not a developer; and businesspeople—at least the successful ones—think about costs. In the following sections, I'll cover three approaches for a micro-ISV to get paid:

- Without having a merchant account, getting paid via PayPal.

- Without having a merchant account, "reselling" your products through 2Checkout.com.

- Having a merchant account with processing provided by VeriSign.

Working with PayPal

PayPal (`http://paypal.com`), as shown in Figure 3-33, is one of those companies online people either love or hate. Started in 1998 and acquired by eBay in 2002, PayPal has grown to become *the* nonbank, payment-processing company today. It does business in 57 countries and has 78.9 million accounts (as of the second quarter of 2005).[9]

It's the nonbank status of PayPal that has in many ways led to the creation of more than a few anti-PayPal sites replete with true horror stories of accounts frozen without explanation, week-long service interruptions, snarling customer service reps, and a reputation for high-handed secrecy. Doing business with PayPal means as a merchant you preauthorize PayPal not only to collect money on your behalf and deposit it into your bank account in any one of 25 different countries but also to remove money from that account, without explanation or recourse.

With all that baggage, why on Earth would a micro-ISV do business with PayPal? Well, it's an excellent way of getting paid!

It has low processing rates (a maximum of 2.9 percent plus 30 cents for each transaction), better than average technical support (at least in the three calls I've made), and no setup fees. And although it used to be that a customer needed to have a PayPal account in order to pay you, that's no longer the case.

In fact, in June 2005, PayPal added a Payments Pro service for U.S.-based merchants, which processes the transaction for you without leaving your site.

For the past six months, I've used PayPal as one of the two ways customers can buy MasterList Professional and haven't had a single issue, customer complaint, or chargeback. I have to say— I'm crazy for how easy PayPal has been to use.

While I may be crazy, I'm not stupid. I also have a payment alternative to PayPal for customers who don't want to do business with PayPal and one business bank account I use only for receiving PayPal payments. As the saying goes, your mileage may vary.

---

9. `http://en.wikipedia.org/wiki/PayPal`

Figure 3-33. *Visiting PayPal today*

Doing Business the 2Checkout.com Way

Another way of collecting payments for your micro-ISV's wares without setting up a merchant account is through 2Checkout.com (http://2checkout.com), as shown in Figure 3-34. This Columbus, Ohio, payment processor charges $49 USD as a setup charge and then charges 5.5 percent plus $0.45 USD per sale.

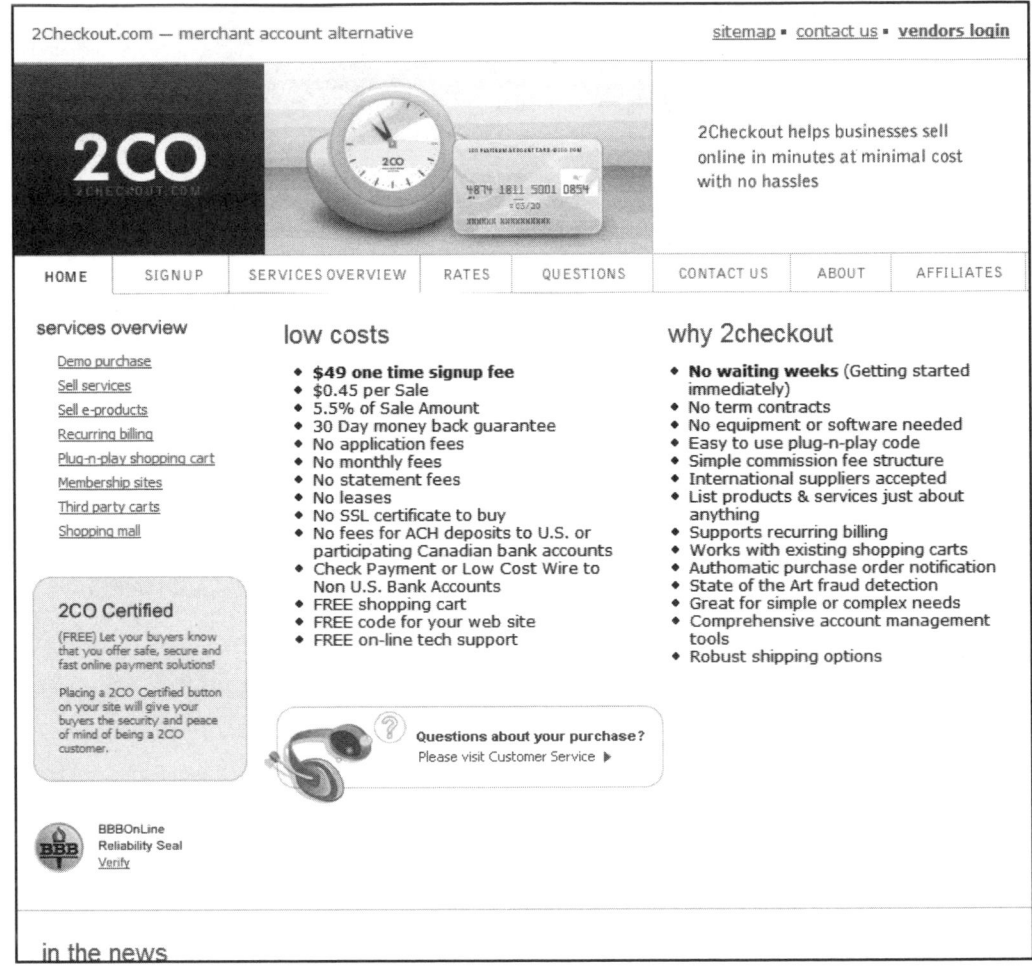

Figure 3-34. *Selling your product via 2Checkout.com*

2Checkout.com is technically a reseller—it buys your software, subscription, or product at a discount and then sells it for the Suggested Retail Price (SRP). This means 2Checkout.com holds 5 percent of your sales for 90 days before paying you as a reserve for returns and other issues. You get this revenue, but it's held for 90 days while 2Checkout.com pays the rest of your sales twice a month.

Unlike PayPal where you can spend money from your account, 2Checkout.com is strictly a payment processor, depositing to your U.S. bank account twice a month your revenue or, for a nominal fee, sending your money via bank wire or check. Also unlike PayPal, 2Checkout.com can handle payment processing for micro-ISVs located just about anywhere in the world (except, as of this writing, North Korea, Cuba, Libya, Iraq, Iran Sudan, and UNITA-controlled portions of Angola).

I've been a satisfied 2Checkout.com (see Figure 3-35) since January 2005 and always have been able to speak to someone knowledgeable, friendly, and helpful when I've called for either technical support or business transaction support.

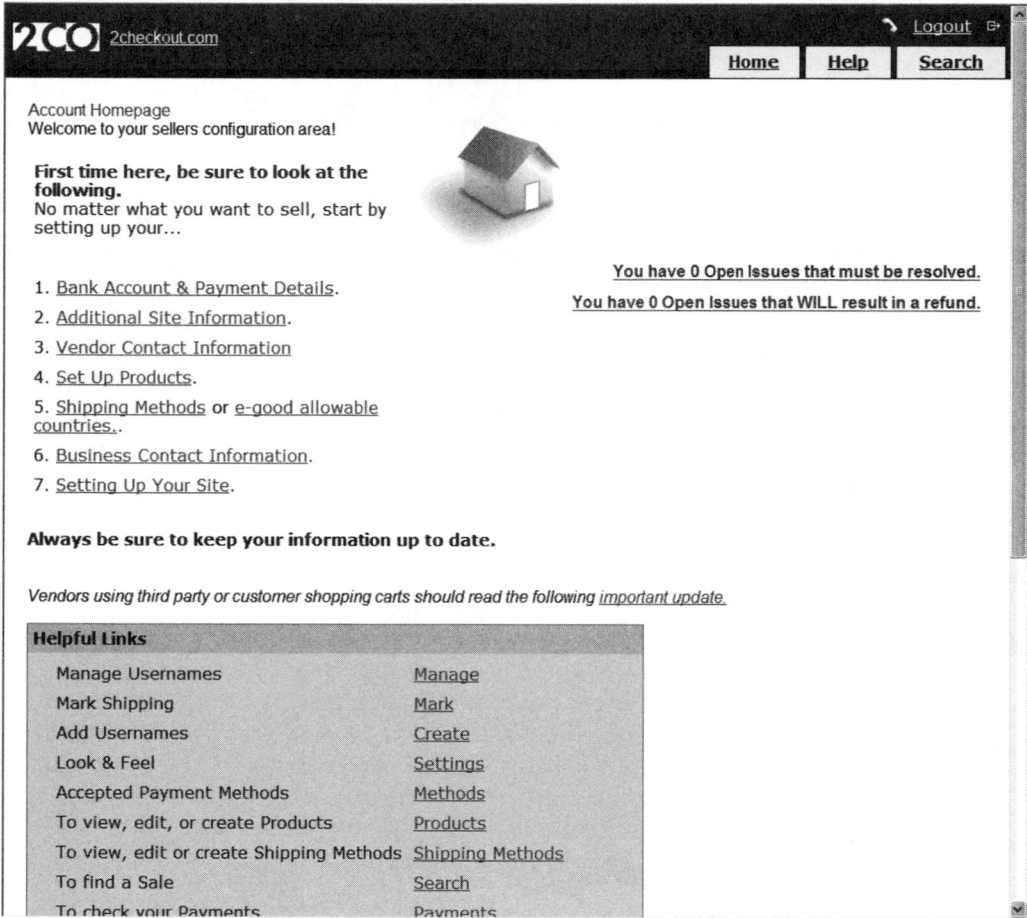

Figure 3-35. *Going inside 2Checkout.com*

2Checkout.com strongly screens transactions for fraud, but unlike some processors that reject the transaction automatically, 2Checkout.com will take an iffy transaction and then alert the merchant to its potentially questionable status while a real person evaluates the transaction, often contacting the buyer by phone and/or email to verify it. In the dozen or so fraud alerts I've received, 2Checkout.com was able to verify all of them within a day as legitimate, none of my customers complained, and one even complimented me on the process.

Any day a company I buy a service from can make my customers happier is a good day.

ALAN HOMEWOOD, CEO AND FOUNDER, 2CHECKOUT.COM

When you read online questions about who should do your micro-ISV's processing, 2Checkout.com often is at or near the top of the list. In this interview, Alan Homewood, founder of 2Checkout.com, explains what his company has to offer micro-ISVs.

Q. In today's business environment on the Web, what are the three best reasons for doing business with 2Checkout.com?

A. Probably the three best are the ease of signing up, the low cost of entry for start-up, self-funded entities, and 2Checkout.com was the same thing, so we understand the business.

Q. Really?

A. Yeah, I started the company in 1999 myself, when I saw the cost of getting paid online was quite steep for a small company that may or may not have large sales or may take a while to start selling. There's the merchant account that's $500 and [then] $50 a month, the SSL certificate, the dedicated servers you really should have to store sensitive information like credit card numbers, the technical resources to manage the servers, and in a lot of cases a shopping cart. I decided there needed to be an alternative where you didn't have the up-front costs, and paid a little more each transaction, to hit that niche market.

Q. What's your history on this? Is 2Checkout.com your first business or your third or....?

A. Personally, I was an Oracle consultant, with a billing background, an antifraud background, a varied background, and I became interested in Web businesses, and that's where the company came from.

Q. Can you give me an idea of how big 2Checkout.com now is?

A. Right now we have roughly 60 employees; we're all located here in Columbus, [Ohio], and at last count we had about 40,000 vendors, we're adding about 2,000 a month, and we do roughly $17 million a month in sales.

Q. I can see that at a certain price point it's more economical to bring payment processing in-house. What's your ideal size client here? How big is big for you?

A. We do have clients at a certain level, but really at $10,000 and below of sales a month is kind of where the breakpoint comes in. Right around that number, I can bring some of these costs in-house and save money; I can pay to do these things directly. Something people don't realize often is that there is a lot of processing that goes on [at] the backend of processing credit cards. There's a lot of overhead and headache people don't calculate in. I roughly say that around $10,000 [sales per month] is the level it might make sense to take a lot of the things we do for them in-house, particularly if they are going to grow and grow and grow.

Of course, we have quite a few clients that stay with us at higher levels because the expense of monitoring fraud can be significant.

Q. Besides the ease of entry and low costs, two things I wondered about was credit card fraud and potential taxes. Can you give me a bit of an education there about what you guys do—especially about fraud?

A. We have a seasoned fraud staff and tools developed in-house over years to help identify fraud. And we pay for a lot of other sources where we get information. We take a lot of that burden away from our clients, most of which are small businesses. They need to concentrate on running their businesses, not being an expert in the myriad ways someone may try to defraud them. There's a massive amount of credit card fraud that goes on on the Internet.

Q. How massive is massive?

A. Just in the United States last year, $400 million to $500 million in losses sustained by merchants; that's not even counting the amount of fraud they stop at the door or the cost of battling the fraud.

Q. Can you give me an idea of what percentage that translates to?

A. I'd say that on a daily basis we catch five to ten percent of transactions as fraudulent. If you are not a bit prudent on the front end, you can catch even more than that. It depends on the product. Some vendors will have one in five orders that come in being fraudulent.

Q. The other question was taxes. Do you get into collecting taxes, or is that something that's not happening on the Internet?

A. It is happening on the Internet; actually, we absorb some tax costs and pay taxes for our clients. In the United States, if you are in Ohio, you sell to someone In Ohio, and you have a presence here or in whatever state you sell in, you are required to pay taxes. But the way we are set up, our relationship with our sellers and vendors is that they resell through us. That basically means that whoever you are, [you are] selling to someone in Ohio, and then we resell the products. That puts the tax liability on us. At this point, we just absorb it; we don't pass it on.

Q. I guess sales tax in Ohio is a lot lower than in California! [Sonoma, California, has a 7.75% sales tax, but Internet sales are exempt statewide.]

A. We pay quite a bit a month for sales that are in Ohio to people in Ohio.

Q. Two more questions. What mistakes do you see start-ups making that they could avoid?

A. I guess the advice I would give is to not give up. It can become difficult early on for a small company. It takes time to grow. In most cases it takes time to grow slowly, and that can become frustrating to a smaller entity.

I guess another problem for smaller entities is that they can become defrauded [and] become the victims of fraud very easily online. That's definitely something to be careful of. And to test the waters online—some things definitely work for some entities and don't work for others. For instance, entities may believe that it's a great use of my investment to pay for pay-for-click advertising. That can quickly add up to a lot of money that doesn't produce any results. In some industries it may provide great results.

One of the most important things to do, at least for start-up online businesses, is to mine the information they get from people coming to their Web site and to constantly ask their clients and customers what they are looking for and try to get information from people who don't buy as well.

Q. One other question. I noticed you made a point of saying all your employees are there in Columbus, Ohio. A lot of financial services companies outsource to India and other places. Is there something here you want to say, or is it that's just how things have worked out?

A. Well, it's a conscious effort. I know [outsourcing] has worked out for some companies, but I prefer to keep jobs here in the community, as long as it's feasible for us. I like to employ people locally, have them here in the office, [and] be able to meet with face to face. I know [outsourcing] works for some companies; it isn't my ideal situation.

Going with VeriSign

One of the key aspects of doing business online is trust. Without the trust of customers in your e-commerce process, you won't have any commerce to process. VeriSign's stock in trade is trust; it manages the .com, .net, .cc, and .tv domains for ICANN (the overseeing board for the Internet), is the foremost provider of Secure Sockets Layer (SSL) certificates used to encode financial transactions on the Net, provides one of the best-known site verification programs on the Net, and performs payment processing for large and small companies worldwide.

VeriSign is one of the biggest, if not the biggest, payment processor on the Net today. In the first quarter of 2005, VeriSign processed 79.21 million transactions worth $10.69 billion.[10]

VeriSign sells two payment-processing services to merchants who plan to use a merchant account and conduct business online, both come with the "Verified by VeriSign" seal:

---

10. VeriSign Internet Security Intelligence Briefing, http://www.verisign.com/static/030910.pdf

Payflow Link: Customers are directed to VeriSign's site where they enter their financial information. Payflow Link costs $179 USD to set up and for a monthly fee of $19.95 will process up to 500 transactions a month.

Payflow Pro: The customer stays on your site, but VeriSign handles the transaction in the background. Payflow Pro costs $249 USD to set up and for a monthly fee of $59 will process up to 1,000 transactions a month.

VeriSign offers a range of add-on services to both Payflow Link and Payflow Pro, as shown in Table 3-2.

Table 3-2. *VeriSign Add-Ons*

Add-On	Features	Price
Basic fraud protection	Includes seven basic fraud filters	Setup: $29.95, monthly fee: $19.95, transaction fee: $0.05 per transaction
Advanced fraud protection	An additional 13 filters and basic fraud filters	Setup: $89.95, monthly fee: $19.95, transaction fee: $0.10 per transaction
Account monitoring	Transaction monitoring by a person	Setup: $29.95, monthly fee: $19.95, transaction fee: no charge
Buyer authentication	Inclusion of the Verified by Visa and MasterCard SecureCode programs	Setup: $150, monthly fee: $9.95, transaction fee: $0.10 per transaction

Although VeriSign provides free, unlimited email and Web support to its customers, it charges anywhere from $12 to $495 a month for telephone technical support.

And speaking of fees, keep in mind if you go this route for handling your sales, you'll encounter the following fees:

Merchant account: Your bank will take a percentage of all the credit card transactions it processes for you, plus probably charge a monthly fee and other charges. For example, Wells Fargo Bank charges for its Online Merchant Services Account a one-time setup fee of $99, a monthly fee of $31, and then 2.40 percent of each transaction. It will also charge you $7.50 for a paper statement and $15 per transaction that becomes a chargeback.

Shopping cart: If your micro-ISV has more than one product for sale, you'll want some form of online shopping cart so that customers can buy more than one product at a time. Depending on how you do this, your shopping cart may be something you code, an open source tool, an application you buy, or part of what Web site the host provider includes in your package. Rest assured, you'll be paying for it one way or another.

SSL certificate: Although there hasn't been one verified instance of an online credit card transaction in the United States, Europe, or Asia as of this writing being intercepted by a nefarious third-party, payment processing without an SSL certificate to encode the data raises instant suspicions on the part of the buying public. If you go with Payflow Link, the processing takes place on VerSign's site, and this is a nonissue. But, if you go with Payflow Pro, you're required to have a SSL certificate, which costs $995 a year through VeriSign. By no coincidence, VeriSign and its subsidiary, Thawte, sell most of the SSL certificates in use today.

MITCHEL VEYS, DIRECTOR OF PRODUCTS, VERISIGN PAYMENT PRODUCTS

VeriSign is one of the commercial Internet's "first-mover" companies, both in terms of domain registrations and e-commerce. In this interview, Mitchel Veys, director of VeriSign Payment Products, talks about what VeriSign offers to micro-ISVs.

Q. What's the argument to be made for a self-funded start-up not to do all the e-commerce functions in-house and to go with a company like VeriSign?

A. A lot of the people I work with are very much like you describe. VeriSign Payment Products is the market leader in this space—we are part of the larger VeriSign corporation—a $1.4 billion company. We have today over 140,000 merchants who are working with us. When I say working *with us*, we are powering their e-commerce. We take care of everything for them. We make it as easy as possible for them to get going and focus on their business.

Since a lot of the feedback we've gotten from merchants is that [what] they want from us is simplicity, a high level of security, reliability, and safety, we are really focused on this middle market [between individuals and large companies] that you describe—people who start their business, who focus on their business, who may have a few employees. We provide everything they need so they don't need to worry anymore about their payment component.

Q. So you benefit from the rest of VeriSign's infrastructure?

A. As you may know, VeriSign runs the .com and .net registry, so that means that there are billions of transactions a day [and] billions of queries that are hitting those servers. And as long as we've been running it, almost eight years now, we've never been down, not a single hour, not a single day. And we're lucky in VeriSign Payment Services to actually benefit from all that infrastructure/investment that has been made in there. So it's a whole piece of the business taken care of, providing very high reliability for our merchants.

Q. So how does this all work?

A. Well, you have two components: a financial component [that] includes having your Internet merchant account, and then it includes the technical component, so that all of the electronic data can be taken in, validated, and transferred within the payment system, so that all the different parties can get paid.

Typically when a small company wants to do payments over the Internet, most of the payments are done with credit cards. About 90 percent of all transactions are done with credit cards. They will need two components— the financial and the technical components. On the financial side, they do need a bank account where the money is going to be deposited—a merchant account. And we can help them with that because we have two partners who do that (as well as the technical side).

Once you're set up on the banking side, you have your account; then on the technical side you typically use a shopping cart. So what we have done is we're integrated with a very long list of shopping carts and all of the leading shopping carts. As you integrate your shopping cart with your Web site, you will have a plug-in that integrates with VeriSign, and we will work with you to activate that plug-in, and you are ready to roll.

When your customer goes to your purchase page and enters their Visa or MasterCard information and clicks Purchase, we will capture that information with Payflow Pro or Payflow Link, validate that information, and send it on through the payment process. There's two pieces to that—an authorization piece and a settlement piece.

On the authorization side, the first thing a bank will do is see if it is a valid cardholder and that the cardholder actually has the funds in his or her bank account to actually make this purchase.

Q. When you say funds, you mean the credit available on their credit card?

A. That's absolutely correct, or it could be a debit card as well as a credit card. What happens next is that the transaction will be passed onto a payment processor that will actually calculate the settlement. The merchant [could be] working with Wells Fargo, but the customer is with Bank of America, so money will have to be transferred from one bank to the other. They will do all that calculation. That's called the *clearing and settlement* process.

These processors are effectively doing the IT functions the banks used to do in the past.

Q. So VeriSign is doing the fraud detection?

A. That is correct.

Q. Without giving away any secrets you don't want to give away, how do you detect fraud?

A. What it means to detect fraud is to actually do a number of checks. We have a whole bunch of filters we've put in place, for example, checking where the IP address comes from. In general our philosophy on fraud is the following: we provide a number of core fraud detection filters in place and then let the merchant decide what decisions we make for that. We can just provide the information to the merchant, or we can stop the transaction at a certain level if the merchant wants that.

In each of those cases the filters will do a number of matches. For example, if the IP is coming from one country and the shipping address is to another country, that looks very suspicious. I'm not saying it's necessarily fraudulent, just that it's very suspicious. If on top of it, say the last three digits are different from the digits that should be associated with the card number, that increases again the probability of the chances of fraud.

If it is being shipped to a freight forwarder or a P.O. box, it again increases the chances of fraud. If it's a certain ticket item, it's going to increase the probability of fraud. If this is the fifth time in a very short period of time that this cardholder has bought, say, a plasma TV, that will increase the probability of fraud.

We have all those filters in place and we will do an analysis based on those filters, and we can say this is very likely to be a fraudulent transaction. When the merchant signs up with VeriSign, they will decide if they want us to stop those transactions or they want us to flag them.

In most instances what we have seen is that merchants are rejecting many more valid transactions they believe are fraudulent than actual fraudulent transactions. So they are better off signing up for fraud protection system that actually has a much higher probability of catching those real fraudulent transactions than those false positives.

Q. So, the payment processors don't get into the business of fraud detection; they take the transaction to be legitimate when they get it. So, someone has to do it—it's either going to be the merchant or VeriSign or someone else.

A. Yeah, again, everything here is a shade of gray. Some payment processors do some of this, [and] VeriSign does a lot of it, because we feel this is a responsibility we have vis-à-vis our merchants. The other thing is that a lot of what VeriSign stands for, a lot of what we do, is being the trusted brand. We are a security company, so this is part of our DNA.

Q. Another part of what you are offering merchants who sign up with VeriSign is that people are paying who they think they are paying—I've seen that "Verified by VeriSign" logo on a lot of sites.

A. Exactly. Very important component. Absolutely. What we have realized is that a large number of cardholders actually go through the whole process, and at the last point when they're asked to fill in their card details, they stop the process if they are not familiar with the merchant. Because we have such a large market share [and] because we power so many Web sites, we know that a lot of those merchants who may not have a well-known brand name actually are real, valid merchants. So what we have done is we have started to push the VeriSign seal into the marketplace, and it's free for merchants to use if they use any of the VeriSign services.

Be it the certificates, the payment services, or any of our other services we offer, we know that is a valid merchant because we have already done all the verification that they are a valid merchant. Then the merchant can show the VeriSign seal on his or her Web site, and that indeed provides that extra level of trust that the consumer needs to make him or her feel comfortable to finish that transaction.

Q. What mistakes have you seen small start-up companies make when it comes to e-commerce?

A. I think we've seen a number of them. For example, with our own products, we have a number of security settings that we encourage people to use, and in some instance either people may not use all of them or they may not update them as their business changes. An example of that is they might start selling small-ticket items, and as their business grows they might start selling higher-ticket items. That changes the mix, that changes the fraud, that changes the risk component…and they may not actually make all those tweaks, opening up the potential for more fraud.

The other thing that we have captured working with our base and all the surveys that we do is that for most merchants, payment needs to be 100 percent reliable, and once it's in place, they really don't want to have to worry about it anymore. So we encourage companies to shop around and find a company that is very stable so they don't have to mess around with payments once they are in place. It's an industry that is shaking up a lot. Lots of smaller companies have started and gone out of business. And a small company just can't afford that.

All in all, most micro-ISVs shouldn't start with a merchant account and either VeriSign or a competing service: it's too complex, too costly, and too time-consuming. Once your micro-ISV is established, revenues are more than $10,000 a month and growing, and you've handled more important issues such as marketing, customer support, and ongoing product development, then you have plenty of time to consider moving to a full e-commerce solution.

For me, the combination of PayPal and 2Checkout.com has worked extremely well, as shown in Figure 3-36. Not all of my eggs are in one other person's basket, my customers have told me they like having a choice, and other than the $49 dollars it cost to sign up with 2Checkout.com, all my costs are a fixed percentage of each sale, not part of the monthly overhead of running a business.

Figure 3-36. *Giving your micro-ISV's customers a choice*

To Host or Not to Host

To wrap up the discussion of your Web site, I'll discuss whether you should host your site yourself or pay a company to do it for you. Now, if your micro-ISV is developing a Web-based application or service, you probably know all there is to know about Web hosting and can skip this section. Or, at least you should know more about it than me!

If you're reading this, odds are good you've never had your own Web site or you're on only your second or third attempt to find a good Web host. I'm currently on my fifth and sixth such companies, having launched my first Web site in 1994.

Before shamelessly plugging the two companies I use, Table 3-3 presents my short checklist for finding the right company or companies for you.

Table 3-3. *Evaluating a Web Host Service*

Questions to Ask	Contender 1	Contender 2
Does the company pick up the phone when you call during business hours?	☐	☐
If you create a technical support request, do you get a reply from a person within one hour?	☐	☐
Can you pay month to month instead of being locked into a quarterly or yearly contract?	☐	☐
Does the company provide support for the technology you want to use to create your Web site?	☐	☐
Does the company offer the additional services (such as shopping carts or online forums) you want?	☐	☐

When you go shopping for a Web host, remember that most times you get what you pay for. I've been lucky to find two good Web hosting companies; Alentus (http://alentus.com), as shown in Figure 3-37, based in Edmonton, Canada, hosts my main site, and Server Intellect (http://www.serverintellect.com/) out of Orlando, Florida, hosts a second site I mainly use for Fog Creek Software's FogBugz bug-reporting/discussion board system.

Figure 3-37. *Getting the Canadian advantage*

Although it's a little unusual to cross international borders to get a Web hosting company, I've found that Canadian-based Alentus has some of the nicest and most helpful staff I've ever encountered.

Meanwhile, the people at Server Intellect offer excellent support for FogBugz, as shown in Figure 3-38, a Web service you'll hear much more about in Chapter 5.

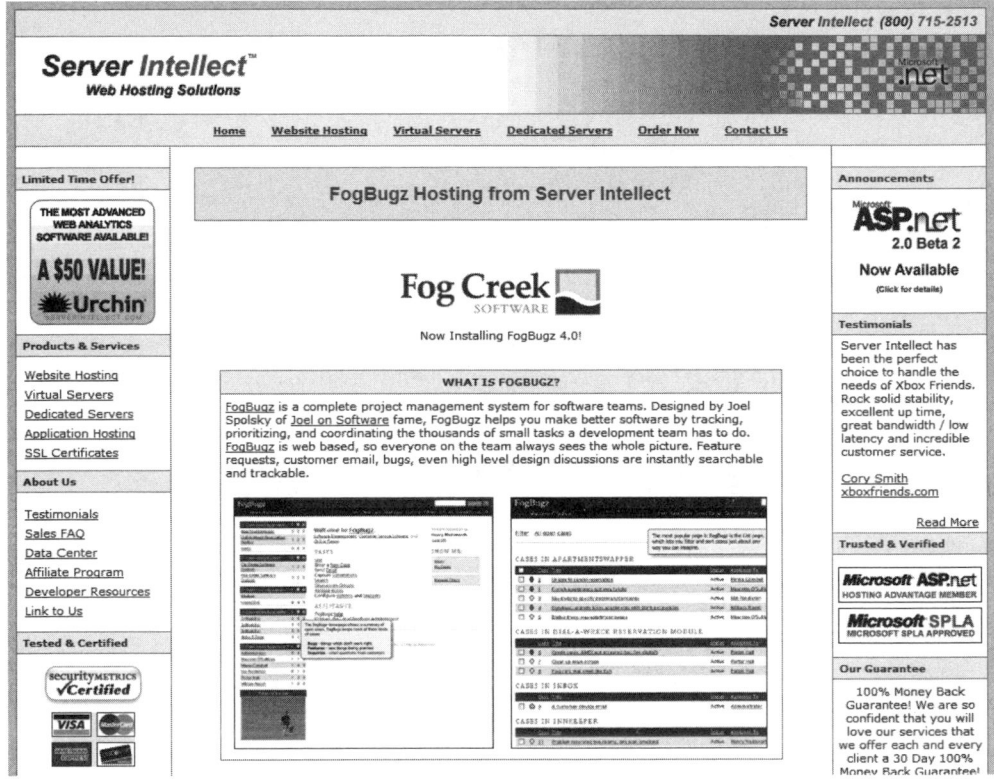

Figure 3-38. *Server Intellect's hosting service offers FogBugz.*

If you decide to pay a company to host your site(s), don't be afraid to "test-drive" their tech support by calling them or contacting a few of their "valued customers" to see just why they value that vendor.

Blogging for Fun and Profit

Finally for this chapter, I'll cover something that is sweeping across the Web this decade—blogging. Short for *Web logging*, blogs are different in four respects from all those billions of other Web pages you see:

- Blogs are written in the first-person, not in a third-person, anonymous voice.

- Blogs let readers post comments about each blog posting.

- Blogs are for the most part fast and immediate—they're the flash wire stories of the Net, not the histories or studies.

- Blogs are red hot, not because an estimated 7 percent of the 120 million U.S. adults who use the Internet have created one, or that 27 percent of Internet readers say they read blogs,[11] but because blogs influence what readers buy, think, and read more than traditional media or "traditional" Web sites.

Influence makes reporters and editors perk up. Influence makes politicians, political activists, and people who follow politics pay attention. And influence, not to mention the attention that the political sphere and media sphere are paying various blogs, rings the dinner bell and gets CEOs and marketing directors salivating at the thought of getting around the market's spin filter to reach customers.

Hi-Ho, Hi-Ho, It's Off to Blog We Go….

Why do people blog? You could pick any one of 15 million blogs Technorati (http://www.technorati.com/) indexes as of right now and find a different reason and rationale: some blogs are rants, some are journals, some are by people who want attention, and some are by people who want to share their interests, as shown in Figure 3-39.

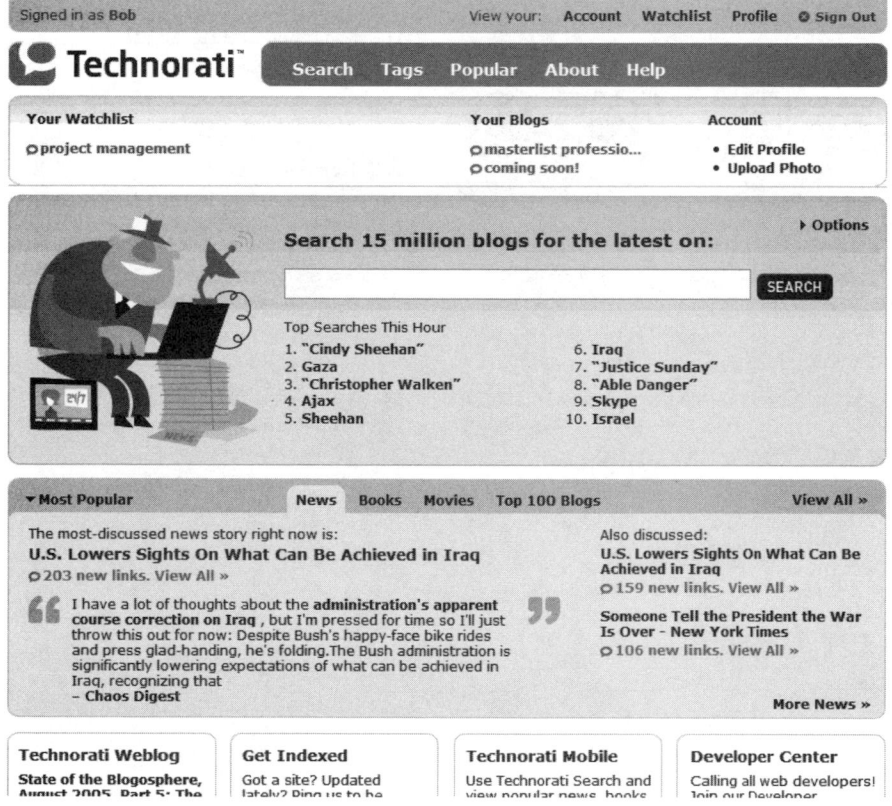

Figure 3-39. *Exploring the blogs at Technorati.com*

---

11. "The State of Blogging," *The Pew Internet & American Life Project*, January 2005. See also http://www.pewinternet.org/pdfs/PIP_blogging_data.pdf.

Why do people read blogs? Again, they read them for a host of reasons: for the latest in information and news about something they care about, for good writing, for provocative writing, and for a different point of view.

The mechanics of blogging are dirt easy. You can host your blog at Blogger.com, a free service offered by Google (`http://blogger.com`), as shown in Figure 3-40, or MSN Spaces, a free service offered by Microsoft (`http://spaces.msn.com/`). You can host your blog via countless smaller companies such as TypePad (`http://typepad.com`) or buy and install a blogging package for your Web site such as WordPress (`http://wordpress.org/`) or Movable Type (`http://www.sixapart.com/movabletype/`), as shown in Figure 3-41.

Figure 3-40. *Welcome to Blogger.com.*

Figure 3-41. *Welcome to MovableType.*

Blogs and Micro-ISVs

So, why should micro-ISVs do a blog? Here's one micro-ISV's (blogged) opinion:

How Blogging Really Pays Off

July 20th, 2005

There's always [a lot] of talk about how to make money with blogs. While I think some people will do OK with advertising and such, the real money is and will continue to be in the indirect benefits of blogging, [in other words,] not getting paid for blogging, but rather the opportunities it provides you. So in my case, [having] this blog has lead to a mailing list for my upcoming product [that] is many times bigger than I had anticipated. Of course, I still have to "close the deal" to make the $, but I now have more opportunity than I would have without blogging.[12]

---

12. http://www.userscape.com/blog/page/2/

For me, my blog (http://safarisoftware.typepad.com a.k.a. http://www.todoorelse.com), as shown in Figure 3-42, has been a way to blow off steam, explain some of the finer points of my micro-ISV product, pontificate on my approach to Getting Things Done and time management, release a few of the interviews done for this book, and show off my cats.

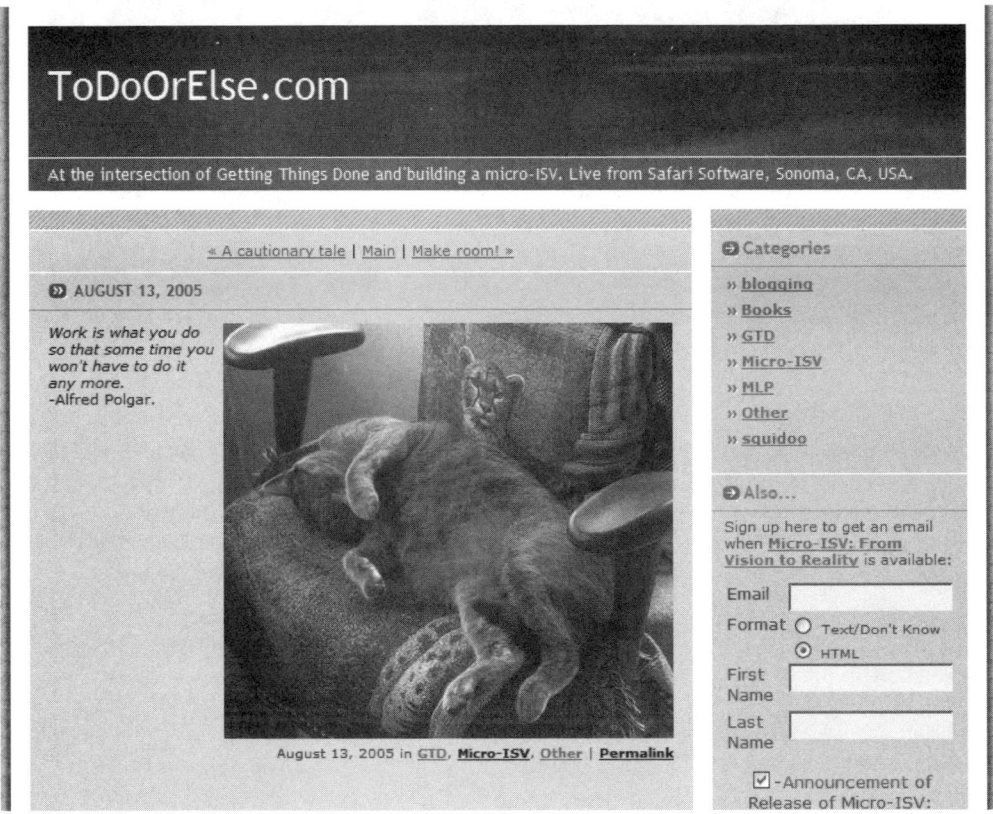

Figure 3-42. *Viewing my micro-ISV's blog*

The most useful part of this blog so far has been the feedback—both via the blog and via email from people reading it—that they like the product I'm bringing to market and wish me well. Being a micro-ISV means all too often long hours alone with your computer with little contact with others.

Being a micro-ISV makes it easy to do what some call a *business blog*. You can write about why you're building a business and selling your product, and that enthusiasm and passion will make for good reading.

MENA TROTT, COFOUNDER, SIX APART

In late 2001, Mena and Ben Trott were running their micro-ISV business from their San Francisco Bay Area one-bedroom apartment when they realized their cute little web logging software, Movable Type, had become a 600-pound tiger called *blogging*. After taking on venture capital funding, launching a blogging service (TypePad), hiring 60 employees, and acquiring several companies, Mena and Ben are at the center of the online whirlwind called *blogging*.

Q. How can a micro-ISV blog successfully?

A. What does ISV stand for?

Q. ISV stands for independent software vendor. *It's a term Microsoft came up with to describe everyone they haven't bought already. It kind of stuck as a label. Let me ask another question some suggested to me: what are three things you should not put in your blog?*

I think the most obvious thing is something that's not new to blogging; it's your company's secrets. When you start a company, or actually you become an employee of a company, it's very understandable that you sign a contract with the company stating you are not going to blog about proprietary information or information that's sensitive. Using that as your basic judgment is one of the easiest things to do. A lot of times when you see bloggers fired from their jobs, they are just writing about things they shouldn't be writing about in any form. They shouldn't be posting it on an email list; they shouldn't be talking about it at a party or on the street. Just the fact there are blogs now just makes it easier to disseminate information, but it's a commonsense thing.

As far as someone running their own company, one of the guidelines we've always said is when you write a post, you should consider that your worst enemy will see it at that moment you post it [and] you wouldn't be able to take it back, so you should always write with the sort of knowledge that anything you are going to write is going to be indexed by Google, it's going to be found right away, it's going to be there forever. And if you're not comfortable with that, don't write in a rage, [and] don't write in reaction to something without really thinking.

Be deliberate but still have that spontaneity that people like, and that's why—and we can talk in a little bit about it—why I think small companies should have blogs.

And also, understand that your blog is a reflection on your company and that personal voice is really important, and it's good to show there are people behind a company and that there's a personality. I write with a personality that may not be corporate, but it's me. But make sure you don't blur the lines and write about something completely random that has nothing to do with the company and that will not bring the company any sort of benefit. Save those sorts of posts for a private blog.

Q. Why should a small company blog?

A. A small company can really leverage bloggers in the sense that bloggers out there are very interested in small companies; they are interested in underdogs, [and] they are interested in people out there doing interesting things. And you can get your customers who are bloggers to be advocates for your product because they are writing about things that interesting to them. Having that sort of connection with your customers is extremely important.

When I attend a blog business conference, one of the things I tell people is that it's not necessarily important to have the CEO blogging or the major executives or the management blog. Having someone with a lot of passion in the company blog is as good if not better than having a ghostwritten CEO's post or a lackluster post. The person who is blogging should be very interested in continuing to communicate with the customers and the readers; it shouldn't be felt like it was an obligation.

I can use Six Apart as an example. I found that with blogging we had a real connection with our customers; we were able to see what they wanted in our products. They used comments and trackbacks to give us feedback. The biggest example was our [Movable Type] 3.0 license.

This happened last May, and we changed the licensing from unlimited authors and unlimited weblogs to restrictions because we found that the license was a little to loose, and we needed to make changes. When we made changes, we really didn't listen to community feedback initially. When we posted the changes, our customers were pretty upset. We allowed them to communicate using trackbacks—they were able to write on their blogs what they felt was wrong with what we doing, and we were able to get that feedback. The point is the posts are all still on our Web site, and a lot of them are very negative.

But the fact is that we are able to know what they wanted specifically and amend our licenses to address those needs. And that helps us a great deal. And it's interesting: we keep all the negativity on our blog, because it's a part of the history of the company, and if we were to delete somebody's negative comments just because they were negative, that would be a disservice to our customers. We have the good and bad. We're very quick to put the good out, and while we don't want the bad posts, we realize that people want an open book. And I think we are one of the few companies that is really doing this.

You need to put everything out there, and you let product speak for itself. There are times we give fodder to our competitors because of this, but at least we know we're proud at the end of the day.

Q. This may be a chicken/egg question, but do blogs make companies more open or are companies that are open more likely to blog?

A. [laughs] That is a chicken-and-egg question. Right now when people start blogs within a company, they have some motivation to do so. And to do that, there has to be some sort of openness to start. I think that once you start blogging and you see the feedback, it tends to make you think, "Wow people are actually reading this!" And it tends to either scare people or empowers them. I think that getting comfortable with being transparent is a hard thing to do, but once you do, it's incredibly rewarding.

Q. So how often should you post?

A. I think it's harder to post if you've stopped posting, because there's a lot of pressure: you're staring at this empty screen and thinking, "All right, this must be an important post because I haven't written in three months." But if you write something once a day, with varying degrees of importance, it gives you the kind of momentum that's easy to sustain.

Q. I'm sure you've been asked this before, but how can I get my blog to the A list? To put a tighter focus on that, how can I get my micro-ISV's blog to be A list?

A. That's probably a harder thing to do than a personal blog; it's associated with business. One of the things you can do is not post things just about your company but post things that are relevant to the space. That's something we try to do especially in our ProNet log (http://www.sixapart.com/pronet/weblog) that's written basically written by Anil Dash, our third employee. He writes about things that are relevant to our users, but he also writes about what people are doing in the blogging spaces as a whole.

If you are running a company, you have to be aware of businesses out there and that there are other applications that are interesting. It can't just be only about you. I think that being able to write an engaging blog in a personal voice is crucial to—I hate to say it—get to that A list. It's crucial, I think, because all the blogs that are popular, you can really tell the voice behind it. It's also putting yourself out on a limb and saying things about the industry you really believe. And being someone respected for your opinion, not just your product.

Q. Then should I lambaste all the lame products out there? Should I name them? Is that being relevant in the space or is that being sort of confrontational?

A. I think that is being confrontational; there are companies that do that, but I don't necessarily respect that tactic. We never say negative things about our competitors—that's just something we've done since 2001. It was something we never wanted to get popular by doing that. I think it's important to raise your company up by pointing to what you are doing right, not lambaste your competitors for what they do wrong. It's always important to stay positive. If there's something to be said negative about your competition, people are likely going to find it out; you don't need to point it out.

Learn from what they are doing, don't do the mistakes, and be content in that you are doing things right. I've learned that the hard way, because you know, we have a lot of competition that criticizes things that we do. But we don't then turn around and say things about the competition, because we wouldn't gain anything. If you go into the mud with them, you just end up dirty.

You can point out things and not necessarily name companies. If you see something that's being done negatively, you can tall about how it could be done positively. Never say things negative just to say things negative.

On Improving Your Blog

Q. Which matters more, comments or trackbacks?
A. On the whole, I think trackbacks are better because people who have taken the time to send a trackback and write in their blog have taken the time to make it part of the contents of their blog. It gives them accountability. I would rather have five trackbacks going off to someone else's site where you could read about the person; you can see the context of what they have to say and write than anonymous hit-and-run comments from people who might visit the site once and never visit it again.

As a whole, trackbacks don't devolve; they're more independent—they stand up. Comments cause sometimes what we call a *pile-on*; I think trackbacks are a more valuable mechanism.

Q. I think that comes back to why and how you become popular in the blogosphere, or not. It's the web of other peoples trackbacks that determines whether you are popular or not, not those anonymous or semianonymous comments.
A. Yes, I think that's right. And I think it's also important that when you're trying to become a prominent weblog, that you let it happen organically. Bloggers tend not to like emails that say, "Link to me." They view it as spam, and they are more likely not only to not link to you but to criticize you. So it's important I think to let people discover you by posting quality thoughts that people find on their own. A trackback would be a good example. If you are writing something clearly relevant to somebody's post and you trackback, that's a way for them to find you. But you should never do it just for us to look at your blog.

Q. Where do you see blogging going in the next two years? Business blogging or personal blogging?
A. Business blogs. I think that more transparency is going to become more and more important. The fact that when you blog and release a product, you pretty much instantly know what people think of it through referrers, through trackbacks, through comments—that's only going to help companies act in response more quickly.

I think more and more companies are—and this can be either a good thing or a bad thing—going to get their company's PR departments involved in creating blogs, and people are going to have to evaluate which blogs they feel are genuine. You're going to see that the blogs that continue to be popular are the ones with strong voices. This is something I've been saying for four years about all kinds of blogs—that knowing the personality behind them is incredibly important.

Blogs right now are used in businesses both internally and externally. One thing I encourage businesses to do is set up internal blogs/set up blogs as an intranet. And let them [all employees] write the posts that they want to write and then take the posts you find that are particularly strong and bring them out externally. For companies who are kind of scared of letting your employees blog, this is a way of allowing people to have the freedom inside and then elevating the people who are doing a good job. And that's the way to find the strong bloggers in your company and promote them.

Q. For a micro-ISV when maybe we are talking one person, maybe three or three or five at most, how often should they blog about whatever space that product lives in?

A. People like to know about the product cycle, about your product development. I know that I said you can't talk about secrets or proprietary information, but you can let people kind of know what's going on. We've been running a beta for Movable Type right now for 3.2 [http://www.sixapart.com/movabletype/beta/], and people are loving the beta blog because we are talking about the release. We are talking about questions people are asking. It's really important that you let people see inside the company.

So for a small company, I don't think you need to post every day, especially if you have RSS that lets people discover your blog and know when it's been updated and not have to go back every day. I think it's important to get a good post or two out every week and map what the company is doing.

Something I've learned is that it's incredibly hard to do blogging when you're doing so many things and you're incredibly busy. "Why should I take the time to do this?" Setting some time to blog is actually a good thing because it helps you process what you're doing. And it helps you kind of realize how the company grows.

If I look back at the archives, I can see what we've done as we've grown from two people—me and my husband—to what we are today. It's journaling in a way. And it's good because it helps shape the company as well.

Q. I see the beta blog—189 comments on one posting?

A. This is the first time we've ever had a beta blog public, and we've been very successful with it.

Q. I notice that you have a web design background. When I look at TypePad, it's very visually and graphically appealing. How much does graphics and design matter in an application?

A. For building applications or your blog?

Q. For either.

A. One of the goals we've always had for all of our products is that we believe you should be able to have a professional-looking blog/a nicely designed blog, even if you don't do anything. You shouldn't have to know how to edit CSS or HTML; you should have the tools that do that. With my design background to try to figure out how the best-looking blogs should be created with the least amount of effort. And I think what we do in TypePad is indicative of that goal. I think it's really important to have a professional-looking site because it's a first impression sort of thing.

If I'm going to a person's site and I realize they haven't done anything to make it look good, or it's covered in ads, it lowers the credibility. It could be the best content in the world, but I might not get that far. So I think for a business, if you don't have the skills to design a site, then I think it's worth it to get a contractor in just to spruce up your blog.

Going from Micro-ISV to "Big Company"

Q. Going from micro-ISV to "Big Company": anything you wish you could email yourself back in 2001?

A. I'm lucky that I haven't gotten to a place where I have regrets. In terms of advice, I would say it's important to keep the drive I've always had but to realize that it is a company. But at the end of the day your life is more important. I've had a lot of stress in the course of four years, and I've realized I've gone to a point right now that the company is running really smoothly—knock on wood—and doing well. What we've accomplished has been incredibly important, and if the company were to fail—God forbid!—we've done so much that we have made a difference, and so I'd be happy with that.

I think if I wanted to give me more concrete advice, it would be staff up sooner than we did. If [you're] growing as a company and can afford to grow, it's important to not be so worried about being too big that you end up doing all the work, because that's connected to the stress. Ben and I were very reluctant to hire, so we did the entire first version of TypePad ourselves, and getting some help in doing that might have made me a little saner in terms of my well being.

Q. You've got something of a complicated pricing model for Movable Type, with a lot of price points. Has that worked out well for you?

A. It actually has worked out well. For businesses, it has been a no-brainer. Businesses are incredibly happy to have structured pricing they can invoice and to know this is what we are paying for. Personal pricing was more difficult—we went from free to free and two tiers of paid. One of the things we limited was that you could not have unlimited weblogs or unlimited authors unless you bought the highest level of Movable Type. In the newest release, 3.2, we've actually taken away the limits for weblogs for all. That was something we realized was not something that needed to be limited, especially since 3.2 has really good blog management.

Q. Have you considered partnering with radio (like subscription radio like XM or Sirius) to have top blogs broadcast in text-to-speech?

A. I wouldn't be against it, but we haven't really gotten to that point. I think that audio is an important component and think one of the ways audio and podcasting can become more adopted is if there are easy ways to parse.

One of the things I find frustrating is that you don't want to sit through an audio recording to find out what it's about. You want to be able to skim. And that's one of the things I think that makes blogs so important—you're able to scan and skim and know what content you want to read really quickly. Audio needs to find a way to do that. We really need some one or some company to figure out a way to do that.

Q. Do you see wikis and blogs converging, or are they going to stay in their separate worlds?

A. I think there are features of both that can be used for the other, but as far as that goes, I think they are different mental models. We have wikis internally and we have weblogs internally, and some people's minds work in a different way. I know that I have to have a more linear structure. Having pages exist in a way that you have to link to them or not find them—that's difficult for me. Both serve different needs; they can co-exist.

Q. Blogs have become the first movers when it comes to influence/politics especially in this country and fashion and other things. Would you say that blogging has climbed to the top of the influence food chain?

A. I think in all areas—in fashion, in film, in music—that there are definitely things that are influencing, and I think that blogs have become a component of it. I don't want blogs to seem trendy. I don't think everyone needs a blog. It's like email. One of our goals is to get blogging as ubiquitous as email.

Q. Do you think there will be as many people blogging as emailing?

A. I think it's very possible. I should explain that more. In terms of blogging, I don't think blogging always has to be necessarily public. There's personal blogging, there's private blogging, and then there's public. More people are going to want to have private weblogs, where they're chronicling events [and] sharing things with small groups. And so we see this with LiveJournal, which we purchased this year. These are small groups of people kind of having a conversation.

My mom when she starts to blog isn't going to want anyone but me and my aunt reading it—and that's an important form. That's why I think blogging is going to be as important as emailing—it's a form of communication that takes the form of archiving, of photo management, of comments, and of RSS, and it allows people to communicate better. There's that group, and then there's the other group that wants to reach larger groups. That will be a lot of businesses, people who have stories to tell or [talk] politics, or just larger communities. Blogging can be used for any purpose.

Q. Any advice to micro-ISV in general?

A. I think definitely read what people have to say about you. Use something like PubSub (`http://www.pubsub.com`).

Q. What's that?

A. It's a service where you basically enter keywords—I have one with *Six Apart, Mena Trott*—and I basically get an RRS feed for anyone who references those keywords. So I'm able to read every day what people are saying about the company, what people are saying about our products, what people are saying about me. And it helps—it helps you gauge the public's perception of your company and of yourself, and it helps you find ways of opening up lines of communication.

One of the things that's really important once you start blogging is to listen to the community out there. And don't be a spammer!

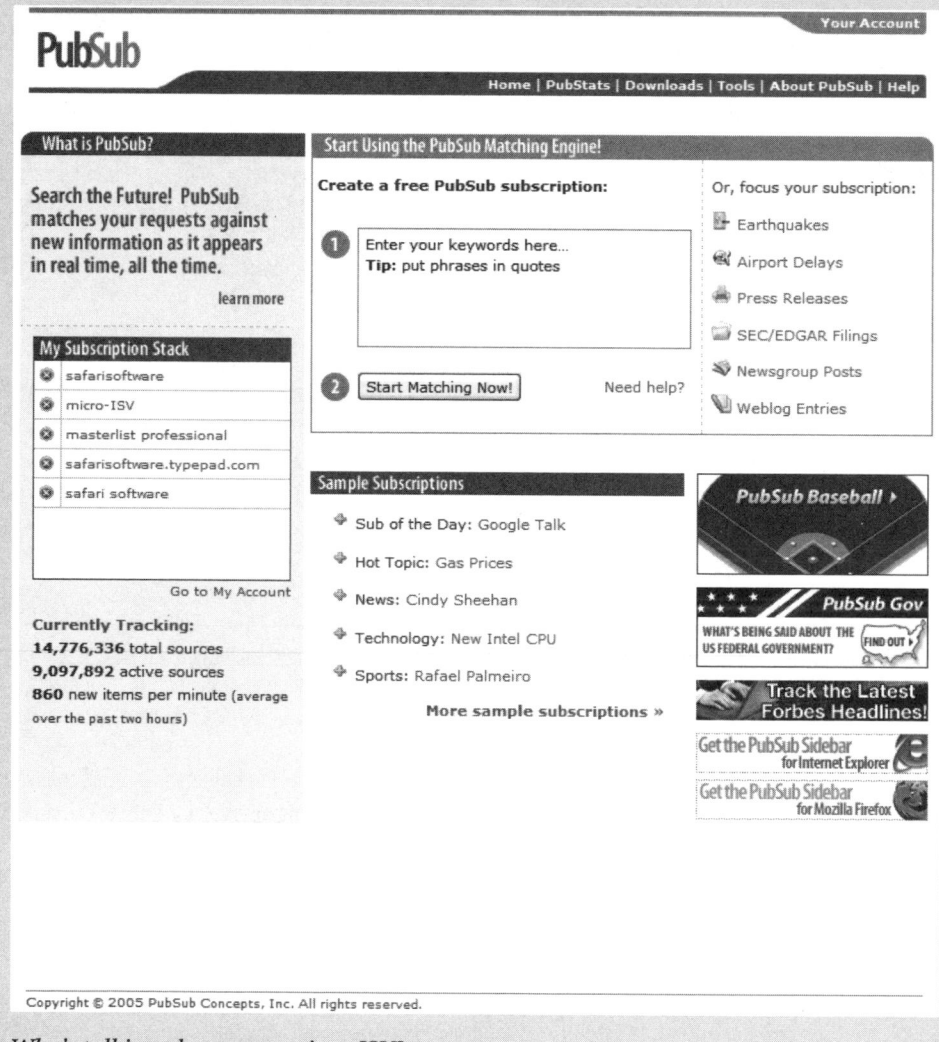

Who's talking about your micro-ISV?

CHAPTER 4

■ ■ ■

Business Is Business

I think maybe in every company today there is always at least one person who is going crazy slowly.

—Joseph Heller, author of *Catch-22*[1]

The point of this chapter is to make sure you're not the one being driven crazy in your micro-ISV by all the rules, regulations, paperwork, forms, requirements, tasks, and projects you're going to have to cope with in order to be in business.

In this chapter, I'll start by covering the foundation of your micro-ISV: what type of business entity are you? I'll then cover the rudiments of the intellectual property law you need to know and why the government is your friend (really!). And, you'll dig into how on Earth you can manage all the tasks and projects you're going to need to do to get your micro-ISV up and running.

Now, most of the business regulation stuff in this chapter is specific to the United States, but please see the sidebars on doing business in the United Kingdom and doing business in Australia. And I apologize in advance to the majority of the world that doesn't speak English for not covering at least one non-English-speaking country in this chapter, but there is a reason for that.[2]

One topic this chapter can't cover is what is best for you and your micro-ISV. Every choice has trade-offs, and your mileage may vary. But Micro-ISVs owners aren't the only people who want to start their own businesses; although I'll highlight a few of the "mainstream" resources available in this chapter and in the appendix, you'll find no shortage of information about starting a business.[3] If you can't find the answers you seek, I strongly recommend visiting the Business of Software forum at Joel on Software (`http://discuss.joelonsoftware.com/?biz`). You'll find many kindred souls there.

---

1. `http://www.memorablequotations.com/heller.htm`
2. When I was in high school, I struggled through a year of German, getting a barely passing grade from my teacher only by promising I would never take German again. In college, I struggled through an intensive summer course of French, getting a barely passing grade from my professor only if I promised not to take French again. A wise man knows his limits!
3. Searching for *starting a business* on Google yields about 60.5 million hits. See the appendix for recommended reading.

You, Inc.

Picking the legal form of your micro-ISV is all about defining who gets what and who's responsible. Before I cover the pros and cons of various ways of setting up your business, the first order of business is nailing down who the *who* is here. If you, and only you, are going to own, create, manage, and profit from your micro-ISV, that's one thing. If *you* means yourself and one or several partners, that is quite another. Both paths can work, but the roads traveled will be different.

Now I must admit to a bias here: my micro-ISV is mine, with no partners.[4] I can see the theoretical advantages of having partners—more people to get the work done and more insights, experience, contacts, energy, and camaraderie. However, for better or ill, that's not the road I've chosen.

If your circumstances are such that you've found the right people to help launch your business, that's good news. In that case, implementing the steps in this chapter is even more important for you: a perennial reason business ventures die early is that the partners haven't confronted and settled the key questions of who gets what and who's in charge.

If you're going it alone, I recommend strongly you get some objective feedback as to whether you're cut out to start a business. Odds are you are if you're reading this, but it never hurts to get a second or third opinion.

The U.S. Small Business Administration (SBA) offers a good, general self-test on its Web site at http://www.sba.gov/starting_business/startup/entrepreneurialtest.html, as shown in Figure 4-1. (I'll talk about the SBA more in the "And What About the Government?" section.)

---

4. Except for my partner in life, Tina. She has a real job!

United States Small Business Administration   search this site   GO
                                                              En Español

SBA   Select a Custom View: Starting Financing Managing Business Opportunities Disaster
                                                          Recovery

■ Starting Your Business   SBA.gov // Starting Your Business // Startup Basics

Startup Basics   ## Entrepreneurial Test

Are you ready?   You need to think about why you would like to own your own business. What makes
Finding a Niche   you think you will be Successful in business?
Buying a Business
Buying a Franchise   Some business development materials start out with a dissertation on the
Protecting Your Ideas   characteristics of the business owner in order to help you decide if you should go into
Product Basics   business for yourself. These questions deal with the basic personality of potential
Startup Guide   entrepreneurs.
Specific Training
                                • Are you "entrepreneurial" enough to build a business?
Business Planning   • Do you know what the meaning of the word "entrepreneurial"?
                                • Are you a risk taker?
Financing   • Did you get good grades in school? Did you know many successful
                                  entrepreneurs did not?
Marketing
                            You are a cautious person and a good student. Should you forget the whole thing?
Employees   That's what some entrepreneurial tests would suggest.

Taxes   However, there are many successful business owners who, as an adolescent, were
                            team players, athletes, school leaders, excellent students, and never seriously
Legal Aspects   questioned the status quo. Often, though, a tendency toward caution is not typical of
                            many successful entrepreneurs. Most entrepreneurs tend to be maverick personalities
Special Interests   with risk-taking vision and courage. Many entrepreneurs tend to be just a bit "off beat"
                            and they sometimes need to be in order to creatively grow a successful business.

Additional Resources   Obviously there is no set formula for success. However, the following entrepreneurial
More Information About Starting   test may help you in your personal evaluation process. You just need to remember that
Your Small Business   this is simply a tool. It is fun to take and fun to interpret, but you should keep it in
                            perspective.
FAQ
Glossary   For each question, click on the answer that best describes you. You must answer ALL
                            questions for the test to be accurate.

                            ### I'm persistent. I am persistent.   ○   ○   ○
                                                                       Yes   Maybe   No
                            ### When I'm interested in a project, I need   ○   ○   ○
                            ### less sleep.   Yes   Maybe   No

Figure 4-1. *Are you micro-ISV material?*

You'll find another good self-test on the Web, courtesy of the Center for Entrepreneurship
at Brigham Young University's Marriott School of Management at http://marriottschool.
byu.edu/cfe/startingout/test.cfm, as shown in Figure 4-2.

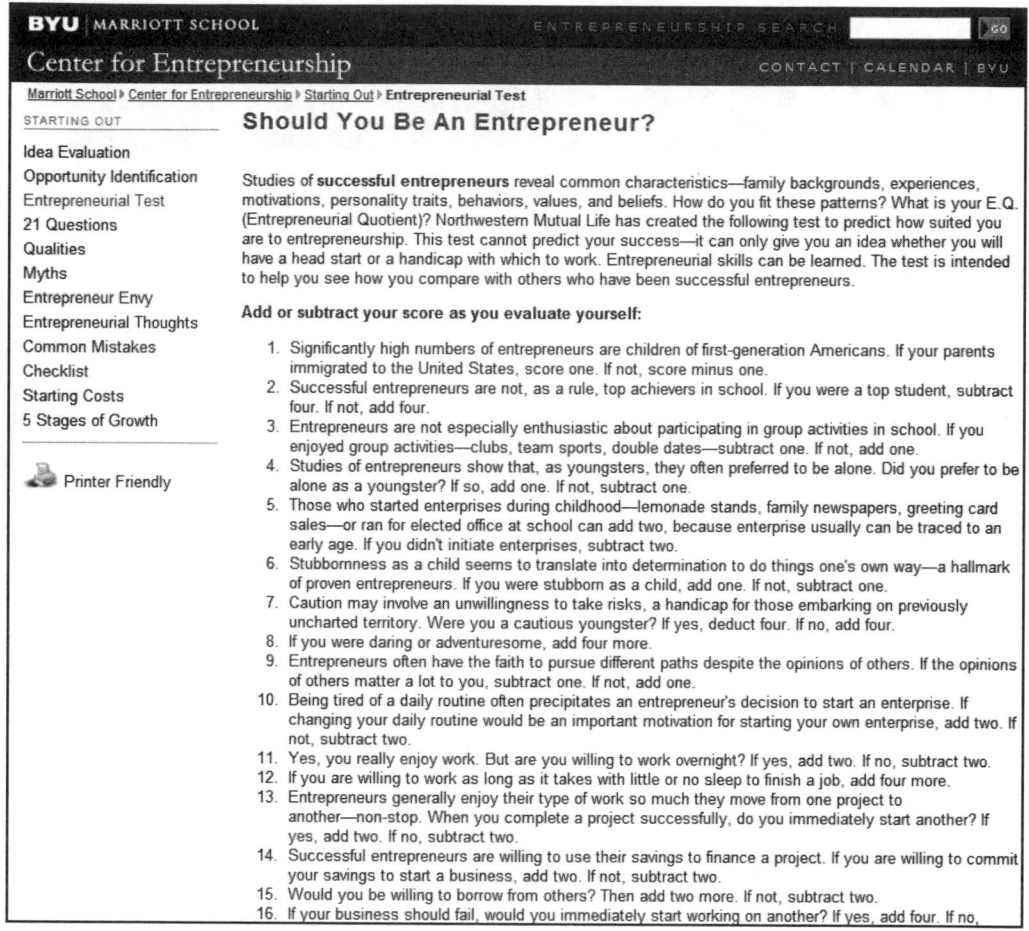

Figure 4-2. *The Center for Entrepreneurship's self-test*

How you run your business is your business, but what form it takes in the United States is set by tax and commerce statutes: sole proprietorship, partnership, Limited Liability Company (LLC), a subchapter S corporation, or a subchapter C corporation. The next sections cover these ways of doing business from a micro-ISV perspective.

Sole Proprietorship

A *sole proprietorship* is the easiest and simplest way for a single person to own and operate a business. Repeat after me: "I am a sole proprietorship." By the power invested in me, I now pronounce you and your micro-ISV legally and financially inseparable.

Now, it may get a little more complicated if you plan on doing business under a name other than your own ("Bob Walsh"); that's when you'll need to register your business's name ("Deerhaven Computing") with your county and take out a small advertisement in a county-approved paper announcing this. But unless you plan on hiring employees or need a small-business license, you're good to go.

Advantages

A sole proprietorship is cheap and simple. And your bank will cash checks written to you. Filing a Schedule C with your Form 1040 income tax return is about all the form filling you have to do. An attorney is unnecessary.

Disadvantages

The disadvantages of a sole proprietorship are significant. You and your business are one. If your business is sued, you and your assets are at risk; in fact, if you're in what's called a *community property state*, your spouse is also at risk.

A sole proprietorship screams small. Some companies will not buy goods or services from a sole proprietorship. Insurance for your business may be either more expensive or harder to obtain.

Bottom Line

Creating and running a micro-ISV means you're all the way in the water, not just sticking a toe in. Risking your assets, and perhaps the assets of your spouse, isn't worth it. Of course, if you're highly allergic to tax forms and other forms of paperwork, this option gets you going. You can always upgrade later.

Setup/Installation

A sole proprietorship doesn't really have setup requirements, unless you're going to have a business name. In that case, you'll need to do one of the following:

- Visit your county registrar's office, check that your desired name is available, fill in the form, pay the fee, take your copy of the filed form to a local newspaper that runs Doing Business As (DBA) ads, and pay to run your DBA ad. The cost will be about $100.

- Go to http://dbaform.com or a similar online service (as shown in Figure 4-3), fill in the form, and pay $95; then you're done.

Figure 4-3. *Online services make it easy to do a DBA.*

STARTING A MICRO-ISV IN THE UNITED KINGDOM

If you're based in the United Kingdom, setting up your business vis-à-vis the government is relatively straightforward. Although no quick summary will cover everything you should know, this sidebar covers the basics you need to consider.

Legal Structures

Your micro-ISV can take the form of three for-profit legal structures: sole trader, partnership, and LLC. Each of these structures sets a different balance between personal liability, ease of setup and maintenance, and capital-raising potential.

- *Sole trader.* This is the simplest way to run your one-person micro-ISV, doesn't require any paperwork other than registering as self-employed with HM Revenue and Customs (HMRC), and makes up the bulk (63 percent) of all British businesses according to Department of Trade and Industry figures.[5] However, no legal separation exists between you and your business; you're responsible for all liabilities, and its income is yours. Also, if you're going to do business under a name other than your own, you'll need to ensure you avoid confusion with other names used by other businesses and certain restricted words. (See the online resources later in this sidebar.)

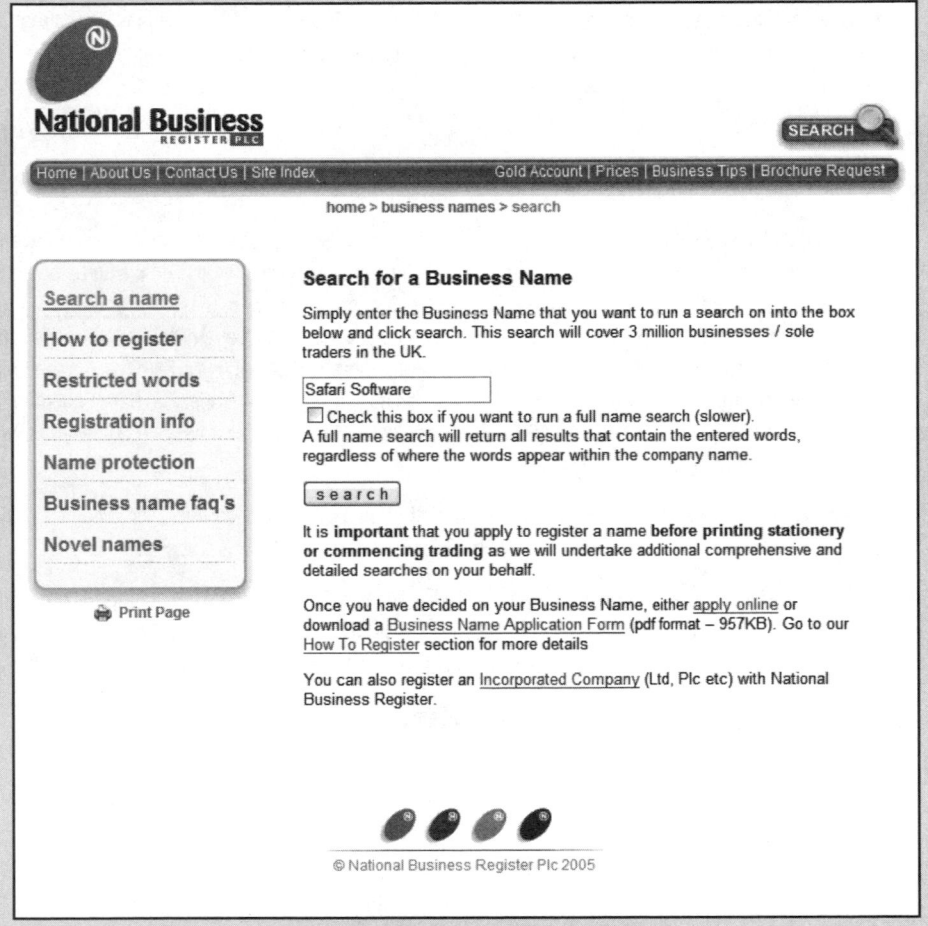

Checking names at National Business Register

---

5. http://www.startups.co.uk/YaY6zhpowhgEFQ.html

- *Partnership*: When two or more people form a business, it's a partnership. Each partner receives a percentage of the income produced by the business, depending upon how much they invested. Like their U.S. counterparts, partnerships are defined by a partnership agreement and strongly need the advice of a solicitor to ensure all foreseeable contingencies are covered. Each partner is fully liable for all the debts of the business, with the exception of a Limited Liability Partnership (LLP), which has members with liability limited to funds invested and designated members with unlimited liability.

- *LLC*: This is the equivalent (and precursor) to U.S. corporations; LLCs legally exist for purposes of liability and taxation in their own right. Shareholders can be individuals or other companies. Two types exist: private limited companies whose stock can't be traded and Public Limited Companies (PLCs) that can be traded. LLCs require registration at Companies House, need directors, and have considerable reporting requirements.

Taxes

Two taxes might affect your micro-ISV even if you do not have employees: income tax and VAT.

- *Sole trader*: As a sole trader, your micro-ISV profits are taxed like any other income by Inland Revenue, under Schedule D, and you're responsible for paying income tax twice a year. You'll also be paying National Insurance Contributions (Class 2) and, depending on your profits, Class 4. If you're making more than approximately £60,000 a year, you'll also need to apply for Value Added Tax (VAT) registration. This means you'll be collecting VAT from your U.K. customers and paying it to HMRC minus the VAT you've paid out in the course of business. You can also opt for the VAT optional Flat Rate Scheme (FRS) if your micro-ISV has less than £150,000 a year turnover and instead pay a flat rate on based on your sales (including VAT).

- *Partnerships*: Profits and losses flow to the members of the partnership. As such, what applies to sole traders in terms of income tax and VAT applies to partnerships and their members.

- *LLC*: As a separate legal entity, your corporation will need to comply with a variety of regulations and be taxed at a rate from 0 percent (less than £10,000 in profits) to 30 percent (more than £1,500,001 in profits). If you're considering forming an LLC, you'll need information beyond the scope of this book.

Worth Considering

The points following are worth considering:

- The FRS can reduce your paperwork and VAT liability.

- Don't muck around with VAT you collect, or you'll be very, very sorry.

- Cash accounting as it applies to VAT can make cash flow easier.

- Be careful using contractual workers hired directly or through an intermediary as if they are employees; you run the risk of Inland Revenue characterizing this as "disguised employment," and depending on the circumstance, you may be at risk for both fines and taxes.

Online Resources

Three web sites bubble to the top of just about everyone's list of online resources for U.K.-based micro-ISVs:

Startups.co.uk at `http://startups.co.uk` has a wide assortment of information about the legal, tax, and human ramifications of starting a business. Note, however, that some information, such as specifics on FRS, is somewhat out of date. Also worth checking is its sister site, MyBusiness.co.uk (`http://www.mybusiness.co.uk`), for information and advice on running a small business.

Start with Startups.co.uk

Another good resource is Business Link at `http://www.businesslink.gov.uk`, offering what it calls practical advice for business. Business Link has a number of interactive tools and forms that will keep you on the side of the angels when it comes to employment, international trade, and data protection regulations.

Next up are the friendly and considerate people at HMRC whose site politely lays downs the law. Find them at `http://www.hmrc.gov.uk` before they find you.

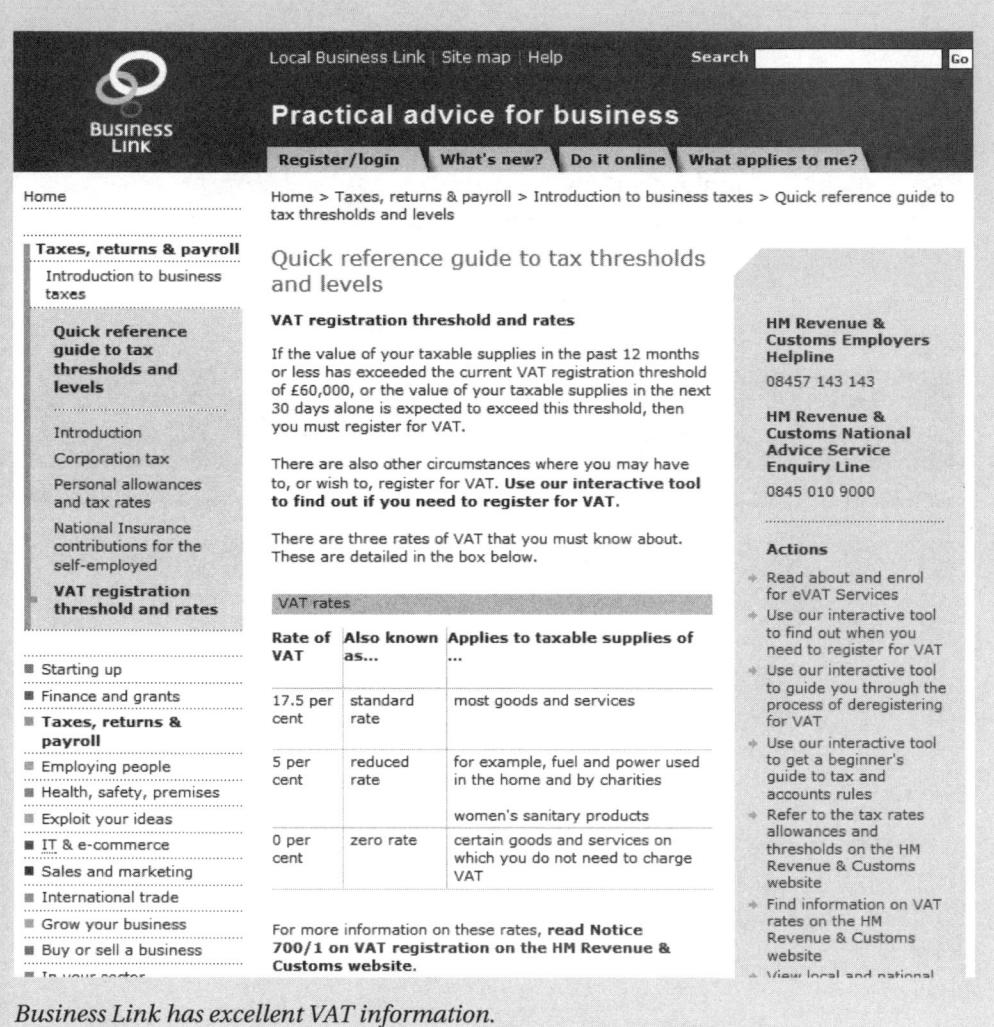

Business Link has excellent VAT information.

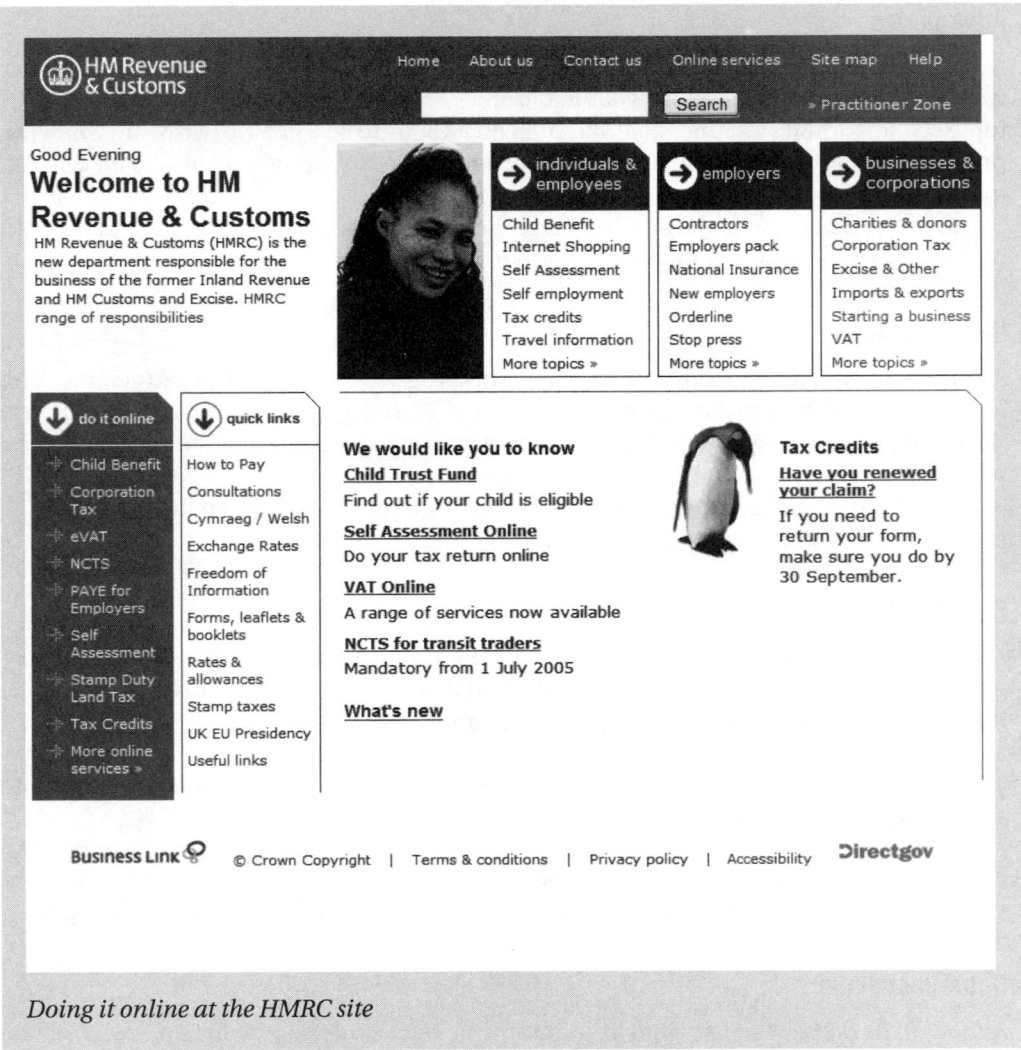

Doing it online at the HMRC site

Partnership

You and your partner(s) are going to own your micro-ISV. It can be a general partnership where all of you manage your micro-ISV and are responsible for its debts or liabilities or a limited partnership where one or more partners don't run the business, have limited liability, get to make money, and usually get to do so because they invested their money in the micro-ISV.

Note that although all the general, active partners are each responsible for the micro-ISV debts and liabilities, who gets what is another matter you all (active and passive partners) get to specify. Once that's settled—and it better be in writing—then all profits and losses "pass through" the company to the partners, at which point the Internal Revenue Service (IRS) and perhaps your state get interested and want information. (Your micro-ISV partnership files each year Form 1065, and each partner gets a Schedule K-1, or Form 1065, to file with their tax returns.)

Advantages

A partnership has two types of advantages. First, having real partners who sweat, toil, and worry alongside of you can mean your micro-ISV is bigger, faster, more profitable, and more fun. Second, forming a partnership with someone willing to be a passive partner in your enterprise in exchange for a portion of the profits may provide the capital you need to make your micro-ISV a successful reality.

If you're dealing with one or more "angel investors," you can expect them to want your relationship to be legally, at the least, a partnership.

Disadvantages

A partnership has many disadvantages. Like a sole proprietorship, all active partners are liable. Also, unless your partnership agreement (which you'll need a lawyer for because every partnership agreement is unique) prohibits it, a partner can sell their interest in your micro-ISV or bequeath it.

Besides the legal issues, a partnership can have personal issues, given the stresses of starting and running a business.

Bottom Line

Although a partnership can work, you and your partners need just the right personality mix to get along and work with each other through good times and bad. If it sounds like a marriage, it is—with the chance of an extremely messy divorce.

Think long and hard about going this route. Settle up front in writing and in no uncertain terms (that's where the lawyer comes in) what each partner is putting into the pot. Trust and shared personal experience are the keys.

The odds are against partnerships, and recognizing that up front is critical to improving your micro-ISV's odds. One partnership that worked out spectacularly well was between a Honeywell employee and a Harvard sophomore with a wild idea and not much money.[6]

Setup/Installation

Although the tax paperwork is only slightly more than for a sole proprietorship, you absolutely need a partnership agreement all parties can live with that's written or at least vetted by an attorney all partners trust.

Limited Liability Company (LLC)

An LLC is a mix of a corporation's legal limits on liability and a sole proprietorship or partnership's tax attributes. On one hand, the partners, called *members*, report profits and losses like they would in a partnership—the LLC isn't a separate taxable entity. On the other hand, if your micro-ISV's LLC owns money or gets sued, only the assets of the micro-ISV are normally at risk.

---

6. Bill Gates and Paul Allen founded Micro-soft (note the hyphen!) as an informal partnership on March 1, 1975; Microsoft didn't incorporate until six years later. See http://www.thocp.net/companies/ microsoft/microsoft_company.htm and http://www.microsoft.com/presspass/insidefacts_ms.mspx.

LLCs are relatively new in the United States, but they're becoming popular since they combine relatively easy tax paperwork with corporate liability protection.

Advantages

Whether you're one person or a partnership, LLCs have some decided advantages. Since profits and losses are passed through the LLC to its members, you do the same tax paperwork as you would for a sole proprietorship or a partnership.

At the same time, your micro-ISV is a legal entity, and if run legitimately, liability is limited to the assets of your company.

Disadvantages

The disadvantages of an LLC are few. Basically, you do the same tax paperwork you would as a sole proprietorship or a partnership.

Depending on whether some of your partners are investors, you'll need the services of a good attorney to navigate through your state's securities regulations and those of the Securities and Exchange Commission (SEC) to the "safe harbor" of exemption from securities law.

LLC law, being relatively new, is less uniform across the 50 states, and you might find in your state that creating an LLC involves a few more steps, or it might be deliberately unavailable to you, as it is for architects, accountants, doctors, and licensed health-care professionals in California.

Bottom Line

This is an attractive way of doing business for a micro-ISV, especially compared to the "naked-ness" of a sole proprietorship or a partnership.

Setup/Installation

Follow these steps:

1. Pick an available business name that complies with your state's LLC rules. Nowadays, nearly every state lets you find a name and reserve it online. For example, you can check in California whether the name you want to give your micro-ISV is taken at `http://kepler.ss.ca.gov/list.html`, as shown in Figure 4-4.

2. File your articles of organization with your state, and pay the fee ($40 to $900 depending on state).

3. Create an LLC operating agreement. You can do this without an attorney if you don't need an attorney's knowledge to advise you about unique issues with your company.

4. A few states require you to run a notice of your LLC's creation in a state-approved newspaper.

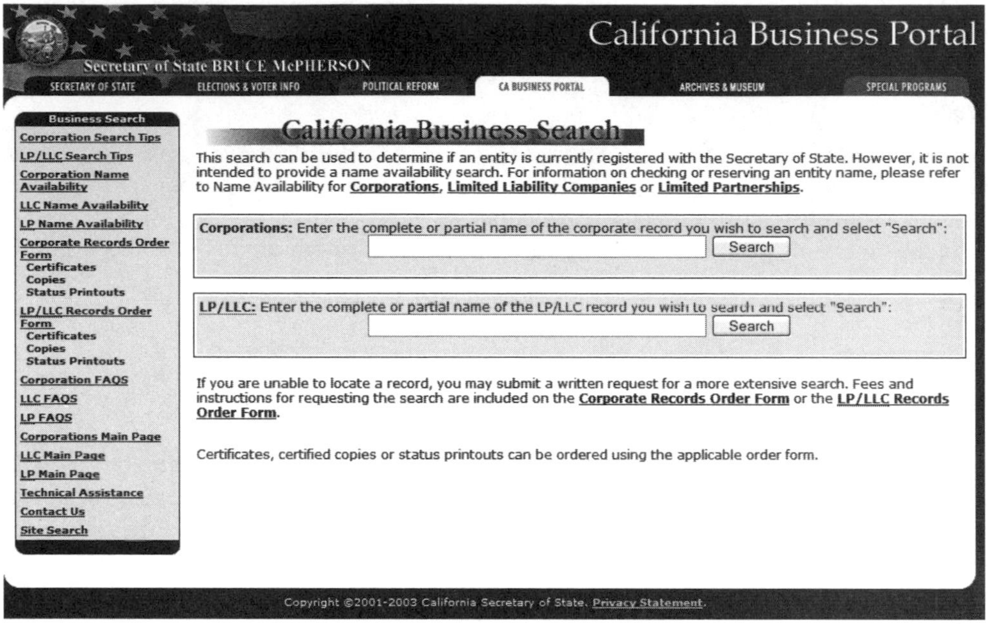

Figure 4-4. *Searching for a California business name online*

STARTING A MICRO-ISV IN AUSTRALIA

More than a few excellent micro-ISVs already call Australia home. This sidebar covers the basics of how yours can too.

Legal Structures

The three most common legal structures for Australian micro-ISVs are sole trader, partnership, and a Proprietary Limited Company (PLC). As in other developed countries, each of these legal structures define a different approach to doing business and a different set of liability, tax, and capital-raising realities.

- *Sole trader.* A sole trader is just that. There is no difference between you and your business for tax or legal purposes. If you're going to do business under a name other than your full name, you'll need to register your business name and pay a fee ranging from nil in the Northern Territory to about $200 for a two- to three-year registration, with $120 being the most common registration fee.[7] Although two sole traders or partnerships can operate with the same name in two different states or territories, two companies can't. Each state or territory maintains its own registration listing, but you can check all using the National Names Index (http://www.search.asic.gov.au/gns001.html) provided by the Australian Securities and Investments Commission (ASIC).

---

7. http://www.incorporator.com.au/business_registration_register_business_name_search.asp

Checking names at the National Names Index

- *Partnership*: When two or more people form a business, it's a partnership, and although there is some flexibility in how income is split, all partners are liable for the debts of the business in general. The main exception to this is limited partnerships, whose regulation and definition vary from state to state and territory to territory but in general limit liability of some members of the partnership to their contribution to it. Limited partnerships are treated for tax purposes as if they were companies.

- *PLC*: With the Corporation Act of 2001, which reduces the number of required shareholders and directors to one, this form of business is substantially more attractive to micro-ISVs. Proprietary companies are separate legal entities that come into existence when the company is registered with the ASIC.

Taxes and Regulations

These are the taxes and regulations that may affect you:

- *ABN*: If your micro-ISV will be doing business with other businesses or the state or federal government, your business will need an Australian Business Number (ABN), which you can lodge online at http://www.business.gov.au. If you don't have an ABN, other businesses are obliged to withhold 48.5 percent from payments to you and send the withheld amount to the Australia Tax Office (ATO) in most cases. The Australian Business Register (http://abr.gov.au) handles the details of registering. (See the online resources later in this chapter.)

- *GST*: The Goods and Services Tax (GST) of 10 percent applies to most things sold in Australia. If your business has a turnover of $50,000 or more a year, you'll need to register for GST. You can do this at the same time as you apply for an ABN on the same form, but you must have an ABN in order to apply because your ABN becomes your GST registration number.

- *Income tax*: Sole trader and partnership income is reported as part of the personal tax returns of the people involved. Companies file their own tax returns, and the general company tax rate on taxable income is 30 percent.

Worth Considering

These points are worth considering:

- Like partnerships elsewhere, a well-written agreement is the foundation you need to have to build a stable business. Strongly consider seeking the advice of a solicitor in this matter.

- Check your state or territory's small-business Web site.

- Don't forget you may need a business license. Check http://www.business.gov.au under Licenses & Permits for each state's and territory's Business License Information Service Web site.

- As is often the case, if your micro-ISV also sells its (your) services, you need to be aware that if your income is derived more than 80 percent from one business, the ATO may determine you're an employee of that company for tax purposes (but not for employment law purposes).

Online Resources

A relatively short guide about GST is available from the ATO at http://www.ato.gov.au/content/downloads/NAT3014-07-2005.pdf.

Victoria has several excellent online resources for starting a business and a strong interest in IT-related businesses. Those sites include Business in Victoria (http://www.bus.vic.gov.au), the Small Business Council of Victoria (http://www.sbcs.org.au/), and Business Victoria (http://www.bizvic.com/index.html).

ABOUT GST FOR SMALL BUSINESS

This guide explains what you need to do to meet your GST obligations if you carry on an enterprise and you:

■ have an annual turnover of $50,000 or more ($100,000 or more for non-profit organisations)

■ have an annual turnover of less than $50,000 but choose to register for GST, or

■ are in the business of providing taxi travel.

TERMS WE USE

When we say:

■ **you**, we mean you as a business entity, for example, a sole trader, a partnership, a trustee of a trust or a superannuation fund, or a company.

■ **sales**, we are referring to the GST term **supplies**. For GST, a sale includes a sale of goods or services, lease of premises, hire of equipment, giving of advice, export of goods and the supply of other things.

■ **purchases**, we are referring to the GST term **acquisitions**. For GST, a purchase includes an acquisition of goods or services such as trading stock, a lease, consumables and other things (including importations).

■ **GST credit**, we are referring to the GST term **input tax credit**. A GST credit is what you claim to get back the GST included in the price you pay for most goods and services you purchase for your business.

Some technical terms used in this guide may be new to you. They are shown in **bold** when first used, and are explained in the list of definitions on page 26.

Throughout this guide you will find important notes (look for the ⓘ symbol) which will help you with key information you should note.

You will also find 'more information' boxes (look for the ❯ symbol) which will show any further steps you may need to take or supplementary information you may need to refer to.

CHECKLIST FOR BUSINESS

Does your business have an annual turnover of $50,000 or more ($100,000 or more if it is a non-profit organisation) or provide taxi travel?

If so, you need to:

☐ register for GST (see section 1)

☐ work out whether your sales are taxable, GST-free or input taxed (see section 2)

☐ include GST in the price of your taxable sales (see section 3)

☐ issue tax invoices for your taxable sales (see section 4)

☐ obtain tax invoices for your business purchases that have GST included in their price (see section 5)

☐ claim GST credits for the GST included in the price of your business purchases (see section 6)

☐ work out whether you have any adjustments (see section 7)

☐ account for GST on a cash or non-cash basis, and (see section 8)

☐ report and pay GST to us (see section 9).

GST in clear terms

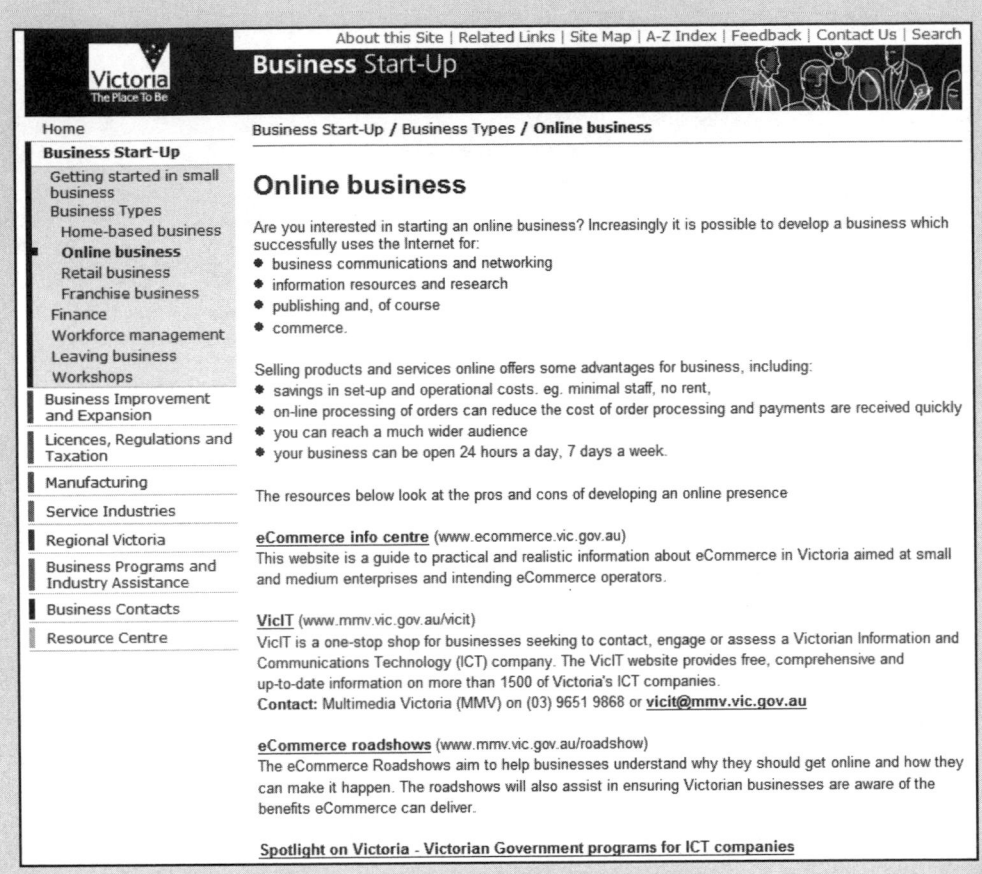

Look for this tasty list at Business in Victoria's Web site.

Not to be outdone, NSW has a good site at NSW Small Business (http://www.smallbiz.nsw.gov.au) covering both the governmental issues and business practicalities of starting your micro-ISV.

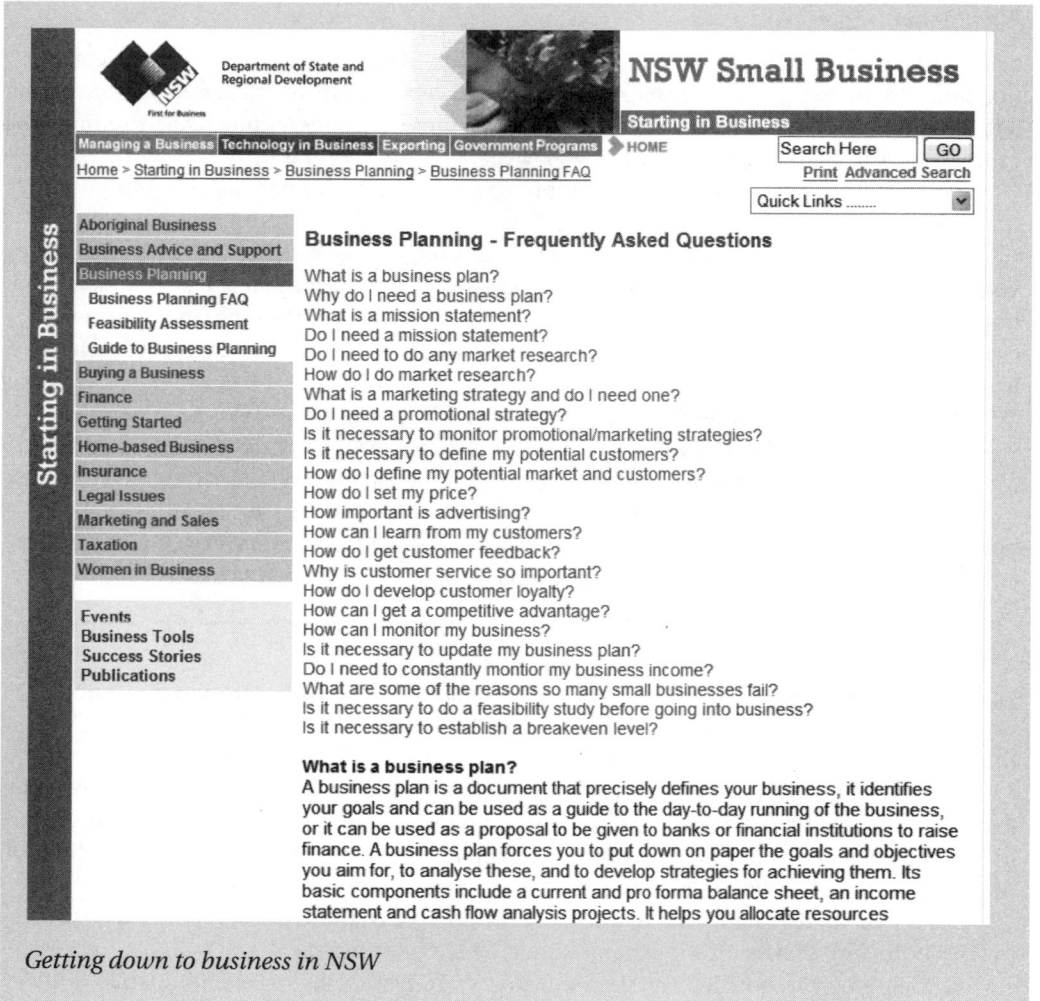

Getting down to business in NSW

Subchapter S Corporation

Up until the last ten years or so when LLCs became fashionable and practical, forming a subchapter S corporation was often the best way to go for a micro-ISV. Your micro-ISV is a real company with *Inc.* at the end of its name, but once the IRS grants you a subchapter S exemption, all profits and losses flow through the corporation to its owner(s) in proportion to their ownership.

Of course, it's not all fun: there is a substantial set of requirements to running a corporation whether the staff is one or one hundred: holding a meeting of the board when you're the board is considerably less fun than throwing a birthday party for yourself. And there's all the other forms you'll need (Pre-Incorporation Agreement, Corporate Bylaws, Shareholders' Agreement, Notices of Shareholders' meetings, Notice of Director's Meetings, Minutes of Shareholder Meetings, Minutes of Director's Meetings, Notices of Consent of Shareholders, Notices of Consent of Directors, and various financial authorizations—to name the basics).

Advantages

Corporations can do all sorts of fun things: issue stock, get corporate travel rates, give new meanings to the term *legitimate business expense*, have corporate credit cards, buy corporate jets, and go on corporate retreats. Of course, most of these activities require real, live employees other than you, a good accountant, a good lawyer, and lots of money.

If you need to issue stock or stock options to attract money or people, going corporate makes sense.

If you are your corporation, you may find it advantageous to be a cheapo employer, paying yourself a lot less than you really deserve in salary (which is taxable just like a "real" salary on both the part of yourself and your micro-ISV) and instead favoring the shareholders in your company (you) with healthy returns, dividends, and distributions that are just coincidently less taxed.

Finally, many companies (corporations) will not buy your micro-ISV's services unless you're a corporate entity. The reason is simple: more than a few high-tech firms—Apple and Microsoft, to name two—found themselves in deep doo-doo in the 1980s and 1990s with franchise tax boards and the IRS over whether a noncorporate independent contractor was really an employee in drag. If these "independent contractors" looked like employees and worked like employees, then that company was liable for paying payroll and other taxes on them.

Disadvantages

For a single person or set of partners launching a micro-ISV, an S corporation is just not the way to go compared to an LLC. Even in an age of "corporation kits" and sites that boilerplate the whole thing for you, it's still a pain.

I incorporated Safari Software in 1994 primarily so I could go after certain types of work for certain customers who did not want to sully their hands with an unincorporated entity. After more than a decade of having schizophrenic written conversations with myself in the form of board meetings, shareholder meetings, and resolutions, it almost feels normal.

But if I decided to start what has become my micro-ISV anew, make no mistake—the initials at the end of my corporate name would be *LLC*, not *Inc*.

Also, although at the federal level your micro-ISV profits and losses flow to your micro-ISV's stockholders, your state may do business differently. For example, Safari Software, a California corporation (subchapter S), gets to enhance the state's revenue each year to the tune of $800 for the privilege of existing.[8] And, if your corporation's annual revenues exceed a certain level ($250,000 in California), your state may have an income tax that applies to your corporation.

Bottom Line

If you're starting a micro-ISV or converting a sole proprietorship or partnership into a micro-ISV, going with LLC and not S corporation status can make your life easier.

---

8. Of course, California also charges LLCs $800 a year as a "minimum franchise tax."

Setup/Installation

Follow these steps:

1. Choose a name not already taken in your state.

2. Appoint the initial board of directors. Depending on your state, you may be able to "triple hat" being president, treasurer, and secretary, or you may not.

3. File the "articles of incorporation" in your state, paying somewhere from $100 to $800.

4. Draft your corporate "bylaws" by spelling out in a totally vague and boilerplate way how your company will do business.

5. Hold your first meeting of your board of directors, where your board officially hires you, issues stock to your stockholders, authorizes opening bank accounts, and more.

6. Elect for S corporation status by filing IRS Form 2553.

Subchapter C Corporation

A subchapter C corporation is a "legal person" and as such pays taxes in its own name, though at lower rates than what actual people pay. This double taxation is seldom favorable to a small company (and hence subchapter S corporations and LLCs).

Micro-ISV and subchapter C are seldom seen together since it rarely makes sense for a fewer-than-five-person company to go this route. However, many subchapter S companies that are successful drop their S status and become full-blown corporations. When, why, and how? Your accounting and legal staff will tell you.

Advantages

The greatest advantage a subchapter C corporation has over a subchapter S corporation is the ability to issue stock to more than 100 stockholders, all of whom have to be U.S. citizens or legal residents.

Disadvantages

Forming a subchapter C corporation is total overkill for a micro-ISV. Don't go there. If you do, make sure you know what you're doing.

Bottom Line

Although it might be fun to fantasize about getting listed on the NASDAQ, hold that thought until you've left the ranks of the micro-ISVs for a bigger (although perhaps not better) future.

Setup/Installation

In theory, the steps for setting up a C corporation are the same as setting up a subchapter S corporation except for getting subchapter S status. In practice, though, setting up a C corporation is far more involved, to put it mildly.

Getting Things Done in Your Micro-ISV

As you've been reading this chapter, the other chapters in this book, and a zillion Web pages that have some bearing on your micro-ISV, you may be wondering, "How the hell am I going to get all this done?"

This isn't a trivial question. One of the hardest parts of going from a company that defines what you do to your own company where you define what needs to get done is figuring out a process for defining, evaluating, and executing what works for you.

After 20+ years of being self-employed yet seeing how things get done (or not) in several hundred companies large and small, I've had to become an expert at recognizing ways to manage my time and workload that yield effective results.

The bad news for micro-ISVs is that the "overload culture" most high-tech companies have where management by crisis takes the place of management and people work until they drop doesn't scale down well. Throwing more staff at a project doesn't work when you're the staff, and endless meetings can't substitute for shipping a sellable product.

The good news for micro-ISVs is that certain people have been thinking quite hard about how to make one person, or a small group, productive in the face of task and information overload, and at the forefront of those thinkers is David Allen.

One of David's books, *Getting Things Done: The Art of Stress-Free Productivity* (Penguin Books, 2001), has become the missing "user's guide to personal productivity." In it, he describes the process he teaches at corporate and public seminars worldwide for becoming more productive with less stress.

"It's possible for a person to have an overwhelming number of things to do and still function productively with a clear head and a positive sense of relaxed control," David says at the start of his book. Like hundreds of thousands of other people searching for better answers, I was hooked. So much so that when I decided to go micro-ISV myself, my products (MasterList-XL, MasterList Professional, and MasterList Professional 2) were strongly influenced by David's Getting Things Done (GTD) approach.

Somewhere, maybe on top of Everest or in a forgotten tomb in the Amazon, a better approach might exist for getting things done, but I've yet to find it. What I have found is that GTD works extremely well for micro-ISVs, and so, based on living the GTD approach and applying it to my own micro-ISV needs, the following sections summarize GTD to give you at least a second-hand guide to getting things done. I strongly advise you to get David's books or, if you can, attend one of his seminars (http://www.davidco.com/products.php). He does a far better job of explaining GTD than I can in just a few pages.

If you'd like to get a taste of what David has to offer, you can watch the Microsoft LiveMeeting Web seminar "Knowledge Work Athletics" at http://livemeeting.com/archive. It's free, it's an hour, and it's a good, fast introduction to GTD.

But you don't need my micro-ISV's products or anything more complicated than paper and pencil to make GTD work for you as a way of getting things done in your business: it's the ideas, not the form, that matters.

GTD for Micro-ISVs: The Overview

The GTD method has five stages: collecting, processing, organizing, reviewing, and doing. Each of these stages is governed by these key insights:

Control your attention: The more tasks you have on your mind and the more tasks, projects, and obligations that have your attention, the less attention you can bring to what you're trying to get done right now. A big part of GTD is clearing your mental desktop so you have somewhere to work. Nothing beats having lots of RAM to use.

Build a comprehensive process: A leaky process is a bad process. If your commitments are scattered over multiple bits of paper, hundreds of emails in your Microsoft Outlook Inbox, and piles all over your office, that's not a process. You're building a process here, and everything that goes in has to go somewhere.

Trust your process: Once you've got the GTD process working without any memory or commitment leaks, you can start to trust it and devote your full attention to what you're doing at the moment. Keeping your GTD process trustworthy means keeping it up to date.

Collecting

The first step in applying GTD to your micro-ISV life is establishing an In basket. Actually, you'll probably have at least two—a physical In basket and the notorious Outlook Inbox. The two key features of In baskets are they're the entry points for all the stuff that comes into your life—information, things to do, ideas, paper—and that stuff gets processed out of your Inbox on at least a daily basis following the GTD process.

Now, collecting everything around your desk that's not reference, supplies, equipment, or decoration, plus writing down or entering all the tasks floating loose in your head—all the things you're suppose to do for other people and all the things you can remember other people are suppose to do—can take a good six hours. "It's not a lightweight amount of stuff that people have committed to," David says during the Web seminar. "[But] that's what we do first, because we don't want anyone's attention on that when we start processing and organizing."

If you can't spare the time to collect everything, pick an area—say your micro-ISV—and collect everything about it. Sooner than later, return to deal with other big chunks of what you're doing: the relief you'll feel by getting everything through this part of the GTD process goes a long way toward stress-free productivity.

Here are some pointers:

- Don't forget to "collect" all the tasks expected of you or on which you're waiting for someone else to finish. You may have to renegotiate them, but these are the tasks that eat at your concentration.

- Favorites/bookmarks are a draining mess on everybody's computer, including mine. Start draining the swamp by creating three folders: In, Reference, and Projects. Put them at the top of your bookmarks/favorites list. Reorganizing all your Web page references is an undertaking outside the scope of this book, but as of now, add only new bookmarks to these three folders.

- As for your email Inbox, one of the goals of the GTD process is emptying it by the end of each day. So, if you have 500 (5,000?) emails, create a new folder called Stuff to Go Through, and move everything but the most recent emails from your Inbox into that folder.

- As for the files on your computer(s), people who start micro-ISVs tend to have a completely outrageous number of files in folders in folders in folders *ad infinitum*. "Collecting" these files can be done, and you can organize them in a way that supports stress-free productivity, but for right now, leave this tar pit for later, and be glad there's Google Desktop.

Processing and Organizing

Processing is just that—working each item you've collected through the GTD flowchart, as shown in Figure 4-5.

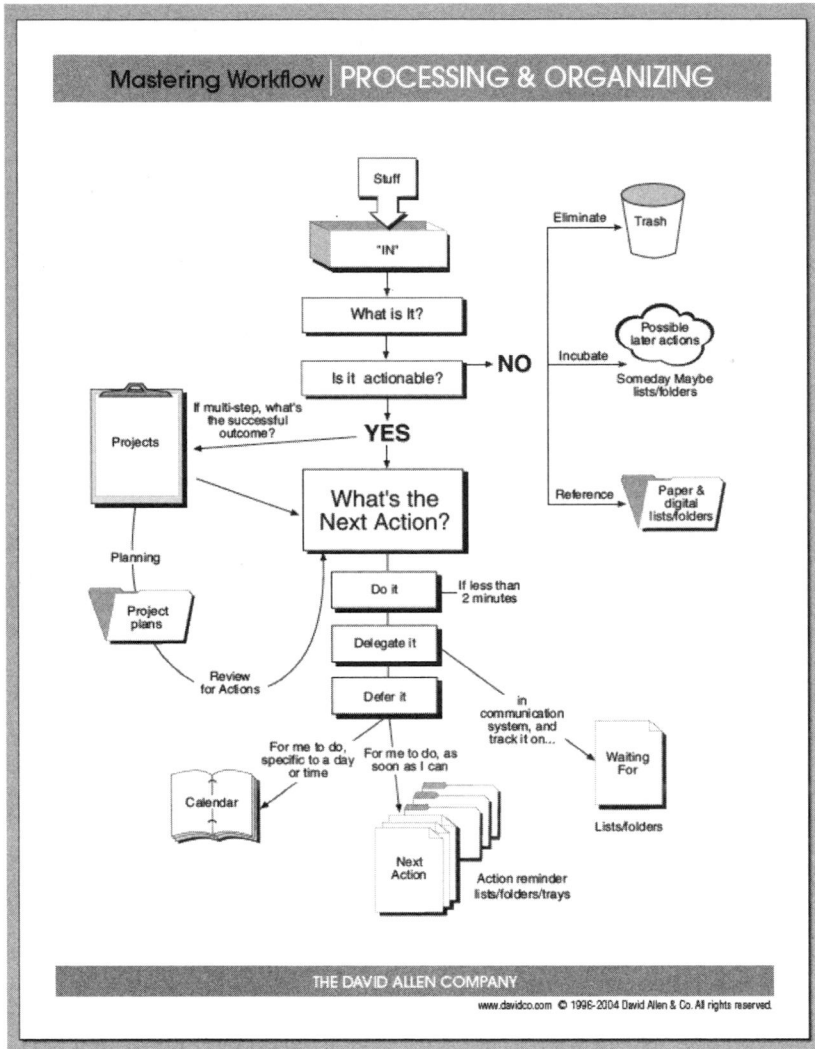

Figure 4-5. *The GTD flowchart*

Ask the following questions for each item in your In basket: What is it? Is it actionable (something you can or need to act on)? If it isn't actionable, that item needs to either be deleted, be filed in whatever reference system you have for that medium, or go somewhere to incubate that you regularly check—the Someday/Maybe folder.

The key question to ask about each item is, what is the absolute next physical action that needs to be done with this item? If the answer is nothing, chuck it, file it, or sit on it for now.

Now, things get a little trickier. Is the item you're processing complete in and by itself? If this item has multiple steps or parts or is tightly coupled with other tasks, it goes over to Projects. It will return, but you're trying to narrow your input to manageable bite-sized tasks, usually quicker than two hours in duration. I'll return to Projects in a moment, but for now let's say you have a simple, straightforward task. What happens to it next?

Proceeding down the GTD flowchart, if the item is actionable, can you do it in two minutes? If yes, just do it, and be done with it. If it can't be disposed of that easily, can you delegate it? Now, delegation opportunities are somewhat thin for micro-ISVers, but theoretically they're possible. If you can delegate it, then forward it, but start a list, the Waiting For list, so you won't lose track of who you sent it to and when they should be done with it.

OK, so you can't delegate it. Now what? You'll have to plan to do it, either by putting a note in your calendar to do it on this date at this time or by putting it on your action reminder list or in a Pending folder.

Organizing your Pending folder gets worthwhile quick. Whatever system you're using—pad and pencil, Outlook, David's GTD Outlook Add-in (http://www.davidco.com/productDetail. php?id=63&IDoption=20, $69.95 USD, 30-day trial), MasterList Professional (http://safarisoftware.com, $24.95 USD, 45-day trial), or whatever—you need a set of filters so you can subset pending but unscheduled action items by at least context, duration, difficulty, and, I would add, value.

Context: At your computer, in the car, at home…each of these are places where doing certain tasks but not others makes sense.

Duration: How long is it going to take to do? If you have 20 minutes before the next thing you have to do, it's helpful to be able to see only your pending tasks that take 20 minutes or less.

Difficulty: Not all tasks are created equal, and after 14 hours straight programming, you might not be equal to the task. Even your laptop knows when it's time to slack off and go slower.

Value: This is one of my filters, used to detect and avoid pouring time into easy-to-do but low-value tasks. The more time you spend on what's valuable, the more successful your micro-ISV will be.

Let's return to the decision point where you decide an item is a single step (and it can be done in two minutes, delegated, or deferred) or multiple steps. This is where the last two parts of the GTD processing stage need building out: your project list and your project plans.

A project is whatever you decide it is, but it does have two characteristics: it culminates in a single outcome, and it consists of multiple steps or discrete tasks. Every "to do" you're processing is going to be either a singleton, if you will, or a part of a project. Each project needs at least one plan—it can be as simple as paper clipping the stack of tasks together you want to do first, or it can be as complicated as you need. Either way, you need to plan when and how these tasks are going to get fed into the What's the Next Action? box.

It may seem equivalent to picking up your refrigerator and going for a run, but processing does get easier. The secret is getting your collection points to empty and then emptying them on a regular, daily basis. "It takes about a half minute a piece to go through that thinking process," David says.

All the emails, all the voice mails, all the meeting notes, all the business cards you collected, all the receipts to process, all the conversations in the hall, all the ideas you had in the shower—if you were responsible for really collecting all those and throwing them into your In basket, it would take you about an hour a day just to keep all this stuff current, just by defining all the stuff you need to do.

If processing and organizing don't sound like rocket science, that's because they're not. "It's actually not that complex a system," David says.

You just need to keep track of projects you're responsible for; you need to keep track of actions you need to do, either on a calendar or some sort of list of actions. And you need to keep track of projects and actions other people are doing.

The organizing part of this system is not that complex, once you've gone through the thinking in the middle of this chart. If you haven't figured out the next action on things, forget it: you're just rearranging incomplete piles of unclear stuff.

Here are some pointers:

- Processing is simple, and the clock is ticking. Don't agonize over whether something is a single physical actionable task; that's a sure sign it's not.

- Good things develop for those who wait. Use, revel in, and honor your Someday/Maybe folder for everything that doesn't fit in now but your gut tells you there might be a place for it later in your life. Put it in the Someday/Maybe folder for now.

- You're going to end up with a least four types of project folders—paper, email, favorites/bookmarks, and electronic (MasterList Professional or a different project management application). Make life easier for yourself—have one master project list, and use the same name for each project across mediums.

- Can't decide what to do with something that's interesting but not actionable—something you "might" need? If it's paper, make a folder called Check on 1st/16th. Put items in that folder, writing a date, say, four months in advance. On the 1st or 16th of each month, cull the folder, and check anything still there after its four-month stay. A few months of this, especially with email, will build up your muscles to the point you won't need this file.

- "People don't throw away enough," is a point David makes often.

Reviewing

At first glance, it might seem that processing and organizing is the heart of the GTD system and the core of what your micro-ISVs needs to do to get business done.

It's not.

Regularly reviewing your project list, your projects, your Waiting For list, your calendar, your Pending folder, and even your Someday/Maybe folder is the heart of this process—pumping things to where they need to be and keeping your GTD system lean and healthy.

The trick to getting GTD reviews right is to review the right tasks at the right time. "It's not that you are looking at everything in your system every hour of every day; you wouldn't get much done," David says. For example, during the course of the day when you find yourself not sure what comes next, you might check your scheduling calendar, project list, and Pending folder. Or check your calendar in Outlook and your tasks by various categories. Or check your Home tab in MasterList Professional. Just enough review to stay on course.

When it comes to reviewing, the next step up is the weekly review, and that's where after a long week of coding, tech support, and marketing, it's all too easy to slip up.

"We coach a lot of people on how to do the weekly review, which is really driven off your project list. Most people are not taking the one to two hours at the end of the work week to sit down and catch up," David says.

> *What are the new projects I need to design, what are the old projects I've finished, what are the action items on the current project, and where do I need to be? That kind of operational review is absolutely critical for stress-free productivity.*
>
> *And it's the behavior most lacking and most needed in the world. Most people don't have a system to review, or they don't have their system populated with enough inventory of their work to review, so it's kind of challenging to review your game if you haven't collected and processed everything. But once you do, this becomes a critical factor of keeping everything alive and well.*

Beyond the weekly review, you'll want to establish your own set of periodic, more comprehensive reviews. It's important to track your projects, but it's also important to focus on a regular basis on the bigger questions: Is your micro-ISV going in the right direction? Is your marketing message getting out there across all the specific marketing projects? Are you going in the right direction?

Here are some pointers:

- Put your first, second, and third weekly reviews into Outlook's calendar where they'll hound you until you do them.

- Want more information on how to do your weekly review? See `http://www.davidco.com/tips_tools/tip16.html` for more information or David's books.

- If you're wondering how to manage those bigger questions you need to review, you might want to supplement your reading with what Steven R. Covey had to say about roles and goals in his classic book, *The 7 Habits of Highly Effective People*, 15th Edition (Free Press, 2004).

Doing

When all is said and done, processed, organized, and reviewed, it's what gets done that matters. "One foot in front of the other," David says, and if you've got your GTD system working, it's just that simple. "It's a lot easier to feel good about what you're doing or not doing if you've collected, processed, and organized everything so you can review it and feel comfortable about your choices."

Remember the filters you set up when organizing? Those filters are your set of tools for determining what's the next task you need to do. Context, duration, difficulty, and, I would add, value help you manage your choices in the moment.

Another tool I've found helpful actually getting things done is a Current list. Now, this isn't the infamous to-do list with *A*s, *B*s, *C*s of traditional time management but a list of the tasks that have your attention in the order you expect, or at least hope, you'll be able to address them.

A second useful toolset for tasks you do day in and day out—for example, tech support, programming, and writing—are checklists. Checklists make it easier to cover everything in a consistent way, whether it be prepping a plane for taking off or ensuring the fewest bugs in the class you just wrote.

A third idea to keep in mind, especially when deciding what to do next regarding your micro-ISV, is driving actions based on revenue. The closer a task is to increasing your micro-ISV's revenue, the more wonderful it is!

Here are some pointers:

- There's nothing magic about getting things done—the trick is managing the process up to that point.

- Have a Current list that gets you through to the next point where you'll reassess where you're going.

- Look for high-value tasks not getting the attention they need, and make appointments with yourself so you can do the best you can on these particular tasks.

DAVID ALLEN, AUTHOR, *GETTING THINGS DONE*

David Allen is the author of *Getting Things Done: The Art of Stress-Free Productivity* (Penguin, 2001) and *Ready for Anything* (Penguin, 2003) and a productivity trainer. He's someone you'll run across quickly on the Net if you're looking for better ways to manage all the tasks and projects you'll need to do to get your micro-ISV off the ground.

David, who started his quest for a better way of getting things done 20 years ago, has become—through his two books, numerous corporate training engagements, and seminars—the unofficial spokesperson for anyone overwhelmed by projects, tasks, and email. His GTD approach toward being productive and stress free works especially well for people facing the challenge of creating their own micro-ISVs.

Q. One thing I've heard time and time again from people starting their own micro-ISV is the problem of email. Any suggestions from a GTD approach for how to deal with email?

A. Well, don't let it pile up. Email is a beast that is out of the barn; you're not going to be able to shove it back in. What you do need to do is quickly get simple ways to make executive decisions about what an email means to you. You've got to decide, "Look, can I delete this?" That's number one.

If you can't delete it, is it some actionable item: yes or no? If it's not, you need to file it as reference. You need to file it wherever you need to file it, but get it out of hand—stop using your In basket as a reference folder. Or, if there's some action you can take later on, you might want to defer it. Now, if it is actionable and it will take two minutes to do it, do it.

Informal studies have shown that 40 percent of your emails are less than two-minute actions. And anything you can finish in two minutes or less, if you're ever going to do it at all, you should do it right then because it will take you longer to track it or look at it again than to finish it. It's a good idea to have a two-minute timer so that you know how long it takes to deal with an email.

And if it's longer than two minutes, you need to ask yourself, "Look, can I delegate this to somebody else?" and so forward it on and have them do it. And if not, you're it. Then you need to organize it in someplace you keep actionable emails. But get it out of your In basket.

Q. Most of the people who end up reading these books practically live on the Web. They spend almost all their waking time on it. How about when it comes to Web sites and blogs and podcasts and RSS and all the rest of the ways of getting information today?

A, Well, it depends on your business. You have to decide what's mission critical for you. And that's a tough call—it's hard to tell. It's a tough enough call even to ask that question. A lot of people don't even ask the question if they need to be doing and reading all that stuff. That's when you have to get hardnosed with yourself: "How important is it that I am reading this?" Because the Web and all the accoutrements thereof can be a black sinkhole.

Q. In the 20 years you've been teaching and training people about productivity, do you think the Internet has made it harder or easier to be more productive?

A. That's like [asking whether] a knife is a good or bad thing. The Web is fabulous—an interactive, live yellow pages. I mean, how cool can that be? It has all kinds of things out there. But it's like anything else—like the morning paper—that can suck you in all day long, just reading the paper cover to cover.

Q. You know a lot of high-tech people. What part of GTD don't they get?

A. Well, I think the hardest thing for high-tech people to get about GTD is that simpler is better and that over-organizing or overautomating doesn't necessarily make it easier. There's a point of diminishing returns about how much structure [and] how much automation actually make a thing easier.

It's not unique to the high-tech people, but the high-tech people are so smart and so lazy that they, like me, want to find that "Gee, if we can automate some of it, let's automate it all." But you can't. Your brain still has to think.

Q. In all the people you've trained who have attended your seminars, have you ever found someone who has achieved a level of GTD that is so far above what everyone else does, and if so, what would that look like?

A. I met a guy once who blew me away. Now, I didn't follow him around in his life, but from everything I could tell by hanging out with him for two days in a seminar, and all the staff who talked to me about it, it seemed he did work that way. This is guy who had taken Outlook, who'd taken the GTD stuff, and had gone into Outlook and customized extra fields so he could list things by priority, by how long they took, by context, and by areas of responsibility in his life. And then he would map it back to a PDA so that when he'd get home, his brain would be semi-toast but could say, "OK, I'm home. I want to do some family things, but I only have ten minutes. Give me all my family things that I can do in less than ten minutes sorted by priority." And—bam!—he'd have those right in front of him.

I mean, God! [laughs] This was a guy who'd come from South America to Florida, spoke three languages, had started up five businesses, and was half my age. I mean, oh, give me a break!

Q. You mentioned in the Microsoft Live Meeting (archived at `http://main.livemeeting.com/demos/web_seminar_archive.cfm`) that you're 60 now and you've been doing this for 20 years. It seems that the pattern in companies is more and more meetings day in, day out, all day, everyday, and people trying to get things done around the edges of that workday. Is that the way productivity should be done? Are we doomed to that sort of rat race?

A. I don't know—it's the knife thing again. How are you using meetings? Meetings can be the best things in the world because they get you focused and because they get you to make decisions you wouldn't by yourself. Meetings are extremely productive in that way.

Meetings can be extremely unproductive because the people aren't focused on what they are trying to accomplish, [and] they are using meetings as a way to communicate inefficiently, with a lot of stuff that could be done much more virtually than in meetings. It's hard to tell; you almost have to take it case by case, meeting by meeting.

And frankly, I don't know. As long as I've been in this game it seems like a universal internal phenomenon. I certainly see a lot of it, certainly in health care. But the same is true in a lot of these places. And a lot of it has to do with how critical it is that you get done what you have to get done out there. The more you know what you're doing, the more you know if you should be going to a meeting or not.

Maybe the reason "meetingitis" got everybody is that I think the speed of change going on out there has accelerated and magnified the amount of ambiguity that there is about what the heck you should be doing and what you should be focused on. It's easy to get sucked into meetings. So, that would be my guess; I don't have anything but anecdotal evidence on that.

The Finer Points of GTD

Q. Let's return for a second to some of the finer points of GTD. It seems that GTD is focused on reacting to things that come in. What's the proactive side of GTD?
A. Well, if you are setting a goal, where does that come from? The proactive side is if you generate something or someone else generates it as a goal, you need to throw things into your In basket. So the CEO part of you is the part that needs to create stuff. It's like, "Hey, where do you want to be five years from now?"

It's all reactive in a way; it's just there's this proactive part of you creating or allowing or noticing.
Q. Reacting to yourself if you will?
A. Sure. Basically there's the CEO part of you and the COO part of you. The CEO has ideas and throws them into the In basket; somebody else can run with them. The COO part shows up and says, "Hi, what's that?" and "What the hell is that?" and "How dumb was I last night?"

If anybody is going to tell me they don't have a committee in their heads, they're not grown up yet.

I mean, you even set goals as a way to respond to a creative energy or a part of you that wants something. Some part of you is contracted or pushed or pulled, right?
Q. Typically, well, I think you start with goals; you have to start with a philosophy you have goals in.
A. Why do you set a goal?
Q. It's a result of your values, I would guess.
A. Yeah—in other words, something is pulling or pushing you to set a goal, right? That's what I'm talking about.
Q. So, you're trying to get control of that In basket, so you're the person who decides what goes in it?
A. Well, maybe. Or you are open to the serendipity of the world. Why not? [The GTD method] is not the key to life; that's just [the GTD way] of processing and organizing. [It] doesn't even include what goes in the In basket. What you let in there, what shows up…once it's landed there and you have some attention on it—here's how you get your attention off of it.
Q. When you have a whole bunch of actionable items, how do you decide what to do next? What's the process for processing decisions, if you will?
A. The way you process is that chart [see Figure 4-5]. Is action required or not? If you're saying, "How do I decide what to ultimately do out of my options of doing?" then that's another decision. That's how you use all of that to make a decision. If you mean by processing what it means to you, that's one thing. If you mean all the other stuff, that's another thing.
Q. I look at things and see that there are things that have little value, there are things that have great value, and often the things that are most urgent have little value. And the things you want to get to have great value. How at any given time do you decide what to do next?
A. Well, there are several criteria that come in. First of all, can you possibly do it where you are? For instance, I have a bunch of things I could do, but I can't do because I'm talking to you on the phone. Right now, you can only do what you can do. If the server is down, forget writing email. Or if you've got no phone signal, forget about making phone calls. So the first thing is, what can you possibly do where you are?

The second one is, how much time do you have before you have something else to do? If you've got five minutes, your highest priority if you want to do something is a 5-minute thing, not try and do a 20-minute thing, [because] you haven't got 20 minutes.

Third, how wasted are you? Are you fresh, or are you toast? There are times when you should not be doing important things or talking to important people because you're not fully there, and you'll screw it up.

Then, all things being equal—assuming you have a choice, and you might not—if you still have a choice, then if you have a choice, which of these things will give me the highest payoff if it's done?

That's when you need to have conversations with multiple horizons: why are you on the planet, what are your core values, where do you want to be short-term, what are your short-term goals, what are your areas of responsibility you want to maintain so that the whole engine works, what are all the projects you've got out of all that, and what are the action items you need to take out of all that?

Those are six different horizons at least that you need to have conversations on.

Q. One thing I've noticed is that it's very easy to forgo that step of the weekly review. And you've mentioned that's a mistake a lot of people make when they try to get the GTD idea right.

A. All the reviews are necessary; it just seems the weekly review [is] the biggest weak step for people trying to get control of their stuff out there. You obviously need to review why you are on the planet every so often. You need to review your yearly goals, because those things matter; you need to review your values too. It's not like that's the only review that people need; it's just that very few people have a project list, and very few people have a weekly review operationally at that metro level up of the actions in the their lives. That's the most missing component for a lot of people.

Q. One thing about traditional time management systems in general: You can end up spending a whole lot of time managing the system that you are using. When you start your day, do you have like a classic to-do list?

A. Well, the first thing I do is look at my calendar, which has the hard landscape for the day. I mean, what will die if I don't do it today? That's the first thing. Assuming I have any time left—sometimes you don't—but assuming you have some time left, I say, "OK, now what are all the other options?" That's why I have a total life to-do list available all the time, so I can pick from. Then you have to evaluate all those things against ad hoc surprises that are not even on your list as they show up.

Then you have to evaluate all those things against one another. So it's a constant self-dialogue/self-reflection about, what are all the commitments, what could I possibly do, what's the new thing I haven't seen before, and how does it map against all the other stuff?

And, yes, every once in a while—I did this last night—I said, "OK, David, you've got a big trip coming up, I've got all kinds of things thrown at me; they're all coming to a head at once." So I just went and did a mindmap real fast of all the things I have attention on right now to make sure I wasn't missing anything. While I have those other lists, sometimes it's necessary to sit down and do another iteration of all the things coming in.

Q. I know MindManager from Mindjet well (http://mindjet.com, from $229 USD). So there are no easy answers?

A. [laughs]

Q. Aww, come on, give me an easy answer!

A. Sure. Just keep track of everything you're committed to. Make sure you are looking at where you're going. And trust your gut.

Q. On that note, if you are doing a start-up business, should you allow time to go wrap up all those open loops from your previous employment or way of doing business?

A. Well, open loops just create drag on the system. It doesn't mean you're not moving or that you can't do it. It's kind of like, how important is it to get rid of drag on the system? Sometimes you don't have time to get rid of drag on the system; you just got to work with a draggy system.

But when in doubt, clean a drawer, because crap is occurring as we speak. Things change, so they change their nature, [and] today's newspaper is tomorrow's fire starter. So as time marches on, so does residue accrue.

Anybody who is trying to ignore that they need to from time to time stop and clean up the open loops and renegotiate them are kidding themselves. But then it's just a matter of how clean do you like to stay? I have a bias towards being as close to zero as possible, because it's easier to deal with surprise with a lot less stress.

If you get surprised with 3,000 emails, that's one thing; if you get surprised with an empty In basket—hey, new opportunity.

Q. Good point. Someone wanted me to ask you, what are some good tips for avoiding procrastination when you're working alone? How do you stay focused? Would I need some "focusum" like Bart Simpson had, or is it simpler than that?

A. It's never that simple. Basically, it's your brain that will screw you up. Procrastination is negative future scenario stuff in your head or your head throwing you into way more complexity than you can control, and you don't want to step into it.

So the idea is stay focused on very specific physical actions you can do and kind of bypass your mental process. Everybody has cleaned the refrigerator by accident. The big key there is to trick yourself into getting engaged physically before your brain freaks you out.

Q. So get engaged physically as a solution to procrastination, but if you are procrastinating, maybe you should be asking yourself, are you procrastinating because the next actionable item is a big, amorphous project you need to do?

A. Yeah, but it has a next action on it. That's the thing, as long as you focus down on to the next action. The whole idea of breaking things down into next actions is to make it something you feel you can control. "I don't know how to do this, but I can set a next action to meet with myself and maybe two to three people and think it through." Or my next thing is to sit down and draft a mindmap about it.

But again, you are up against all the issues everyone has got, called, "Gee, I don't feel I'm capable of it." There's also subtler issues that people have—"Gee, if I actually went and did it, I might create success and move out of my comfort zone."

Going with Your Gut

Q. Put yourself in the shoes of someone who has decided to start their own business today for a moment. Where would you start?

A. I have no idea.

Q. Espressos and trust in God?

A. All that.

Q. Would you get yourself the world's biggest whiteboard and start writing?

A. That's not a bad idea. I mean, basically get moving. That's the key. It's a lot easier to change direction if you are in motion than not.

Q. So often you see online discussions of people who want all the answers to starting a business before starting a business.

A. Yeah, but nobody ever started a really successful business with a business plan I think, except FedEx. I think you just have to pay attention to the fire in your belly if you've got one.

Q. OK, a couple of more personal questions. You've been doing this for about 20 years. Why did you decide to focus on productivity as the thing you do in life?

A. Ah, gee, it's not a bad job. It beats waiting on tables most of the time. I was fascinated by human behavior, and also I was fascinated by how you actually get things done with as little effort as possible. It's a combination of my lazy factor, and also, I think I've got educator in my DNA. I've always liked being an educator—to facilitate stuff and help people out and to help them with something valuable to them.

And it was nice to find something that was valuable to everybody, or most people anyway. That I really didn't have to change my song no matter who I was talking to. If it dealt with a universal issue, kind of like teaching people about gravity, all I had to do is point out basic principles and how to make it work, coaching people along the way. And it turned out that I latched on to something almost transformational for a lot of people. That's fun.

Q. Leaving aside the people who have attended your seminars and read your books, do you think business-people in the United States are more or less productive or more or less organized than they were 20 years ago when you got started with all of this?

A. I really have no idea. I've sort of noticed what I've been noticing, but I've not been like a formal researcher. Anecdotally, the issues I deal with and teach people about people have always had.

Q. Will there be a new book by 2006?

A. There might.

Q. You mentioned during the LiveMeeting seminar you are getting more and more interested in "train the trainer" sort of things. Broadening the reach, if you will. Do you see your company sticking with, for lack of a better term, a corporate focus? Or do you see it heading more toward consumers or single people?

A. It's actually both. My basic philosophy was just raise the flag and see who was going to salute. Make it as much as the world wanted or as little as the world wanted—that would be fine with me. So, a lot of it has been seeing who's going to show up.

The education itself is what's important to me, and it turns out that the corporate world has in itself adult education going on. It's a venue for that, it has the most happening, and it also pays for it so it's not a bad place to be, if you are into education. Some of the best education development on the planet is going on in corporate education programs in the United States. But I could just as easily work with churches, with school systems, with the military; it doesn't matter. I'll work with whoever's interested. It's good information, so I'm not particularly wedded to one venue or another.

Q. If you could tell some software developer out there what the perfect GTD solution would be and have them come up with it, what would you tell them?

A. Well, I've drawn a number of screens myself back 11 years ago. I drew a bunch of screens and said this is what the software should do to clear your head. We actually started a company called Actioneer (http://www.actioneer.com) [that] was designed around trying to do that. It turns out that to make that happen takes an awful amount of lines of code, or it least it did back then.

Mitch Kapor is trying to grapple with that right now, trying to create an open source PIM operating system (http://wiki.osafoundation.org/bin/view/Projects/ChandlerHome), where cool stuff could be done without having to reinvent the wheel every time you do something cool.

Q. The world does not need a calendar program that can't talk to your outliner program?

A. All that stuff. There's a lot of connectors that need to happen in terms of how you do GTD, and those connectors require a lot of sophistication to make it happen. Now you could have fooled me, but I'm not a software engineer. But it could be done; it could be easily done. I know what the model is, but I don't think the markets are mature enough yet to want it.

Q. It's too advanced for everyone?

A. Most people don't think they need GTD, much less the software version of it.

Q. How is your cat, Nikos?

A. He's cool. He's growing up. He slept with us last night.

Q. You're talking to a committed cat person here, so I understand that one real well. I was curious because I read about Nikos on your blog, and I'm also curious about how is this blogging stuff working out for you.

A. The jury's out. I think when I changed its name to "Between the lines…" and I say, "Hey, look." When I very first started, I said, "Look, there's no commitment to this." I have no idea of what this is going to look like. It is kind of nice. I like sharing just stuff with people and chatting, hanging out, and BSing with cool folks. I figure [the blog] is a virtual way to do that. It's weird, though. Once you get notoriety like I'm starting to get, like GTD is starting to get, it's a mixed bag.

I share how cool our $99 wallet is, and people say, "There are people starving in India; why are you doing this?" And I'm going, "Who needs this? Go get a life or something. Go help them out. Why are you reading a blog? And whose computer are you typing on?"

So, the jury's out. I think there's a group of people out there that look to me as something of a model in terms of what the "GTD lifestyle" is like, and so letting people know I'm a real person like everybody else gives permission that they can have the same thing, so I've found there's a lot of value in that. I've gotten a lot of positive feedback on it; people love it.

Q. Does this guru thing bug you?

A. Not really. The good news far outweighs the bad. Anything [that] gets people to pay attention when you have something to say is nice when they pay attention. It's fun to be called a guru, and then people find out there really isn't a guru. I'm just like them.

Q. I guess there is one question that everyone kind of wonders. You've given so much thought to this—you live it, you teach it, and you train it. Is your life easier than everybody else's?

A. I don't think so. I mean the better you get, the better you'd better get. I can overwhelm myself, and then I think, "Gee, didn't I write a book about stress-free productivity? I need to read it." I get myself in trouble as much as anybody. I just know how to get out, so that's the difference.

The Government, the Law, and You

Finally, I'll cover briefly a few of the legal considerations and government-funded resources you should know about and put on your master micro-ISV to-do list for further research. A full treatment of these areas are books themselves—you'll find a list of recommendations in the appendix.

Your Product's EULA

End User License Agreements (EULAs) are those bits of legal boilerplate you've agreed to by clicking I Agree or by opening the box on practically every program you own. Now, it's you who will need a EULA for your micro-ISV product.

There is a right way and a wrong way of doing a EULA. The wrong way is to copy and paste another company's EULA into your installer after doing a search and replace. EULAs are legal documents, and most major software vendors (you know who I mean) have tailored their EULAs to do exactly what they want. Doing this can come back and bite you.

The right way is to start at the Electronic Frontier Foundation's white paper on bad EULA practices (`http://www.eff.org/wp/eula.php`). Suffice to say, this white paper covers the topics you don't want in your EULA unless you enjoy being sued, vilified, and pilloried online.

Next, you need a clean, generic software license template in one of two flavors: open or closed. You can find open source licensing information in several places, but the best place to start is the Wikipedia open source license article at `http://en.wikipedia.org/wiki/Open_source_licenses`, as shown in Figure 4-6. You, as a micro-ISV, need to be aware of certain important subtleties.

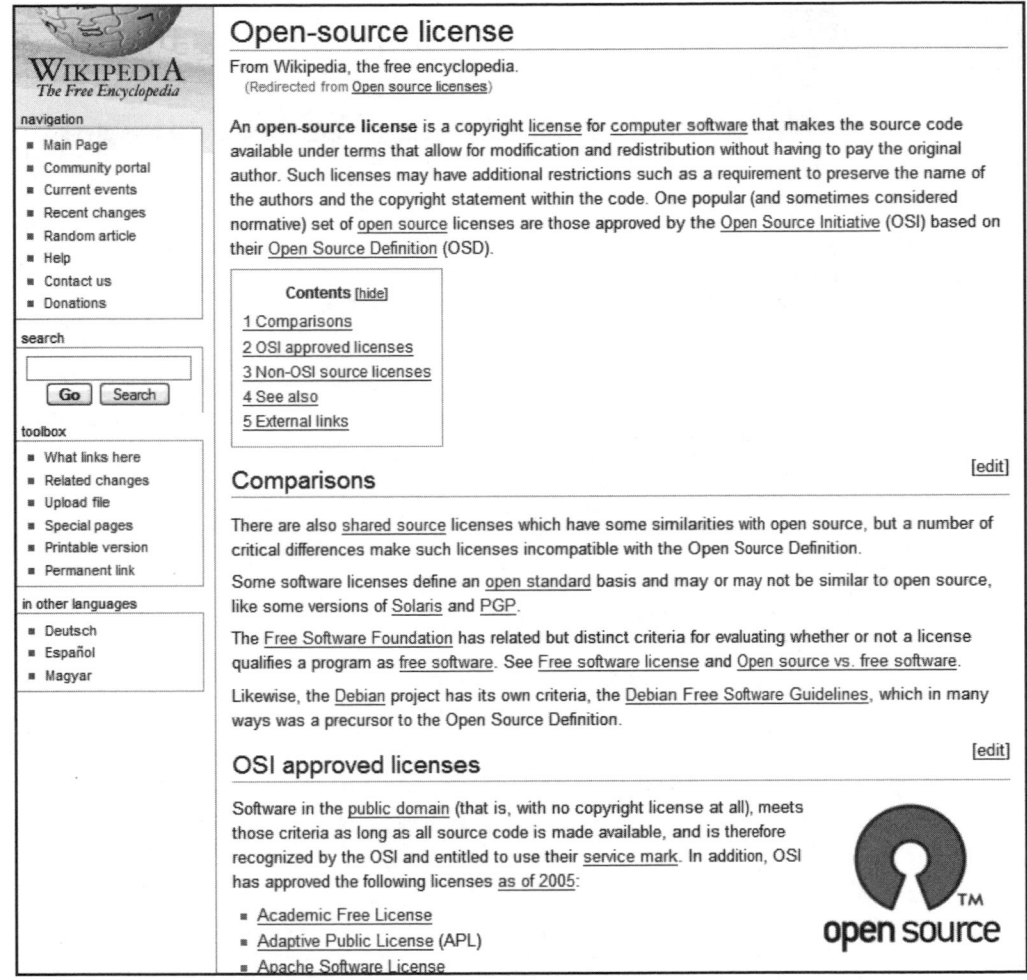

Figure 4-6. *Starting at Wikipedia*

As for closed (that is, shrink-wrapped, proprietary) licenses, I've found only one intrepid soul willing to provide a free generic EULA at `http://www.soft14.com/upload/software_000039.htm`, which might be too generic for your needs. As an alternative, you might want to buy a EULA template from MegaDox.com at `http://www.megadox.com/documents.php/589?a_id=74`, as shown in Figure 4-7.

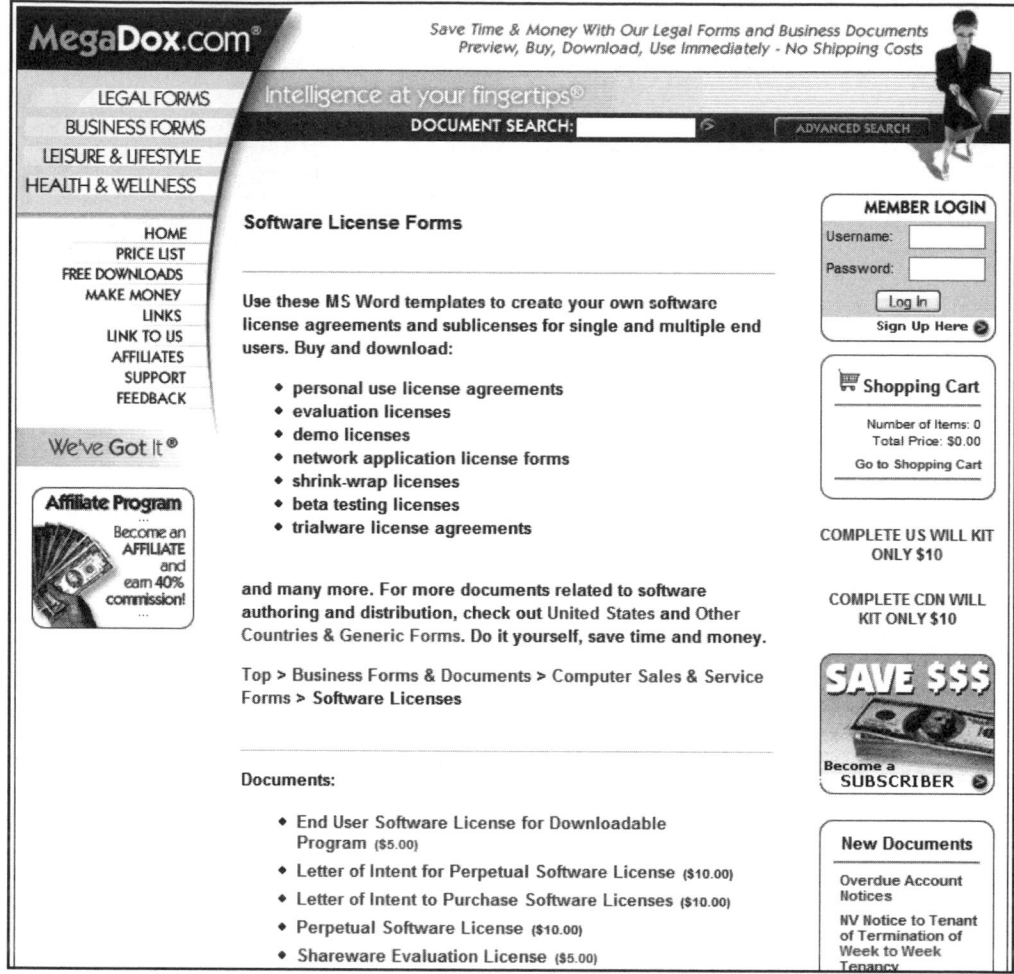

Figure 4-7. *Buying a clean EULA*

Legally Protecting Your Software

If you're in the closed software camp (as I am), of paramount concern is making sure you have as much legal protection of your Intellectual Property (IP) as possible. Practical protection will depend on how you design your software or Web service, but in theory, legal protection depends on copyright, patents, trade secrets, and trademarks.

Of course, the difference between theory and reality is that in theory, there is no difference! Patents—which give the person a 17+-year monopoly on the use and distribution of what has been given the patent—aren't a game for micro-ISVs for two reasons. First, it usually takes two to three years to successfully complete the process of applying for and being granted a patent by the U.S. Patent and Trademark Office (PTO). Second, it can take a lot of money; $100,000 is a good starting figure.

Trade secrets are another tool in the IP arsenal, but they're really relevant to a micro-ISV only if your former employer decides to sue you, citing your alleged misuse of their proprietary information to benefit your micro-ISV at their expense.

Copyrights and trademarks do matter to micro-ISVs. *Copyright* is a legal device for letting the author of a literary work control how that work is used. Software, for the purposes of this law, is a literary work, and you automatically have a copyright on software you write. That means, in theory, no one can copy, distribute, display, or adapt the work without your permission. If someone infringes on your copyright, you can sue to make them stop and to pay. As usual with the law, however, the devil is in the details. Although your software automatically is copyrighted, unless it has been registered, the amount you can recover from an infringer in federal court is in most cases limited to actual damages you can—with difficulty—prove. If you've registered your software with the PTO, sue, and win, you'll be able to collect your attorney fees, court costs, and up to $100,000 per infringement (*statutory damages*) without having to prove what damage you actually suffered.

Registering your software usually costs $30, doesn't require an attorney, and in effect serves notice on would-be evildoers that messing with you will make them fresh meat for a contingency fee-minded carnivorous member of the Bar.

Trademarks for your software products and *service marks* for your Web-based micro-ISV service are another effective IP protection. A trademark or service mark establishes your legal right to the name, logo, or symbol of your product; costs from $275 to $375 per filing (depending on how its filed); and can take 18 months to approve.

Although you can file online with the PTO (http://www.uspto.gov/teas/index.html), numerous online services such as LegalZoom.com (http://legalzoom.com), as shown in Figure 4-8, are competing for your business and can make the process of finding a trademarkable name or symbol and filing the correct paperwork relatively pain free.

Figure 4-8. *Using LegalZoom.com*

Now, you may be wondering what with all the online legal services and the multitude of self-help legal advice books from Nolo Press (http://www.nolo.com/index.cfm) and other publishers whether you actually need a real, live lawyer. Read on.

PATRICK CUNNINGHAM, ATTORNEY

Attorney Patrick Cunningham runs his solo attorney practice from next to the old Pacific Stock Exchange in downtown San Francisco. I've known Patrick for more than 15 years, and as I was putting together this section of this book, I wanted to ask him about what a good attorney can do for someone starting a micro-ISV.

Q. What can an attorney do for someone starting a micro-ISV that they can't do online today?

A. Well, I think the counseling aspect is critical. People don't want to hear this, but you can give a macro view because of your experience whether the business they are proposing to do really makes sense compared to his other clients, some of whom have made money, some of whom have lost money. He can maybe give you some initial input on that. Then of course one of the critical things that any attorney can do is the tax angle. You can't make a business decision without considering the tax consequences. A lot of business owners don't think about that when they are just starting.

Another thing related to the taxation is what type of business entity is going to make the most sense for you.

Q. Let's take the issue of partnerships. On several occasions I've seen a couple guys get together to start a software company only to have it turn into a mess. One partner wants more, another wants out, and so on. What can an attorney do to help?

A. They can create a partnership agreement that will really work. And the first step is to have a written agreement. A lot of people don't. But if you have a written agreement, then you have to think about what you're going to write in that agreement and hopefully you think it through very clearly.

But even if you have a very, very simple written agreement, at least you have the basics of an agreement between the two of you that's signed, and when you do fall apart—as nine out of ten will—you've got a place to work from that's not 100 miles from where the other guy is coming from.

Q. Do attorneys often negotiate partnership agreements between partners?

A. They can, but in a very small setting what often happens is two partners go to an attorney and say, "We want to become partners. Can you draw up the papers?" and the attorney can't negotiate because which side is he going to be on? He can only ask them, why don't you two come up with an agreement, and I'll help you make that into a legal document?

Q. What else can an attorney do for an aspiring young business?

A. Number one is, make sure there's a written agreement. Make sure it's in the proper form. Make sure they have the proper business permits. They can introduce you to an accountant, which will probably be helpful to organize your accounting records [or] at least get a structure set up. Familiarize yourself a little bit with the laws of trademark and trade names so you don't run afoul there. Talk with you about accounting and taxation. Talk to you about insurance for your business; maybe introduce you to an insurance broker or agent.

Q. Should small businesses find small law firms or go with big law firms?

A. Well, probably the very large law firms don't want the very small business, and the small businesses can't afford a larger law firm, for the most part. I do think for the smaller entrepreneur having a solo practitioner or a small law firm—fewer than ten attorneys in the law firm—would be better. You would have a more personal relationship with your legal counsel. And you can afford the rates a little better. It's a little cheaper—maybe a lot cheaper.

Q. Should that business owner find a lawyer when they need them or before they need them?

A. Absolutely before you need them. If you have a lawyer who helps you with the business when you start it—and you should budget for legal when you start your business—when a problem arises, you'll have someone you can call who may be able to help you directly with the problem or refer you to someone who can.

So you're going to have that kind of security blanket, that kind of member of the team.

Q. If someone you knew were going to start a micro-ISV, and they came to you and asked, how do I find a good lawyer? What would you tell them to do? Just pick a name in the phone book?

A. I think the first step is to contact a lawyer, maybe someone you have some kind of relationship with, a personal or family relationship or some pre-existing relationship, and get a referral. Most lawyers do have a network of acquaintances in different areas of law.

Another good place to start is local lawyer referral organizations; for example, in San Francisco there's BASF—Bar Association of San Francisco—they have lawyers who participate in their panels divided up according to practice areas.

Q. OK, so let's say you find John Smith, esquire. What would the lawyer expect you to ask?

A. The lawyer would expect you to ask if he had a firm résumé; some of the smaller firms do have them, some do not. You could ask them about any specializations they have; the state bar specializations in different areas. You can ask them what additional degrees they may have beyond their law certificate. You can ask him what percentage of his work is dedicated towards business organizations. You might even ask them if he can name to you any of his, shall we say, model clients.

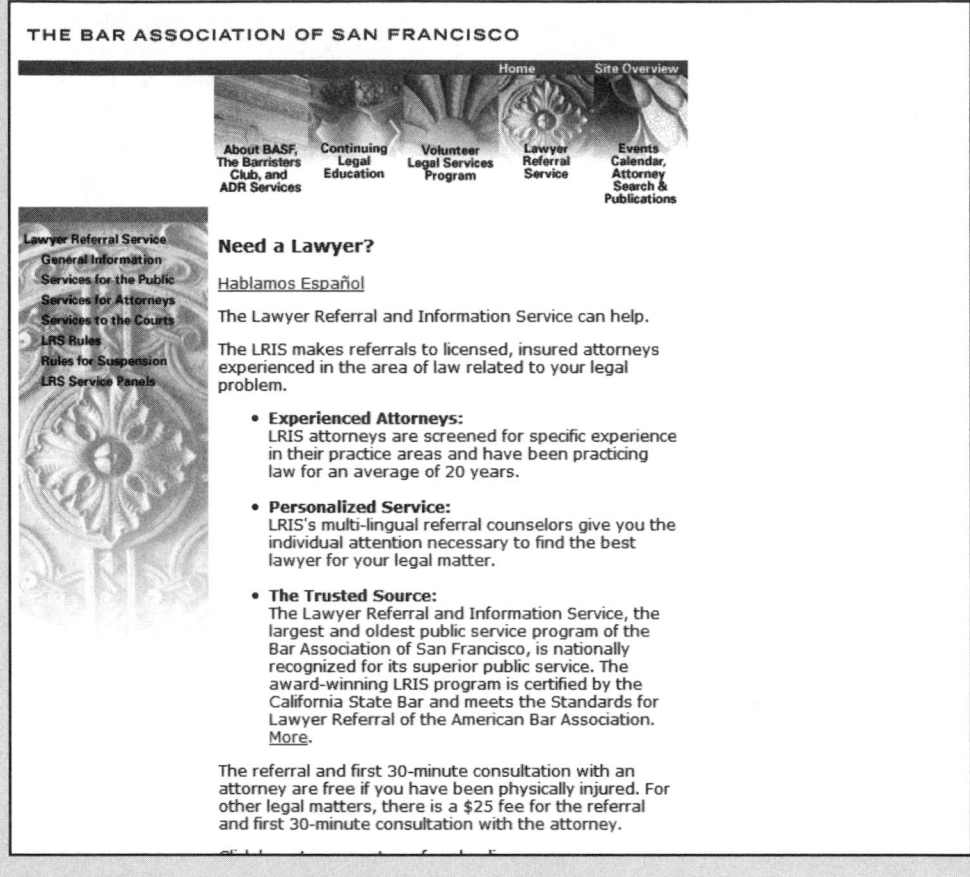

Need a lawyer, start with your local bar association.

Q. Any other advice you'd give to someone starting a micro-ISV?

A. Well, one piece of advice I have heard that I think is valid is that before you hire your first employee, have an employee manual. Oh, and this is critical if you do nothing else—before you hire your first employee, have workers' compensation insurance set up before the person sits in his chair, or her chair, so that she's insured for worker's comp.

If you have an employee—or anyone working for you for that matter—who you may call an independent contractor and that person trips over a chair in your office and, say, sustains a brain injury, you're facing catastrophic financial repercussions, if you're not insured for comp. If you are insured for comp, it's not a problem for you. Worker's comp insurance is not as expensive as you think.

Q. I'm confused. I thought someone had to be an employee to be covered by worker's comp?

A. In California the law presumes that someone doing services for another is an employee. And then it's the burden of the employer to prove that the person is not his employee but an independent contractor. Generally speaking, it's difficult to carry the burden when you're up against the presumption of employment.

It's going to be heard in the Workmen's Compensation Board with that presumption of employment, and in fact the Comp Board is required to let us, say, favor the employee in a comp case. It's very likely that the person you thought was just your part-time independent contractor is in fact your employee.

Q. Gotcha!

A. Yeah. And suppose you have a part-time independent contractor doing some work for your firm, and he's working for you 20 hours a week on a regular basis but he's an independent contractor; that's the way you arrange it. And you send them down to Radio Shack to pick up a computer cord. And on the way, he hits a pedestrian in the crosswalk. And then you find out he doesn't have insurance. You're going to be sued. And again, you're probably going to lose, because of the presumption of employment.

Q. *Well, these are the sorts of things it might be good to know about before they happen.*

A. Before it happens. Before it happens. You're in business to make money, right?

Q. *Right!*

A. And you want to make money, but at the same time you don't want to lose money…lose your financial future. So you have to approach it with some degree of caution.

Q. *So this is why you want to have someone—I'm not going to say adult supervision—but somebody who knows what they are talking about.*

A. Yes, absolutely.

And What About the Government?

Finally, I interviewed Teri Takahashi, the training manager for the Florida Atlantic University Small Business Development Center (FAUSBDC, and you thought computer acronyms were bad!), and she has some advice for micro-ISVs worth passing on.

FAUSBDC, as shown in Figure 4-9, offers 450 classes and clinics a year, the vast majority for free, for start-up businesspeople in the areas of business planning, marketing, financing, accounting, bookkeeping, taxes, import/export disaster recovery, and more. The classes—typically two to four hours, the most expensive of which is $100—then get followed up with one-on-one mentoring between you and SBDC staff, for free.

For example, FAUSBDC has a business plan clinic: "It's four hours, in which you get your template started, what is a business plan, and why do [you] want one type of thing," Teri says.

> *We don't do extensive training; our training is two to four hours, and that's it—a one-shot deal, you come in, and you're done. Our training seminars are set up so you get good information in as short a time as possible, [and] then we encourage you to follow that up with one-on-one consulting forever, for as long as you want.*

> *Say you come in and come to the Introduction to Business Plans seminar. After you go there, you get a good, basic idea of what you need to do, then you come in and work with somebody one on one. It's always free, we're the federal government.*

"Your tax dollars at work," she emphatically adds.

FAUSBDC is part of a network of federally funded Small Business Development Centers (SBDC) funded through the SBA. They all offer classes for people who want to start their own business, and most offer one-to-one mentoring as well.

Although the SBDC near you will be clueless regarding the ins and outs of programming, they know a lot about the business side of being in business and can give you some objective advice on whether you really are the type of person who can start a business or would be better off staying within the structure of an existing company.

To find the SBDC near you (and there is one, believe me) at the America's Small Business Development Center Network site at `http://asbdc-us.org/`, click Lead Centers at the top. Click the FastTrac link, especially the FastTrac Tech information. As a matter of fact, you'll find a lot of interesting to micro-ISV links listed here.

Figure 4-9. *One of 450 members of the SBDC network*

CHAPTER 5

■■■

Focusing on the Customer

So far in this book I've focused on how you'll define, construct, beta test, and market your micro-ISV's first product. And I talked about customers and would-be customers in a general way: how they can help you define your application, service, or product as beta testers, why your Web site needs to be customer-centric and not product-centric, and so forth.

All this work in producing your micro-ISV has been to get to this point, when you can start focusing on and creating paying customers.

This chapter will dig deep into three major marketing topics: how to find your customers, how to interact with them, and how they will find you. I'll start with how to locate the sometimes-elusive customer by researching offline habits and online haunts, how they see the world, and how you reach an identifiable collection of them. This is the stuff MBAs like to call *market research*, *market segmentation*, and *marketing plans*, and I'll use those same terms but gear the approach to the Internet and the realities of being a micro-ISV.

Next, I'll cover how to interact with customers and potential customers via email and, most important, via your technical support process. Finally, I'll show you how to make sure potential clients can find you, the trial version of your product, and other people interested in it.

Your Marketing Re-Education

Although you may think you know what marketing is, don't bet on it. Remember all those jokes and Dilbert cartoons about marketing people? Surprise! When you get past the marketing of marketing and the fluff, a lot of well-tested, repeatable, applicable techniques consistently yield results you can take to the bank, if you apply them.

So, as a first step, put aside the usual IT bias against marketing, and keep in mind you're about to start having a new type of relationship with (you hope) a whole lot of people all over Earth. Customers aren't employers, managers, bosses, project managers, or clients. And they're not co-workers, friends, buddies, or even acquaintances. They're something else entirely, and you need to learn the ins and outs of this new kind of relationship if your micro-ISV is going to succeed.

The next step is to stop thinking about the supercolossal, megabig monster called The Market and start thinking about small slivers of people who, if they know about your product and what it could do for them, could become your very own market. You don't need, don't want, and can't cope with 20 million customers at your online door today; one in twenty of all the left-handed accountants in firms of fewer than ten people will do quite nicely for your bank account for starters.

The final step in your marketing re-education before you start working on how to market your micro-ISV is to firmly ignore all the ways large companies have marketed to *you*. Ditch all the television, radio, newspaper, magazine, billboard, and online banner advertising you've been taught in your lifelong education as a consumer. All that advertising and marketing you see every day (it's estimated that a person in the United States sees from 245 to 6,000 marketing messages a day[1]) is completely irrelevant to how you and your micro-ISV will market. Why? If for no other reason, you can't afford it.

That's the bad news. Advertising works—that's why millions of businesses worldwide spend hundreds of billions of dollars on it each year. The good news is you have something that can work better than advertising: you have value and a story to tell. The trick—and the first part of this chapter—is about finding the right people to tell in the right way about that value.

Marketing for Micro-ISVs

In Chapter 1 you started scoping out the market for your micro-ISV's vision. To briefly recap, I covered how to do the basic online market research to determine whether other people (those with money!) might be interested in your product, and you identified at least three market segments you could target later.

It's later!

Now, if you skipped ahead because you already have your vision and what you need are real, live customers, and you need them *now* because no one is buying your software, I understand. That's the situation I found myself in back in spring 2005 when my Microsoft buddy Jason Hermitage started taking the time to gently hammer into my programmer brain that a business needs to identify specific markets and address them to succeed.

"Bob, think about who needs MasterList Professional," Jason would say during our twice-a-month phone calls. "What do they do for a living? Who do they hang out with? Who do they associate with? What do they want?"

You'll hear more about Jason in Chapter 6; he's a genuinely Smart Guy. Right now, it's time to get down to the particulars of how you discover, understand, connect to, and get known in a specific Internet market.

Internet market? What's that? Well, it's the place your micro-ISV lives, and unfortunately, it's a place few of the "How to Start Your Own Business" and "How to Create a Marketing Plan" authors and experts understand.

I'll focus on two information tools I've created because micro-ISVs need to research, create, and implement marketing plans: the Specific Internet Marketing Segment (SIMS) Planner and the Marketing Segment Action Planner (MAP). You can find free versions of both these planners at this book's Web page at `http://www.apress.com/` and at `http://www.microisv.com/`.

Here's how to use SIMS and MAP: take a look at your research from Chapter 1, and pick one of the smallest, least critical market segments you identified there. Or, define one right now. Why small and (to be polite) least critical? Micro-ISV marketing, like performing surgery on yourself, should first be done on a nonvital part of your anatomy. Once you get the technique down and your confidence up, you can move on to bigger and better.

---

1. How many advertising messages (from all media sources) is the average American exposed to on a daily basis? See `http://answers.google.com/answers/threadview?id=56750`.

These planners are starting points, not stone tablets. Undoubtedly, as you work through them, you'll find ways to make them work better for your micro-ISV. But by working through them, you'll take the most valuable step to making a rootin'-tootin', revenue-producing success of your micro-ISV: identifying a specific market segment and doing the work necessary so the market segment learns about your software, Web service, or product.

Starting with SIMS

Now, if you were reading this online at one of the ever-multiplying "Get Rich on the Internet with Our Secret Formula" sites, here's where I'd tell you that SIMS will make you 247 percent richer in only a single afternoon while watching your favorite spectator sport if—*and only if*—you send me your $79.87 right now.

Nope. Sorry. No secret sauce here. Although I'd be happy if you sent me your money, SIMS is just a set of pretty logical questions you'll have to answer for your micro-ISV. Rather, think of SIMS as being a set of those fiendishly clever puzzles companies such as Microsoft and Google like to spring during job interviews, only they are nowhere near as hard.

SPECIFIC INTERNET MARKET SEGMENT (SIMS) PLANNER

The goal of SIMS is to define in as much practical detail the attributes, characteristics, influences, and needs shared by a specific online group of people who have an unmet need your product fulfills. The keyword in that sentence is *practical*: fill in what you can, define these people in a way that can be marketed to, and go from there.

Preliminary Definition

- What is the general term for this market?

- What segment of that market am I focusing on?

Characteristics/Demographics/Market Size

- Professional, amateur, nonprofit, consumer, small business, company, enterprise, multinational?

- What language do they use?

- What occupation titles describe what they do?

- How many of these people are employed?

- Is the number of people in this market segment increasing, decreasing, or holding steady?

- How many of them are on the Net?

- How old are they?

- How do they become part of this market segment? How do they leave?

- Are there educational, training, or other requirements to join this market segment? Who controls those requirements?

- What's the size of the market?

Purchase Habits

- What goods are bought by this market segment?

- What services are bought by this market segment?

- What things do people need to have access to in this market segment?

- What things do people in this market segment buy on the Net?

- Do they buy for themselves, or does someone buy for them?

Needs and Wants

- How do people in this market segment define success?

- What do they need to be successful?

- What unmet or undermet needs do people in this market segment have?

The Internet

- How do people in this market segment connect to the Internet?

- Where do people in this market segment connect from?

- What are the top community/portal Web sites people in this market segment currently visit?

Associations (Online and Off)

- What associations (industry, professional, nonprofit) specifically serve this market segment?

- Which ones have Web sites?

- Does this market segment have one or more active mailing lists?

- Does this market segment have one or more active Usenet groups?

- Does this market segment have one or more active Google Groups?

- Does this market segment have one or more active Yahoo Groups?

Trade Press/Trade Shows

- What publications (magazines, weeklies, dailies, or newsletters) do people in this market segment read offline to keep up to date?

- Which of these publications have Web sites?

- Which writers or editors for these publications have blogs?

- What trade shows are held regularly for members of this market?

Blogs

- What blogs can I find about this market segment at Technorati.com?

- What blogs can I find about this market segment at Blogcatalog.com?

- What blogs can I find about this market segment in Google Directory?

- What blogs can I find about this market segment at Feedster.com?

Competitors

- What competitors for my potential customers' time are there in this market segment?

- What competitors for my potential customers' money are there in this market segment?

- Who are the top competitors in this market segment?

- What are their strengths compared to my product or service?

- What are their weaknesses compared to my product or service?

- How do my competitors sell to this market segment?

- What do my competitors charge?

My Selling Proposition for This Market Segment

- How can my micro-ISV's product make people in this market segment successful?

- What is different and better about my product than my competitors in this market segment?

- What's my Unique Selling Proposition (USP) to this market segment?

- What are the key benefits of my product or service for people in this market segment?

James Thurber, a great 20th-century humorist once said, "It is better to know some of the questions than all of the answers." By asking the right questions about one small sliver of all the people on the Net who might want to buy from your micro-ISV, you'll be well on your way to answering the question your relatives, friends, and former co-workers will ask: "Are you making any money?"

Hand Me the MAP, Please

Once you've worked through the questions about your target market segment, you can start planning and implementing how you connect with your target. MAP is one way to define the objectives and tasks you'll need to execute in order to get results, as shown in Figure 5-1.

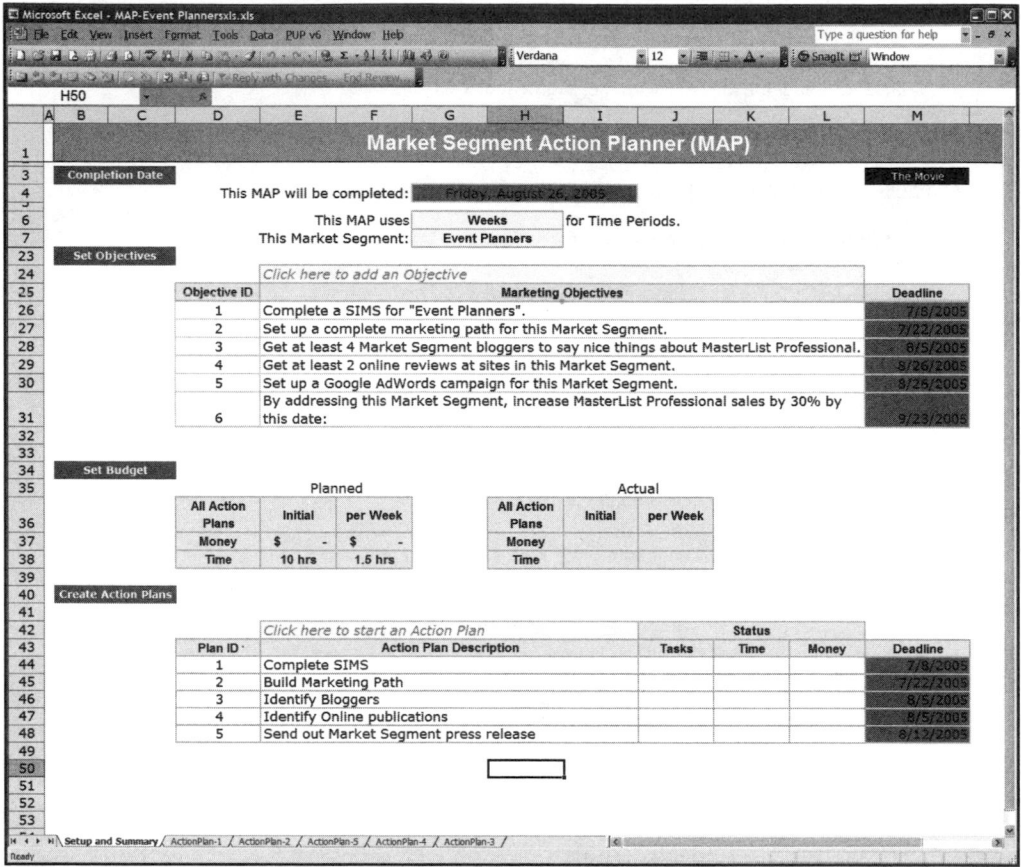

Figure 5-1. *MAP your marketing to event planners.*

Although the MAP I've written in Microsoft Excel has a few nice touches to make it easier for you to define your marketing objectives in measurable terms, parse those objectives into specific tasks, and track those tasks through execution, the best MAP is the one that works for you. If you're not already using some tool (the MAP template, a big whiteboard, Microsoft Outlook, an open source project manager, or maybe even your own product), now is the time to start tracking the specifics of marketing your micro-ISV.

The specifics of your MAP will turn out differently than the one shown in Figure 5-1, but here are a couple of MAP tips to keep in mind:

Get specific: With your SIMS, you've gotten a lot of information about your target market segment. Now it's time to define specific objectives about how to connect with that market segment and to schedule the time you need to do the work.

Make your target market segment feel special: Make the effort to build a landing page for that segment, along with a customized set of benefits that make sense to them. One sure-fire technique is to create one or more online demos where your product addresses one or more of your target market segment's problems.

Identify your target market segment's bloggers and trade press, and reach out to them: I'll cover in more depth how to deal with the trade press and mainstream media in the section "The Influencers" later in this chapter. For bloggers, the best way is simply to email them, explain why your product is interesting to them and their readers, and go from there.

Find and execute ways to bring your micro-ISV's existence directly to the attention of potential customers in your target market segment: Later, in the section "Google, Relevancy, and Your Micro-ISV," I'll cover one of my favorite ways of doing this: Google AdWords. But whether it's participating in online forums, joining mailing lists, writing online articles for Web sites where your market segment hangs out, or doing some other form of marketing, take steps to get visible.

Email: Retail, Wholesale, and You

Starting a micro-ISV may make you richer, happier, and more fulfilled. But I guarantee starting a micro-ISV means you'll be spammed like never before. Worse, if you don't plan ahead, people will start accusing *you* of being a spammer.

The purpose of the following sections is threefold: develop a plan for handling an order of magnitude more email you'll get as an micro-ISV, learn the rules and tools you should follow and use now that you're a business, and finally look at how you should and shouldn't communicate with your customers—potential and otherwise.

You Have Mail—Lots of It!

Being a micro-ISV means you need to change how you deal with email and spam. For starters, a whole bunch of people not on your email whitelist are going to start firing off messages to you: they're called *customers*, and you want to respond to every one of them in a timely manner without going nuts.

Second, *anonymous seller* is an oxymoron. If you plan to sell your software, hardware, or services on the Net, customers will expect to be able to contact you, which means you'll need at least one public email address spammers will have ten minutes after you post it to your Web site.

So, depending on how you get/filter email now, you may need to change spam filters, your Inbox configuration, and your email addresses to meet the demands of your business. Table 5-1 gives you a checklist of email tasks to do.

Table 5-1. *Checklist for Reconfiguring Your Email World*

What?	Why?
Set up a new private email address.	This is the address you'll be giving to family, friends, and loved ones and will never, ever use for business.
Set up, at a minimum, four new micro-ISV addresses: techsupport@, sales@, info@, and you@.	These should be new addresses at your micro-ISV's domain (Hotmail/Gmail isn't acceptable); these are the roles you'll need to play.
Turn off/unsubscribe from any service you now use that requires new correspondents to prove they aren't spammers.	Potential customers will not stand for it.

Table 5-1. *Checklist for Reconfiguring Your Email World (Continued)*

What?	Why?
Configure your spam filter to hold, not delete, supposed spam.	Even the best Baysian spam filters will bag some inquiries from potential customers; you'll need to review all spam to catch these "false positives."
Prepare a signature file.	This is a small sales/CAN-SPAM notice that needs to be at the bottom of each original email from your micro-ISV. (See the "Current Email Marketing Realities" section for more about the CAN-SPAM Act.)
Reorganize your email folders to be aligned and streamlined to your micro-ISV.	The specifics will vary with your micro-ISV and email client, but you want to separate your email into an Action folder for what you need to do or respond to in your micro-ISV, a Reference folder for nonaction emails relating to your business and receipts, and a Nonbusiness folder for everything else.

Also, it's a good idea to put in place an automated bug-tracking system that manages your tech support email as part of your overall email strategy. (See the section "Technical Support Is Customer Support" later in this chapter.)

You Can't Say That Anymore!

Now that I've covered how to reconfigure how you handle your email, I'll cover how to reconfigure you—or at least the part of your brain you use to write and respond to email. You need to realize that the rules for permissible/acceptable/desirable emails changed when you started working for yourself, and worse, you're now the dreaded email cop.

Put another way, you'll be swapping emails with hundreds, if not thousands, of strangers from all over the world, and you need to develop or at least refine your "email voice" so that it's effective and, well, businesslike.

This doesn't mean you need to sound like a commercial or be boring or dull. It means you need to keep in the back of your head two thoughts:

- The purpose of any email you write is to further your business.

- Law 1440 never takes a break.

Table 5-2 provides a short list of business email dos and don'ts to copy and stick by your keyboard until they become second nature.

Table 5-2. *Business Email Dos and Don'ts*

Do	Don't
Do focus on the reason for the email.	Don't ever curse, insult, or swear, no matter the provocation. (And you'll get people who write you long emails along the lines of "Your software is a pile of crap, and you're a worthless human being for writing it.") Your first instinct may be to sear their eyes out of their head with a flaming email. Don't. Either drive them crazy(ier) with a "Thank you for your input" one-liner or ignore them.

Table 5-2. *Business Email Dos and Don'ts*

Do	Don't
Do be cheerful, helpful, and unapologetic.	Don't be defensive, sullen, or argumentative.
Do be clear in what you're telling them or asking them to do.	Don't assume their primary language is your primary language.
Do make clear what you want from them and or what you'll be doing.	Don't make assumptions about gender or nationality based on the person's name. (In fact, gender, nationality, politics, religion, and personal stuff in general has no place in your business emails.)

TOOLS FOR LEVERAGING EMAIL

This sidebar introduces four mail-related tools to help impress your customers with your micro-ISV's email responsiveness and (not incidentally) reduce the amount of time you need to spend.

The first tool you can use to leverage email is an autoresponder. Whether you set up autoresponders within your email server, your ISP's email management tool, or a third party, autoresponders are an excellent way to automatically respond to an email and provide stock information to current and prospective customers who, for whatever reason, did not find what they needed on your Web site.

A nice feature of the actual content of your autoresponse is you can write it once and then repurpose it or write the content for other reasons and repackage it. Here are a few typical autoresponder topics:

- *Policies*: For example, support information, upgrade information, how to run your software on more than one computer, transferring ownership, and returns.

- *Sales information*: For example, general sales, corporate/site sales, nonprofit organization sales, and governmental entity sales.

- *Guides*: For example, a getting-started guide, a reviewer guide, and an integration guide.

- *Email courses*: For example, this is a good technique: write a "How to Get the Most Out of Our Software in Five Easy Daily Lessons" set of five one-page HTML emails. You can offer the emails on your site and include a mailto link at the bottom of each one linking to the next lesson.

Note that you should clearly state that the content comes from an autoresponder email address. And, you should clearly state either that the emails of people who tap your autoresponders fall under your general antispam/privacy policy or, better still, that they will not be used or saved for any purpose except sending the requested information. I know, most micro-ISVs' first inclination is to persist any and all data, but resist it: autoresponders will work only if the potential customer is assured they won't be pummeled with advertising.

The second tool I'll cover is for Outlook users who use Microsoft Word as their email editor: capturing and reusing stock information using Word's AutoText tool. With AutoText, you can capture your product's name, main benefits, or a complete description as an abbreviation that Word will automatically expand. Here are two articles I've written about using AutoText: http://www.safarisoftware.com/fTip3.htm and http://www.safarisoftware.com/fTip36.htm.

AutoText is nice, and it's free if you own Microsoft Office. But the next two tools take leveraging your text much further.

Using AnswerTool from DTLink Software (http://www.answertool.com) could not be easier; after writing something you want to reuse, go to AnswerTool, create a new topic, and paste it in. When you want to reuse that text, go to AnswerTool, select the topic to put the text (plain or HTML) on the Clipboard, and then paste it into your email. At $29.95 USD (as of this writing) and available for a free 15-day trial, AnswerTool might be the right solution for you.

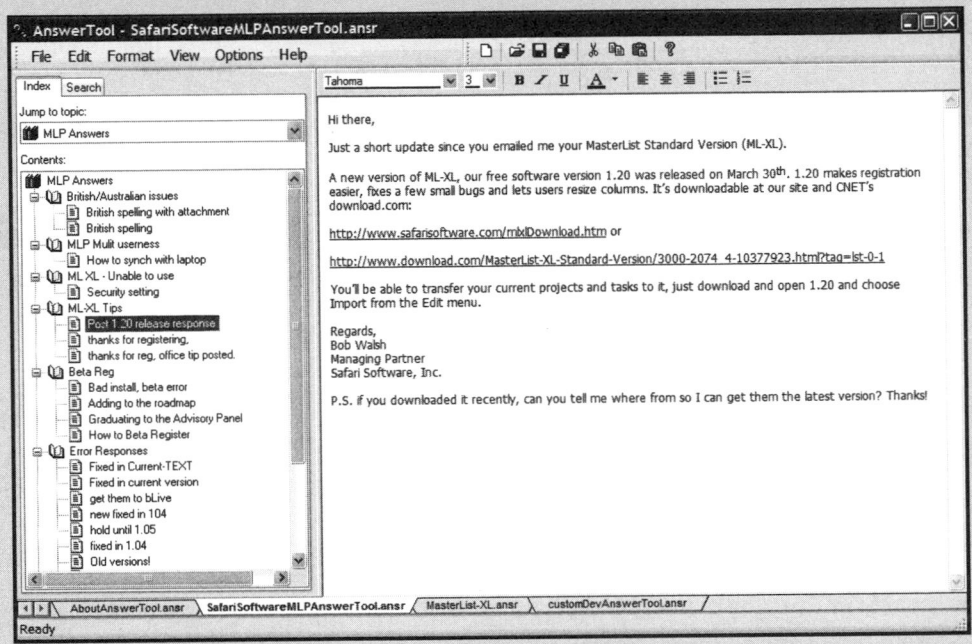

AnswerTool makes it easy to build a library of responses.

The fourth email tool is ActiveWords (http://activewords.com, three versions starting at $19.95 USD, 60-day trial). ActiveWords is like adding a universal command prompt to your computer. The concept behind ActiveWords is deceptively simple: you type a word—say, *blurb*—and activate it by pressing F8, and the word is replaced by your 200-word product description. It doesn't matter whether you're replying to an email, posting to your blog, submitting information to a Web site, writing in Word, or creating content in your HTML editor. Type the word, hit F8, and get your text (or run a program, open a uniform resource locator [URL], or run a script).

Or type **maps+F8** to pull up Google Maps. Or type **email+F8** to see Outlook open a new email editor window for you. Or type **buy+F8** to choose whether you wanted to go to Amazon, Best Buy, or CDW (my personal choices, as is F8). As you start getting the hang of it and enlarge your ActiveWords vocabulary, you'll wonder how you ever got anything done without it.

One final word about ActiveWords: the two-man micro-ISV behind the product, ActiveWords Systems, does an extremely good job of marketing via email—it's worth downloading the 60-day trial just to see what good email marketing looks like.

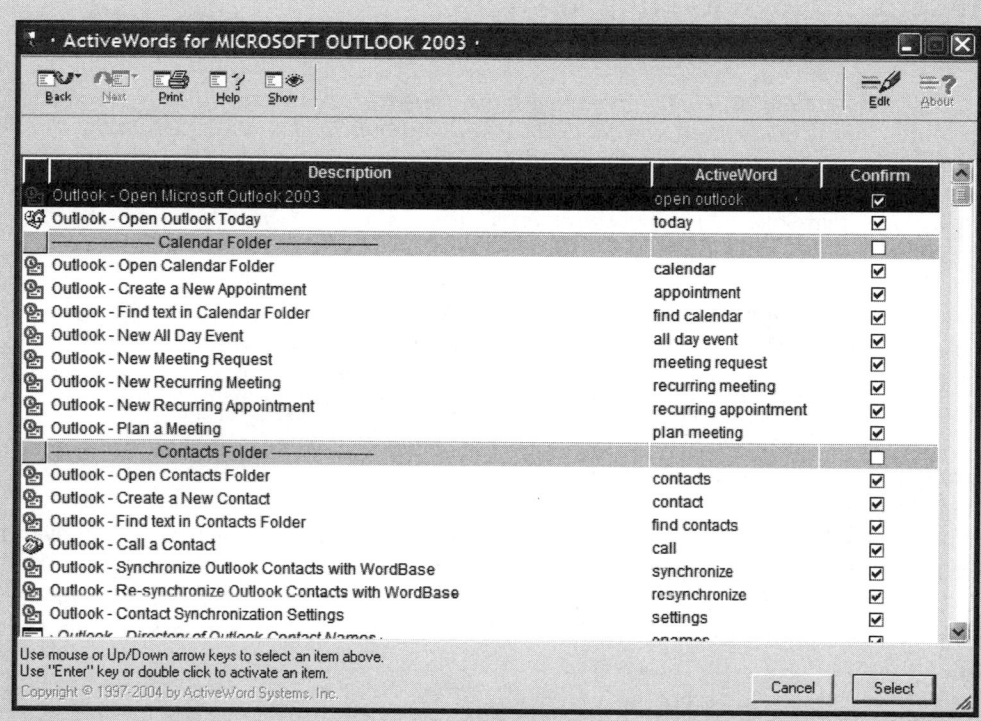

Some of the activewords used for controlling Microsoft Outlook

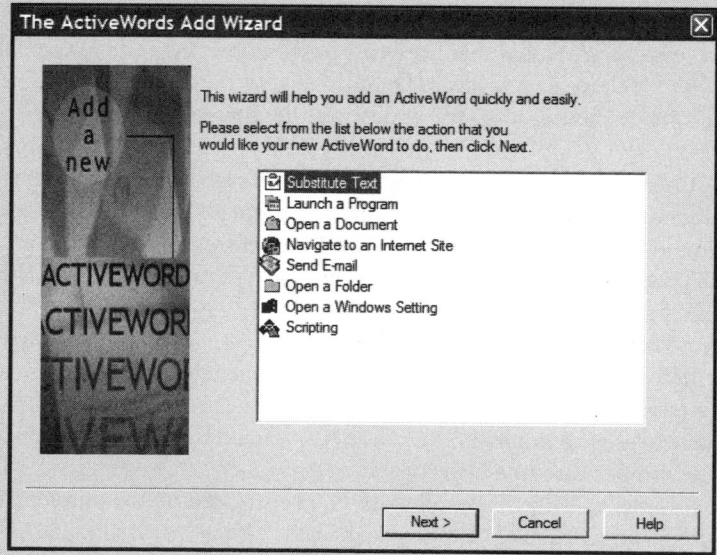

Things you can make your PC do easily with ActiveWords. Notice the scripting.

Current Email Marketing Realities

(Washington, D.C., May 26, 2008)—The Centers for Disease Control announced today the eradication of the last-known spammer in the United States, Melvin Bulleseye, pleading that he didn't really mean to send 25,000 emails announcing his new MelvinBull 2.0 to the end, was put to death in the now traditional way of being locked in a room with 1,000 starving rats and a lawyer. "After I stripped him of his assets, the rest was easy," said Jennifer Gotem, 24, when she emerged from the room. "The rats did most of the work," she added modestly.

Done right, email marketing can bring smiles to your customers' lips and money to your micro-ISV's bank account. Done wrong, and you get to join Melvin. I simply can't overstate how vital it is for your micro-ISV's continued existence that you understand what you should and shouldn't do when it comes to using email as a marketing tool.

Email is an essential tool for a micro-ISV, but as of mid-2005 the carcinogenic spread of spam has forcefully rewritten the rules; these rules, at least in the United States, have become federal law.

The CAN-SPAM Act now requires those who send commercial email (that's you) to provide in each email a way for the recipient to opt out of receiving any further emails, to identify the email as an advertisement, and to include the sender's valid physical postal address. It prohibits using fake originating headers, deceptive subject lines, or harvested emails from sites that have posted a notice (http://www.ftc.gov/bcp/conline/pubs/buspubs/canspam.htm).

Now, in case you just searched for the CAN-SPAM Act on Google and found various blogs, news stories, and other comments that the act has no teeth and no one but flagrant professional spammers have been pursued by the Federal Trade Commission (FTC), consider two points. First, in the United States, the typical way consumer protections such as protections against deceptive advertising, unfair debt collection practices, and being stuck with a terminally defective car become part of the business culture is that first Congress passes a law, then the FTC nails a few flagrant violators, then the FTC tweaks the law to be more realistic, then the states start passing various supplemental laws, and finally everybody gets the message that it's Not Good Business.

Second, the U.S. Department of Labor's Bureau of Labor Statistics estimates between now and the year 2012 the number of lawyers (currently estimated at about 500,000) will increase about 10 to 20 percent a year. Just how long do you think it will be before a "SueTheSpammer.com" lets you click a button to have the site scan your offending email and you receive the first of many unpleasant legal communications?

My point here is not only should you follow the letter of the law when it comes to how your business emails but the spirit as well. And following business best practices unless you have a very good reason not to is a good way to stay in business.

So, what are the best practices for a micro-ISV that wants and needs to email current and prospective customers? The number-one rule is to comply with CAN-SPAM, even if you think you can get away with not complying. This means all your email correspondence should use real headers, descriptive subject lines, include your physical postal address (as of May 2005, the FTC wanted to tweak this to allow P.O. box addresses), and a clear means to opt out from being emailed by you.

Although managing a customer database tied to an unsubscribe form in your favorite programming language (PHP, ASP, and so on) is fairly easy at first, the devil (and the distractions from your core activities) is in the details. Managing your mailing list is another one of those activities that lends itself to paying someone else to do it right.

MailerMailer (`http://www.mailermailer.com`) is one company in the business of managing a company's mailing lists. "We actually have a lot of software companies using our system," explains Raj Khera, CEO of MailerMailer. "And one of the things we've found is just the ability to be able to communicate with your customers on a regular basis is very critical in differentiating you from the competition, because not everyone will necessarily keep in contact with you after you make a purchase."

MailerMailer—which was started as a post-dot-com micro-ISV by Raj Khera and his brother, Bivek Khera—handles the opt-in process of subscribing to a company's mailing list and then sends a confirmation email to the supposed subscriber email address. It also gives the subscriber an easy way to opt out of your mailing list at any time and automatically includes this information in any emails (such as marketing promotions, upgrade announcements, and email newsletters) you send your list through MailerMailer.com.

This is according to Raj Khera:

> One of the big benefits of using a double opt-in list like MailerMailer.com is that you've verified everyone's intent of being on your list. There's no chance someone could download some software, put in a fake address just to get access to your software, and then just go about on their merry way. This way [double opt-in], they've actually confirmed their address, and you know you have a real person you're talking to.

Like a lot of micro-ISVs, MailerMailer has a free trial available—you can send 200 emails a month free. The paid service starts at $29.95 a month for 20,000 messages and goes up from there. MailerMailer has a nice control console that makes making and managing mass emails easy, as shown in Figure 5-2.

As for CAN-SPAM, which doesn't require double opt-in, Khera says this:

> At MailerMailer.com, we try [to] follow the best practices, which happens to include the law, but there's actually many more things we do on top of the law to try [to] make it a better experience for both the list manager and the recipient.

Khera's take on where email marketing is going is worth considering: "You hear these reports that spam is going to kill email marketing, but frankly, we just don't see it, and our numbers back us up." MailerMailer actually has the numbers, analyzing more than 200 million emails from more than 2,000 email marketers in 2004. Available at its sister site (`http://emailmarketingmetrics.com`), MailerMailer releases an "Email Marketing Trends" report every six months with industry-by-industry data on what makes an email work, how quickly permission-based email gets opened, and more.

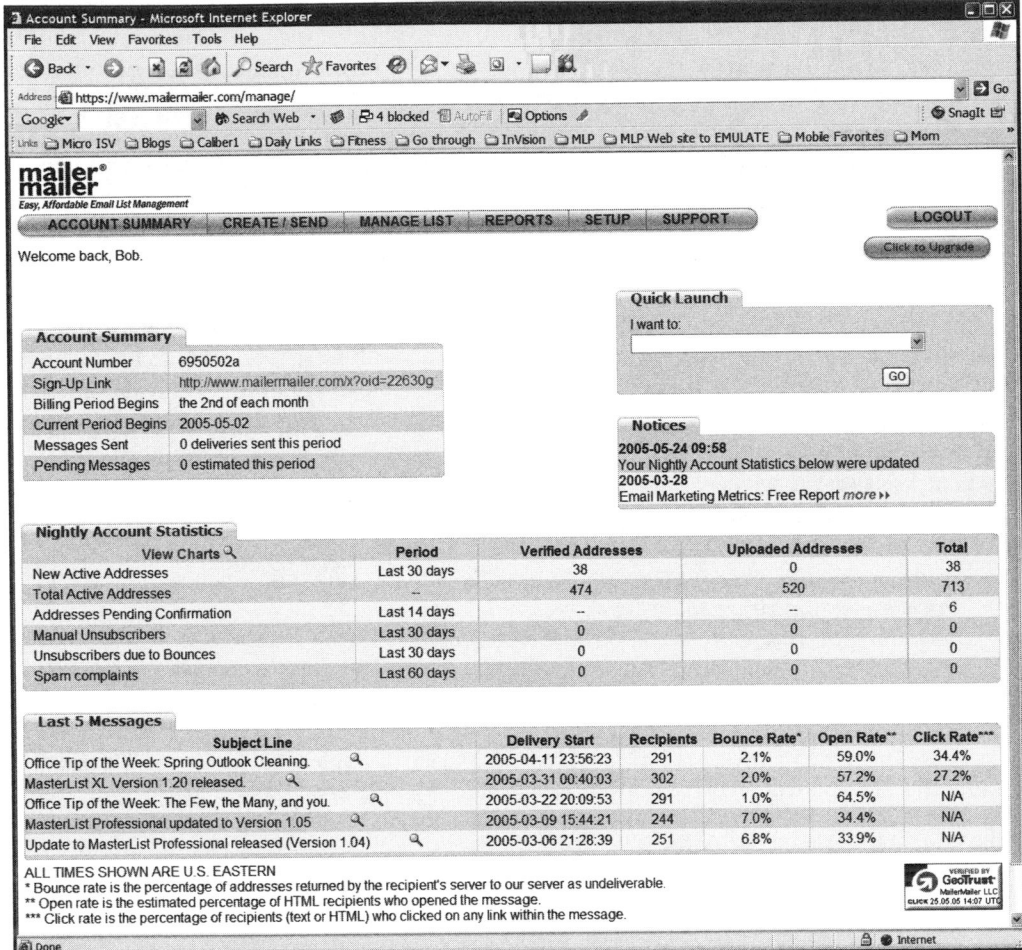

Figure 5-2. *The MailerMailer control console: notice the Open Rate and Click Rate columns.*

Khera advises that instead of looking at it as email marketing, look at it as a way of effectively distributing the traditional marketing tactic of company newsletters, without the printing costs and with the large advantage of being able to track who is actually reading your material.

> *Long before the Internet got commercialized, people were sending newsletters as a way of keeping in touch with their customers. What technology now allows you to do is save your money on print and production costs, and for a tiny fraction of what it costs to do a newsletter, you can do an email one and actually quantify your results. You'll know who's clicking on what. And that kind of data for the cost is invaluable [market research].*

One other point Khera makes is that while it varies from industry to industry, HTML emails have a higher click-through rate than plain-text emails, although plain text is favored by people in the computer industry.

Khera's advice to micro-ISVs pretty much sums up business emailing strategy today:

For everybody who downloads the product or purchases it, ask their permission to be on your email list. Then send regular notices—it could be monthly, even quarterly, although once a quarter is about the lowest frequency you want to go with—something to a least just say "hello" to your clients.

Maybe you're providing them with an online demo of your software, industry trends about that particular kind of product, or something to just touch base with those people every month or so. That alone will increase [the] loyalty of your customers. There's an old saying that if you're talking to your customers, they can't be talking to your competition. If you are talking to them, then you have a much higher chance of retaining their loyalty.

Technical Support Is Customer Support

"Well," like my dentist said as he started to remove the last for four wisdom teeth, "this next bit might be a kind of painful."

If you're reading this, odds are good you've already spent more of your life than you want to remember providing technical support at some company somewhere. At the least, you've spent some of your life trying to get technical support for something you bought or were thinking of buying.

But the painful fact is no matter how great your vision, how elegant your code, how robust your testing, you—yes, *you!*—will need to provide technical support for your micro-ISV's product. What's more, unlike large software and hardware vendors, you have to provide good—nay, *great*—technical support that sets you apart from your competitors.

No Sympathy for the Devil

Remember the last time you needed technical support? I do. About a month ago after replacing my computer with a spiffy laptop, I decided I wanted to change from streaming music and instead play a bunch of those 99-cent tunes I'd bought over the past year from an online music service that will go nameless. So, I loaded the software, added the tunes to the playlist, cued up "Sympathy for the Devil," and got the message "Permission denied. You do not have a valid license to play this music." What?

So, off I went to Nameless's Web site. I log into my account, figuring I could at least download again what I paid for, right? Wrong. Sometime between when they gleefully sucked 99 cents from my credit card and when I ungleefully found out which digit is extended when it comes to Digital Rights Management (DRM), these suckers had dumped my purchase history.

No purchase history, no rights. No rights, no music. So, I can either kiss off 40 bucks worth of music or hope that Nameless's tech support was better than their database programmers. I mean, they couldn't be as clueless, right? Ha.

Four times I emailed them, explaining I just wanted to play the music I bought on my new notebook, and I'd even go download them all, one by one—just give me something I could click. And four times I got back the same "read the following to fix your problem" email explaining why DRM is *good* for you and all I had to do was click the songs listed in my purchase history to download them again.

I would have been better off rolling up two twenties, wedging them up my nose, and setting them alight. To say I'd rather have my toenails ripped out than spend another dime at Nameless.com is a gross understatement.

I'm sure you've had at least one such descent into technical support hell yourself. Too many big companies have made a pact with the devil, and in exchange for somewhat lower costs, they consign your soul to voice mail, email, or Web "knowledgebase" hell.

Those companies may be able to get away with that, although I suspect not forever. You can't, not for much as a day. You're too small. And that's good—really, really good.

By providing your customers with great technical support, you'll convert many of those customers into raving fans instead of raging enemies. And those fans will put the *word* in word of mouth for you, both online and off.

Doing Tech Support Right

So, just how do you, a micro-ISV, provide great technical support without going nuts or broke or both? If you happen to be sitting next to a CEO of a multinational company while you're reading this, and they glance at this page, their answer is to offshore it—as far away as possible, as cheaply as possible.

Wrong answer.

I'll leave what's wrong with offshoring to my fellow Apress author, Bill Blunden, whose book *Offshoring IT: The Good, the Bad, and the Ugly* (Apress, 2004) does a great job of covering offshoring, both for and against, and instead focus on the micro-ISV practicalities:

- As a micro-ISV, you can't afford to offshore.

- As a micro-ISV, being close to and responsive to your potential and actual customers is too important a function to trust to others.

- As a micro-ISV, you can provide great technical support relatively easily if you plan for it: when the going gets tough, the tough use software.

If you're a entrepreneur first and a technical person second, think of technical support for your micro-ISV not as overhead or as a secondary priority but as a way of creating a vast, enthusiastic, believable, and unpaid sales force that will, without further supervision on your part, go find business opportunities, new market niches, and revenue for you.

And if you're a programmer first and a businessperson second, look at technical support for your micro-ISV not as the pain of dealing with dumb people who haven't a clue but as the error checking and code handling for your program—something that separates the amateurs from the professionals.

Whichever way you choose to view tech support, you'll want to put in place a comprehensive system for receiving, responding to, resolving, and learning from tech support incidents. And although many good help desk/tech support programs are available, if you've already read Chapter 2, you'll know what I'm going to say here: get Fog Creek Software's FogBugz (http://www.fogcreek.com, $129 per user, free 45-day online trial, 90-day money-back guarantee).

Tech Support Is Like Beta Support, Only More So

Put simply, you'll need all the same elements you needed to make beta testing during development work for you, only more so. If you didn't put in place a system then, now is the time for a quick review of what you need from your tech support system if you're going to succeed.

As I suggested in Chapter 2, baking error reporting into your software or Web site is one of those Really Good Ideas: it shows people you're ready, willing, and able to take bugs seriously.

For example, I'll walk you through what happens when an exception gets raised the hard way in my software. Figure 5-3 shows an error report automatically generated by MasterList Professional.

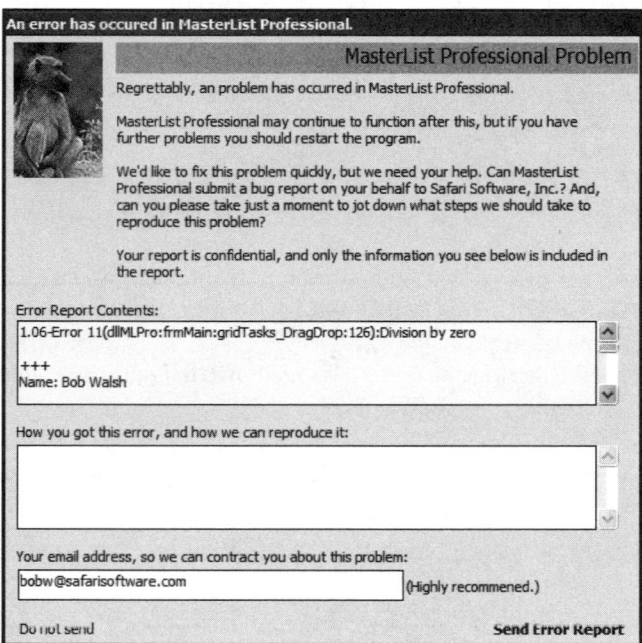

Figure 5-3. *Tech support starts within your application.*

The point of this error report is to immediately *respond* to the error just visited upon this person. Never mind what the error was, whose fault it was (probably mine), or whether it's something I'm going to fix right away, for the next build, or maybe even never. The point is my tiny company is already treating this seriously, something most companies forgot to do long ago.

Notice three other features of this bug report: I populate it with information as to where the bug happened, I ask the user how they received the error and how to reproduce it, and I practically beg but don't require their email address.

From your micro-ISV's point of view, you need some clue as to how to reproduce this error, and the best time to get this is the minute it happened when it's freshest in the person's memory and their motivation is the highest. Tech support systems where you submit an trouble ticket, go fill in an online form, or get directed to some god-awful "knowledgebase" are *prima fascia* evidence that not only doesn't the company care about customers but it doesn't care about the people who are supposed to fix the problems.

OK, flame off—back to the error walk-through. When the person clicks Send Error Report, the bug gets posted to my FogBugz and a few seconds later they get back a message within the program, as shown in Figure 5-4.

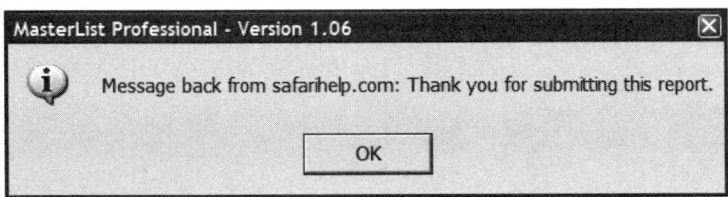

Figure 5-4. *Message received.*

Now one of the many nice features of FogBugz is I can customize this message, and if I'd already gotten this bug, I could say "Do this," "Do that," "It's fixed," "Download the current version," or anything else that makes sense.

While they're reading this message, I'm getting one of my own, as shown in Figure 5-5, and it's going to the top of my list of bugs in FogBugz, as shown in Figure 5-6.

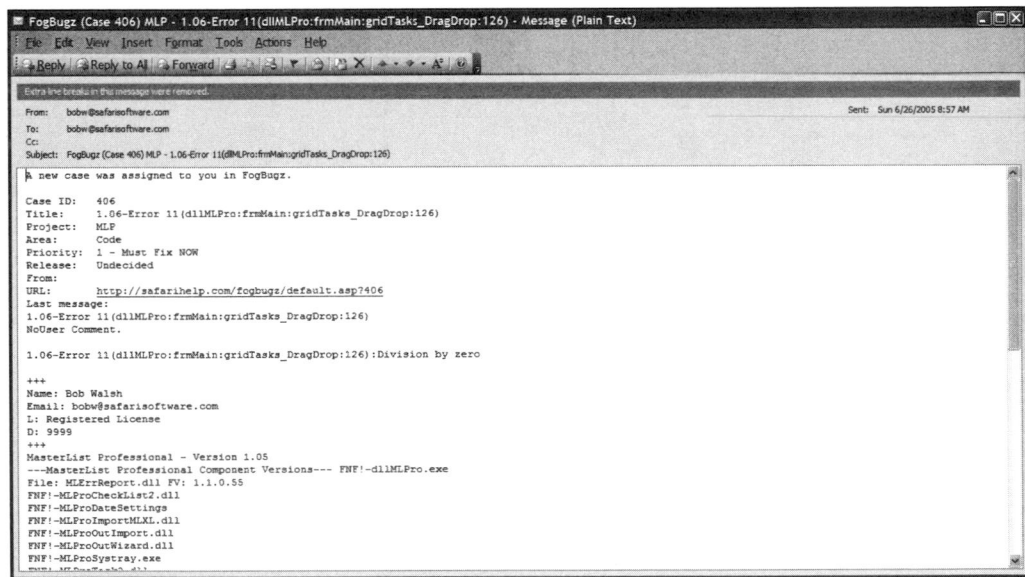

Figure 5-5. *You've got mail–Oy!*

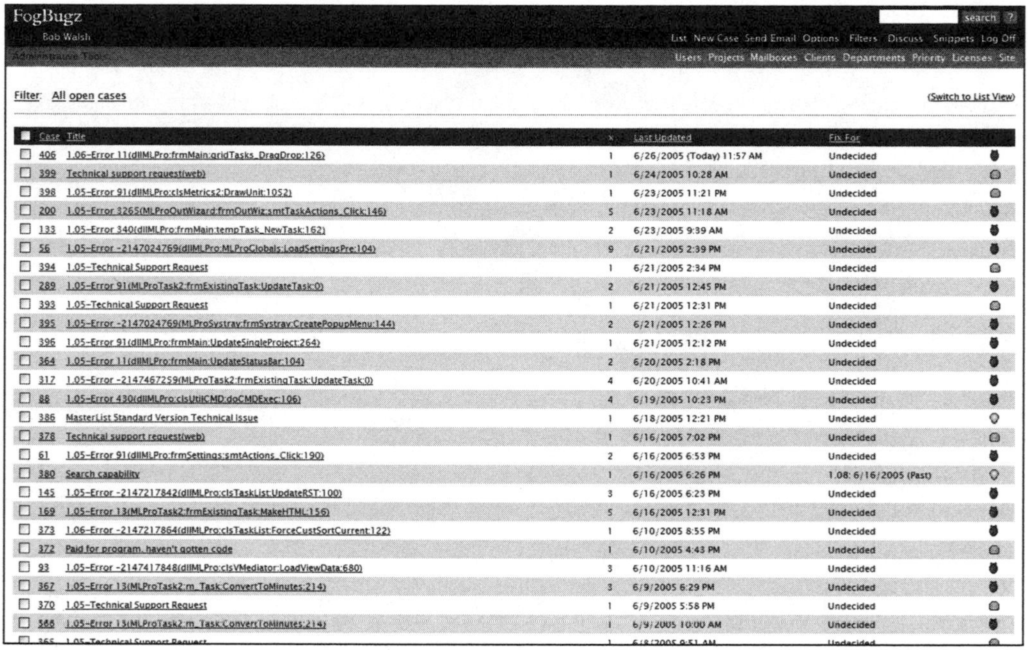

Figure 5-6. *My FogBugz list*

What happens next depends on the message. If I'm lucky, I get enough information to find and kill the bug. Then I do the following:

1. Click once to edit the bug, changing the automatic response line.

2. Click Reply, and type **fnr`**, which FogBugz expands to "Thanks for reporting this bug. I've found the problem and corrected the code. This bug fix—along with others—will be automatically available to you with the next free update of MasterList Professional, due out in the next few weeks."

3. Click one final time to send and close the bug.

If I'm not lucky, then I continue the conversation, getting more information if I can about where they were in MasterList Professional when it went boom.

You'll see more about FogBugz in the next section when I cover discussion forums, but I'd be remiss to not mention an excellent book, *Painless Project Management with FogBugz* (Apress, 2005), by my fellow Apress author, Mike Gunderloy, that covers FogBugz far better than this one does.

Two more quick points before leaving this topic: First, the following sidebar provides a short checklist of points to consider when you plan your tech support system. Second, you'll find a free Tech Support Planner Excel workbook at this book's page at Apress's Web site (http://www.apress.com) and at http://mymicroisv.com to help you plan this important part of your micro-ISV.

TECH SUPPORT PLANNER

Here's a checklist of points to keep in mind when setting up your micro-ISV's tech support system and doing tech support in general:

Core System Requirements

- Captures all bug reports, feature requests, and inquiries.

- Gets information I need to reproduce bugs.

- Takes as little of my micro-ISV's staff time as possible to manage.

- Requires as little effort from customers and potential customers as possible.

- Can run 24/7.

- I can afford it!

Managing Tech Support

- Define when and how often during the business workday new bugs will be reviewed and responded to.

- Define a workday, and communicate that on Web site, voice mail, and email.

- Set who is responsible for processing new tech support requests.

Basics of Good Tech Support

- Find out how to reproduce the bug.

- Customers will tell what triggered the bug. They are often right, and they are often wrong.

- Not all bugs are worth fixing, but all customers and potential customers are worth listening to.

- One bug can be operator error; the same bug more than once is not.

- Never belittle a customer. Ever.

- Never tolerate abusive people. That's what refunds are for.

Discussion Boards: Listening to Your Customers

In the previous section I covered how to do one-to-one technical support right. But the Internet is more than a two-way street, and it's at least equally important, especially for micro-ISVs, to listen to your potential and actual customers and talk with them in public.

If you're reading this book, odds are good you've seen at least a few dozen discussion boards or forums and perhaps have participated in several. Figure 5-7 shows Thraex Software.

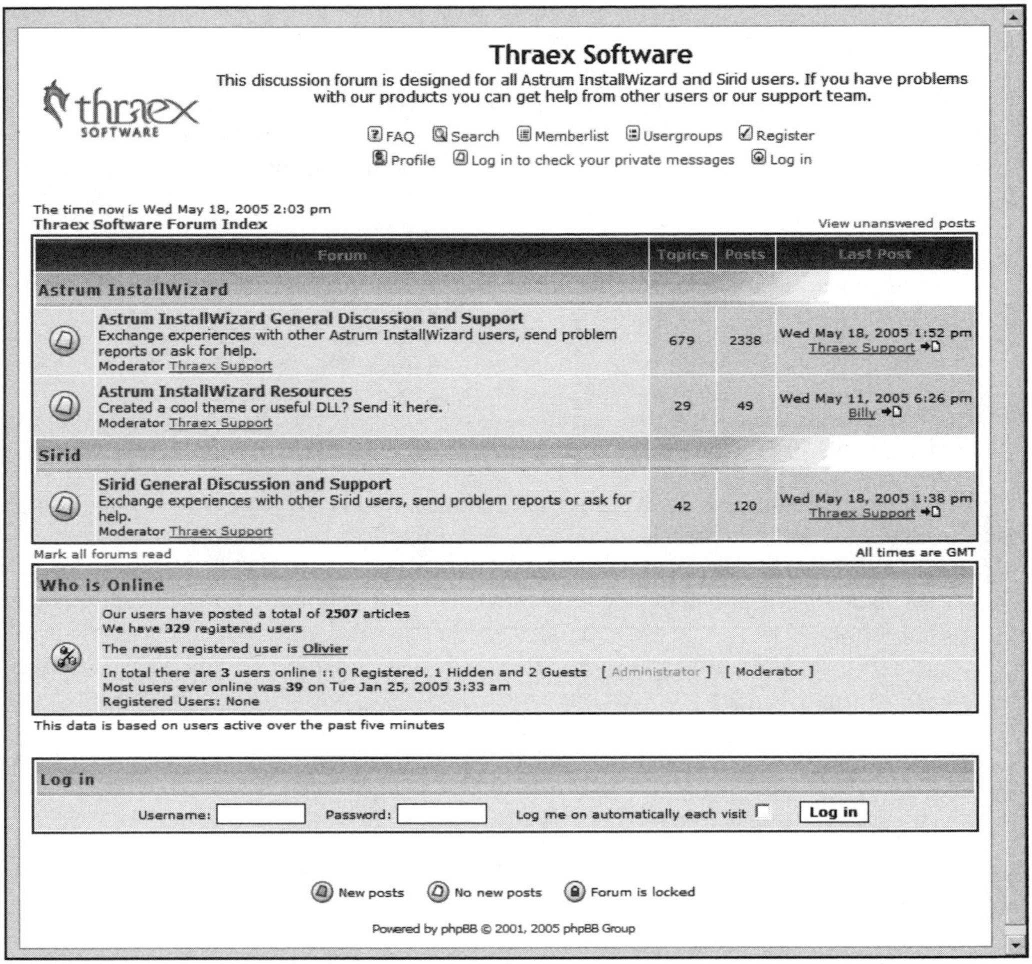

Thraex Software

This discussion forum is designed for all Astrum InstallWizard and Sirid users. If you have problems with our products you can get help from other users or our support team.

thraex
SOFTWARE

? FAQ   Search   Memberlist   Usergroups   Register
Profile   Log in to check your private messages   Log in

The time now is Wed May 18, 2005 2:03 pm
Thraex Software Forum Index   View unanswered posts

Forum	Topics	Posts	Last Post
Astrum InstallWizard			
Astrum InstallWizard General Discussion and Support Exchange experiences with other Astrum InstallWizard users, send problem reports or ask for help. Moderator Thraex Support	679	2338	Wed May 18, 2005 1:52 pm Thraex Support →▯
Astrum InstallWizard Resources Created a cool theme or useful DLL? Send it here. Moderator Thraex Support	29	49	Wed May 11, 2005 6:26 pm Billy →▯
Sirid			
Sirid General Discussion and Support Exchange experiences with other Sirid users, send problem reports or ask for help. Moderator Thraex Support	42	120	Wed May 18, 2005 1:38 pm Thraex Support →▯

Mark all forums read   All times are GMT

Who is Online

Our users have posted a total of **2507** articles
We have **329** registered users
The newest registered user is Olivier

In total there are 3 users online :: 0 Registered, 1 Hidden and 2 Guests [Administrator] [Moderator]
Most users ever online was **39** on Tue Jan 25, 2005 3:33 am
Registered Users: None

This data is based on users active over the past five minutes

Log in

Username: [   ]   Password: [   ]   Log me on automatically each visit ☐   [**Log in**]

New posts   No new posts   Forum is locked

Powered by phpBB © 2001, 2005 phpBB Group

Figure 5-7. *Supporting applications via a discussion forum*

Discussion boards have emerged as one of the best ways to have and foster two-way communication on the Web. Established brands such as General Electric, Microsoft, and even 125-year-old Pillsbury have discussion boards for tech support. These companies aren't run by fools; if they're doing it, it's for good reason and not an Internet fashion statement.

Here's one of those points to write down and stick above your computer where you can see it every day: "Done right, a discussion board is a strategic advantage for my microISV." Simply put, a good discussion board will build a loyal following, discover which aspects of your product sell, supply a legion of nonpaid Quality Assurance (QA) testers, provide you with new ideas to build and expand your company, and even recruit potential employees.

But notice the "Done right" part of the previous motto. Done wrong, and your discussion boards will offend customers, repeal buyers, consume countless hours of your time with no bottom-line return, and become a painful experience for all.

The key factor isn't what you think is a great discussion board but what the people who spend their time on your board think. It's the user experience, which means you have to take into account the types of people you want to attract, their habits, and their practices.

That said, it's up to you to consciously decide what type of discussion board you want and whether that board will be primarily a many-to-one or a many-to-many relationship. The many-to-one (the one being you) can start looking similar to tech support but with three advantages:

- Some—but by no means all—of your tech support queries will get answered before they arrive in your Inbox. This is a good thing.

- You can repurpose both your answers and their questions as Frequently Asked Questions (FAQs), best practices guides, demo scripts, and more. This is also good.

- Potential customers see you're not afraid to support your product in public and that you listen to them. This is a very good thing.

The many-to-many type discussion board is frankly harder to create and isn't likely to work until you've built a set of many-to-one relationships. You have to have a fairly sizable number of people interested in your product, and the problem it solves; also, the people must share a set of habits and practices that pull them together as an online community for this kind of forum to work.

Luckily, for you, any forum software worth considering is going to let you build subforums for one-to-one tech support, and then when forum members start talking with each other, you can add other forums defined as many-to-many places.

Here are two more facts to think about before you learn about four discussion board software packages for your micro-ISV: what are the base business requirements for a discussion board, and when should you start one?

What to Look For

Although seemingly endless variations of this list exist, you really need to consider only the following four items to make your discussion forum shine:

You need participants: For your discussion board to work, it needs to provide value to those who use it and be easy from their point of view to use. At the beginning, this value—in the form of access, information, tips, advice, and expertise—will come from you and the rest of your micro-ISV. If you require users to register before they post to prevent spam, keep it simple, and above all keep it fast. If you're not going to automate your discussion board registration process, don't make forum members register, and plan to kill spam when it appears.

You should logically organize information for the benefit of participants: Paradoxically, the biggest problem a forum can have is too much information—too many "please help!" postings, too many loose discussion threads, and too much noise, not enough signal. Creating the right organization of your discussion board is key to concentrating discussions into useful information. A few subforums (Tech Support, Future Enhancements, and General Discussion) with clear editorial policies and purposes is better than a pack of little subforums.

You or someone you trust has to take responsibility for it: This means you or one of your partners has to be responsible for answering posts, cutting off flame wars, nudging posters back to the stated topic, and eradicating spam in any way, shape, or form. This isn't a chore to be taken lightly; you're trying to build a relationship with people interested in your product, and relationships take time and commitment. It's far worse for your sales to leave questions unanswered for days or weeks than it is to skip doing discussion forums altogether.

A discussion forum complements but does not replace the need for tech support: By all means, use your forum to provide information. No matter what you do, people will post tech support issues on your forum, so have an easy way to move discussion postings into your bug-tracking system. But pushing customers into a forum when they have a technical issue almost guarantees their dissatisfaction with your product even if it solves their immediate problem.

When to Do It

When should you start your online discussion forum? The short answer is concurrently with your first external beta version—or right now if you already have a product available. By launching your discussion board at the same time you start your first public beta, you leverage your efforts: just limit your forum to beta testers who do double-duty testing both your product and your discussion board.

Furthermore, as discussed in Chapter 2, you want to establish a close relationship with your beta testers. Starting your forum with them means they're a part of your venture from the start; don't be surprised if some of them become evangelists, forum moderators, and perhaps even employees down the road.

If you're already selling a product, launching (or relaunching) a discussion board is a high, if indirect, priority. It's a high priority, because more and more potential customers now look to discussion boards as an expected adjunct to your product. But it's indirect, because while having a discussion board will lower tech support costs and increase sales, there is no easy way of measuring these benefits directly.

Finally, it takes time to build a good, active discussion board. It takes a bit of time to plan it, a little more to implement it, and then lots of time for it to grow as people find value in participating or at least reading it. It can take months before your discussion forum really takes off, and this time is something most programmers unconsciously overlook.

As you read through the following sections, which cover the four ways of implementing your discussion groups, keep the business points I've covered firmly in mind.

Approach 1: Code It Yourself

Unless you plan to create, market, and sell a discussion board application, resist the urge to code it yourself. You may be just as good a PHP, ASP, .NET, Java, or whatever programmer as the (mostly) guys who wrote the next three offerings covered, and you may be a damn sight better. But, every minute you spend here is a minute you can't spend on your product and its marketing.

Approach 2: Open Source, Kind Of: phpBB

Started in June 2000, phpBB is arguably the most well-established open source discussion board package available today. With its choice of database backends (MySQL, SQL Server, PostgresSQL, Access/ODBC), easy-to-use interface, and open source nature, phpBB is often the first choice of programmers and in many ways has defined what a discussion board should look like.

Figure 5-8 and Figure 5-9 show a typical phpBB implementation. The discussion board for phpBB is an example of an extremely successful discussion board with more than 162,000 topics and more than 763,000 posts to its main discussion group.

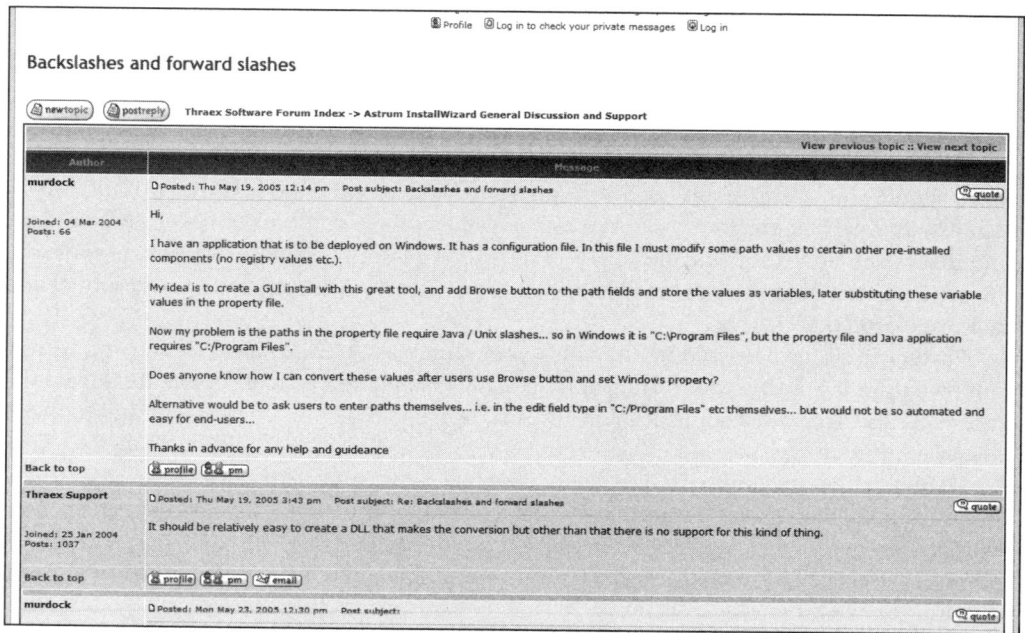

Figure 5-8. *A post and a tech support response within phpBB*

To implement phpBB, all you need to do is either go with a site hosting service that offers phpBB or learn enough to set up, configure, administer, and maintain it from the wealth of documentation at `http://www.phpbb.com/support/` and then download the source code from `http://www.phpbb.com/downloads.php` to run this Web application on your own server. As of this writing, the 50 or so people who maintain the phpBB project have just released phpBB2, a more robust, security-aware successor to phpBB.

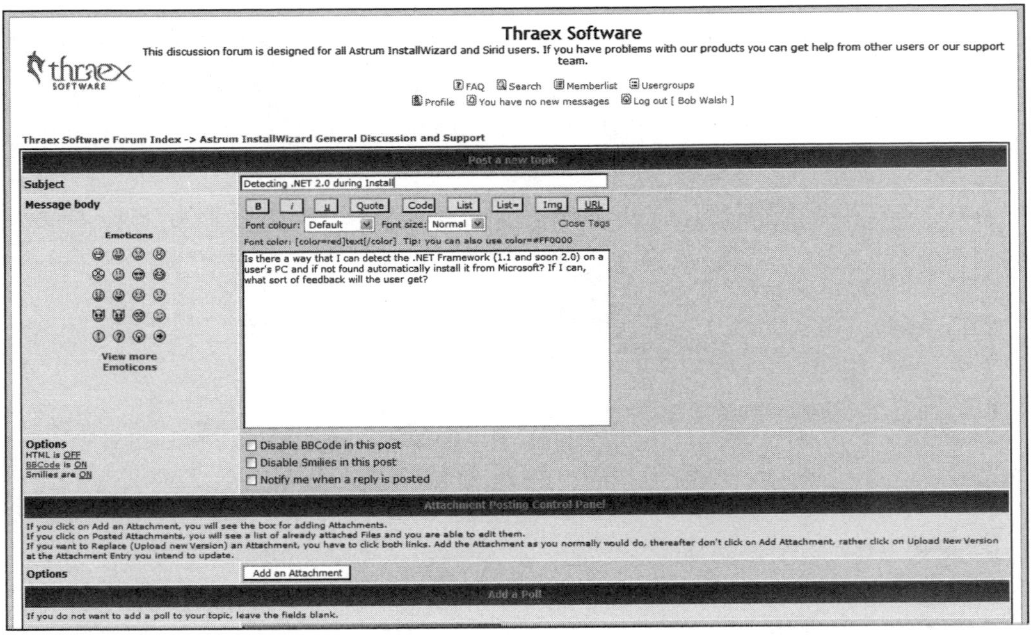

Figure 5-9. *Posting to a phpBB board*

Approach 3: Outsource to Invision

As good as phpBB/phpBB2 is, there's always room for improvement and monetization. Invision Power Services (http://www.invisionboard.com/) of Forest, Virginia, is one such company, offering its own PHP-based discussion board products; offering free telephone support, installation, and upgrades; and offering hosting for your board.

Invision's excellent technical support system is worth the $69.95 USD for a one-year license for the software, and many tech-related discussion sites use it, as shown in Figure 5-10.

As with many products, you get what you pay for; from my own experience I can say that Invision delivers an extremely robust and highly customizable discussion board, and its tech support lives up to its online reputation.

But, in March 2005 before even contemplating this book, I was not a happy Invision camper. Although I had used Invision during the initial beta period of MasterList Professional, board maintenance was taking too much of my time, my users had to jump through too many hoops to post, and too many users were posting questions that I would have to answer but would never see again.

I was ready for a different approach, and then Fog Creek Software released FogBugz 4.0.

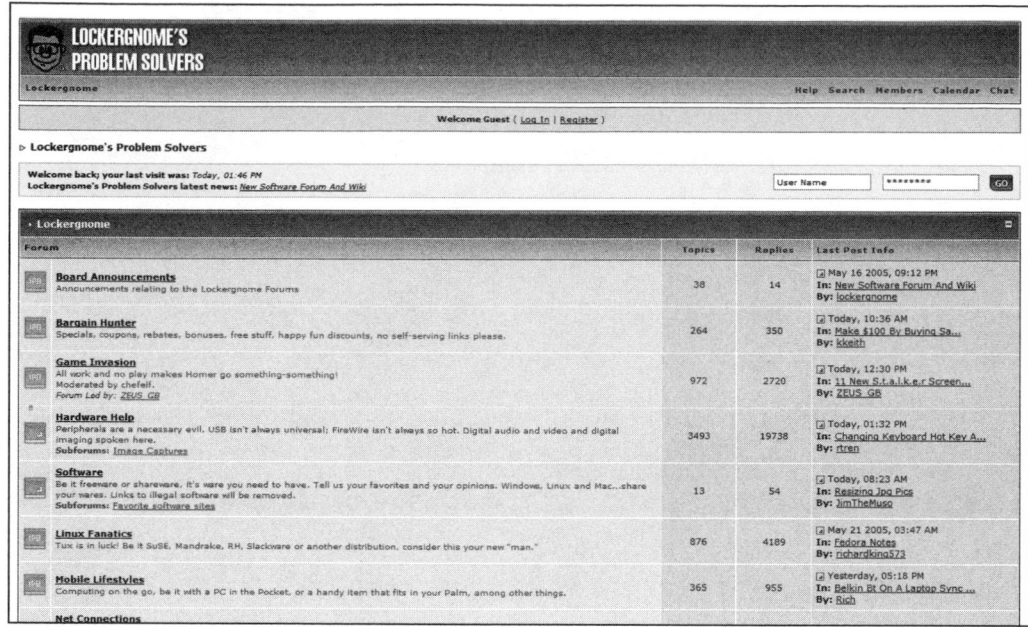

Figure 5-10. *Lockergnome's Problem Solvers site is powered by Invision.*

Approach 4: By, for, and of Micro-ISVs

As you've read the previous three approaches, you've seen more and more complex program-ming, features, and functionality. Now it's time to talk about something that will work for micro-ISVs.

Although the first three approaches make sense in general for discussion boards, in my opinion, Fog Creek Software's FogBugz 4 (http://www.fogcreek.com/FogBugz/, $129 USD per user base price, 45-day trial available) has discussion forum functionality that is by far the best way for a micro-ISV to organize and maintain its conversations with current and potential customers.

FogBugz has four characteristics that specifically help a micro-ISV:

- The amount of time you'll need to spend moderating has been cleverly reduced to the lowest possible value.

- Through specific user interface decisions, FogBugz discussion boards keep people coming back to them and rapidly build the many-to-many relationships that make an online community work.

- It's cheap; in fact, you can think of it as free if the main reason you buy FogBugz is to track bugs.

- By combining automatic Bayesian filtering found in antispam email applications with a bit of poetic justice, spammers, like cockroaches, check in but never get to check out.

Now, are these four characteristics lucky, unintended consequences? Nah. As Michael Pryor, president and cofounder of Fog Creek Software tells it, they were the products of really thinking about the problem they were trying to solve.

One of the things we try to do is make our software work in a social context. What is the problem that we are trying to solve, and how will the software solve that?

A lot of the time as programmers you look at the problem, and you try [to] break it down into logical steps that will solve the problem. For example, when you have a discussion forum, you get troublemakers. You know, people who are going to write prose, they're going to write posts that really don't belong, they're going to harass other people, and a lot of the discussion forums out there try to solve the problem by just giving moderators the right to delete posts.

That gets rid of the post, but it doesn't solve the real problem, which is to try [to] keep the troublemaker out of the view of everyone else. Because if you delete their post, they come back and post again, now saying you're violating their free speech rights: you create ten posts for the one you deleted.

So one of the things we did in FogBugz to solve the problem of how do you get the person to go away and leave you alone is, well, you take their post and make it invisible to everyone else, but they still see it. They won't know they've been deleted. There's no one fanning their flame. You can't get into a flame war if no one responds to your criticism. So they get silenced and eventually just go away.

Poetic justice indeed! But how effective is it? Pryor continues:

We have several ways of telling if they come back, and it's been proven to be extremely, extremely effective. Say a spammer posts to your board and then they come back to check if it's still there, and they see it—to them it's still there—but no one else sees it, so they're not bothered by it.

Besides applying social engineering to spammers, Fog Creek Software decided to apply a solution from another area that works well on the problem of unwanted messages:

The other thing we did was integrate deleting those posts with Bayesian filtering, so once you start teaching the forum what sort of things are off-topic, it learns, and it will autodelete them. And all you have to do is go in occasionally and tweak how you trained it. So if some spammer comes along and posts a "Make Money Quick," no one will ever see it because their post will start out deleted.

FogBugz, compared to other discussion board packages, is positively minimalist: you start a topic, and other people post after you. There's no threading, no autoquoting, and no way to even change your posting, as shown in Figure 5-11.

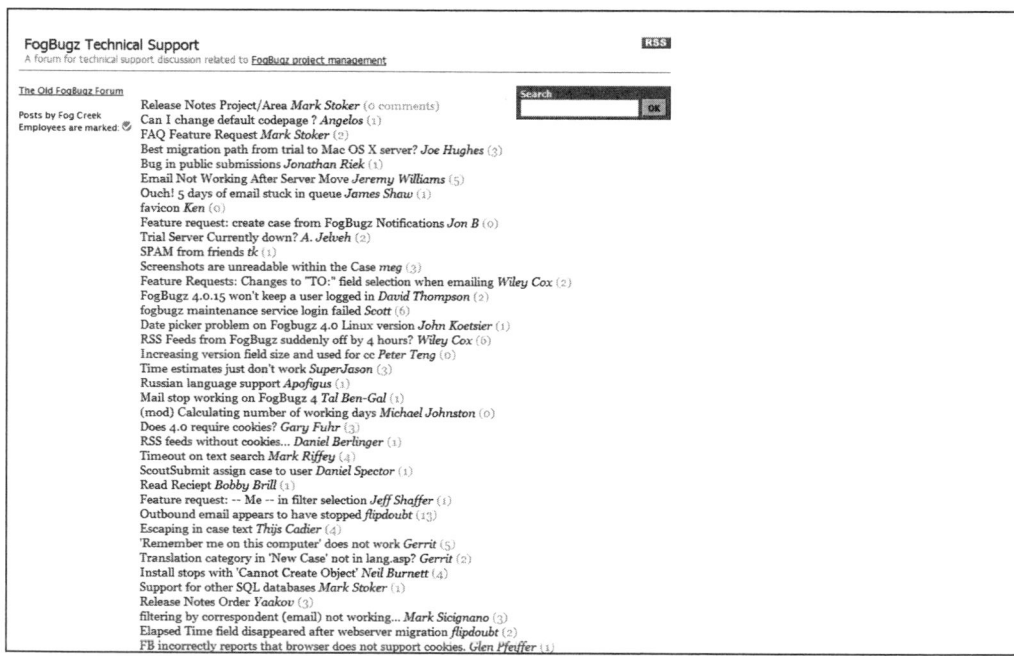

Figure 5-11. *The FogBugz minimalist discussion group*

Why?

This gets back to the whole idea of creating a community with the software, and in order to make that happen, we made a lot of decisions. We didn't say, oh, we want to make a discussion board, and let's look at what else is out there and copy that. The goal of the software that runs the forum was to provide technical support for our product. That really guided the design of the software. So features like threading are things we decided to not do, and we will never add that because we think it gets in the way of having a conversation—an online conversation but a conversation [see Figure 5-12]. We're trying to get into the idea that you are talking with someone, but you just happen to be online.

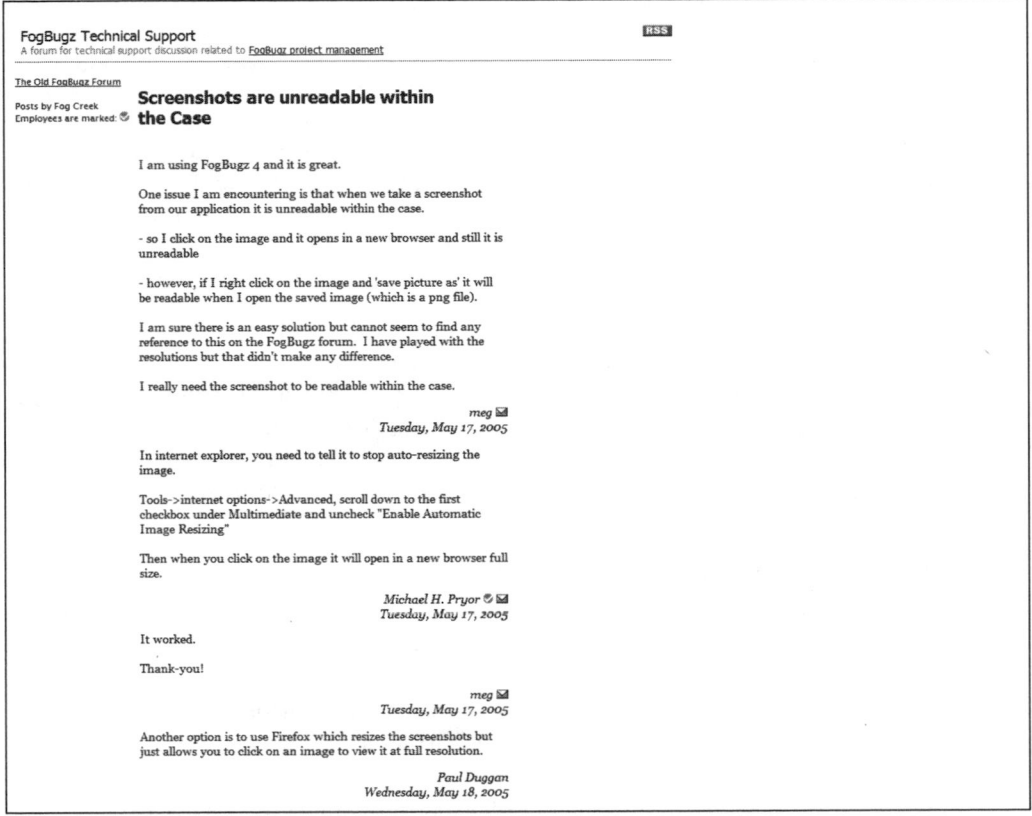

Figure 5-12. *Notice the nonmoderator chiming in at the end of this question.*

All in all, FogBugz's discussion board functionality is well suited to the needs of a micro-ISV.

Where Your Customers Start

For micro-ISVs, understanding how your potential customers will look for you and making sure you're there to be found are critical to your success. Simply put, it's up to you, not your customers, to make sure they can find you, which means you need to see the process from their point of view.

In this section, I'll cover three major ways your customers will find out you exist and (you hope) try to perhaps even buy your micro-ISV application:

Search engines and directories: I covered the basics in Chapter 3 of building a good Web site home page—making it easy for large search engines such as Google and MSN to find and correctly list you. But the Web is a big place, and many of your customers will use a wide variety of search tools and specialized directories, so you need to develop your site submission strategy to cast your potential customer dragnet as wide as possible.

As useful as these specialized directories are, Internet search reality is now defined by Google. Google AdWords are such an important tool for micro-ISVs that I'll talk with Emily White, the Google AdWords product manager, in the "Google, Relevancy, and Your Micro-ISV" section.

Download sites: Although search engines are important, they cover every imaginable topic. Savvy Internet users turn to software download sites and so should you. Later in this chapter, you'll look at three major download sites—CNET Download.com, Tucows.com and Microsoft Office Marketplace—and get the scoop from Kelly Morrison of CNET about what these sites can provide micro-ISVs (see the "CNET Download.com" section).

The influencers: Finally, don't forget traditional media, trade media, and the new medium of blogs as way to connect to your customer. In a world with too much media and too much information influencing the influencers, the reporters, editors, and respected bloggers are critical parts of your strategic marketing plan. I'll talk with a mainstream tech reporter and an online software reviewer to better understand how these information matchmakers see the world and companies like yours (see "The Influencers").

How to Do General Site Submission Right

Few topics show just how much the Internet has grown and evolved than the ins and outs of getting listed on the Internet over the past ten years. First there was Yahoo!, where you could submit a site description, and that was that. Next, other directories started to spring up. Then directories became portals to offer you all things Internet. Next came the search *engines* rather than *directories*, which were the next hot thing until the boom went bust and Google redefined the whole game.

Although it used to be you could handle, with a day or two of work, making sure your product was being found in the general places people would look, now you need a year or two. The rules are fundamentally different. Here's how the game is played today: First, while you can still submit to the places you really want to be—Google, MSN, Yahoo, and a few others— these companies are in the business of finding you for their customers, if you're relevant. So, one part of the puzzle is "optimizing" your company's Web site so it's relevant to potential customers. Part of this I covered in Chapter 3, when I discussed your Web site, but Search Engine Optimization (SEO) needs to be part of your submission marketing plan.

Another recent site submission development is popular directories such as Yahoo, HotBot, Lycos, Ask Jeeves, and LookSmart "monetizing" (charging for) inclusion. Depending on your product and especially your market, it might make sense to include one or more of these in your annual marketing budget. Then again, it may not.

What I'm focusing on right now, however, isn't on the top few places people use to find sites on the Net but on the many places you probably never heard of. How many of these places exist? According to Google Directory, as of June 2005 at least 340 specialized search engines and 844 directories exist. That's a lot—too many to manage manually. So, you have an information management problem, and that's something every programmer understands.

Now, before you reach for your favorite database tool to solve this particular information management problem, stop. Yes, you could probably whip up an app that does this, but should you? Unless you happen to be planning to sell a site/blog submission tool, it simply is not a good use of your time—remember Law 1440?

Instead, it's time to go shopping for the right tool or online service. Keep in mind that like all things Internet, site submission is an evolving field, and what worked last year may not work this year. In fact, over the past few years many site submission services and applications have withered away as search engines and directories counter their own form of spam—bulk automatic site submissions generated in the hopes of improving search engine scores.

So, with this warning in mind, here's your short-and-sweet shopping list:

- Needs to work in a manner currently acceptable to search engines and popular directories.

- Needs to be well supported, up to date, and evolving as the Internet evolves.

- Needs to be able to tell you where you're listed and not on an ongoing basis.

- Cheap is better than expensive, all things considered.

In the following sections, I'll cover three such tools—one online, one desktop, and one a company that offers both. Then, for those who want to dig into how search engines work, I'll cover one of the top search engine watcher's Web site. Certainly more tools exist than I can cover in this chapter; you can find a good set of links at these four Yahoo pages:

- `http://dir.yahoo.com/Business_and_Economy/Business_to_Business/`
  `Marketing_and_Advertising/Internet/Promotion/`

- `http://dir.yahoo.com/Computers_and_Internet/Internet/World_Wide_Web/`
  `Searching_the_Web/Search_Engines_and_Directories/Submit_a_Site/`

- `http://dir.yahoo.com/business_and_economy/business_to_business/`
  `marketing_and_advertising/internet/promotion/Software/`

- `http://dir.yahoo.com/computers_and_internet/internet/world_wide_Web/`
  `Site_Announcement_and_Promotion/`

Tool 1: Submit Express

Submit Express (`http://www.submitexpress.com/submit2500.html`), as shown in Figure 5-13, offers two submission tools: a free submitter script that will send your URL and email to 40 major directories and a more tailored subscription service where your home page will be reviewed by Submit Express for its level of SEO and then submitted to more than 75,000 search engines, directories, and Free For All (FFA) links pages.

Submit Express also offers SEO consulting services, apart from assessing your site if you use their paid submission service.

As of May 2005, Submit Express will submit your site a single time for $24.95 USD or (as they recommend) monthly for six months ($99.95), monthly for a year ($189.95 USD), or quarterly for a year ($69.95 USD).

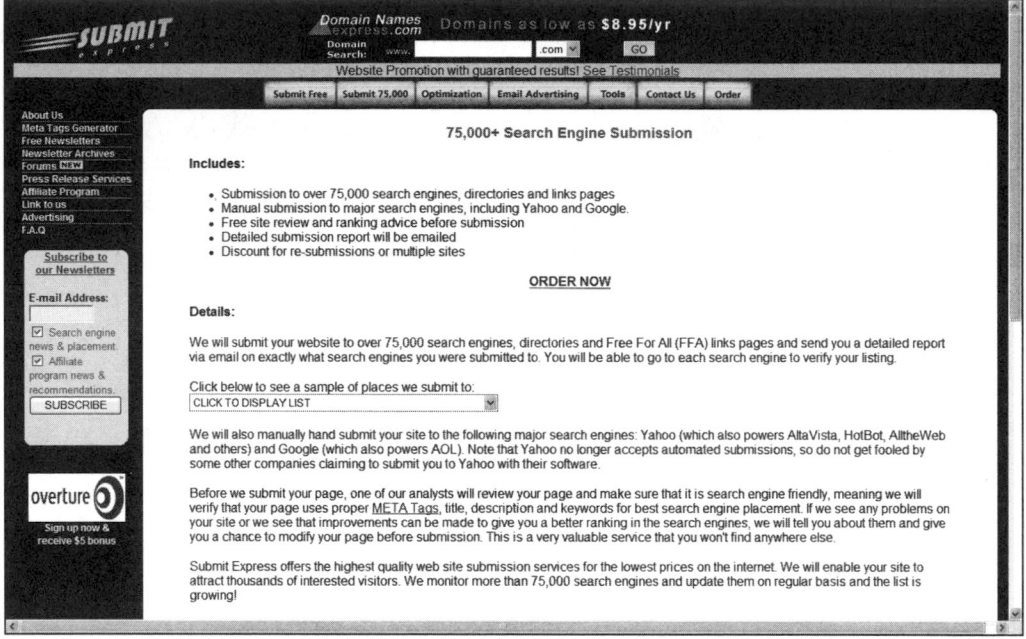

Figure 5-13. *Submit Express' value proposition for micro-ISVs*

Tool 2: IBP

Internet Business Promoter (IBP) (`http://www.axandra-web-site-promotion-software-tool.com/index.htm`) is a Windows desktop application with 16 optimizing, promoting, and tracking tools and three tools (search engine, directory, and topic sites submitters) designed to make your site submission process effective.

Unlike several other applications, IBP recognizes that most popular search engines verify that a real person exists at the other end of the submission process by either presenting a "machine-unreadable" image of a string you need to type in or by sending a confirmation email or both.

What IBP excels at is managing the process and filling in as much of the information as possible for you, once you've targeted the all-important keywords your customers will use to search.

The tool's clever Top 10 Optimizer, as shown in Figure 5-14, shows you the optimization techniques of a competitor. For example, let's say you're launching a new time management application. You feed IBP your URL, select the search engines important to you from a large list, and enter the single search term your customers are likely to use. Then IBP goes out to the Net and compiles a list of the current top-ten Web sites for that keyword.

Next, IBP analyzes each site's search engine optimization techniques—such as the correct use of meta keywords and description, <h1> and <h2> headline text, and <img> tag attributes—and compares it to your site, presenting you with your own SEO report showing the differences between you and your competitors, as shown in Figure 5-15.

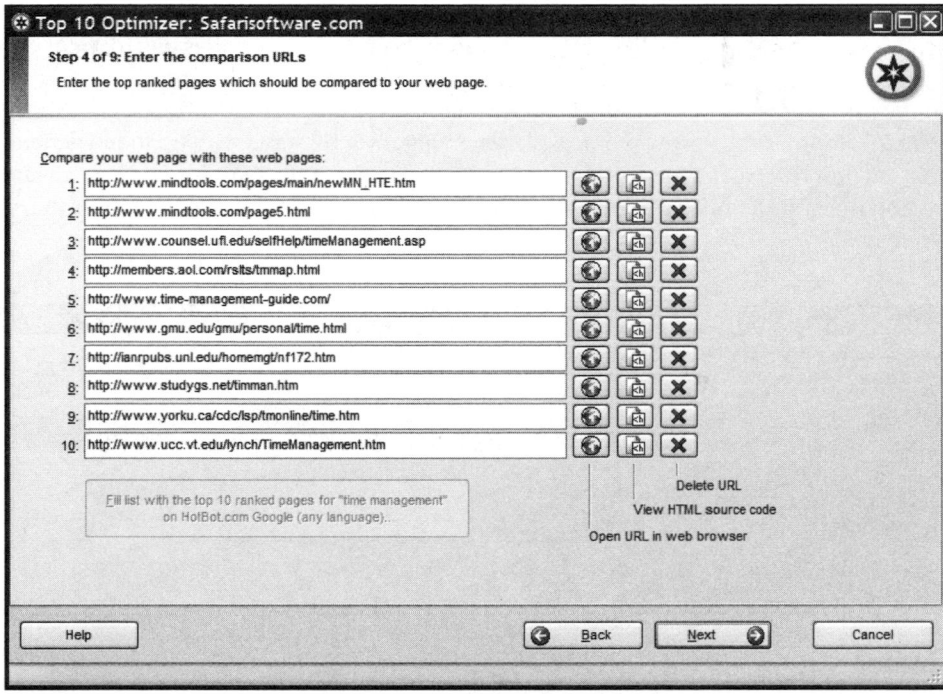

Figure 5-14. *IBP 8's Top 10 Optimizer report prepares to analyze your competitors.*

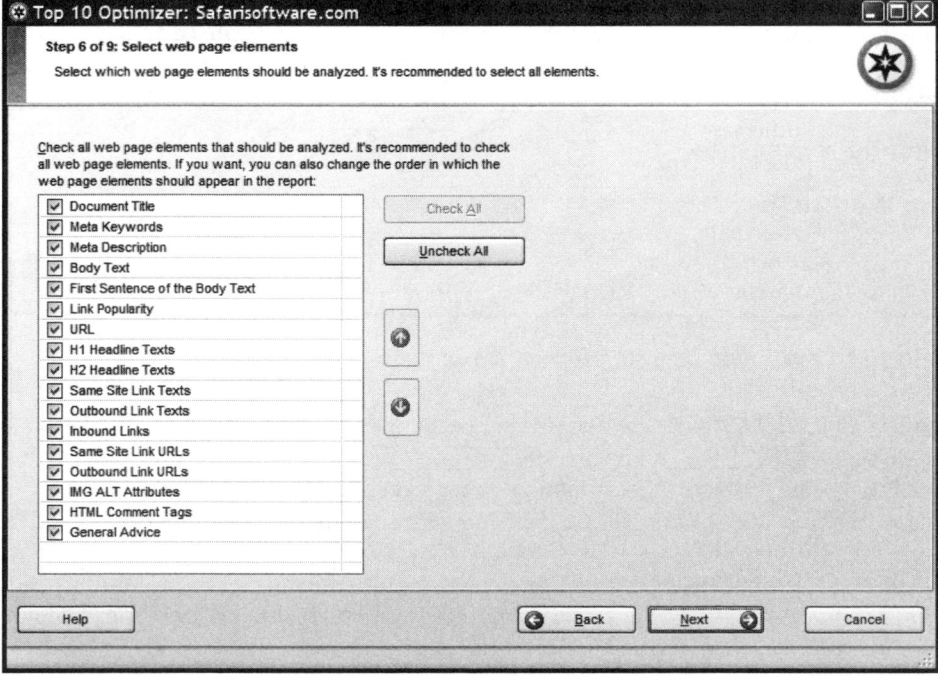

Figure 5-15. *IBP 8 checking your site for SEO*

Another aspect of the Internet marketing game IBP plays well is its recognition that most major search engines rank sites at least in part based on how many other sites link to them. So, if you're a micro-ISV, one of the best ways to improve your visibility is to find and ask sites that focus on the same topics as your product to link to you.

IBP's Link Popularity Improver tool, as shown in Figure 5-16, starts with up to ten general keywords that describe what your product covers. Then you check the search engines you want to target, and the app compiles a list of sites that you can contact via the tool to request they link to your site.

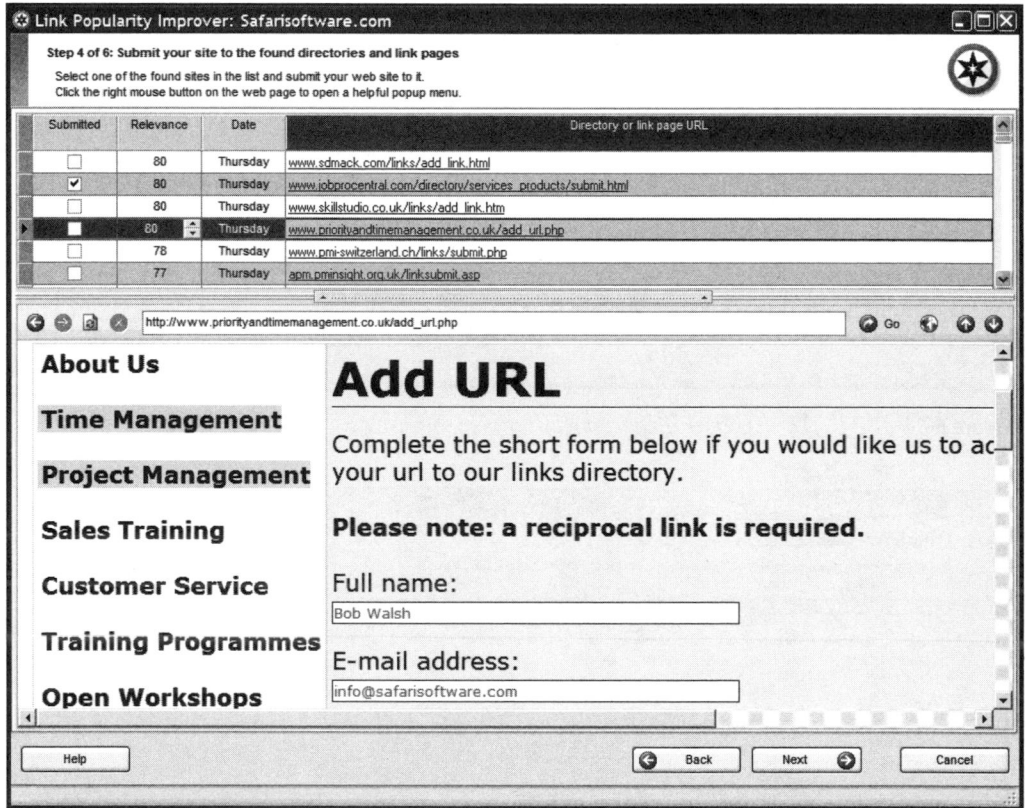

Figure 5-16. *IBP 8's Link Popularity Improver can find you sites to request links from.*

Axandra, the micro-ISV that created IBP, sells a companion product called ARELIS that expands on this linking idea by managing the process of requesting and granting links with other sites, including intelligently automating creating requests, verifying that your links appear on other sites, and creating HTML pages for your site using your template or a standard template.

Together, IBP and optionally ARELIS can powerfully manage most of your site submission and optimization chores, with one exception: what to do about the major directories that now charge for inclusion.

Tool 3: SubmitWolf Pro

Trellian Software is another survivor in the site submission business. Its approach is threefold: PrioritySubmit.com (`http://www.prioritysubmit.com`), an online submission service for sites that charge to be listed; SubmitWolf, software for submitting to more than 1,000 directories using its rules, which are constantly updated; and an SEO toolkit (including SubmitWolf for optimizing your pages).

SubmitWolf's (version 6 as of this writing) (`http://www.trellian.com/swolf/index.html`) approach is to define for each search engine and directory it covers a specific "submission engine" that automates as much as possible the process. Although SubmitWolf is attractively priced ($169 USD including one year's worth of updates), it isn't as robust as IBP 8. However, where Trellian shines is its PrioritySubmit.com service. If you decide to go the pay-for-inclusion route, it's far easier to have one service that manages all your submissions.

PrioritySubmit.com has relationships with Yahoo Search Submit Express, about 15 mid-level search engines, and about 20 regional search engines. You can submit to, say, All-business (Netherlands) and WebWombat (Australia) at the same time.

Signing up with PrioritySubmit.com is free and a good way to make your pay-for-inclusion search engine budget go further.

Google, Relevancy, and Your Micro-ISV

> *Rel-e-vant—adjective. Having significant and demonstrable bearing on the matter at hand.*
>
> *—Merriam-Webster's Collegiate Dictionary*, 11th edition

When something like one billion people go looking for what they want in something like 9 billion Web pages, relevancy is the force in the universe that will bring the right pages to the right people. This little insight turned out to be worth about $14 billion to the founders of Google,[2] the search engine that in many ways redefined how things work on the Internet this century.

Your job as CEO and Marketing Vice President of your micro-ISV is to learn, live, and breathe who your product is relevant to; how to present your product as relevant to the market you're focusing on; and where to spend your limited budget to highlight that relevancy. For many online companies, Google has been the tool for defining, shaping, and marketing their relevancy.

I covered how to correctly design your Web site's home page to properly display your application's relevancy in Chapter 3, and I discussed how to use Google to find and define your market. Here, the focus is on the one form of advertising I recommend for micro-ISVs—Google AdWords and their copycats.

In case you've been unconnected for, say, the last four years or so, Google AdWords are small, text-only advertisements that appear separately from the results of your search in Google but that are based on the same logic that returned those results. As an advertiser, it costs you nothing for the ad to appear; you're charged if and when someone clicks the embedded URL in that ad and goes to your designated Web site page.

---

2. 2005 World's Richest People List, Forbes.com

How much do you pay for that click? That's up to you: it can be from 5 cents to 100 dollars. How much does it cost per day? Your daily budget can be from 5 cents to whatever limit you want to set. Who decides which ad is at the top of the first page of search engine results for a particular search? Google's code base does, based on the maximum Cost Per Click (CPC) you set, the Click-Through Rate (CTR) of your ad or ads, and most of all how relevant your ad is to the person who queried Google in the first place.

The appeal of Google for small advertisers such as yourself is you can't be shouted down by big competitors. Your minuscule ad budget, some time learning the ins and outs of Google's ad "programming language," and most of all your clear definition of relevancy are more powerful than the truckloads of money others use to advertise.

Google does an extremely good job of explaining AdWords mechanics at its AdWords site (http://adwords.google.com). Recently, Google started offering new advertisers in the United States a tempting deal. Google specialists will look at your site and create a Google ad campaign for you. The program, currently called Jumpstart, costs $299, plus whatever you set as your ad budget. But, Google credits your ad budget $299, and you're free to modify your campaign in any way you want. Essentially, for $299 in advertising, you get a professionally designed AdWords campaign.

As of this writing, Jumpstart is limited to new U.S. advertisers targeting customers in English, but expect this to expand. In the meantime, Google has also put together a slew of suggestions covering how to optimize your site for Google, how to design ad campaigns, and how to do much more. The information is part of Google's new Advertising Professionals program and is called the Learning Center at http://www.google.com/adwords/learningcenter/, as shown in Figure 5-17.

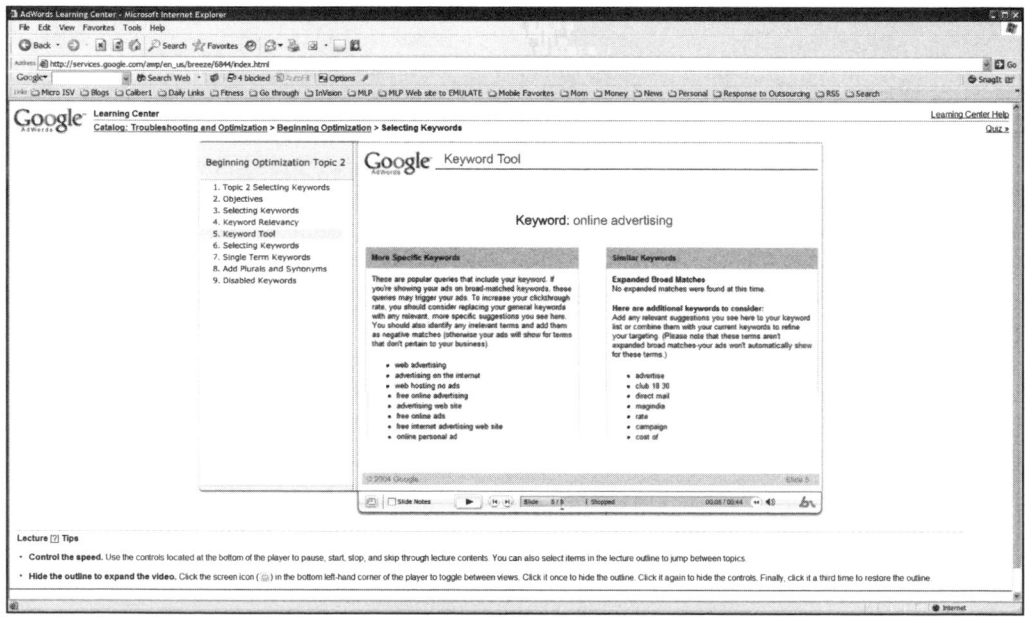

Figure 5-17. *Google's Learning Center—a free keyword training course*

EMILY WHITE, ADWORDS MANAGER, GOOGLE

As Google continues to redefine search on the Internet, confound Wall Street predictions, and give traditional advertising a run for its money, I had the good fortune to talk to Emily White, the manager of AdWords about what AdWords has to offer micro-ISVs.

Q. What can AdWords do for a start-up company?

A. AdWords is a great product for advertisers like that for a few reasons. First, we have a very large audience on the Internet. People come to Google looking for something very specific, and in return, Google gives them that certain specific thing, whether in terms of search results or ads. So there is a lot of reach Google provides advertisers.

Google provides a lot of control to advertisers too, especially the people you're talking about because they can create and edit an ad campaign at any time. For $5 and 15 minutes, anyone can get their campaign up and running. Advertisers have the flexibility to change their audience. They can experiment, and they can also control their budget. They set a daily budget, which sets how much they want to pay for any day's worth of traffic, and that can be a dollar [or] a hundred dollars—it can be any amount the advertiser likes.

Q. Is Google AdWords only for big advertisers? Don't established companies in an area pretty much lock out start-ups?

A. I would say absolutely not for a couple of reasons. First, the way we rank ads is the maximum cost per click the advertiser is willing to pay for that keyword multiplied by the click-through rate, or how popular that ad is. What that means is if an advertiser spends the time to find the right keywords for that account, they can get higher on that page and pay less for that position. There's no locking in of positions at all: the positioning is completely dynamic for all the ads on that page and really depends on how relevant that ad is to the keyword the user is searching for. This essentially levels the playing field so that small advertisers and large advertisers alike can run on the same keyword.

Q. So how can a micro-ISV find the right keywords?

A. A couple of pieces of advice: we have a keyword tool that returns similar keywords to the keyword you want expansions of. It returns keywords we have found to be related, so it's a great way to find what people are looking for within that industry.

We also suggest that advertisers use multiword keywords. Ads that run on two or more words as a keyword tend to do better than advertisers who run on singular keywords, and here's why: singular keywords tend to be more general. The more specific the term is to the product being sold, the better.

Q. So you mean the more specific keywords are, yet covering variations of that keyword, the more likely they are to meet with good results?

A. Exactly.

Q. What mistakes do beginning AdWords advertisers often make?

A. One mistake that some small companies make is running [an ad campaign] on a term they know or their product's name. They may know what it means, but not that many people will. So what we suggest is that people use much more descriptive words of what their product is and also look at things like their Web logs and see how people are finding their site. What kinds of things are they searching for? What are industry terms for what you are selling?

Successful advertisers tend to experiment with many variations of keywords and, once they have been running their campaign, go back into their account and see what's working and what is not.

A couple of other common ad mistakes: one would be not to define your metrics out [of] the gate, [such as] advertisers going into the program thinking, "Oh, I want to capture the top ad position, and even though my product sells for $50, I'm going to set a CPC of $100." Now, that's a bad example, but in general, people don't tend to go into the AdWords program knowing what their goals are [or] how much they are willing to pay for a click, for example.

Also, advertisers will run on their product's name when it is not very well known yet, or they will run on keywords that are really untargeted. Also, in some cases advertisers believe that running a snazzy ad that is somewhat misleading—you know, like *free software*—that sometimes that will get people's attention. That tends to lead to clicks but no purchases.

Q. Truth pays?

A. Truth pays—definitely. Especially when it comes to conversions.

Q. If my micro-ISV's AdWords campaign isn't performing, what can they do?

A. We provide a service for advertisers who have a campaign and it's not working as well as you like. We call it In-house Optimization. So, if the advertiser emails us through the Contact Us form on our Web site, and they say, "Hey, can you help me with my campaign? It's not performing as well as I would like. Here are my goals," we will actually have an optimization specialist go into the account, evaluate it, and publish suggestions for that account, such as additional keywords they might want to ad, keywords they might want to delete, or ad text that might work better for that industry.

So we currently provide services to help advertisers get back on-track, and that's free actually. That's not a paid-for product.

Doing the Download Tango

A core reality for micro-ISVs is that the more ways your potential customers have of downloading your software, the better. And that means submitting—and sometimes paying for—your software to be available with one if not all of the current leading download sites CNET Download.com, Tucows.com, and Microsoft Office Marketplace—as well as a slew of lesser-known sites, especially those relevant to your customers.

CNET Download.com

As with a lot of things on the Net, quantity has a quality all its own. CNET Download.com (http://www.download.com) started in 1996, adding one of the first file download sites, Winfiles.com, in 1999 and never looking back. Now, along with Tucows.com, Download.com is one of the key places to go to corral trial software applications based on a given category or keyword, as shown in Figure 5-18.

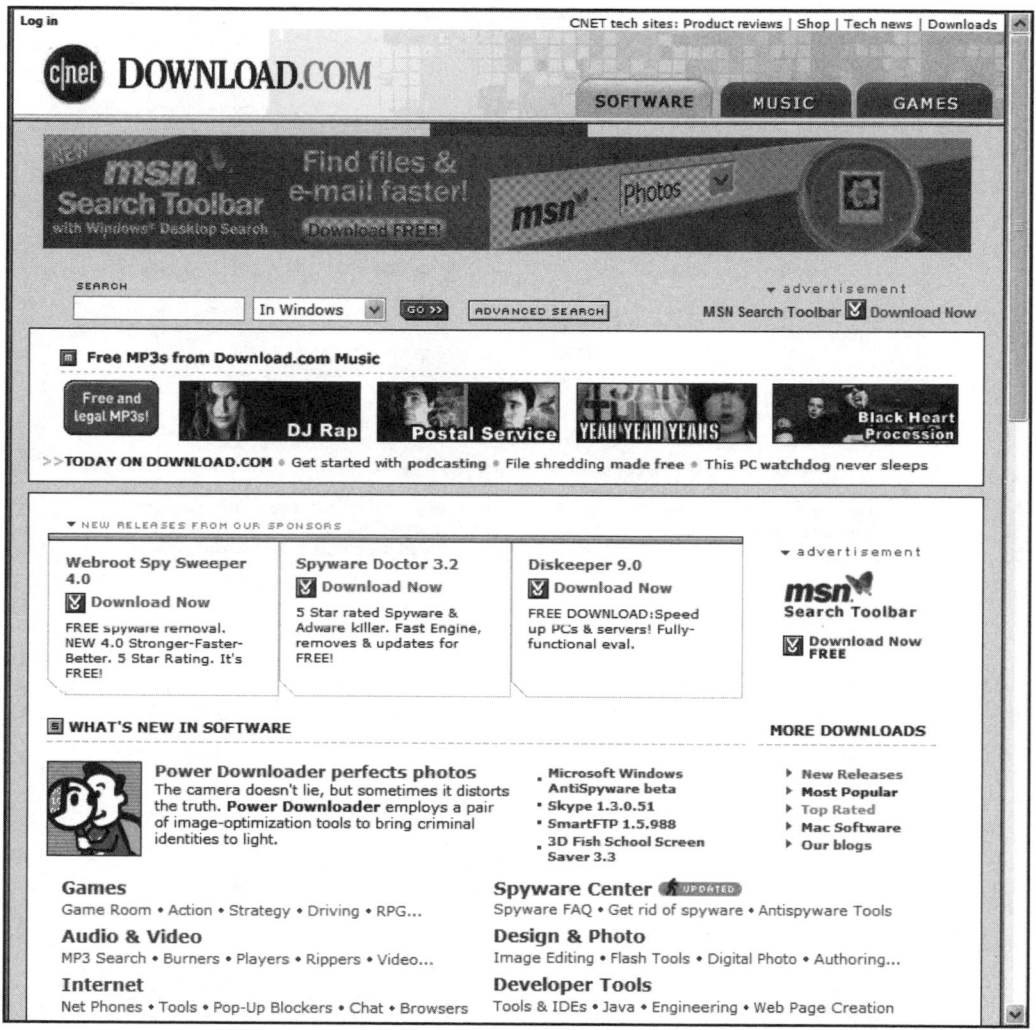

Figure 5-18. *Welcome to Download.com.*

Although you can list at Download.com for free, and a free listing is better than no listing, most micro-ISVs will want to go with either the Basic ($9/month USD) or the Premium ($99/month USD) listing service. All listings mean you can offer potential customers a one-sentence pitch in the listings, a trusted source to download a virus-free file up to 15MB, a screen shot, and your 200-to-1,000-word description, as shown in Figure 5-19.

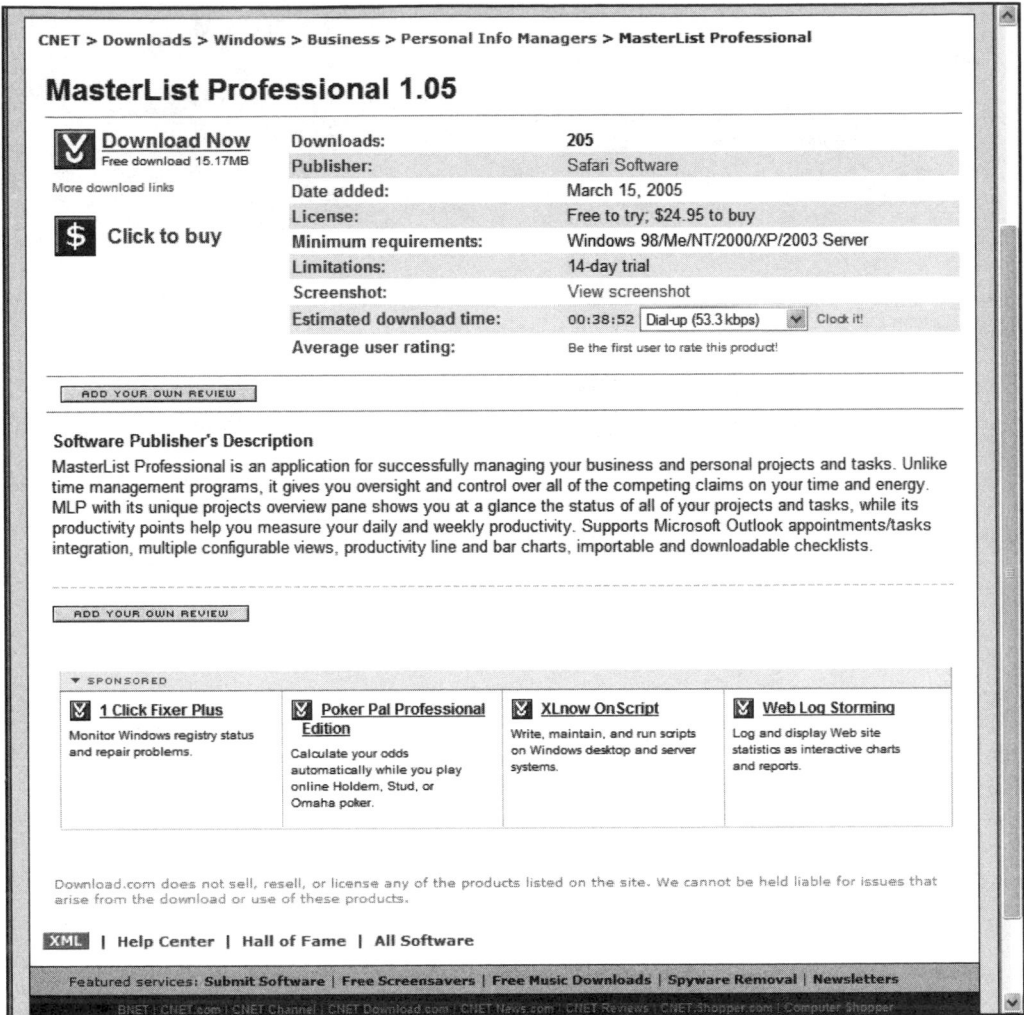

Figure 5-19. *Welcome to your Download.com category*

I've use the Premium service for both MasterList XL Standard and MasterList Professional—a cost of almost $200 a month. Why?

The Premium service gives me the ability to suggest up to five keywords for Download.com's site search function, and being able to control my keywords to some extent means I can keep the path between my applications and potential customers as short as possible.

Another benefit is being able to update MasterList Professional's listing in a day, instead of 5 to 15 days as with free listing. Each time I do an update, I've seen a spike in downloads.

Even though MasterList Professional is out, and MasterList XL is and always was free, I still fork out $99 USD a month to list MasterList XL because over the past two years I've made more than twenty times the cost of listing from custom software contracts for companies that found me via Download.com.

KELLY MORRISON, DIRECTOR, CNET DOWNLOAD.COM

If you want to download and try legitimate software, the place to go is Download.com. Kelly Morrison, director of Download.com, explains what micro-ISVs have to gain from listing their software at Download.com.

Q. How many downloads does Download.com get in a day?

A. About 2.5 million (this includes software, games, and music).

Q How many applications are posted currently at Download.com?

A. Just under 35,000.

Q. If you're a start-up software company (a micro-ISV), why make a trial version of your app available via Download.com?

A. The try-before-you-buy model has become a standard for software in the nine years since CNET Download.com launched, and it has been extremely successful for both small and large publishers. Over those nine years, Download.com has proven that it can put small publishers on the map with new-to-market products that would not have gotten distribution through other channels.

At this point, I would say that offering a downloadable trial is essential for new products, especially considering the massive shift to online software purchasing that we've been seeing over the past several years.

Q. What are three mistakes to avoid when listing at Download.com?

A. • This is probably obvious, but make sure you have a stable product release before you list on Download.com. Our editors review a vast number of products on the site, and a negative review can seriously hinder a new product's success.

  • Make sure the product has reasonable trial functionality and duration. For example, a one-day or one-use trial is not sufficient to make the user comfortable with it. A 30-day trial, or a trial in which output (say, printing) is disabled or watermarked in some way, would be preferable.

  • Don't include adware of any kind. We scan all incoming submissions, and we will decline to list products that contain adware.

Q. I notice there are some new things at Download.com—Merchant Services and Pay-per-Download. What do these services mean to a micro-ISV, and where is Download.com going?

A. Pay-per-Download is a promotional program that allows software publishers to get more exposure and distribution of their product. In essence, publishers go to `http://www.upload.com` and can bid in our monthly auction environment for top placement on listing pages (by subcategory). We award the top-five listing spots to the top bidders, based on download volume, cost per download, and spend cap. We currently have about 400 publishers in the program.

Merchant Services is a self-service platform that allows software publishers the ability to configure their product with trial functionality, registration, merchant services, and copy protection on a postcompile basis. In other words, it helps publishers establish a trial version of their product, capture customer registration info, transact a purchase, and protect the trial version with top DRM functionality—all in a self-service platform.

Tucows.com

Another important download site is Tucows.com. Unlike Download.com where most listings go unrated by either CNET or downloaders, every software application submitted to Tucows.com gets reviewed. A coveted "5-Cow" rating can ignite your sales and is well worth highlighting on your Web site; to even be listed, a software app has to score at least a 50 percent (3-Cow) rating.

Tucows.com goes to some lengths to make sure the software its readers see is worth their time, as shown in Figure 5-20.

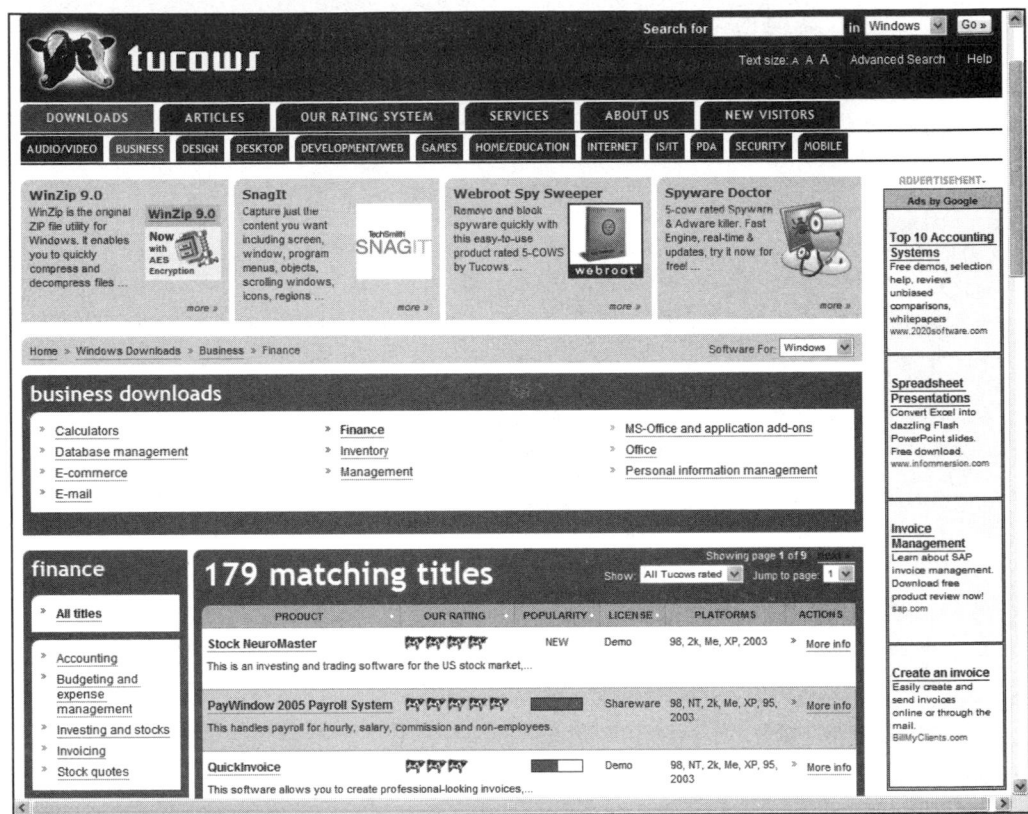

Figure 5-20. *Welcome to your Tucows.com category...*

The Tucows.com submission process is relatively straightforward, but how fast your application will be reviewed, and whether you'll have a shot at getting it rereviewed, depends on what you're prepared to pay. And, keep in mind, as you see in Figure 5-21, you're not paying for a guaranteed listing but for how soon your product will be considered for listing.

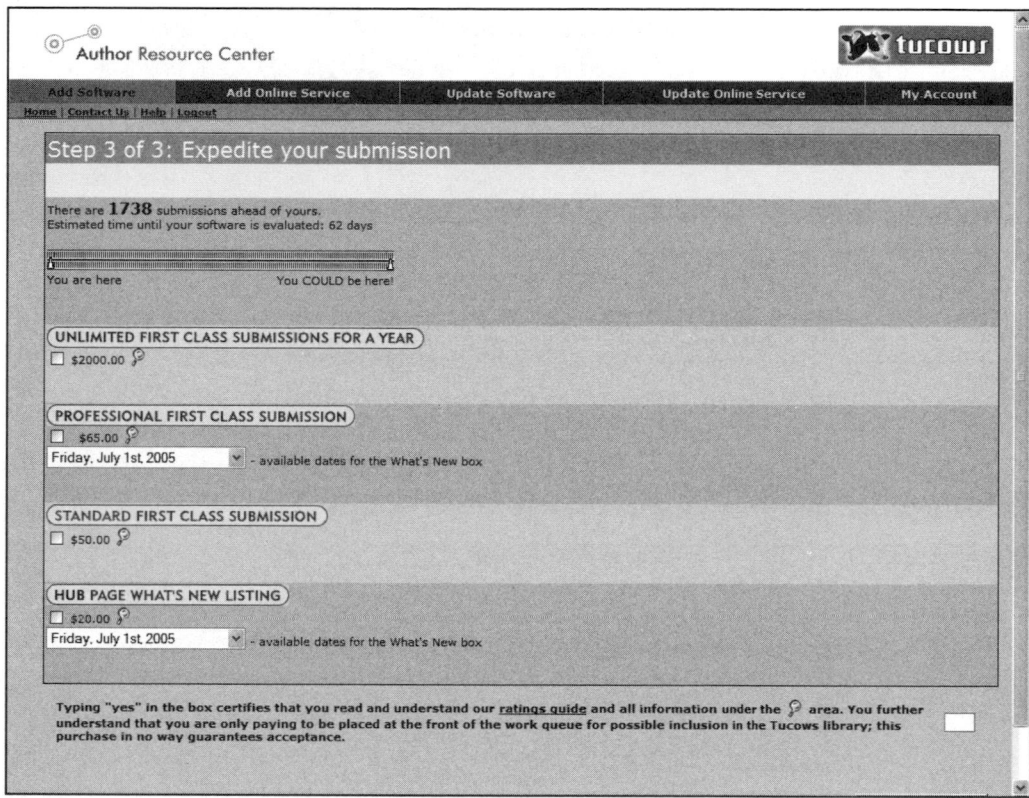

Figure 5-21. *...once you're considered for listing.*

Microsoft Office Marketplace

As with many, many other markets, Microsoft arrived on the software download scene late and by virtue of being Microsoft became a major player. That said, if your micro-ISV's application in any way, shape, or form relates to any part of Microsoft Office, pursuing a listing at `http://office.microsoft.com/en-us/marketplace/default.aspx` is well worth the effort, as shown in Figure 5-22.

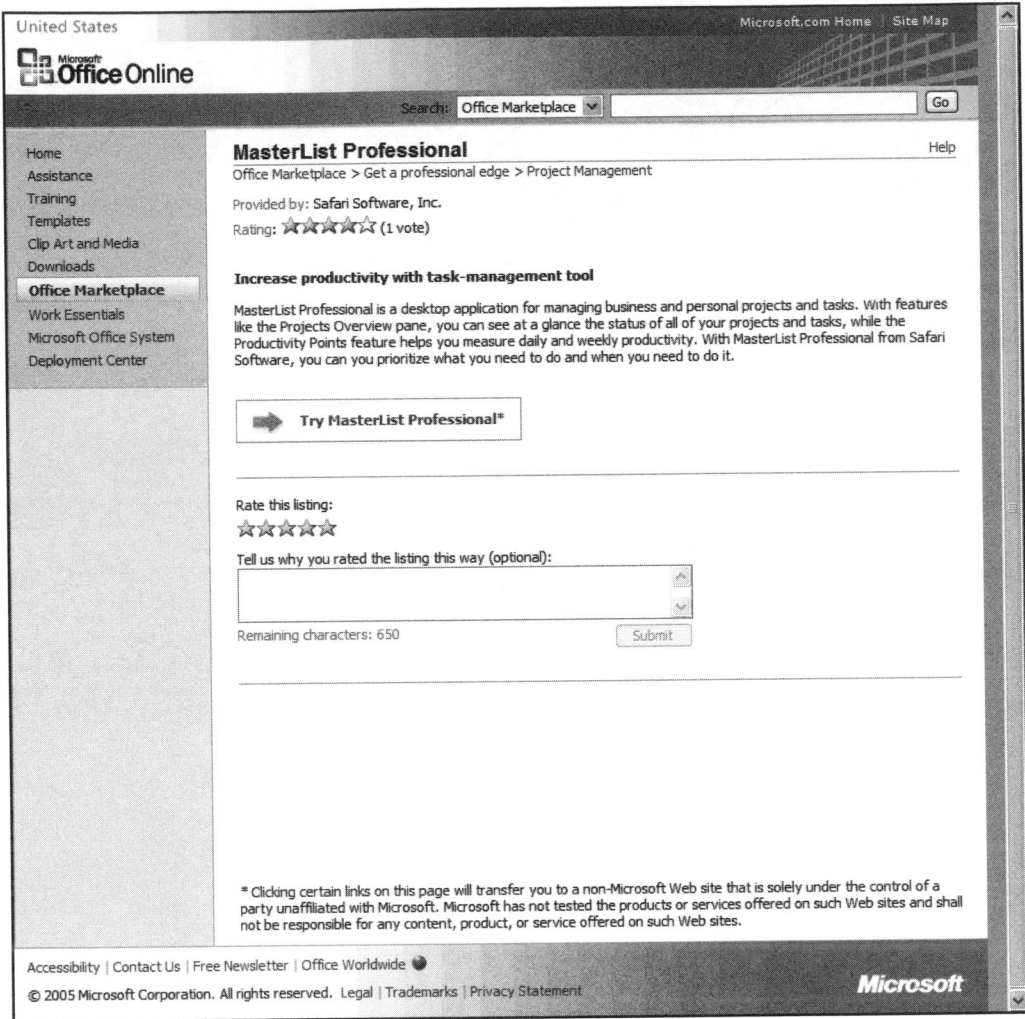

Figure 5-22. *A typical Marketplace listing*

After the strong dose of monetization you'll find at the previously mentioned download sites, Marketplace's lack of ads and free listing is a nice change of pace. Of course, one could say the entire site is a giant ad for Microsoft, and that's true; I'll have more to say about coexisting with Microsoft in Chapter 6.

One interesting aspect of how Marketplace does business is its requirement that you have a dedicated landing page on your site for visitors who click your listing in Marketplace, as shown in Figure 5-23. As discussed earlier in this chapter, dedicated landing pages are an excellent way of making specific audiences welcome, and with more than 20 million visitors (about the entire population of, say, Australia[3]) a day to Marketplace's parent site, Office Online, this is an audience you want to roll out the red carpet for.

---

3. http://www.photius.com/rankings/world2050_rank.html

Figure 5-23. *A dedicated landing page for Microsoft Office Marketplace*

JEANETTE FISHER, BUSINESS DEVELOPMENT MANAGER, MICROSOFT OFFICE ONLINE

If your software application connects in some way with Microsoft Office, Microsoft wants you. In this interview, Jeanette Fisher, the business development manager for Microsoft Office Online and the gatekeeper for Office Marketplace, explains why.

Q. What is Microsoft Marketplace? How many people go there?

A. We have 50 million unique users worldwide each month who visit not Marketplace directly but Office Online, our parent site (our mothership, so to speak). Of those 50 million users, about 2 to 3 percent trickle through to the Office Marketplace.

Q. What does Marketplace have to offer micro-ISVs?

A. We have one of the highest known conversion rates in the history of the Internet at our Web site. That means customers who come to a partner's site from our site are much more likely to purchase—to become a paying customer in some way—than anywhere else because we send qualified leads to our partners. The average conversion rate for Internet sales is around .2 percent; we see conversion rates of between 1 percent and 19 percent.

Q. How many listings are there at Office Marketplace?

A. Right now there are over 600 unique listings in the U.S. market. If we are talking worldwide, then we are close to 1,000.

Q. Is Marketplace only part of the main U.S. Microsoft site?

A. Office itself is localized in at least 47 different languages, and Office Online is available in most of those. I think now 42. But Office Marketplace, because we need to have a substantial number of both customers and partner listings in a given market before we launch a full Marketplace, that's a much smaller number. We are in 19 different regional markets.

Q. Why does Office Marketplace exist?

A. Microsoft Office Marketplace exists as the customer connection for partners who build atop the Office platform. Marketplace was an initiative to connect customers with those solutions because the idea of Office Online when it was launched was not just to provide assistance in the way of help articles and tips and tricks, and things like that, but to do anything we can to boost the productivity of an Office customer as they use the Office system.

Q. How connected must a product or service be to Microsoft Office to get listed?

A. Obviously we [get] some listings that are not downloadable solutions built on Office, that are not code. Examples of those are books, training services, [and] consulting services that help a customer deploy Office in their environment. The main criteria are whether or not it is relevant to the customer's use of Office.

For example, I had an application that came in today for an educational product, but there was nothing in the product or service that related to Office. The customer did not need Office to get this product running, and also there was nothing on their Web site that said anything about how they integrate with Excel or Word. The email I sent back to this potential partner was, "I don't see any relevance for the customer using Office at the same time as your product." That's really what we are looking for.

Q. Only the core office apps, or do you cover the "extended family" of Office like MapPoint?

A. Anything falls within that extended family of Office, like SharePoint, Project, Visio, InfoPath, all of those.

Q. I noticed that there are no ads presently at Marketplace—is that a firm policy?

A. It is something as a business development team we are revisiting—we are very aware of the size of our customer base and the potential for projects like revenue sharing and advertising, so that [no ads] may change.

Q. Is it a level playing field? In other words, you have two companies—one with one person, the other with a thousand people. Are their listings going to be any different?

A. Nope. It is a level playing field. We consider ourselves to be an open and fair marketplace. We don't give preferences—it's really about free marketing for everybody. The promotion opportunities on the site—for example, today there's a wine cellar template being promoted—we change those every week. And some of the recommended downloads change daily. We try [to] do a constant rotation. We may be changing that in the future (as the number of partners grow). For example, we may give more promotion to partners who offer free trials than partners who don't.

Q. How does one of your listings pitch you to be one of your featured promo spots?

A. Really at this point it's a compelling story about how they integrate with a part of the Office platform. They usually need to have good customer data about how they increased productivity or customer satisfaction. They have to be willing to put together or modify the jump page we link to so that a customer's experience is the best possible when we link to their site from ours, and again the free trial is always one of the criteria we call out.

Q. *That's interesting—you don't usually think of Microsoft and free in the same sentence....*

A. We definitely believe that people should be able to try software first, and you'll see that reflected in the rest of Office Online. All of our products are available for free trial now. We strongly believe in our products, and if people experience it, they will want to keep it. We would like to believe that our partners have the same confidence in their offerings.

Q. *A lot of developers have a love-love, love-hate, or a hate-hate relationship when it comes to Microsoft.*

A. Very true.

Q. *What do you say to a small developer who is more than a little bit paranoid that their software is going to turn into the 753rd feature in Word someday?*

A. We try to be very up front with all of our partners and all our potential partners. We clearly state that you providing this service to Office customers does not preclude Office someday from building a similar feature. And most of the time when that happens, at least in my experience in the last six years here, I can honestly say that I have never seen a partner offering being evaluated by the product team and see the product lead say, "Oh, that's a great idea. We should build that in directly."

Usually what happens is that we are the process of building a feature in and a partner comes to the front with that feature in existence, and we say, "Great, they can fulfill the customer's needs until we have the time to build it ourselves."

Q. *Would you recommend that micro-ISVs make the effort to get listed with Office Marketplace?*

A. Absolutely! Because if for no other reason, it's free marketing. And it's free marketing across several different companies if they are willing to localize their jump pages. And it's free marketing that has the potential of hitting 50 million customers on a monthly basis.

Q. *Office Marketplace wants a dedicated landing page. Why?*

A. There's a couple of reasons for that. The primary reason is customer experience. We want to make sure that the cognitive load on the customer is as minimized as possible. For example, when a customer searches our site for *FrontPage templates*, finds one, and clicks it, the first and foremost thing they should be presented with is the fastest and easiest way to get FrontPage templates. When the customer is arriving at one of our partner's jump pages, they've already gone through that filtering process—the worst thing to do to them is to throw them back to the "everything possible" situation.

All the Rest and Lessons Learned

In this section, I'll make a couple of final points about download sites. As with search engines, don't fixate on the top few and ignore the lucrative many, as shown in Figure 5-24. This especially applies if your micro-ISV is focusing on an application or service of interest to a particular industry and or country. Hundreds of other download sites large and small will welcome you with open arms, if you make the effort.

Next, and this especially applies to Download.com, when you update your software, update your software's listing. Updating your listing will at least for a time move it to the first page of listings for your primary search category, and updating your listing shows you're serious about improving your product.

Finally, if you want to kick-start your download site program, download the Download Site Planner from this book's page at Apress's Web site (http://www.apress.com).

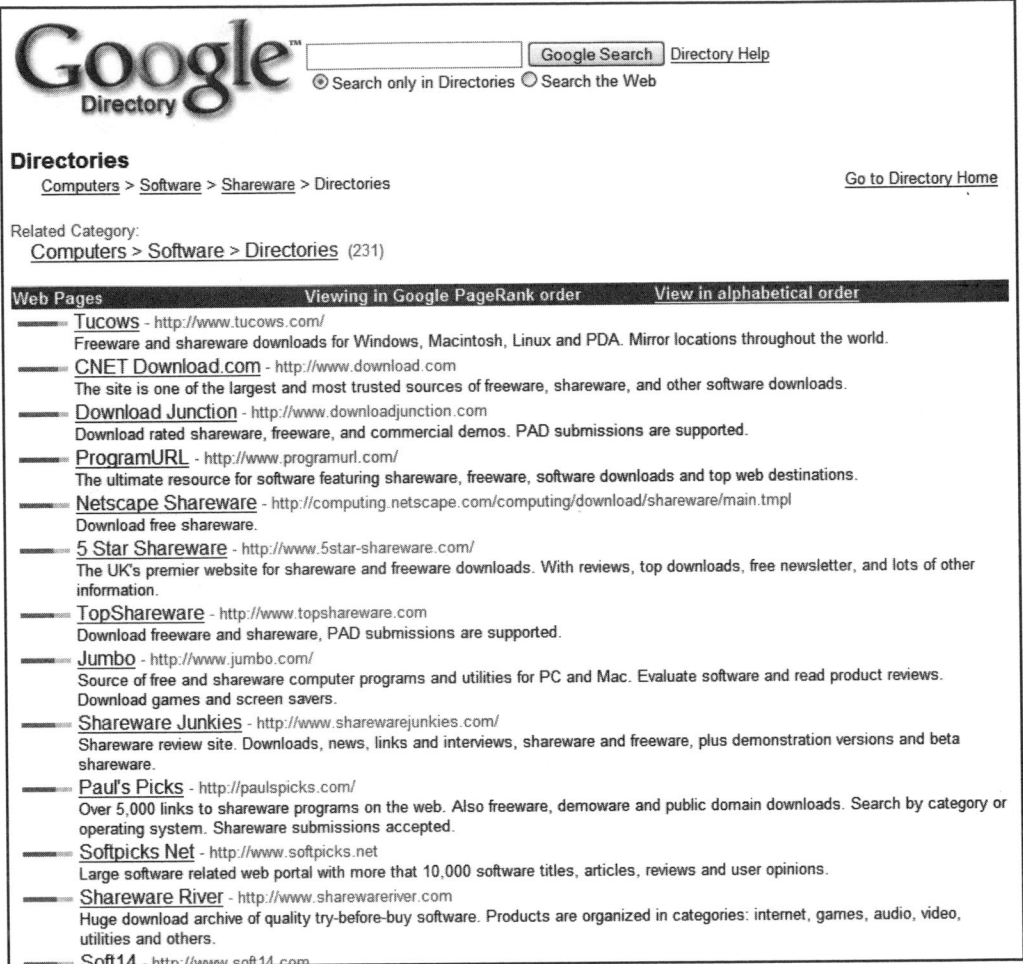

Figure 5-24. *272 and counting...*

The Influencers

Although the Internet has removed many of the intermediaries between you and your customer, if you're going to be successful, you need to pay attention to and understand the needs of the *influencers.*

In this case, influencers are the mainstream, trade, and Internet media—the newspapers, trade magazines, and blogs that significant portions of your target audience respect and follow.

Don't underestimate the power of these people to make or break your product. I remember a time in the late 1980s when I was a contract programmer for a company bringing to market a network label printer. The company had secured millions in venture capital funding, worked out the technical issues, and was ready to ramp up to a 100-person company.

Then the first review of a preproduction unit came out in a major trade publication. It lambasted the product for shoddy performance, poor print quality, and being unworkable. The next day when I arrived to meet with my manager, the company that had occupied an entire floor of a Silicon Valley office building was gone. The chairs were pushed into a herd in one corner, the computers were stacked four up in another, and no one was left. The venture capitalists had pulled the plug on the company, based on the Kiss of Death review.

In those days, perhaps 20 trade publications followed the industry in the United States; mainstream press was trying to explain what a LAN was, and blogging was something you did after you drank too much at a party. Now, 53 *categories* of online trade publications are listed in the Yahoo Business Directory,[4] most newspapers and television stations have at least one technology reporter, and blogging is still something you do after a party, except it can influence a national election or send half a million people to your Web site.

Your job as media relations person (a.k.a. flack) for your company is to first understand how to work with mainstream, trade, and Internet reporters and editors and then to learn how these people, if properly approached after you're prepared, can be inordinately helpful to your micro-ISV.

I'll talk to a reporter and an editor next so that you can start seeing how things look from their perspective, what to do and not do, and how to prepare your product for review.

LESLIE BROOKS SUZUKAMO, TELECOM AND TECHNOLOGY REPORTER, *ST. PAUL PIONEER PRESS*

I've known Les Suzukamo since we both started as cub reporters at UCLA's *Daily Bruin* oh so many years ago, and he graciously agreed to spill the beans to me on what reporters covering tech want from the companies they cover: real news.

Q. Tell me what you do, what you cover?

A. I cover telecom and local technology companies. Since we're part of Knight-Ridder, the second largest newspaper chain, we get a lot of big technology news that way. My editor doesn't think it's the best use of my time to be one of thirty reporters chasing the same national story. If it's something that affects us locally, then I'm on that.

Q. Let's say I'm two guys in a heated garage in St. Paul, Minnesota, and we've just whipped up the newest, latest, and greatest application for Windows. We're local guys, and we think, "It'd be great to read about us in the Pioneer Press.*" What should we do?*

A. Well, something we always ask is, "So what?" Just because you have a new product doesn't mean you have a compelling story to tell. There's another guy at the newspaper who does product reviews, and this would go over to him.

Q. At some point, I'd like to talk to him about how he decides what to review; but the other part of this is the local angle making news. Let's say a company donates 50 copies of their new digital organizer to a school and calls you. I'm wondering if as a reporter this is the sort of thing you would go for or wouldn't touch with a ten-foot pole?

A. We try to stay away from manufactured news. Nobody is interested in that sort of thing.

---

4. http://dir.yahoo.com/Business_and_Economy/Business_to_Business/News_and_Media/Magazines/ Trade_Magazines/

Q. Well, what types of stories do make the news?

A. Here's an example: Each weekend I write a piece on a local entrepreneur. This local firm takes Microsoft Great Plains software—a back-office, HR sort of thing—and customizes for schools. They had worked with a local school for a year to develop this product for an underserved market, and they were preparing to start selling it nationally. That was kind of interesting—I could call the school and find out how the software was working, and they were a local firm about to go national.

Q. By the way, how did they contact you?

A. They had a PR person contact me.

Q. And nowadays are paper press releases obsolete and email press releases are the way to go?

A. Most people in the business much prefer emails. Email is the way to go.

Q. Is it OK to call you?

A. That's fine, especially to follow up an email. But don't call me at 4 p.m. That might be a good time for you make your calls, but my day is kicking into high gear at that point. And don't have PR people cold-call me—they're just going off a script their client gave them, and they can't tell me anything if I get interested.

ROB VAMOSI, SENIOR EDITOR, CNET NETWORKS

When it comes to online coverage of all things tech, the best known and the most comprehensive coverage is at CNET's two main web sites, CNET.com and ZDNet.com. Rob Vamosi, a senior editor at CNET, shares his perspective with micro-ISVs.

Q. What do you do at CNET?

A. I'm the lead editor for software, security, and Internet services. It's a big territory to cover. My background is more in security, but I've been working in software for the last four or five years, so I'm familiar with the breadth of software, and I recently started picking up Internet services. I work with a number of editors and associate editors who take on pieces of that.

Q. From your vantage point in the industry, is desktop software dead? Is everything going to move to the Web?

A. I think I sort of answered it when I said I'm taking on Internet services. I don't want to proclaim that desktop software is dead; I think ownership is a big part of it—that you want to load and run software on your machine. I think the idea of it being hosted elsewhere is personally scary for a number of reasons, but I think there's going to be a lot of growth in Web services in the next few years and perhaps consolidation and shakeout in desktop software.

Q. Are you seeing more and more software or less and less? Are you seeing it all coming from bigger and bigger companies or smaller and smaller companies?

A. I think, if we are talking about [the] desktop again, we are seeing less; there [were] perhaps more a few years ago. And, again, it's because of the consolidation that's going on. For instance, I'm looking here at a box from PowerQuest; they were bought by Symantec, so Drive Image is no more, except as bundled with Symantec.

Q. So do you get a stack of press releases on your desk every day?

A. Here's the thing—over the years, it's all gone email. I don't get anything via the U.S. Postal Service anymore; and if I do, it's very odd. That said, people will send me software unsolicited and on occasion eye-grabbing promotional things. Given where CNET falls on the media spectrum, we see everything here, and we have to be very selective when we pick and choose what we can and cannot cover.

Q. How do start-ups get you interested in something?

A. I can come up with two examples, one being Spybot Search and Destroy. There's a little product that generated just a lot of buzz when it came out a few years ago. I think it got picked up on Slashdot; people were talking about. It wasn't that it was just available on CNET Download.com that brought it to my attention; it was the sheer buzz around it that made me want to go and review it. There are a lot of antispyware products out there. It really came to my attention because of the positive response that people were giving it.

The other product that springs to mind is something called EverNote; it's like Microsoft OneNote. There again there was a bit of buzz, but they were going after an existing product from Microsoft that had relatively no competition, and it seemed this was a logical direction for software to move into.

Q. How should micro-ISVs contact you to pitch their story?

A. My preferred method of contact is email, and I think that's true for a number of my colleagues. Send your press releases, PDFs, whatever, and if it's going to fill a niche we are looking to fill, if it's going in a direction we are going anyway, it will really catch our attention, and we will follow up with you on it. I don't necessarily like phone calls. I discourage them as much as possible. I like to look at the nitty-gritty, if your press release has specs. I'm not swayed by testimonials; testimonials don't always win me over.

I can also say that going out and hiring a PR firm is probably not always the best way to get your point across with someone like me. I think I have a really good spin filter in place; I can tell when I'm being snowed. Sending me a box full of T-shirts and pen holders and whatever, it doesn't move me in any way. It's basically, is this a good piece of software, and is this something we should be telling people about because it again fills a niche or represents where technology is moving in the next few years?

People who come up with software solutions for already crowded niches, I think are kind of, well, they have to be really, really good to knock the existing players out of the ballpark. For example, I've been hit with a lot of antispyware in the last few months, and it seems to me the window for that was a couple of years ago. It's a really crowded market, and for someone new to come along and convince me that they're better than these guys, I'm going to be really skeptical.

Q. It sounds like part of what CNET sees its mission as is not just feeds and speeds but where is the technology going?

A. Yes

Q. What would you say are the three stupidest things people ever did trying to pitch their product to you?

A. Number one would be not taking no for an answer. I will respond to email solicitations, and oftentimes it's "This is not within our content coverage for 2005." And people will write back and parse my response, writing "But! It really does this!" and I will say no again.

I guess another would be not being familiar with our site and spamming all the editors with requests. And I guess the third thing would be referring to my work as Download.com, again not knowing CNET's structure. I get a lot of email that's intended for Download.com, and I have a great relationship with the people on that floor. They do review products, but their criteria are different than ours.

Q. Any last advice for micro-ISV's dealing with CNET or life in general?

A. Well, like I said, I have a pretty good spin filter in place. If the work is there, if the product is really good, it will show through, and once you've got the foot in the door, the product is going to make it all the more easy to be reviewed and talked about and so forth. Put all of your work into the product.

And I'll just add to that: we have checks and balances as well. We may be on this mountain looking out over the software industry, and so forth, but if I go out and declare something an Editor's Choice and people download it or buy it, and it just didn't perform the way we said it did or the way the box said it did, they respond, and it's on the site. And everybody can see it.

Q. Do editors read those comments?

A. Yes. You'll be going to update something, and you'll notice that you gave a product a 7 and the readers gave it a 4. It will merit some investigation. If there's only two or three people writing in, and the reviews have been up for a while, I might discount that as sour grapes. But if there's a lot of people writing in, and the problems are fairly common, then, yeah, it's a wake-up call. We missed this somehow—how did that happen? So there [are] checks and balances here. We can't go out and promote a product if it really doesn't work the way it's supposed to work. And that's a very good thing.

CHAPTER 6

■ ■ ■

Welcome to Your Industry

Joint undertakings stand a better chance when they benefit both sides.

—Euripides, ancient Greek poet[1]

So far, you've been focused on you, your customer, and your micro-ISV. It's time to broaden your horizons and take a look at the resources and opportunities of working with other software companies, how to and why you should keep an eye on your competitors, and some of the organizations and Web sites you should know about as you build your micro-ISV.

What About Microsoft?

Whether you hate or love Microsoft, from a developer's point of view, it's the 900-pound gorilla in your room. Maybe the gorilla likes you, and it will share all sorts of goodies with you. But maybe the gorilla doesn't like you and spends every waking moment thinking about how to crush you.

It's a matter of record that in software market after software market, Microsoft has gone from uninterested bystander to market dominator. For example, at the time of this writing, Microsoft was beta testing two products: Microsoft OneCare (an antivirus, backup, and firewall subscription service), as shown in Figure 6-1, and Microsoft AntiSpyware. These two products have the potential—and in my opinion, the likelihood—of driving several major companies and dozens of others off a financial cliff to the sharp rocks below.

It will not be the first time. (Remember Netscape?) And it will not be the last: any fair reading of computer press would put large and small companies in the customer relations management "space," RSS reader vendors, and of course Google on Microsoft's endangered species list.

The weird thing for micro-ISVs about Microsoft is one of the keys to its immense power has been its long and substantial commitment to developers. From providing developers with virtual megatons of technical information and dozens of marketing programs (designed at least in part to assist other companies) to having a new religious zeal for blogging on a developer-to-developer level, Microsoft has by any estimate one of the best, if not the best, developer programs.

---

1. http://www.brainyquote.com/quotes/quotes/e/euripides149001.html

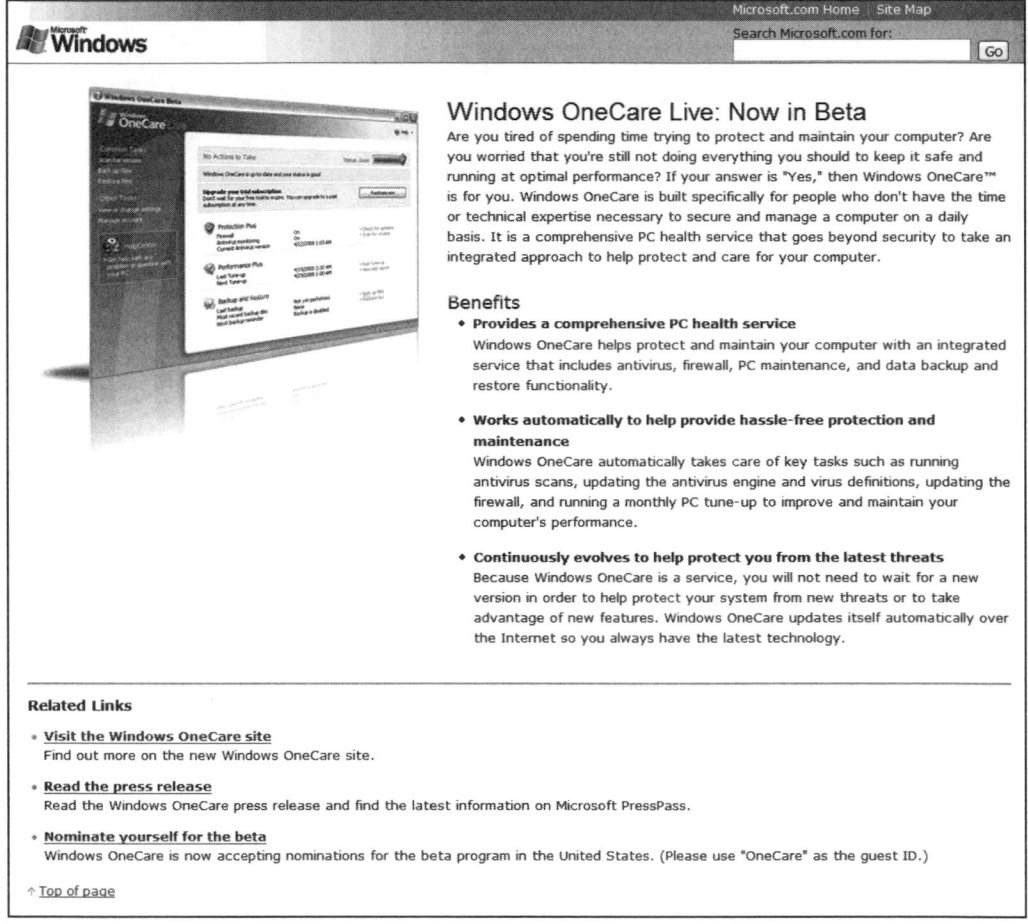

Figure 6-1. *Bad news for competitors*

The sheer volume of developer information Microsoft makes available is mind numbing. For example, leaving aside all the pages of information at Microsoft Developer Network (MSDN) (http://msdn.microsoft.com/), all the various events and conferences Microsoft sponsors, all the newsgroups Microsoft participates in, all the Software Development Kits (SDKs) it offers, and all the sheer technology it offers, consider just one number: as of this writing, 2,044 active Microsoft employees are blogging (as shown in Figure 6-2) about what they did today at Microsoft.[2]

Make that a talkative, 900-pound, schizophrenic gorilla.

Books could be—and have been—written about whether Microsoft is "bad" or "good." This isn't going to be one of those books, because the focus here is making your micro-ISV successful. Instead, you'll look next at four specific Microsoft programs of considerable interest to micro-ISVs and several Web sites that should be on your daily list, even if you're developing a completely non-Windows application or Web service.

---

2. http://blogs.msdn.com/Bloggers.aspx?GroupID=2

Blogs	Last Post	Authors
Microsoft Bloggers		
Alex Lowe's .NET Blog Taking feedback to the next level....	Blog moved....	AlexLowe
Notes from the field... William Zentmayer - Architect Evangelist	Doing SOA without Web Services? Part II.	William Zentmayer
Michał Cierniak Rotor, Semiworks and other interesting topics	Moving to a new blog	michalic
.NET Banana Developer Happenings in Pennsylvania, Delaware, Maryland, DC, Virginia, and West Virginia	.NET Master Class in Reston, VA	gsnowman
Communiverse All about Community		ThomasFi
Kirk Allen Evans' Blog .NET From a Markup Perspective	Where's the Outlook Demo for Beta2 and Beyond?	kaevans
Michael Murray's .NET Blog weblog.NET, radio "nyet"	The Other BlogX?	mimurray2
greggm's WebLog	Reflections on 64-bit	greggm
Baiju Nair's Blog on Visual Web Developer	Recent changes in web conversion tool	Baiju
Love that ASP.NET and SQL Server Ben Miller's Developer Experiences	SQL Server party at Tech Ed Europe	benmiller
Alex Ingerman's WebLog All the news that is fit to blog		AlexIngerman
Yun Jin's WebLog CLR internals, Rotor code explanation, CLR debugging tips, trivial debugging notes, .NET programming pitfalls, and blah, blah, blah...	Trivial debugging note - using WeakReference in finalizer	yunjin
shrini Kulkarni's WebLog on Software Testing	Logging Off	shrink
GisliO.net [MSFT] .net on Ice	Do you want to show off at PDC?	Gislio
Point2Share Daniel McPherson's Blog for Casual Comment on SharePoint	Maurice is in London AND having a Pint2Share	danielmcpherson
File it! Brian Dewey's Blog: All about file systems, storage, and miscellany	Setting up DFS at home? Learn from Charlie.	Brian Dewey
shawn's blog LOAD"",1	MyBlogLog	shawnmor

Figure 6-2. *Microsoft employees blogging: 2,044 and counting*

The Microsoft Empower Program

If you plan to develop software or a Web service for Windows[3] and your micro-ISV isn't already a Microsoft Certified Partner, you should consider applying for the Microsoft Empower program, as shown in Figure 6-3.

For $375 USD you get a slightly downscaled[4] annual MSDN Universal subscription to almost all of Microsoft's technology for the purpose of developing a new software application. Compare that to the suggested retail price for an MSDN Universal subscription—$2,799 USD, or £260, versus approximately £1900 in the United Kingdom. After the first year, you can apply to stay in the program for another year.

Besides saving a few thousand dollars, you get another benefit from the Empower program: you get ten hours of "advisory support" per year.

"This phone-based consultative service helps you develop applications using Microsoft technologies. Services include ad hoc development advice, best practice recommendations, code samples, [and] limited technology architecture or application design reviews," says Microsoft's Empower site.

---

3. Or any of the other Microsoft operating systems, such as Xbox

4. No tech support incidents. Your license to use all the software provided as part of your subscription ends the day your enrollment in the Empower program ends.

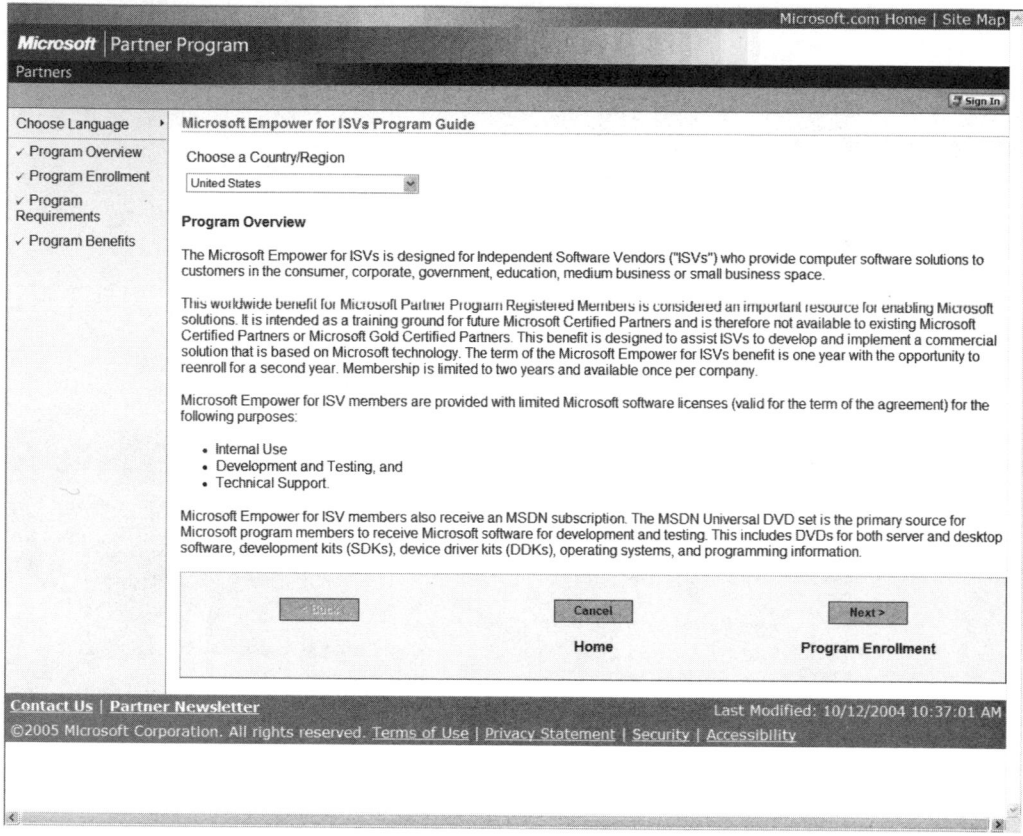

Figure 6-3. *Microsoft Empower program*

Full disclosure time: my micro-ISV, Safari Software, is in the Empower program. About two weeks ago, I got a call from Raj at Microsoft, asking how Safari Software was doing and whether my development efforts could benefit from some one-to-one technical help from one or more Microsoft employees. I declined—but only until I can figure out the best way to use this valuable resource.

The Microsoft Buddy Program

I wholeheartedly recommend another Microsoft program to micro-ISVs: the Microsoft ISV Buddy program (`http://msdn.microsoft.com/isv/isvbuddy/default.aspx`), as shown in Figure 6-4. The 900-pound gorilla—or at least this part of it—*really* wants to be your friend, seriously.

I signed up just when the program started in September 2004. Signing up is free and easy. To qualify, your micro-ISV needs to be "actively developing software solutions on Microsoft platforms/technologies for one or more external customers."

My first Microsoft buddy was Jane Pratt, a Microsoft U.K. employee working in the Developer Tools Support Team. Jane was invaluable not only for finding some fairly obscure technical information but for talking with me via email like I was a real, live, genuine developer.

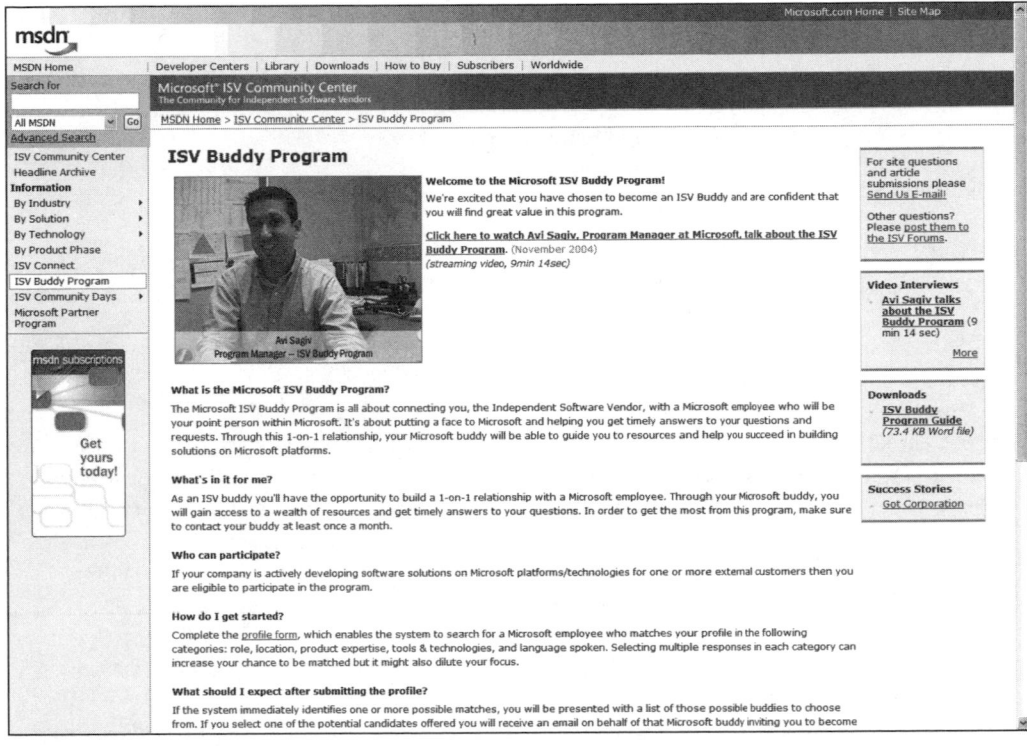

Figure 6-4. *Microsoft ISV Buddy program*

Jane "unbecame" my Microsoft buddy because of other commitments (the Microsoft Buddy program is unpaid and doesn't replace the Microsoft employee's regular workload). This turned out to be a blessing in disguise, because my second Microsoft buddy, Jason Hermitage, is a senior product manager in the Windows Server Product Marketing Group.

Marketing isn't something that comes easy to me or most developers. Jason has been absolutely great in our various conversations not just for getting me involved with some of the multitude of marketing initiatives at Microsoft but in showing me how a Sharp Guy thinks about marketing.

I highly recommend this program to any micro-ISV.

AVI SAGIV, PROGRAM MANAGER, MICROSOFT BUDDY PROGRAM

While Avi Sagiv, a program manager for the Microsoft Buddy program, was on parental leave and out of the country, he kindly took the time to answer the questions I posed to him about the Microsoft Buddy program.

Q. What are the goals of the Microsoft Buddy program?

A. • To put a friendly face on Microsoft through one-on-one connections between ISVs and Microsoft employees.

   • To help ISVs grow their businesses and succeed in building solutions on the Microsoft platform.

   • To help ISVs find answers to questions they might not be able to find anywhere else.

   • To better understand the challenges ISVs face when partnering with large companies like Microsoft.

Q. What has been the response of developers—how many are in the program?

A. We've had good participation from both sides. Current numbers:

- 2,190 ISVs requested development in their profiles.

- 2,804 total ISVs matched.

- 514 Microsoft developers.

- 1,941 total Microsoft employees enrolled.

We also have a valuable line-up of employees with expertise in product usability, marketing, sales, business development, localization, [and] user assistance/documentation.

Q. What has been the experience of the Microsoft employees to and in the program?

A. We've heard from many Microsoft Buddy program [participants] that this program has been a fun and valuable learning experience for them. In many cases, interacting directly with the companies that build products on Microsoft technologies has helped them and their teams make product and process improvements and get a better understanding of the obstacles ISVs run into when developing on Microsoft technologies.

Q. As you go forward, are there either plans to expand the program or to cap the number participants?

A. At this time, we plan to continue the program and recruit more Microsoft employees.

Q. Any advice for self-funded software startups (micro-ISVs) regarding the program or anything else?

A. Take advantage of any program that enables you to forge relationships with employees to get the answers and insights you might not find anywhere else.

Explore all of the programs and resources available to you, for example, Empower and other levels of the Partner program, ISV Community Days, ISV Royalty program, MSDN ISV Community Center and Forums, MSDN Developer Centers, etc.

Also, here are a few recent quotes we've received from happy ISVs:

- "You are a gold mine, my friend! Thanks a million! That was it...have no idea who came up with this Buddy program...but I am grateful to them and you!"

- "This was a great idea and to me shows a real commitment by Microsoft to help people learn their platforms. There are times when all of the experimentation and reverse engineering in the world won't answer the whole question, and at those times it's great to have this kind of access."

- "Although we only use [our buddy] infrequently, he has helped to shape our development program for the new 64-bit servers, and for a small company this was very important."

- "Our buddy can get to people for answers who we don't even know exist."

- "Wow! This Buddy program rocks! I've never had such fast interaction (and results) with Microsoft."

The Other Microsoft

Like a lot of large multinational companies, two very different Microsofts exist, and micro-ISVs can benefit from learning about and connecting to what I call "the other Microsoft."

Besides all the technical evangelists, development advisors, and support engineers located in and around Microsoft's corporate headquarters in Redmond, Washington, there's the other Microsoft in Phoenix, Arizona; Alpharetta, Georgia; and Columbus, Ohio. It's the other Microsoft that's also in Argentina and China and even Auckland, New Zealand.

The other Microsoft is just as committed to the goals, values, and bottom line as the Microsofters who work in Microsoft office buildings, eat Microsoft food, and live in Microsoft suburbs and drop their kids off in the morning at Microsoft day care. Absolutely!

They are just a wee bit more approachable, a wee bit more used to making their own decisions, and, if you are lucky, a wee bit more interested in you.

NIGEL PARKER, DEVELOPMENT ADVISOR, MICROSOFT NZ

I came across Nigel Parker, the development advisor for Microsoft NZ, when I went looking to put a human face on the other Microsoft. Nigel was kind enough to spend a chunk of his Saturday (my Friday) responding to questions from 10,000-odd miles away.

Q. In what sort of ways do you evangelize Microsoft to developers in New Zealand?

A. In New Zealand the Developer and Platform Evangelism Team is small and multifaceted. We have distinct roles within our group focusing on all the different components of the industry. We have focus on academia, community and professional developers, independent software vendors, Web hosting organizations, IT professionals, architects, business decision makers, and citizenship initiatives.

Although we are proponents for Microsoft technology, we are furthermore proponents for the innovation that drives the IT industry to change the way we work and live. One of the activities that I drive in New Zealand is rolling out early-adopter programs to independent software vendors. This enables those companies to get support in building their applications on our new platforms well before they ship. Those customers get the ability to make suggestions and change our platform to fit their real-world requirements!

The process of matching passionate individuals to exciting technology is really rewarding. My MSN Messenger just flashed up with a message from a customer: "Dude, thanks so much for the Expression Studio nomination. I've got an email from the PM [Product Manager] to kick the process off. It's greatly appreciated...I'm extremely excited...expect to see some great evangelism from me in the future with it...UI and design is a major passion of mine!"

Q. Do you have any sort of local developer events?

A. Of course! Every year our team organizes Tech-Ed. Tech-Ed is the premier developer event in New Zealand. For the last few years this event has followed a global pattern and been a sell-out. Over the space of a week we trained 700+ students, 2,000 developers with 77 speakers (from all over the world), 8 tracks, 128 sessions, and 1 big party.

In addition to Tech-Ed twice a year we run a Microsoft Connect event that spans three cities and is well attended by close to 5,000 professional developers. Microsoft Connect is traditionally a free or minimal-charge event that has greater reach to the regions than our Tech-Ed event. As a team we also sponsor New Zealand–based user groups that support Microsoft technology. Last year the .NET user groups of New Zealand combined to create an incorporated society (http://www.dot.net.nz) to facilitate growth and manage programs including seminars, workshops, Webcasts, and support mailing lists. Our team has committed to provide three Microsoft-based speakers each year to tour and talk at these user groups.

Q. What sort of Microsoft resources might a New Zealand developer not know about that you do?

A. I will cover the Microsoft business start-up and Partner and program resources below. For this question I will focus on the training and technical resources that we provide. First of all, I am the editor of a fortnightly newsletter called MSDN Flash. MSDN Flash has a wealth of useful resources and links to topical events and Webcasts. If you are not a subscriber of MSDN Flash, make sure you sign up at http://www.microsoft.com/nz/msdn, and then click "subscribe to MSDN Flash" under the resources menu.

Visit Microsoft Learning (https://www.microsoftelearning.com/). We often run free hands-on training that you can complete in your own time. Do you know about our hosted servers (http://msdn.demoservers.com)? You don't need to install anything. Just go here, and try out our new tools through your browser. Did you know that you can get technical support online? Do you know about the Microsoft Technical Communities (http://www.microsoft.com/communities)? If you are an expert in a field and you spend a bit of time helping people, here you might even get yourself recognized as a Microsoft MVP (http://www.microsoft.com/communities/mvp).

If you are working with beta software, you can report bugs or make suggestions at http://lab.msdn.microsoft.com/productfeedback/. This is the best way of getting your questions in front of the product teams. They are measured on how quickly they can respond to bugs or report on features.

One word of advice is that if you are submitting bugs, make sure that you submit clear steps required to reproduce the problem.

If you are excited by beta software and you want to become a beta tester for a program, go to http://beta.microsoft.com/, and follow the on-screen instructions. Getting into early betas is a great way to influence the development of a product and gain a competitive advantage in the field.

Q. Any advice you'd give to a New Zealand developer interested in starting their own self-funded company?

A. If you are a New Zealand developer interested in starting your own self-funded company, don't look past the business incubators (http://www.incubators.org.nz)! Microsoft New Zealand and Incubators New Zealand, unveiled at Tech-Ed, is a New Zealand 3.5 million technology sponsorship package that will provide 100 incubator companies and 16 incubator organizations with access to software technologies to support their business ambitions. This sponsorship package is being distributed amongst both technology-based and non-technology-based start-ups.

Prior to the Incubators New Zealand program, Microsoft helped create KiwiStartup (http://www.agitavi.com/kiwistartup/english/), an initiative where Microsoft, HP, Vodafone, and TelstraClear all joined forces to provide technology resources for New Zealand start-ups that want to pursue a technology-based innovation or initiative.

The Microsoft NZ Partner page (`http://members.microsoft.com/partner/nz/`) has a heap of resources and links that you should take a look at. This partner portal page gives you a vast array of tools and information for building products and businesses that leverage Microsoft technology.

In terms of getting access to these tools and resources, the first thing you need to do is to sign up as a "registered member." This is the first step in getting into the Microsoft Partner program. You can do this at `https://partner.microsoft.com/global/program/levels/registeredmember/`. The Partner program gives you access to some great tools including Channel Builder, which allows you to look at organizations overseas and in New Zealand and see what their specialties are. This creates a forum for communication that you can leverage to open new channels for your product or business. As you move up the levels in the partner program, you gain more access to Channel Builder and other resources.

Once you've done that, you can sign up for the ISV Empower program at `https://empower-isv.one.microsoft.com/isv/programguide/`. For 810 NZ dollars, per year for a maximum of two years, you get a Visual Studio Professional 2005 with MSDN Premium Subscription media kit with five user licenses. There are some requirements you must meet when you sign up—these are listed on this page. One of the main requirements is that you must commit to developing a resalable product that will support one of the specified Microsoft products while you are a member.

In addition to these programs, consider getting a business plan together—don't make it too big—just two pages to start with. Key things to think of:

- What will I sell?

- What business problems does it solve?

- What is the problem you are fixing?

- How will you sell this to customers?

- How will you charge for the product?

- Consider a sales model (subscription, product, maintenance, etc.).

- How will you support the product?

- When will you get cash flow positive?

- How will you grow the company?

- How will you allow for investors to invest?

- What will the company look like in 12 [or] 24 months? In 5 years?

- How will you get out?

The main reason to have a business plan is so that you can set goals and think about outcomes. It will probably change from month to month, but just keep writing it down—you'll be surprised how many times you'll be asked for it.

The Microsoft Digital Locker Program

One of the facts you should understand about Microsoft is that it is such a huge organization, new programs, opportunities, and resources spring up all the time.

One such new program, still in beta as of October 2005, is the Windows Marketplace Labs' Digital Locker, as shown in Figure 6-5 and Figure 6-6. Awkward name, hot news: Microsoft wants to sell your micro-ISV's software at its visible Windows Marketplace site for you.

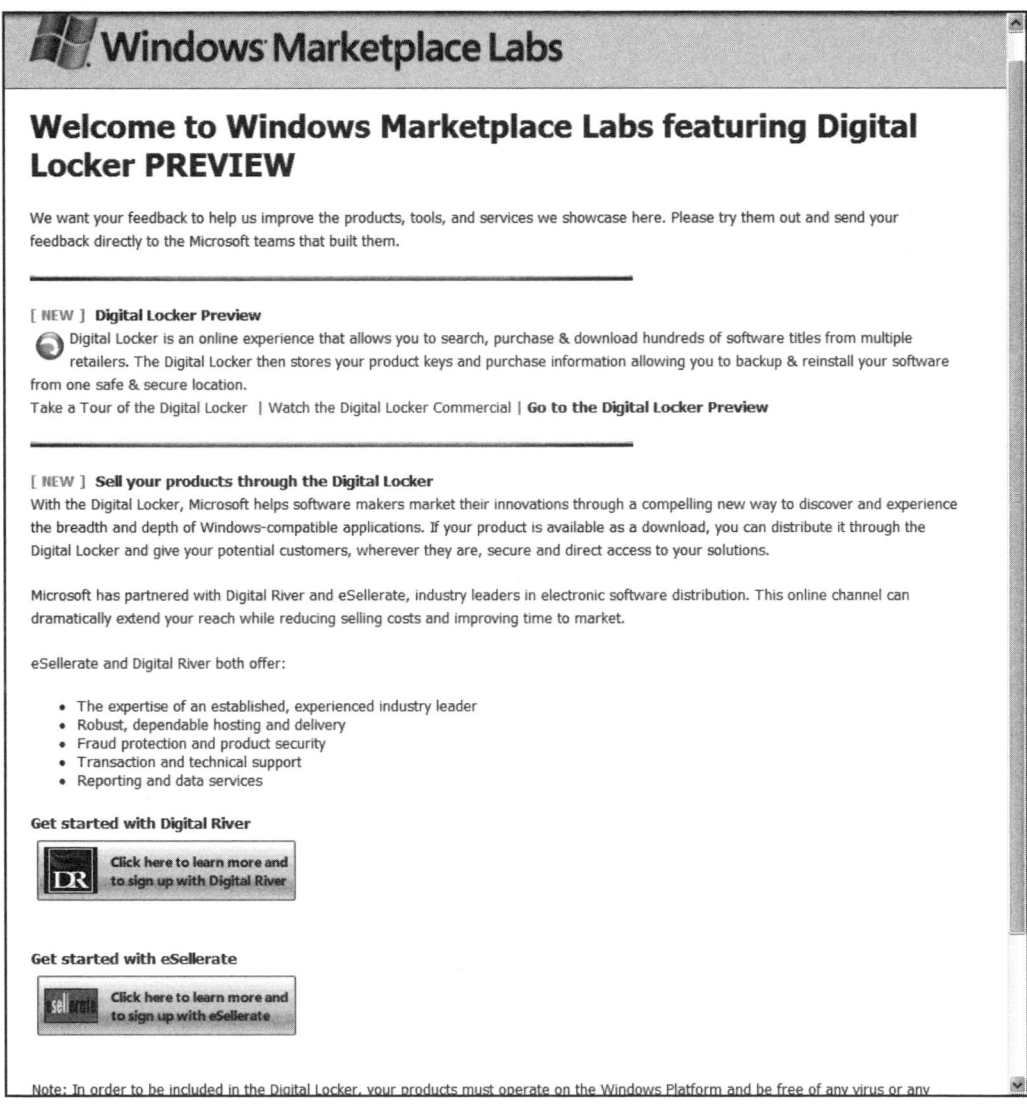

Figure 6-5. *Microsoft's Digital Locker*

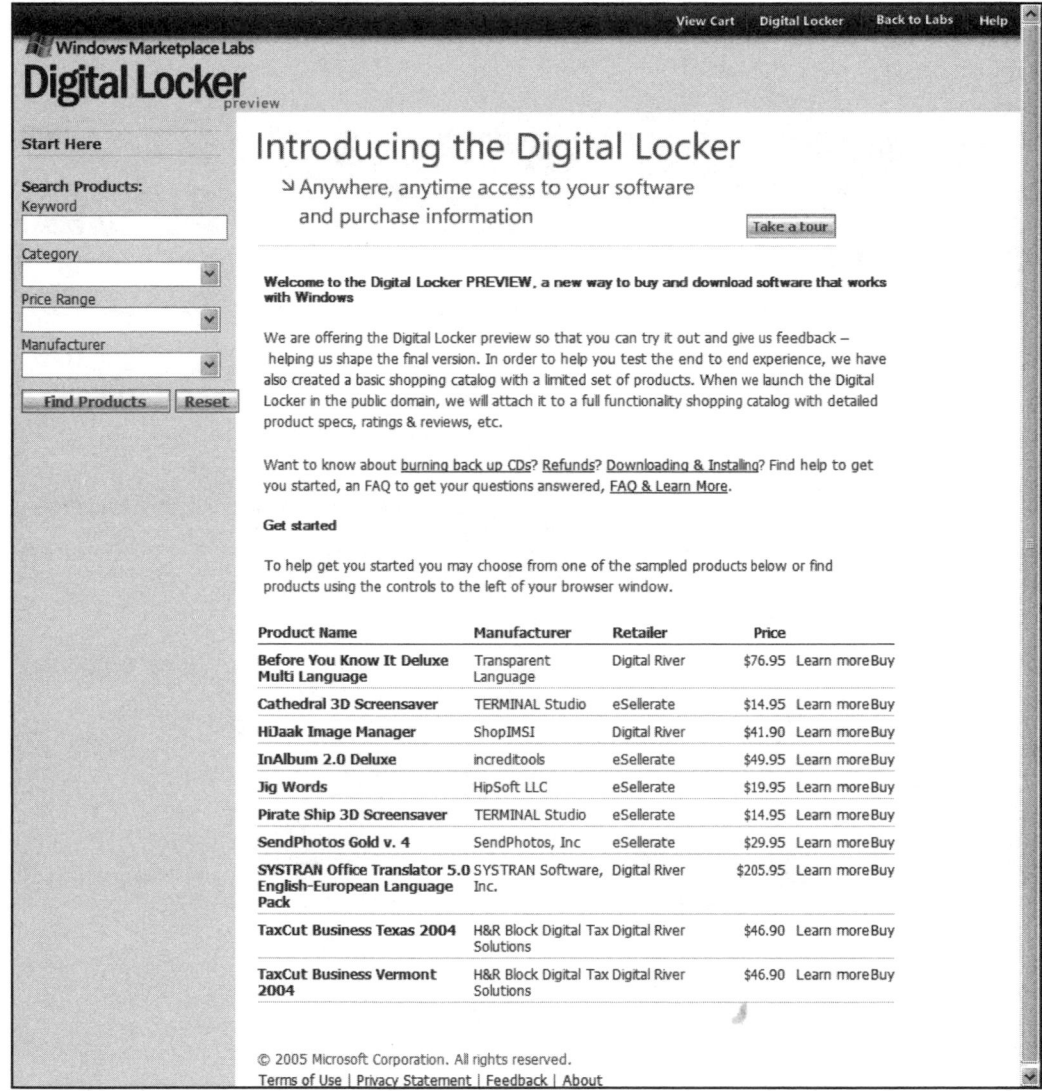

Figure 6-6. *Consumer view of Digital Locker*

"The goal of Digital Locker is to provide a way for our partners to grow their business," said Raj Biyani, product director of Digital Locker. Here's how it works for a micro-ISV: you sign up—or already do business—with one of two electronic distribution companies, either Digital River or eSellerate.

If your software runs on Windows, you arrange with either Digital River or eSellerate, as shown in Figure 6-7, to be listed in the Digital Locker when it goes live. From consumers' points of view, they'll get one place to shop for software online, with the added features of being able to retrieve their purchased software and back it up to CD from anywhere.

From a micro-ISV's view, you get a major new channel for distributing your downloadable Windows software, can skip all the messy details of payment processing, and get to ride Microsoft's multimillion-dollar, multiple-medium global marketing coattails.

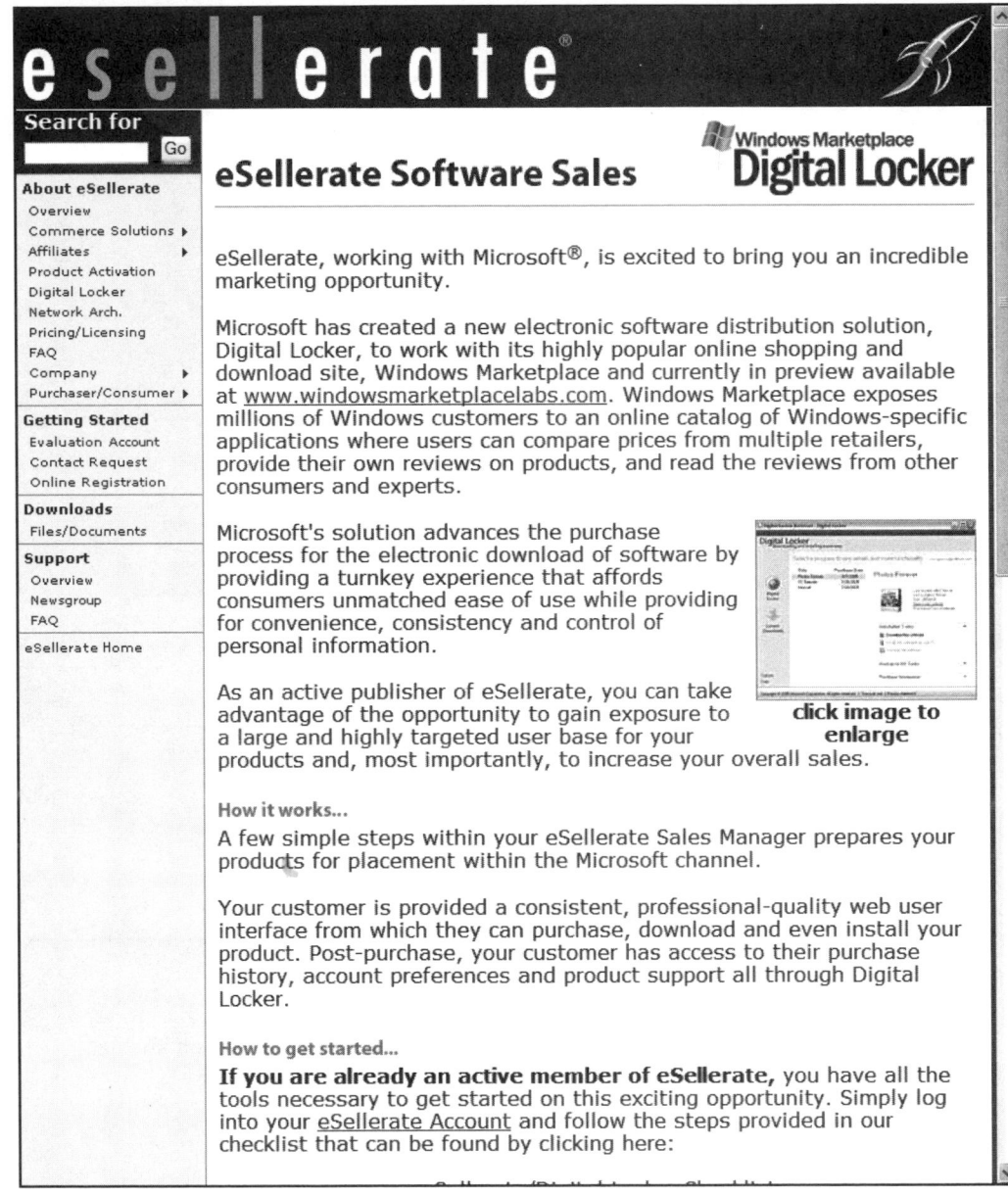

Figure 6-7. *eSellerate's half of Digital Locker*

RAJ BIYANI, PRODUCT DIRECTOR, WINDOWS MARKETPLACE LABS' DIGITAL LOCKER

Microsoft is seriously interested in selling your micro-ISV's products for you, according to Raj Biyani, the product director of Microsoft's Digital Locker. Although it's too soon to tell if this will be a success, Microsoft's marketing muscle could be a big assist to you in reaching the revenue zone.

Q. What's the idea behind Digital Locker?

A. Brick-and-mortar shelf space is becoming increasingly more limited, and in turn, distribution of software is becoming more challenging for ISVs, especially micro-ISVs. Electronic Software Distribution (ESD) is an increasingly more popular method for ISVs to get products to their customers.

Microsoft's goal is to help ISVs bring the products they are developing for Windows to their customers by making the consumer experience for buying and downloading software easy and safe. Digital Locker is all about making it very easy for third parties to deliver their products so customers can easily purchase and download software from the rich portfolio of micro-ISV products that are available on the Windows platform. The goal of Digital Locker is to provide a way for our partners to grow their business.

Q. What other Microsoft initiatives for small developers does Digital Locker link up with?

A. On September 13, 2005, at PDC, we launched a preview of the Digital Locker for ISVs and announced that the next version of Windows Marketplace, in the Windows Vista time frame, will have integrated ESD capabilities through the above feature called Digital Locker. Windows Marketplace will enable easy software download and purchase with a new streamlined and consistent shopping experience across a broad offering of merchants.

Digital Locker offers a single place to store all online software purchases with an integrated download manager and the ability to easily back up software to a CD. The service is adware and virus free. In short, the new Windows Marketplace will make online purchasing of software safer and easier than ever before for consumers—thus helping our ISV partners.

Q. Will you be adding other "retailers" besides Digital River and eSellerate?

A. Microsoft has chosen Digital River and eSellerate as the initial service providers to support the Digital Locker preview. eSellerate and Digital River are making this new channel of distribution via the Digital Locker available to their ISV partners and are motivated to help sell more of their ISV partner products. We will be working with more retailers/delivery partners in the future. For our launch of the Digital Locker preview, both Digital River and eSellerate were willing to work very closely with us to deliver a great customer experience, and both are considered industry experts.

Q. Any advice to micro-ISVs re Digital Locker or anything else?

A. Note the following advice:

- *Micro-ISVs*: Windows Marketplace Digital Locker gives you the "go-to market strategy in a box" to extend your reach to an installed base of over 300 million users on Windows XP.

- *For your customers*: Make it effortless for your customers to try, download, and purchase the software you have developed for the Windows platform.

- *Digital Locker preview*: You can preview the Digital Locker, obtain detailed how-to information on selling your products, and give us your feedback at http://www.windowsmarketplacelabs.com.

The Office Marketplace Program

I covered Office Marketplace, as shown in Figure 6-8, in detail in Chapter 5, but it's worth mentioning again here. If your particular software application or Web service integrates or works with some part of Microsoft Office, you can get your product listed at Office Marketplace for free.

How useful is that? Well, in the eight months since releasing MasterList Professional and shortly thereafter listing it at Office Marketplace, Office Marketplace has been the number-two or three referrer to my micro-ISV's Web site each month.

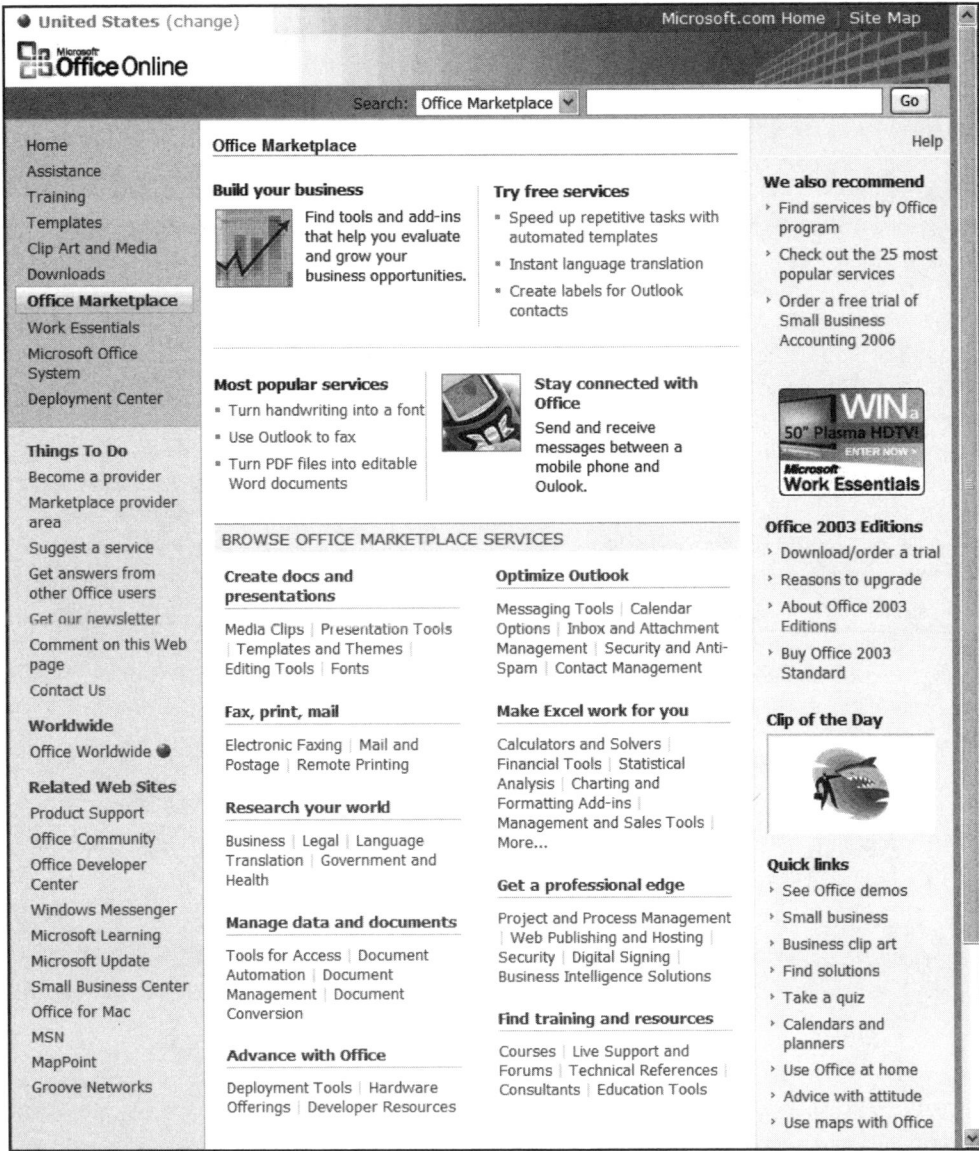

Figure 6-8. *Microsoft Office Marketplace*

Microsoft Wants You! (Maybe.)

Just about every micro-ISV at one time or another after too many hours of staring at an LCD screen drifts off and has The Microsoft Daydream. It goes like this: Bill Gates calls you up to say he just loves your latest release and Microsoft wants to buy your company, lock, stock, and source code. As you're stammering out how you can't possibly sell your company for less than Ten! Million! Dollars! Bill says, "Great, hold the phone; let me put Steve Ballmer on to finalize the deal and give you the FedEx address to send your company to us."

"Developers, developers, developers, developers!" Ballmer shouts at you. "Ten million? That's peanuts! That's nothing! Are you crazy?!? We'll buy it for $20 million and not a cent less! Take it now, or we'll have 1,000 programmers writing our version of everything you've ever coded!"

At this point, your idyllic daydream dissolves into a cold sweat. Microsoft might want to buy you. Microsoft might run right over you without you knowing it until too late. I'll talk about what to do to prevent the latter in a moment, but thanks to blogging, the veil of secrecy about why and how Microsoft buys companies is gone.

DON DODGE, EMERGING BUSINESS TEAM, MICROSOFT

In years past, the why and wherefore of which company Microsoft wanted to buy was the stuff of much speculation in the software industry. Every so often, a book or press release would come out about acquisition telling exactly nothing, but happy platitudes would break the silence. That was then, and this is now. Don Dodge is one of several members of Microsoft's Emerging Business Team not just spilling the beans about what Microsoft is interested in but spelling out exactly what's on the shopping list in hopes software developers will come in from the cold.

Q. When I came across the Microsoft Emerging Business Team and your blog (at http://dondodge. typepad.com/), I wondered, is this exclusively for ISVs that are VC-funded?

A. It tends to be, yes, although I spend a lot of time with angel investor networks and self-funded start-ups. We try to get involved with start-ups as early in the game as possible. A lot of times that means they don't yet have investment, or they have friends of the family type of investment, bootstrapping, or angel investing.

The Emerging Business Team itself tends to spend a lot of time with venture-backed start-ups because there are thousands of start-ups, and we to place our bets with companies we think are going to succeed long-term and have a pretty big impact on the ecosystem of Microsoft in general. We've found that VC funding is one of the filters we use to determine who will be successful long-term.

Q. It sounds like the Emerging Business Team is kind of like a specialized protein that goes out and find the right molecules to hook up to the main DNA of Microsoft to fill in the gaps that may exist at any given time, either through acquisition or partnership or just support in a general manner.

A. Yep, you've got it exactly right. That's pretty much what we do.

Q. I seem to remember there are 80,000 companies registered as Microsoft Partners now.

A. That's true.

Q. And would you say that the Emerging Business Team is the leader in Microsoft as to where Microsoft will put its acquisition dollars?

A. Well, we tend to be. What we try to do is find the emerging companies before everyone else does. We try to find the leading-edge technologies where innovation is happening and companies that are going to be leaders in their space. So our job is to find the golden nuggets amongst the thousands and thousands of little start-ups. And surface those to the product groups back in Redmond so they are aware of them, so they can work with them. They may work with them on a partnership basis, or it may graduate to a licensing, cross-promotion deal. In a few cases it results in acquisition.

Q. Do you think over the next five years more of these "holes" are going to be filled in the latticework of Microsoftdom by acquisitions or by sort of pointing ISVs and VCs at each other and letting them fill that hole?

A. Much more the latter. It's very, very few we will acquire. Very few. Less than one percent. The vast majority is going to be where there are partner opportunities. We have another whole section of Microsoft we call *Channel Builder*. It's a way for partners to be introduced to other partners, for partners to be introduced to system integrators, [and] for software partners to be introduced to other software partners where there's synergy. So by far, most of it will happen at the partnership level.

Q. Is Channel Builder something micro-ISVs should be looking at?

A. Yeah, I think it is. You become a Microsoft Partner, then you self-identify who you are, what your competencies are, and then you can match up with other companies.

Q. How do you hear about these emerging companies?

A. As a matter of fact, Bob, I just wrote a blog about that (`http://dondodge.typepad.com/ the_next_big_thing/2005/10/innovation_is_b.html`). Basically, I spend all my time with start-ups. I did five start-ups myself, so I'm from the start-up world; I just joined Microsoft a year ago. I go to Dow Jones VentureWire, to a conference on emerging ventures just a week ago. And I go to conferences like that all the time. I'm a member of three different angel investor networks where we see 10 to 15 companies a month. So I get to keep my finger on the pulse of what's happening out there and get a really early look at what's going on. So I spend all my time going to VC conferences [and] emerging business conferences—that's where I spend my time. I don't see every company, but I try.

Q. It does seem, scanning your new blog quick, that you see another big upswing in software innovation is going on.

A. Yep. It's pretty exciting. We've been stagnant for four years. After the Internet bubble burst, VCs and entrepreneurs got pretty hesitant and retrenched. Now we're seeing lots of new companies come out. You know, I'm just seeing them now; they started a year ago, and now they have something to show. So we're emerging from the slumber, and the after-effects of the tech bubble burst. We're seeing lots of good companies [and] lots of interesting things emerge.

Q. Is this more than Web 2.0?

A. Web 2.0 is an overused term. It generalizes quite a bit. As I said in my blog, these companies that are emerging are emerging in a different way than they did during the Internet bubble, from necessity. Back in the Internet bubble, you could take a PowerPoint presentation and a couple people and go to a VC and get money to start a company. That's not happening anymore.

Now we're seeing companies emerge that are all bootstrap. The innovators have built the technology themselves with their own time. They are not looking for VC money. They are typically doing Web services, introducing their product over the Web. They aren't spending a lot of money on infrastructure or development. They typically have working code or applications they've exposed on the Web, so they're building a user audience and getting market feedback very early in the process.

Then, when they see market uptake and interest, and they need to expand quickly, then they are going to angels and VCs and getting money. And even then, they're not seeking $25 million. They take $2 million, and go back and develop the company and the product before coming back for a second round. It's a much more rational way of building companies. It's the way software used to be.

Q. It sounds to me like you see a shift in the positioning of VCs to start-up ISVs. If they're not looking for VC money, what do they get from a VC?

A. Well, I would say they are not looking for VC money early in the game, like they used to. VCs help when you start to get market traction, and your idea catches on. Then you need to move quickly to capitalize on the idea. You can't generally bootstrap it anymore.

Q. So it sounds like the Emerging Business Team is almost like the big brother to the Microsoft Buddy program.
A. That's essentially what we do. So it works both ways—where the VC has found a company and funded it, and they want us to help them be successful at Microsoft. And the other way, where we find companies pre-VC, and we match them up with the right VC.

Q. You're asking people to come out of the woodwork and come see you—how should they contact you?
A. We run the danger of being inundated, but I'm not worried about that. That's my job—I have to sort through hundreds and hundreds of companies. If they contact me by phone or by email (ddodge@microsoft.com) or respond to my blog, great. I'm going to take a look at them.

Q. Is there a set of things that Microsoft uses to decide if they should acquire a software company?
A. Yep. I wrote a blog about that too: `http://dondodge.typepad.com/the_next_big_thing/2005/10/microsoft_will_.html`.

Q. If you wanted to sum that up, what would you say?
A. We look to acquire companies that add value to existing Microsoft products in places where we haven't gotten to it yet or we didn't think of it. We're looking to acquire companies that fill in a hole—that's one class of companies.

Q. Sure, for instance, Vermeer becoming FrontPage.
A. Right. If you read that blog, you can see some of the acquisitions that Microsoft has made and that has resulted in tremendous products for us.

Q. Those tend to be the big holes catching up. That's one class of acquisition. But every so often there seems to be a very small, quiet acquisition like Giant Software.
A. Right. There are a lot more of those then there are of the big ones. That was part of the point of that post. We make lots of acquisitions that sort of happen under the radar, which don't get a lot of publicity but fill in the holes, and Giant is one of those. And that's what I try and do. I try go find these companies that are doing some very interesting, innovate things, and acquire them for 20, 30, 50 million dollars before they get VC money in.

Once they get VC money in there, then you're talking multiples of that number.

Q. What's the smallest company in the past year Microsoft acquired?
A. Giant was pretty small. Giant is kind of a misnomer. They called it Giant Software, but it was only, like, five people.

I can't name them off the top of my head, but it is not uncommon for us to acquire companies that are five to ten people. It's not uncommon at all.

Q. Do you ever acquire one, two-person companies?
A. Yes, but that is in the second category. We talked about the first category—fill in the hole. Probably most acquisitions happen for the reason of acquiring people, not technology. Software is all about people and great developers. And when we look to acquire a company, we are looking for a great team of people—technical people, business people, people who can build a software business.

So when we do these very small acquisitions, a lot of times we are acquiring the people more than we are acquiring the product. We know these guys have demonstrated innovative ideas, so what would happen if we took this same team of people and put them on an existing Microsoft product? What kind of leverage do you think could happen there? Well, that's the idea.

Q. Tell me if you want developers to do this, you're neutral, or you don't want people to do this: should they look at Microsoft's structure, find something overlooked, develop it, get it out on the Web, and then say to you "Buy me!"
A. Well, a lot of people do that.

Q. Does it work?

A. It works, but I wouldn't have that be my strategy from day one. Because it's very risky. We don't acquire that many companies.

Q. How many in a year would you say? Of the small ones?

A. We acquire anywhere from 10 to 25 companies a year, altogether. So it's not a great strategy to start a company—you need to have multiple exits. You need to think about the companies that would most likely value your company.

Q. What would be a better strategy?

A. I would do the old-fashioned way. And I think is more in line with your micro-ISV kind of thing. In the old days, the way you built a company was you had a great idea and you went to potential customers and showed them the idea and asked them for development money, to customize the product for their needs. And basically what you've done is raised money from a customer. The customer gets an early release customized for their needs, and you get to keep all the intellectual property. That's the way it used to be done, and that's what I'd suggest they do.

Q. Well, a couple people out there, for instance, Joel Spolsky, have pointed out it's easy to become a consulting-ware company. You come up with a product and customize it so much that you end up with a consulting company rather than a product company.

A. Right. That's the balance. Two things happen: one, you become more of a consulting company than a product company, and two, because of the customizations, you paint yourself into a corner where you now have a very specialized product, not a generalized one, that we might be interested in. So those are the things you have to be careful of when taking that strategy.

Q. OK. Now I get to put on my devil's advocate hat on. You may have noticed there's a lot of people out there that who don't love Microsoft, especially in the developer community. These are people who have little voodoo dolls on their desk of Bill Gates.

A. Sure.

Q. So why should anybody trust Microsoft? Why should any developer show what they are doing to Microsoft? Won't Microsoft just do it themselves and say, "Thanks! Have a nice day!"

A. Well, I think there's a misperception about that, and it's happened over the years. I think we're different now than we used to be. Number one: we are much more focused with working with partners. We have 80,000 partners. And we know that partners drive a lot of our revenue.

Number two, that happened because we were not real open and out there about where we were investing. In the past, we would have people working on technologies inside our development organization or our research organizations for a year or two, and we would say nothing about it. And other start-ups would be out there doing the same things, thinking they were the only ones doing it. They didn't know that Microsoft had gotten on to that idea and had been building it. It's just that Microsoft is such a big company it takes two to four years from the time we start working on something to the time you see it in the marketplace.

It's not that Microsoft stole an idea, they didn't. It just took them two to four years to get it out because the product cycles are much longer in a big company.

Q. Well, I know there is now something like 3,000 Microsoft developers or technical people blogging, according to MSDN. That's a lot of people to be blogging for one company.

A. Yeah, and we are pretty serious about it. And I think that's a good thing. We need to have a personal face on Microsoft. You've read my blog; there are thousands and thousands of Microsoft employees who are also blogging. And we think it's important that the public and the technical community has a personal and direct connection to people who are working and leading Microsoft.

Q. So that would be the answer to why should a developer trust Microsoft. So why should a developer trust the VCs they meet through the Emerging Business Team?

A. Well, again, I think there are misperceptions there. VCs see hundreds and hundreds and hundreds of companies. They've seen every idea that there is out there. Anyone who thinks they go to a VC and they're the first ones who came up with this idea, 99 percent of the time you're wrong.

VCs—their whole business is built on trust. A VC couldn't stay in business very long if they got the reputation that they were stealing ideas. I trust VCs. I work with them every day, and it's a pretty small community. I think you can trust VCs; it's just that people don't understand what they do and how plugged in they are. Some of these entrepreneurs live in a world where they think they are the only ones doing something, and they're not.

Q. Would you advocate start-ups be more public or more private, given what you've said?

A. I would recommend they be more public. The stealth-mode stuff—I think that's ridiculous. Again, that breeds from these entrepreneurs thinking they are the only ones who have this idea, they've got to get it out there before anyone else, the first-mover advantages are paramount, and all that stuff.

I met with an entrepreneur last week. And they had this stealth idea of what they were going to do. And I started asking them questions. And it was pretty obvious that he had not talked to the potential customers of this product. I asked him some pretty obvious questions that he didn't have answers to.

I asked him, "Why haven't you talked to your potential customers?" "Oh, it's not ready yet. I don't want to show it to them until its ready to go." It's a mistake: they get so far down the path, spend a lot of time and money, and they're making a huge mistake.

Q. You're working with a lot of VCs. I've seen published reports that if you want VC, you'd better plan to outsource your development to India. True, false, bogus?

A. False, bogus.

Q. OK, what are you hearing about outsourcing and VCs?

A. There are some VCs who are hot on India, outsourced development for low-cost kind of stuff, but that's bogus. That's analogous to saying, if you want to get funded in today's environment, you should use open source or Linux or whatever.

Q. That was my next question....

A. The VCs don't care what platform you use. They don't care what development model you use. What they care about is do you solve a problem uniquely that no one else does? Is it going to be a big market that can grow tremendously? Is there a team in place, a management team that can execute, that can make it happen? Those are the things they care about.

Q. Finally, any other advice for micro-ISV? On funding, not funding, what color to wear, anything?

A. Not other than what I've already said. You need to figure out what path you're going to take—if you're going to try to bootstrap it as far as you possibly can, or maybe all the way. Or are you going to try to walk the fine line of being a consulting company versus a product company? That's a good route; you just have to be careful about how you walk it. Or if you want to go the traditional VC route. There's several ways to build a company. You just need to focus in on which one of those paths you're going to take and which one fits your style, product, and pace. Any one of them can work.

Keeping an Eye on Microsoft

Before I leave the subject of the 900-pound gorilla, we should stop by the Web sites of a couple of people who have made tracking the gorilla's movements a full-time job.

First up, there's Microsoft Watch (http://www.microsoft-watch.com/), as shown in Figure 6-9.

Figure 6-9. *Microsoft Watch*

Begun and run by Mary Jo Foley, a journalist who covered Microsoft for many years at various publications, Microsoft Watch comes in two flavors: the free Web site shown in Figure 6-9 and a premium subscription-only newsletter featuring much deeper analysis costing $899 USD a year. The goodness of this site isn't just repackaging Microsoft press releases; you'll find good solid analysis of what moves Microsoft is contemplating—moves that might mean your micro-ISV is at risk.

With a more technical and less business news bent than Microsoft Watch, there's Steven Bink's Bink.nu, as shown in Figure 6-10. Over the years Microsoft has jerked Steven's chain about him releasing screen shots of various Microsoft operating systems and products before their official releases, and Steven does a great job aggregating not just Microsoft's news about itself but how other key industry events affect Microsoft and news Microsoft would rather you not dwell on.

Figure 6-10. *Bink.nu*

Finally, if you want to get a taste of what's really going on inside Microsoft, the anonymous Mini-Microsoft blog (http://minimsft.blogspot.com/), as shown in Figure 6-11, is the site to visit.

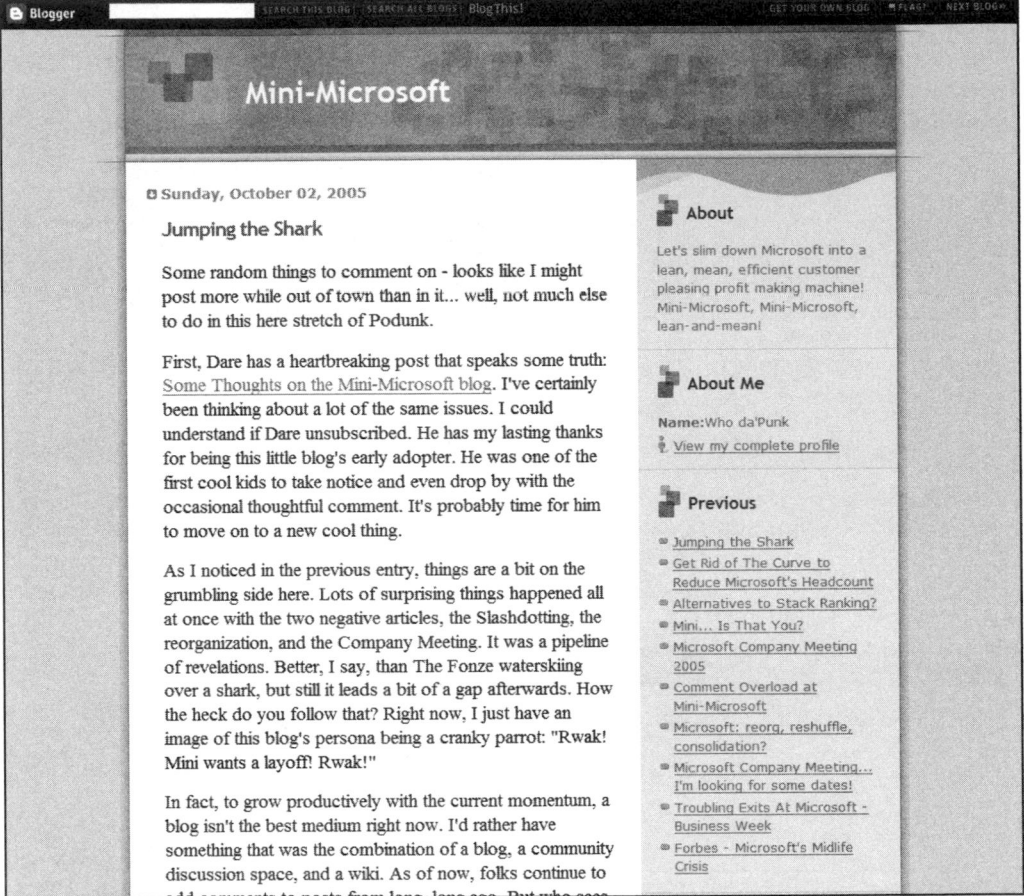

Figure 6-11. *Mini-Microsoft*

Supposedly edited by an anonymous Microsoft employee, Mini-Microsoft is an underground newspaper of stupidities, blunders, and bureaucracy within Microsoft, written for the most part by current employees.

Before moving on, here's a final wrap-up of what I think you as a micro-ISV need to know about Microsoft:

- Without a doubt, Microsoft can instantly crush your micro-ISV, either because you are so foolish as to compete directly against it or because it shifts in some direction and sucks the oxygen out of the room you're both in.

- That said, more than a few Microsoft business programs exist that can significantly improve your micro-ISV's revenue. These are places where your interests and Microsoft's coincide, and you should take advantage of them.

- Yes, Microsoft could decide one day it wants to buy your company. It's estimated that Microsoft spends an average of $1 billion to $2 billion a year, acquiring companies to enhance Microsoft's revenues. But I wouldn't plan on your company getting bought.

- Keep an eye on Microsoft as one of your business intelligence foundational tasks. Think *business intelligence* is an oxymoron? Read on.

Business Intelligence Is Intelligent

Business intelligence is a polite way of saying monitoring your competitors. I'm definitely not talking about industrial espionage here; I'm talking about doing the least amount of information gathering you need to do to know what your competitors are doing in public view. Business intelligence for micro-ISVs is mainly about three issues:

- Initially identifying your direct competitors and understanding how you compare to them.

- Monitoring who is talking about you, about your product and your company, and about your competitors' products and what they are saying.

- Keeping an eye on broad trends that might affect the market for your product or Web service (see the discussion of Microsoft in the previous section).

Now, some of this you probably already do this. But what I'm talking about here is doing business intelligence in an organized way. This means you need to do some initial analysis on your competitors and their products, and then on a regular basis you'll need to check up on them.

The Initial Analysis

The first task you need to do is make a list of your direct competitors. These are the companies—large, medium, and micro—that sell a product or Web service, as perceived by your market, that is the same product or service as you do.

Note that phrase, "as perceived by your market." You need to draft your list based on what your market sees, not based on what you think. One good way of doing this is to scan your tech support incidents for inquiries such as "Do you do X like Y does?" Another is to ask some of your customer privately who they think your competition is. They know.

■Note You'll find an Excel template, the Business Intelligence Tracker (BIT), at this book's Apress page (http://www.apress.com/book/bookDisplay.html?bID=10057).

Next, visit each of your competitors' Web sites. You want to learn the following bits of intelligence:

- The product's name and development history (is it being actively improved, or has it been put out to the cash-cow pasture?).

- The full price of the product (sales price, plus tech support price, plus upgrades, and updates price).

- Their Unique Selling Proposition (USP). (It should be the clearest message on their home page.)

- How do they do tech support (forums, telephone, or something else)?

- In their home page's HTML, what keywords and phrases do they use?

Strengths, Weaknesses, Opportunities, and Threats (SWOT)

Now that you have the basic stats on each of your direct competitors, it's time during your initial analysis to ask yourself some hard, but illuminating, questions: compared to each competitor and to your competitors as a whole, what are your product's and company's Strengths, Weaknesses, Opportunities, and Threats (SWOT)?

What do I mean by this?

Strengths: Does the competitor's product cost more, do less, have a harder-to-use interface, offer less functionality, have a harder setup, provide less documentation, have oddball restrictions, or encompass all of the above? What's wrong with your competitor's public relations, marketing, or selling? How about their Web site—any glaring mistakes there? Is their selling process hard to navigate? Do they bury prospective customers with too much information or starve them with too little?

Weaknesses: How much bigger is the competitor? How many more employees do they seem to have? Do they have partnerships you don't? Are they bragging about specific major customers in your industry you don't have? Is their product better than yours? Cheaper? Does it have a better interface or more functionality? Does their product have unique features that better solve their customers' problems than your product?

Opportunities: What parts of the problem aren't your competitors solving adequately? Are they all overpriced, leaving a gap for a much less expensive product from a smaller competitor (that's you!)? Are they all underfeatured, solving the problem as it was five or ten years ago but not what customers are dealing with now? Do they fumble addressing part of the problem you've heard your customers complain about or wish for?

Threats: Which competitors have announced price reductions? Which have announced or blogged that a major new version of their product is just months away that will do everything your product does and more? Has a competitor been bought out by a presumably more intelligent company that might decide to get serious about dealing with upstarts such as you?

SWOT analysis has been around a long time, but it's invaluable to ferreting out the things your micro-ISV has to do to be competitive and make money. Like I said, doing the SWOT analysis can be uncomfortable. But it's the only way you're going to get a clear picture of your competitive advantages and disadvantages.

Once you've invested the time to do your initial analysis of identifying your competitors and doing your SWOT analysis, plan to return at least once a month to check the following:

What has changed? For each competitor and competing product, are they a stronger or weaker competitor? Do you need to add new competitors to your business intelligence brief? Have they refreshed, improved, streamlined, or enhanced their Web site?

What have they done? For each competitor who said they were improving their product in either minor or major ways, have they? Are the getting less technical support postings (if visible) or more?

What have you done? Given the opportunities and threats you identified last month, what have you done? This is probably the most important question of the entire SWOT process.

Talk, Talk

The second big facet of business intelligence is keeping up with what people are saying about you, your company, your products, and, to a lesser degree, your competitors. As you might expect, this is all about what people are saying on the Internet, and therefore it's part of the whole rapidly evolving blogosphere.

Currently, I recommend three free tools for regular doses of self-examination: PubSub, Technorati, and Google Blog Search.

PubSub

PubSub's (http://www.pubsub.com) approach is different from a search engine. You create a (currently free) subscription and enter keywords or phrases you want to monitor, as shown in Figure 6-12. PubSub then reads on an ongoing basis some 16 million blogs, 50,000 Internet newsgroups, and all SEC (EDGAR) filings for mentions of one or more of your search terms.

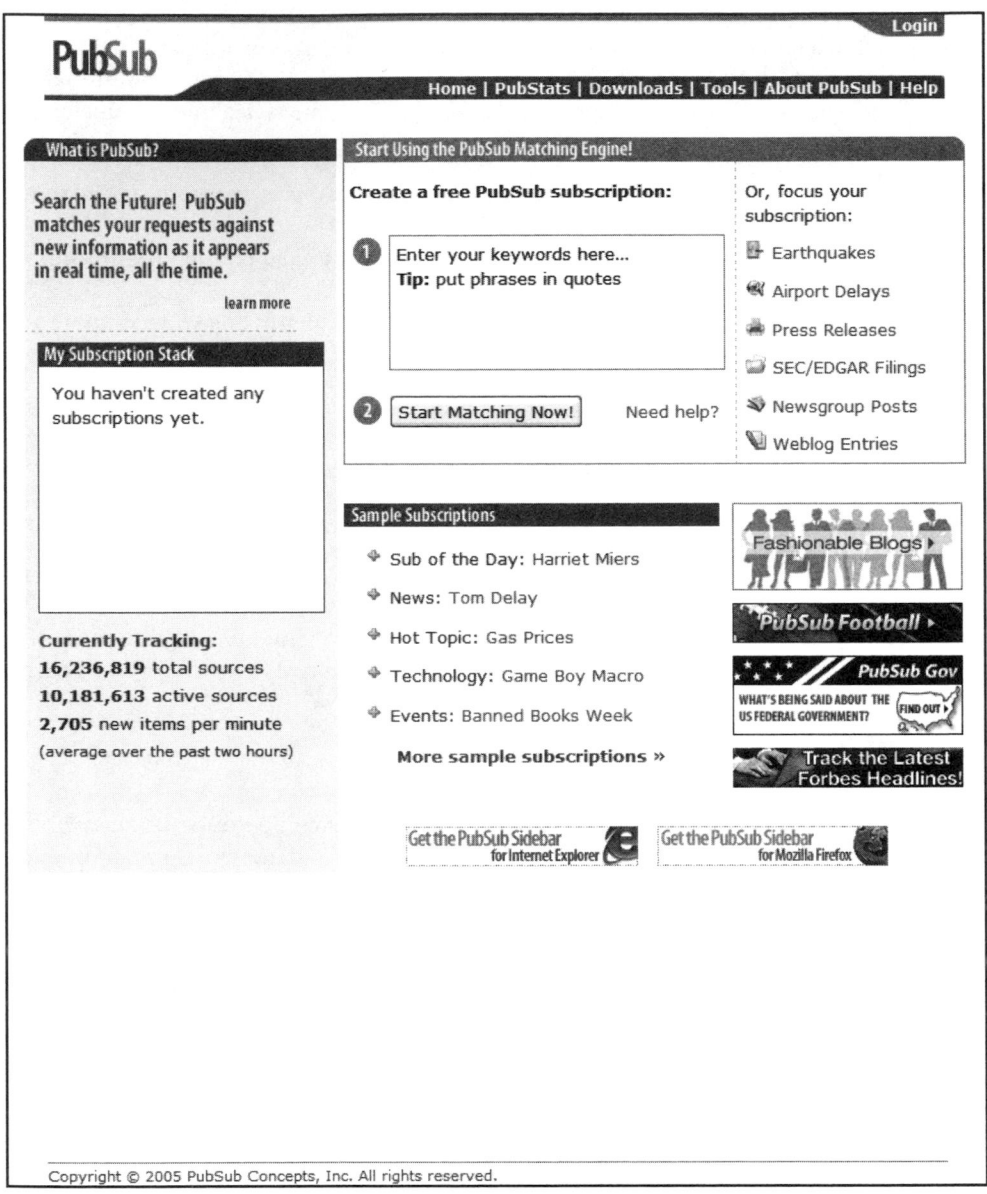

Figure 6-12. *PubSub's start screen*

When PubSub gets a match, it turns on a PubSub button in your Internet Explorer or Firefox Web browser and gives you a link in its PubSub Sidebar.

For example, I just checked my PubSub Sidebar in Firefox because the little blue PubSub button had turned orange and found two new mentions of MasterList Professional, as shown in Figure 6-13.

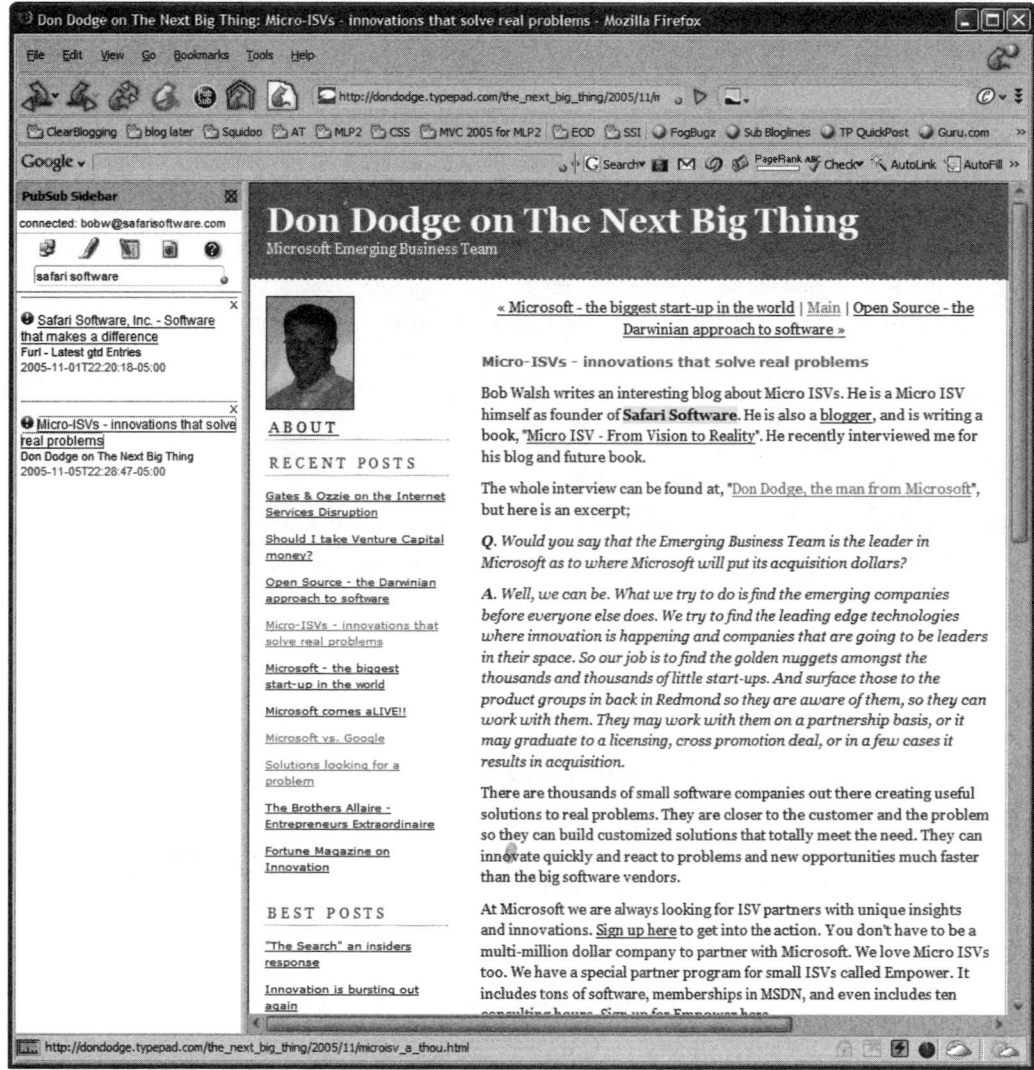

Figure 6-13. *PubSub delivers*

The two limitations I see with PubSub is that you need to keep your keywords very specific and few or otherwise you'll be bombarded by PubSub alerts. The other limitation is that PubSub can be another thing clamoring for your attention—not good for either developer or business productivity.

Technorati

A couple of years old, Technorati (http://technorati.com) was among the first blog search engines. With it, you can perform several blog-related searches. First and foremost, you can search for specific terms in blogs, as shown in Figure 6-14, and see how many blogs link to an entry that mentions that term. Second, you can "claim" your blog so that photos and profiles appear on Technorati's site whenever a search involves your blog. Technorati is adding other blog search features at a steady clip.

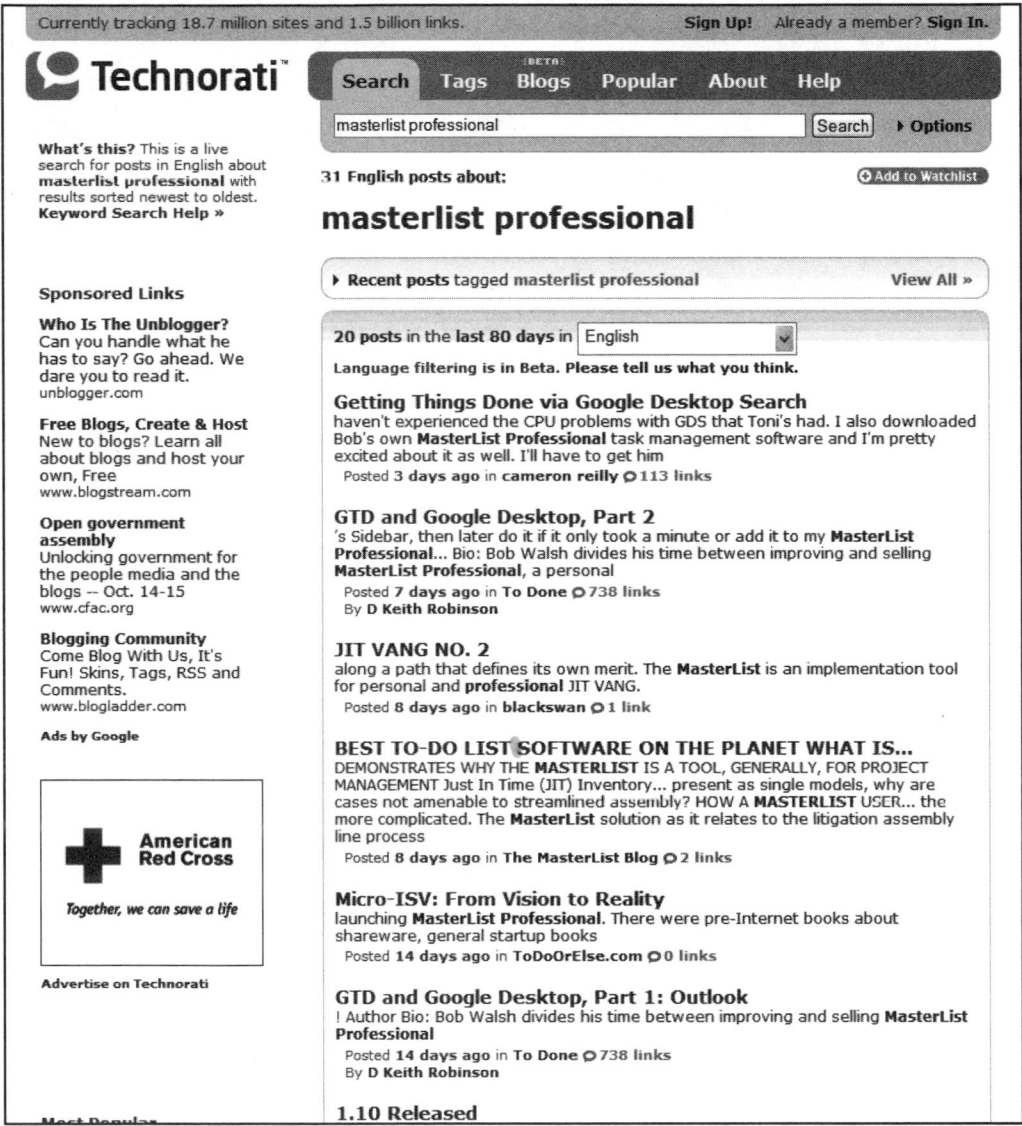

Figure 6-14. *Going with Technorati*

Although some bloggers obsess over how Technorati ranks them overall in the blogosphere, I've found Technorati to be a great way of doing business intelligence.

Google Blog Search

Starting in June 2005, Google created a separate index/search page for blogs (http://
blogsearch.google.com/). In addition to the usual Google search tricks, Google Blog Search
can restrict results to finding a particular phrase in the name of a blog or a blog posting or
finding blogs by author or URL.

Figure 6-15 shows what a search for *MasterList Professional* looked like while this chapter
was being drafted.

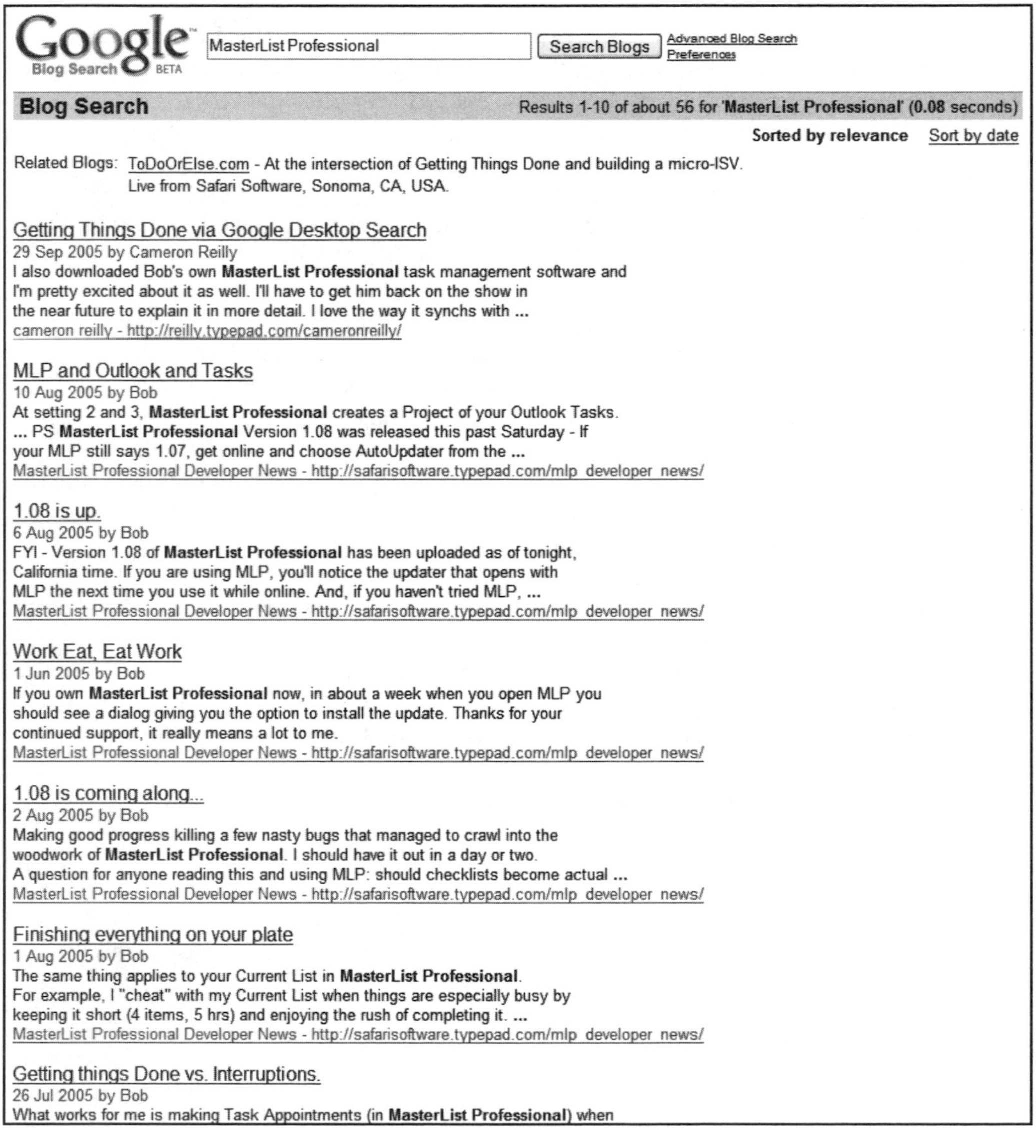

Google Blog Search BETA   MasterList Professional   [Search Blogs]   Advanced Blog Search
Preferences

Blog Search   Results 1-10 of about 56 for 'MasterList Professional' (0.08 seconds)

Sorted by relevance   Sort by date

Related Blogs: ToDoOrElse.com - At the intersection of Getting Things Done and building a micro-ISV.
Live from Safari Software, Sonoma, CA, USA.

Getting Things Done via Google Desktop Search
29 Sep 2005 by Cameron Reilly
I also downloaded Bob's own **MasterList Professional** task management software and
I'm pretty excited about it as well. I'll have to get him back on the show in
the near future to explain it in more detail. I love the way it synchs with ...
cameron reilly - http://reilly.typepad.com/cameronreilly/

MLP and Outlook and Tasks
10 Aug 2005 by Bob
At setting 2 and 3, **MasterList Professional** creates a Project of your Outlook Tasks.
... PS **MasterList Professional** Version 1.08 was released this past Saturday - If
your MLP still says 1.07, get online and choose AutoUpdater from the ...
MasterList Professional Developer News - http://safarisoftware.typepad.com/mlp_developer_news/

1.08 is up.
6 Aug 2005 by Bob
FYI - Version 1.08 of **MasterList Professional** has been uploaded as of tonight,
California time. If you are using MLP, you'll notice the updater that opens with
MLP the next time you use it while online. And, if you haven't tried MLP, ...
MasterList Professional Developer News - http://safarisoftware.typepad.com/mlp_developer_news/

Work Eat, Eat Work
1 Jun 2005 by Bob
If you own **MasterList Professional** now, in about a week when you open MLP you
should see a dialog giving you the option to install the update. Thanks for your
continued support, it really means a lot to me.
MasterList Professional Developer News - http://safarisoftware.typepad.com/mlp_developer_news/

1.08 is coming along...
2 Aug 2005 by Bob
Making good progress killing a few nasty bugs that managed to crawl into the
woodwork of **MasterList Professional**. I should have it out in a day or two.
A question for anyone reading this and using MLP: should checklists become actual ...
MasterList Professional Developer News - http://safarisoftware.typepad.com/mlp_developer_news/

Finishing everything on your plate
1 Aug 2005 by Bob
The same thing applies to your Current List in **MasterList Professional**.
For example, I "cheat" with my Current List when things are especially busy by
keeping it short (4 items, 5 hrs) and enjoying the rush of completing it. ...
MasterList Professional Developer News - http://safarisoftware.typepad.com/mlp_developer_news/

Getting things Done vs. Interruptions.
26 Jul 2005 by Bob
What works for me is making Task Appointments (in **MasterList Professional**) when

Figure 6-15. *Using Google Blog Search*

As usual with Google, you get results immediately that are fairly well targeted. Keen observers will note that Google isn't serving Google AdWords to Google Blog Search. Yet.

Finding Others on the Road

One of the less appealing aspects of starting a micro-ISV is that at least in the early stages, it can be a lonely job. You may have left a job with co-workers you could talk to, or you might be starting your micro-ISV "on the side" and can't talk about it. You're neither fish nor fowl, betwixt and between.

But you don't—and you probably can't—build your micro-ISV alone. In the following sections, I'll cover several online communities for micro-ISVs. My advice is to browse them, get to know the people in each community, and find one that works for you.

Joel on Software

First on the micro-ISV community hit parade (and probably no surprise at this point in this book!) is the Business of Software forum at Joel on Software (`http://discuss.joelonsoftware.com/?biz`), as shown in Figure 6-16.

You'll find a lot of great information, plenty of sharp people facing the same issues you are, and some humor. Most important, you won't find any spam at the Business of Software forum. This is so unique in online communities that it's worth repeating: over the past two years of participating almost daily on this forum, I've seen exactly one "spammy" posting that disappeared within a day. No, the forum's moderator (a "graduated" micro-ISVer), Eric Sink, doesn't spend 15 hours a day playing Whack the Spam Mole. Instead, a Bayesian filter is built into the forum (which by the way is the standard FogBugz discussion forum) to filter out the crap, *except when the spammer looks at the forum.* Talk about poetic justice!

While writing this book, I posted several requests for good sources of information on legal structures in the United Kingdom and Australia and within hours received great URLs from people who had been there and done that.

Three other forums at Joel on Software are worth getting to know: the Joel on Software forum where a menagerie of computer stuff gets discussed, the Design of Software forum where software design and usability topics get kicked around, and the .NET Questions forum devoted to, well, .NET questions.

These are all highly recommended.

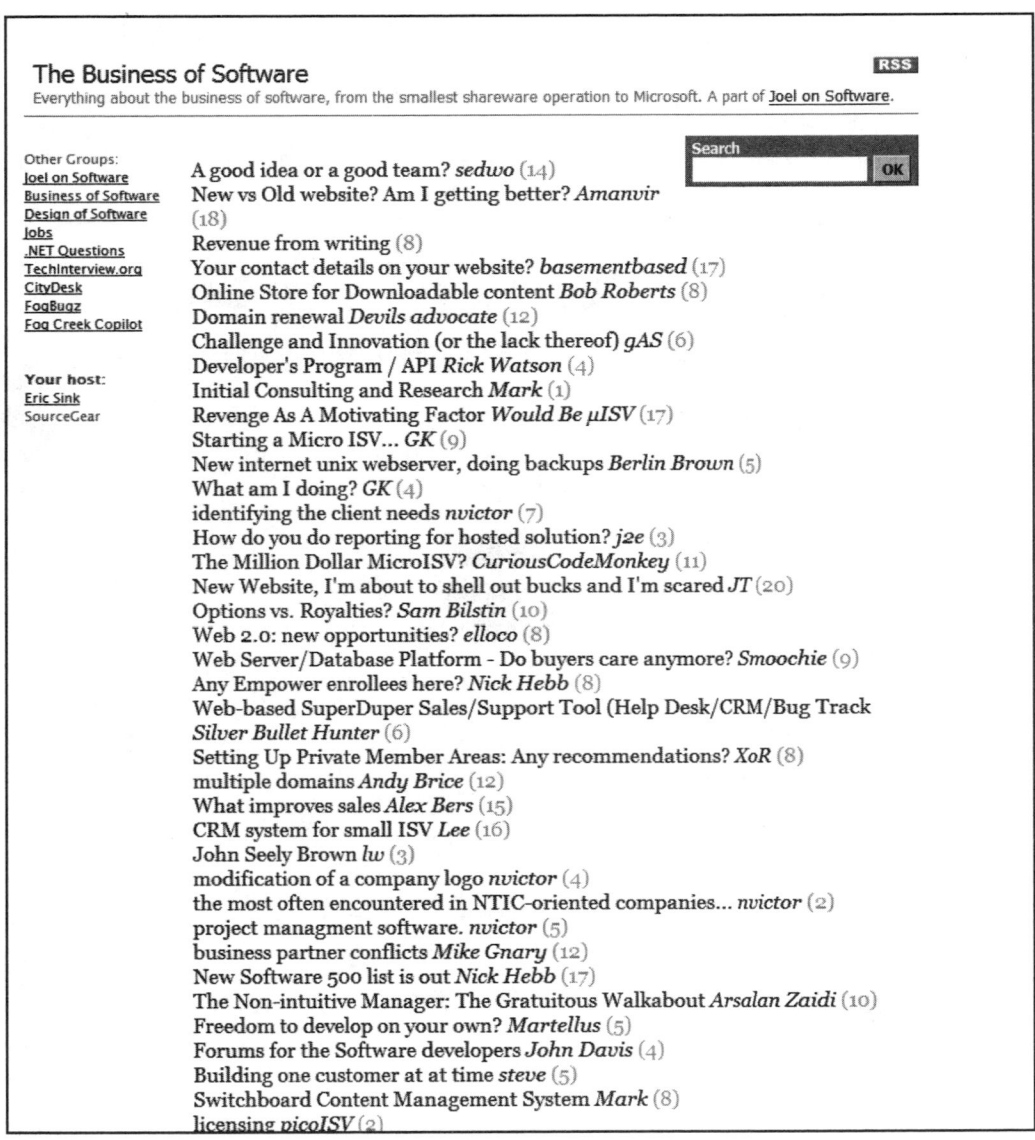

Figure 6-16. *The Business of Software*

Association of Independent Software Industry Professionals (AISIP)

Relatively new, the Association of Independent Software Industry Professionals (AISIP) (http://www.aisip.com/), as shown in Figure 6-17, is another good hangout for micro-ISVs. AISIP is a private forum: it costs $24 USD a year, and it has a fairly strict policy about privacy. But the benefits are considerable:

- You get access to a community of other small software vendors who share tips, advice, resources, and camaraderie.

- There's a slew of discounts from members to members.

- The Business Book Club, where one business book relevant to micro-ISVs is discussed chapter by chapter, is an excellent way to dig deep into a subject in a fun and productive way.

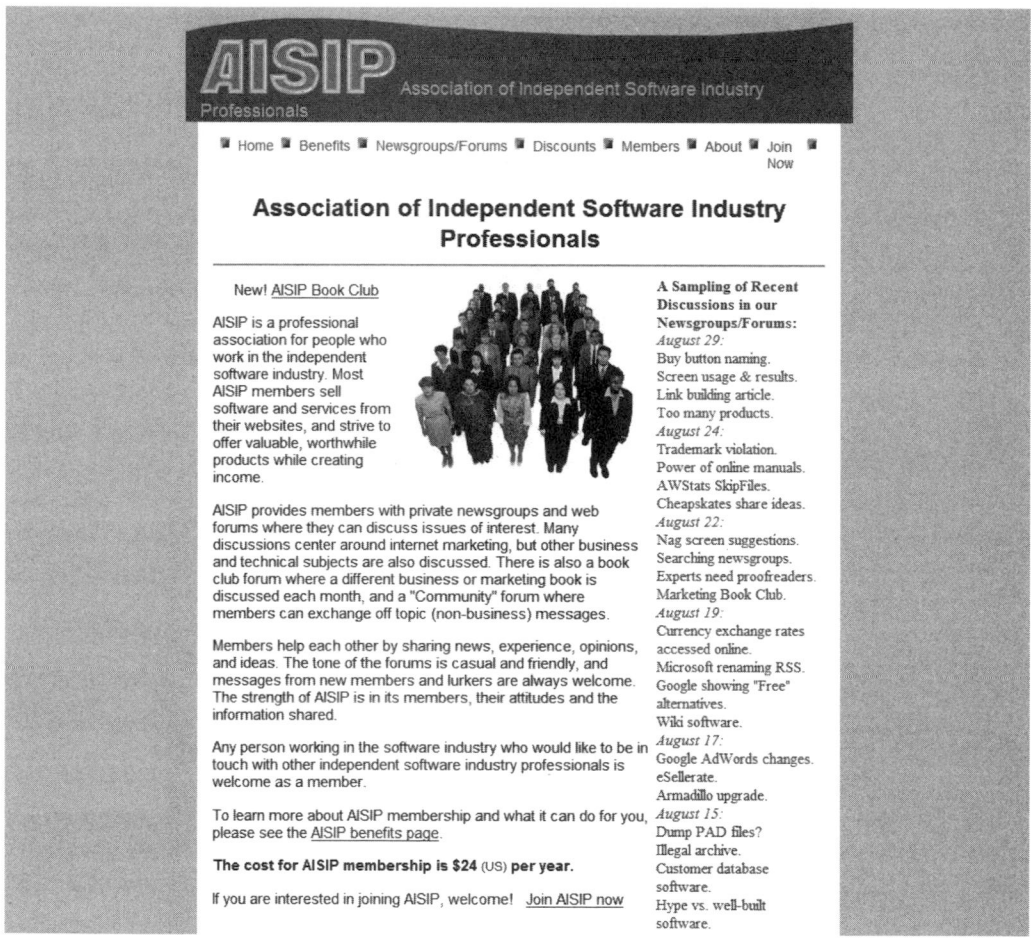

Figure 6-17. *Joining the AISIP*

Association of Shareware Professionals (ASP)

Started in 1987 to foster, publicize, and promote "try-before-you-buy" software, the Association of Shareware Professionals (ASP) (http://www.asp-shareware.org/) is a 1,400-member organization and one of the best small software vendor forums. Don't let the "shareware" part of the name throw you; a micro-ISV rose smells as sweet by any name.

Although I'm not a member of ASP (dues are $100 USD a year), as shown in Figure 6-18, I've heard from three micro-ISV founders who rave about the quality and quantity of great information available in the private forums of the ASP.

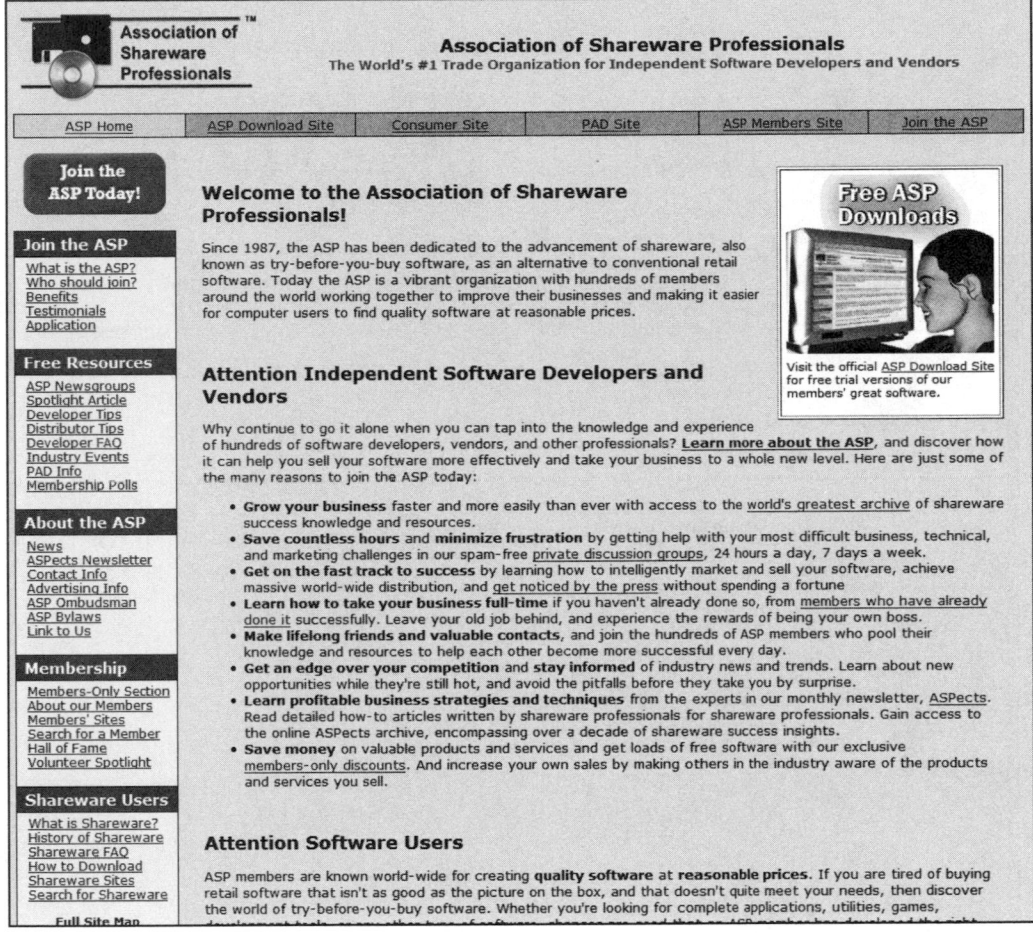

Figure 6-18. *Joining the ASP*

One service that the ASP has provided to all companies that distribute trial versions of their software is the Portable Application Description (PAD) format, as shown in Figure 6-19. By creating a PAD file for your application using PADGen (provided free by ASP), you can easily load upload to sites such as CNET Download.com with information—a handy timesaver.

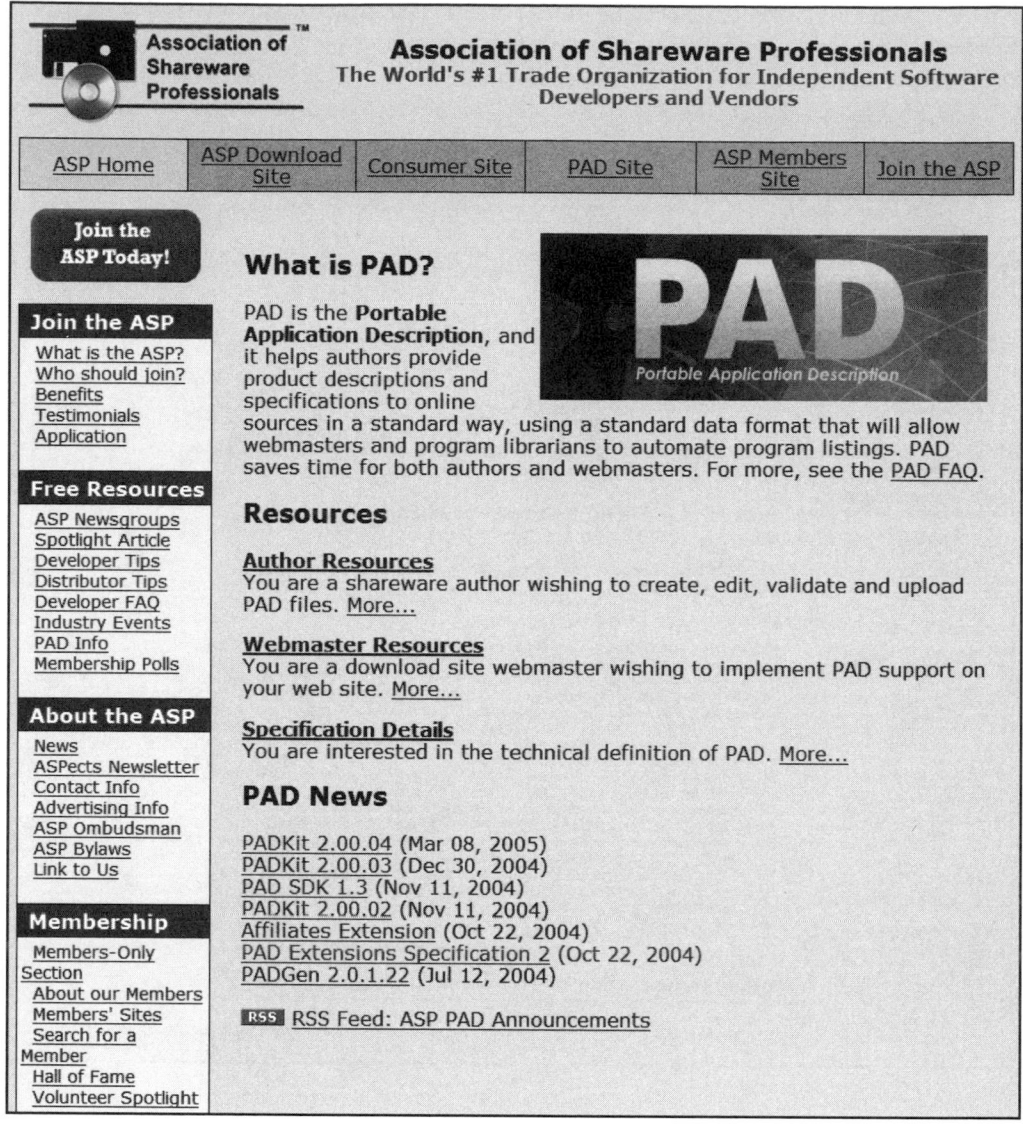

Figure 6-19. *The ASP created and popularized PAD*

Educational Software Cooperative (ESC)

One more online organization gets an honorable mention: the Educational Software Cooperative (http://www.edu-soft.org), as shown in Figure 6-20. Started in 1994, ESC is a nonprofit organization focused on better developing, advertising, distributing, and selling educational software. Basic annual membership dues are $35 USD ($40 outside North America).

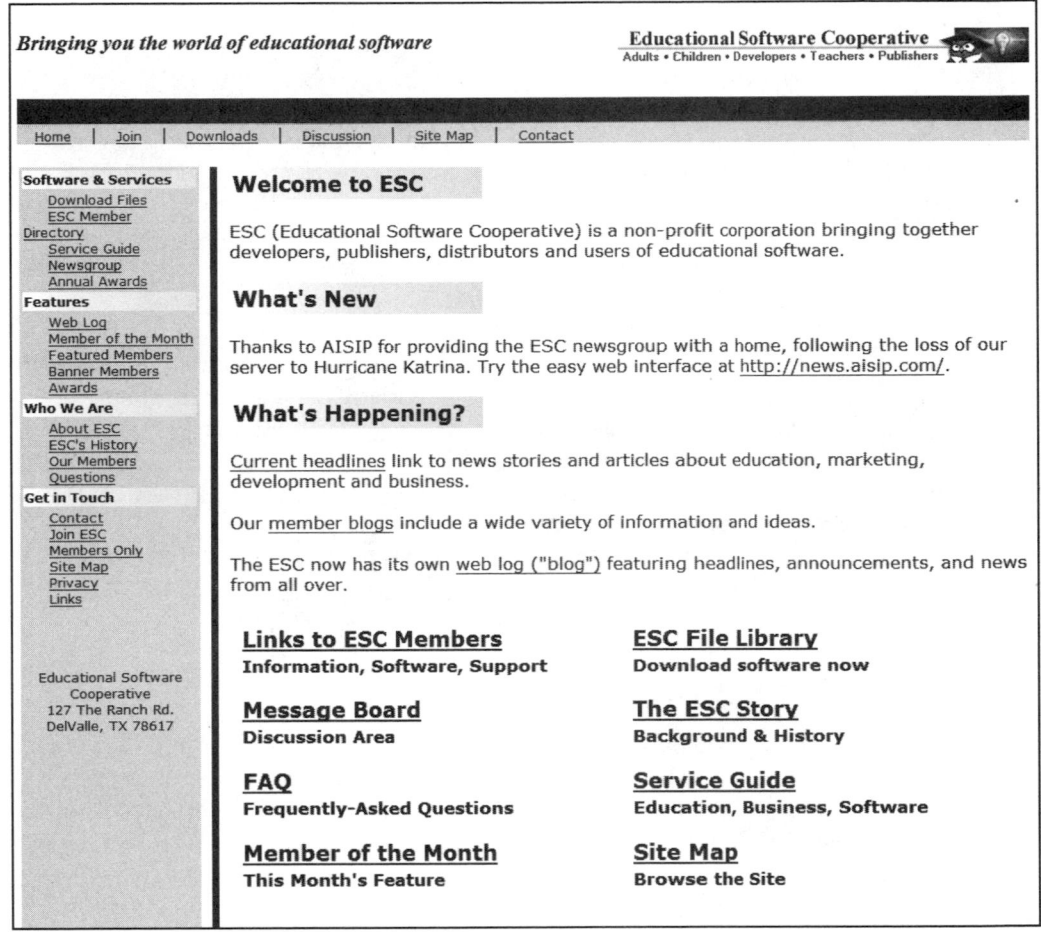

Bringing you the world of educational software

Educational Software Cooperative
Adults • Children • Developers • Teachers • Publishers

Home | Join | Downloads | Discussion | Site Map | Contact

Software & Services
Download Files
ESC Member
Directory
Service Guide
Newsgroup
Annual Awards
Features
Web Log
Member of the Month
Featured Members
Banner Members
Awards
Who We Are
About ESC
ESC's History
Our Members
Questions
Get in Touch
Contact
Join ESC
Members Only
Site Map
Privacy
Links

Educational Software
Cooperative
127 The Ranch Rd.
DelValle, TX 78617

Welcome to ESC

ESC (Educational Software Cooperative) is a non-profit corporation bringing together developers, publishers, distributors and users of educational software.

What's New

Thanks to AISIP for providing the ESC newsgroup with a home, following the loss of our server to Hurricane Katrina. Try the easy web interface at http://news.aisip.com/.

What's Happening?

Current headlines link to news stories and articles about education, marketing, development and business.

Our member blogs include a wide variety of information and ideas.

The ESC now has its own web log ("blog") featuring headlines, announcements, and news from all over.

Links to ESC Members
Information, Software, Support

Message Board
Discussion Area

FAQ
Frequently-Asked Questions

Member of the Month
This Month's Feature

ESC File Library
Download software now

The ESC Story
Background & History

Service Guide
Education, Business, Software

Site Map
Browse the Site

Figure 6-20. *Joining ESC*

ESC is more than just an online community; it's a real-world organization with elected officers.

ROSEMARY WEST, PAST PRESIDENT AND WEBMASTER, ESC

ESC is one those small, market-specific organizations whose influence far exceeds its online presence. Rosemary West, past president and current Webmaster of ESC, filled me in.

Q. For a self-funded start-up (a micro-ISV), what resources are available through ESC?

A. For many of our members, being linked to a top-rated Web site is a very high priority. Paying for a [Google] AdWord for *educational software* would cost a fortune. ESC consistently comes up above the fold in a search on that term (usually in the number-two or number-three slot on Google).

The newsletter and the download site (where customers can find evaluation copies of members' software) are two benefits that our members always mention as their favorites.

Our service guide (list of nonsoftware goods and services from members), Webring, blog page, and member-of-the month program are all ways we help our members become more visible and market their products. We also offer banner advertising to premium members, sponsor annual awards, and cooperate with other organizations of projects of interest.

Q. Have you found that the networking among ESC members helps break into the educational market?

A. There is no way to place a high enough value on the advice from members who have experience with the educational market (or marketing in general). Schools often have special needs or ways of doing things that are different from other businesses.

I have been told again and again how specific tips and suggestions have helped ESC members do a better job of selling software to schools, learning how to handle purchase orders, making more effective Web sites, etc.

Q. What advice would you give to a micro-ISV, be they starting in the educational market or not?

A. Make the best product you can. Keep making it better.

Be unique. There are too many people doing what has already been done. Being unique applies not just to your product, but how it is presented. At a recent educational conference, the same stock photo of students appeared in three different companies' booths. This was not impressive. It's always worth the time to be creative and look for a different approach.

Don't assume that your customers think the way you do or that their needs are the same as yours. Investigate your market and learn how to give your customers what they want.

Remember that it is easier to sell to existing customers than it is to find new customers. Be creative and energetic about postsale marketing.

Your Micro-ISV Industry Cheat Sheet

I know you probably think you have enough to do getting your micro-ISV up and running without having to thumb through this chapter again and again for the topics you need to remember about the industry you're now in, so Table 6-1 offers a quick cheat sheet of important points to remember.

Table 6-1. *Your Industry and You*

Question to Ask	Resources
What is Microsoft doing in my market?	Check Microsoft bloggers, especially Don Dodge (http://dondodge.typepad.com/the_next_big_thing/) and Microsoft Watch (http://www.microsoft-watch.com/).
Am I taking advantage of Microsoft in every way possible?	Check Microsoft's Partner page (https://partner.microsoft.com), and ask around at Joel on Software (http://discuss.joelonsoftware.com/?biz).
What are other big companies doing in my market?	Check Google News (http://news.google.com/).
Who are my main competitors and what are they up to?	Check where you're listed in Google Directory (http://directory.google.com/) and Technorati (http://technorati.com).
What are other people saying about me and my micro-ISV?	Check Technorati, PubSub (http://www.pubsub.com), Google Blog Search (http://blogsearch.google.com/), and your favorite RSS aggregator.
Who have I commiserated lately with online or over a beer?	Check Joel on Software, ASP (http://www.asp-shareware.org), and local small business groups—they'll understand about the long hours.

CHAPTER 7

■ ■ ■

What Happens Next?

Some things have to be believed to be seen.

—Ralph Hodgson, author and poet[1]

Most worthwhile endeavors, be it mastering a new programming language, writing a book, or starting a successful micro-ISV, have at least two mandatory components: a great deal of work and the belief you can do it. In Chapters 1 through 6 I covered just about all the tasks you need to master in order to make your micro-ISV a success; in this chapter, I want to get at the other component—believing you can do it.

Now, I could have you chant "I can do it! I will do it! I am doing it!" a couple hundred times each morning. That works—except your co-workers might talk. Or I could send you off on a "Discover Your Inner Strength" seminar and charge you up that way. That would also work.

Being an old "just the facts" type of ex-reporter, I decided the best way to show you that you can build a successful micro-ISV was to go out and interview 25 micro-ISVers who are making money—sometimes a lot of money. Seeing is believing.

I conducted the following interviews in September 2005, so by the time you're reading this, things may have changed for each of the micro-ISVers who were kind enough to let me interview them via email. I've organized the interviews into three groups:

- Micro-ISVers who are just starting out and have not yet seen big bushels of money come their way.

- Micro-ISVers who are humming right along making money and growing.

- Micro-ISVers who are either doing extremely well as micro-ISVs or have recently "graduated" to full-blown companies.

Most of these interviews started with the same set of questions and then spun out from there, so the juicy bits tend to be toward the end of each interview. Please excuse the length of this chapter; in some ways this is the most important chapter in this book. Each of these micro-ISVs has useful lessons to pass on, but here's the most important take-away: if they can do it, so can you!

---

1. http://www.quotationspage.com/quote/674.html

Emerging Micro-ISVs

The first group of interviewees is on the first furlong of the micro-ISV race and is just starting to see, or will soon see, revenue. As you read these nine interviews, you'll see a couple of common themes emerge:

- It takes more time and effort to get a micro-ISV started than you might have predicted.

- If you're hoping for instant riches, you're better off playing the lottery. Building revenue is a multimonth, sometimes multiyear, process.

- Doing everything yourself might not be the best solution, unless of course it's the only solution you can afford.

Of all these interviews, I have to confess to being most impressed with Ian Landsman's studied, careful, and meticulous approach. Since I conducted that interview in September 2005, Ian's product HelpSpot has gone live and by all accounts is doing very well.

ANDY BRICE, FOUNDER, ORYX DIGITAL

Micro-ISV: Oryx Digital
Web site: http://www.perfecttableplan.com
Blog: "Not yet"
Interviewee: Andy Brice, founder
What it sells: PerfectTablePlan, a Windows and Macintosh software application for planning seating arrangements for weddings, conferences, and other events.
Location: High Wycombe, England (about 30 minutes west of London)
Q. Can you tell me a bit about the software or Web services or products your micro-ISV sells?
A. I sell PerfectTablePlan, desktop software for doing table/seating plans for wedding receptions, corporate events, charity dinners, etc. Currently it is available for Windows, and I am just about to release a Mac version.

I got married last year, and I found doing the seating plan for the wedding reception a real nightmare. And we only had 60 guests. I looked around for software to help me, but I just couldn't find anything appropriate. There were a handful of products, but they were too expensive, [they were] too difficult to use, and I didn't think they were very well marketed. I realized there was a gap in the market, so when I was made redundant from my dot-com job, I took the plunge.

Particular interests of mine include usability, optimization, and cross-platform development, and PerfectTablePlan was interesting because I was able to combine all three. (It uses a genetic algorithm to automatically seat guests according to who you want them to sit next to.)

So far feedback from customers has been very positive. The main problem is that most people don't even realize that there is a better way to do a seating plan than using scraps of paper or cutting and pasting into a spreadsheet. I have to try [to] educate the market with a minimal marketing budget.

Q. Is revenue a) less than what you hoped, b) about what you predicted, c) exceeding expectations, or d) you're going to buy a small Pacific island later this year? Can you share your sales per month?

A. When I started, I had little idea how many I would sell and through what channels. But I divided my living costs by the expected margin for each sale, and I thought it was achievable. As a target I drew a graph of monthly revenue starting at £0 in month 1 and the equivalent of my salary as a full-time software engineer in month 12. Sales have increased linearly every month, and so far I have reached almost every monthly revenue target, with the help of some consultancy in the first few months.

However, I should stress that this revenue goes to the company, not to me.

I have paid myself very little so far for working very long hours and have mostly been living on savings. Thankfully, I have a very supportive wife (thanks, Claire!). If money is your primary motivation, I wouldn't recommend micro-ISV as a career path.

Q. What has been the biggest surprise in getting your micro-ISV started?

A. I've had a few surprises. It is a process of discovery, and that is part of what makes it interesting. I've learnt so much in the last eight months!

I had assumed that my Internet sales would be four in the United States for every one I made in the United Kingdom, but so far it has been the other way around. I think this is partly because many Americans (especially from the Midwest) don't do table plans for their weddings. They regard it as too formal. I guess I should have done more research, rather than making assumptions.

I thought the obvious sales channel for PerfectTablePlan was department stores with wedding gift lists. I managed to interest one but was flabbergasted by the deal that was suggested. I calculated that if they sold 1,000 units of PerfectTablePlan, I would owe them £1000. And this didn't even include my support, shipping, and printing costs. I felt that this was more of an insult to my intelligence than a business proposal.

Q. Do you have a marketing plan?

A. Yes. I thought quite a bit about how I was going to market PerfectTablePlan before I wrote the software. It's mostly in my head, rather than written down, though. It also evolves as I find out more about the market and what works and what doesn't.

I have quite a few ideas on how to make PerfectTablePlan more useful to customers, how to broaden the market, and related services I can offer. But I obviously don't want to say too much about future strategy.

Q. In what ways do you market PerfectTablePlan?

A. Mainly Google AdWords, search engines, and magazine ads.

AdWords is great because you can get really quick and detailed feedback on what works and what doesn't. Also, you can get it up and running in a few hours. However, it does require a lot of tweaking, and I still end up paying for click-throughs from people who are looking for seating plans for Yankee Stadium or Boeing 747s.

I found that it took months of waiting and quite a bit of tweaking of my Web pages to appear anywhere on the major search engines. But the effort was worth it, as I now get quite a lot of traffic that costs me nothing. I didn't pay anyone to do search engine optimization for me—all you need to know is out there on the Web.

Magazine ads probably don't make sense for a lot of micro-ISVs. However, I am selling to specific niches in the consumer market that are well served by magazines. Also, some of my customers might not think to surf the Web, and I need some way to reach them. Unfortunately, it's difficult to measure the success of print ads. I am trying to use a different URL for each ad so I can monitor the response.

PerfectTablePlan by Oryx Digital

Q. Given your experience so far, are you planning a second product?
A. Yes. I already have a basic prototype that I am using to help me with my work. Like PerfectTablePlan, it's a tool that solves a well-defined problem. However, I am unlikely to do much beyond developing it for my own use in the next few months—I am too busy with PerfectTablePlan.

ANDREY BUTOV, PRESIDENT, ANTAIR

Micro-ISV: Antair
Web site: `http://www.antair.com`
Blog: `http://www.antair.com/andrey`
Interviewee: Andrey Butov
What it sells: Chinchilla, a developer product.
Location: New York City, New York; United States

Q. Can you tell me a bit about the software or Web services or products your micro-ISV sells?

A. Antair's one and only product right now is Chinchilla. It is a desktop application geared toward .NET developers [that] allows them to extract class inheritance diagrams from within .dll and .exe .NET assemblies. There is an educational product in the works and a Mac/Linux port of Chinchilla for the Mono project.

Q. Is revenue a) less than what you hoped, b) about what you predicted, c) exceeding expectations, or d) you're going to buy a small Pacific island later this year? Can you share your sales per month?

A. Considering that Chinchilla was literally released last week and is only in the beta release program stage, I would say *a* for actual sales but *b* for expectations. I really don't know what to expect but am optimistic. I am looking into marketing options but expect later products to generate more revenue than Chinchilla has the potential for. No sales as of yet.

Q. What has been the biggest surprise in getting your micro-ISV started?

A. How much noncoding work there is. I had no idea how much effort it takes to take care of all the infrastructure and administrative work surrounding the launch of a business...even a one-man operation. From incorporation to bank accounts to marketing, I find myself going deeper and deeper into areas I was not trained to deal with.

Q. Why a chinchilla?

A. *Chinchilla* was chosen primarily for acoustic aesthetics. *Antair* is completely meaningless. I wanted the company name to stand on its own...meaning the word would have no meaning associated with it aside from the company. Chinchilla sounded well when spoken after *Antair*.

It doesn't hurt that the creatures are cute. I knew the resulting logo would come out nicely...and it did. I am much happier with Chinchilla's logo than with Antair's logo.

Q. What's your approach to marketing to developers?

A. I am warier of marketing than of any other noncoding aspect of the business. With all other administrative and business foundation matters, one can get advice from other start-ups, message boards, or people who own non-IT businesses. Marketing is the only thing that is not only product specific but also directly hits your pocketbook. If you make a mistake in marketing, you not only lose money in the attempt but you also lose time, which in a one-man operation is the most limited resource.

I intend on doing a lot of research, trying small, noncostly avenues of advertising and hoping that word of mouth spreads. From what I've read thus far, word of mouth brings more sales than any other form of advertising.

Q. Do you see a growing (little? lot?) Mac/Linux market via Mono?

A. I think as far as percentage of sales with respect to downloads/visits, the Mac market should be higher. The Apple community has a way of standing behind its developers. I find myself spending more on software for the Mac, even though my primary machines are Solaris and Windows. Visual Studio 2005 offers a similar feature to Chinchilla. Chinchilla is meant to be an affordable, stand-alone replacement. Since there is no Visual Studio on a Mac, it offers a more appropriate market. I think Mono could gain ground on the Mac platform, but the lack of a Windows Forms implementation might just prevent that. Gtk is just not satisfactory when you're writing .NET code. After many years in the IT industry, I am no longer naive enough to believe that there is a market for this in the Linux community. I don't think Mono will ever catch on in the UNIX derivative market.

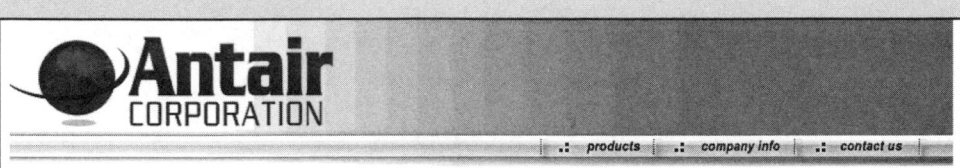

products .: company info .: contact us

We're proud to announce the release of Chinchilla 1.3

Sign up for our beta test program, and grab the full version of Chinchilla at 50% off.

[Chinchilla Information]

[Beta Test Information]

Copyright © 2005, Antair Corporation. All Rights Reserved

Chinchilla by Antair

BORIS YANKOV, FOUNDER/OWNER/CEO, VIRTUOZA

Micro-ISV: Virtuoza

Web site: http://www.virtuoza.com

Blog: http://www.borisyankov.com

Interviewee: Boris Yankov

What it sells: A task management application, a Windows start-up manager, and a time management application.

Location: Bulgaria

Q. Do you have one Web site or several?

A. My main Web site is http://www.virtuoza.com. I had my products listed there, but now they all have their own Web sites. They are

- *InControl*: http://www.get-in-control.com

- *Smart To-Do*: http://www.smarttodo.com

- *OverSpy*: http://www.overspy.com

Q. Can you tell me a bit about the software or Web services or products your micro-ISV sells?

A. I wish I could say I had some great strategy defined before creating my applications. It isn't so. InControl is a start-up manager. I created it back in 2001. Smart To-Do is a lightweight task management application. And OverSpy is report-remotely, computer-monitoring software.

I will not advise anyone to create several applications differing that much.

Q. Is revenue a) less than what you hoped, b) about what you predicted, c) exceeding expectations, or d) you're going to buy a small Pacific island later this year? Can you share your sales per month?

A. Before I started Virtuoza, I was doing some projects on Rent-a-Coder. [A] few of the jobs I did there made me more familiar with the current state of shareware. So I decided diving in myself [would] be the smart move—the way to getting rich.

When I started my micro-ISV, in July 2003, I hoped to start earning $1,000/month almost immediately. Far from it. What happened was that I began getting an average of a sale a month. It turned [out] that creating and marketing software is much harder than I anticipated in the beginning. As I learned later, most micro-ISVs started very slowly too, at just [a] few sold copies a month.

So, I needed to continue doing projects on Rent-a-Coder; my micro-ISV wasn't going to pay the checks for long. But I continued to invest time in developing software and learning how to market it better. Finally in March 2005 I began getting more serious. The sales went up from two to three a month to ten, then twenty, then thirty. I currently make about $1,000/month, but this is just a temporary position I am in. It is already a success for me, because now, I can devote my full time on my business, which will help me grow it much faster. I estimate sales of $2,000 to $3,000/month until the end of next year (2006). Or if I get lucky—much more.

Q. What has been the biggest surprise in getting your micro-ISV started?

A. The biggest surprise was that it would take me that long to start earning good money. Don't get me wrong—now I am quite happy. Even if $1,000/month doesn't seem [like] that much, think about one important aspect: I don't need [to] do almost anything in order to keep [this] money coming. I need to spend few hours a week answering customer emails, and I will keep [this] coming for a long time.

Have you considered joining the Association of Shareware Professionals? It helped me tremendously, and at $100 per year it is almost a no-brainer.

Q. Regarding ASP, how has it helped?

A. To the outsider, the ASP does not offer too much value. You may think that the private newsgroups, which are its biggest asset, are nothing too good. The difference comes from the people in it. There are about 1,500 members currently (and rising every year). Most of them have released a product and have real experience. A good portion is doing this full-time. The difference to the Business of Software forum on Joel's site and the public `shareware.authors` newsgroup that you can find on Google is this: when a topic is discussed, most of the people giving opinions have already successfully implemented the things they advise. There are a lot of smart people in Joel's forum, but most of them are not actually a micro-ISV.

I can preach this for long time, but the bottom line is this: it brought much more value to me than the $100 I spent for the membership.

I blogged my initial impressions nine months ago here: `http://borisyankov.blogspot.com/2004/12/should-you-join-asp-for-some-time-i.html`.

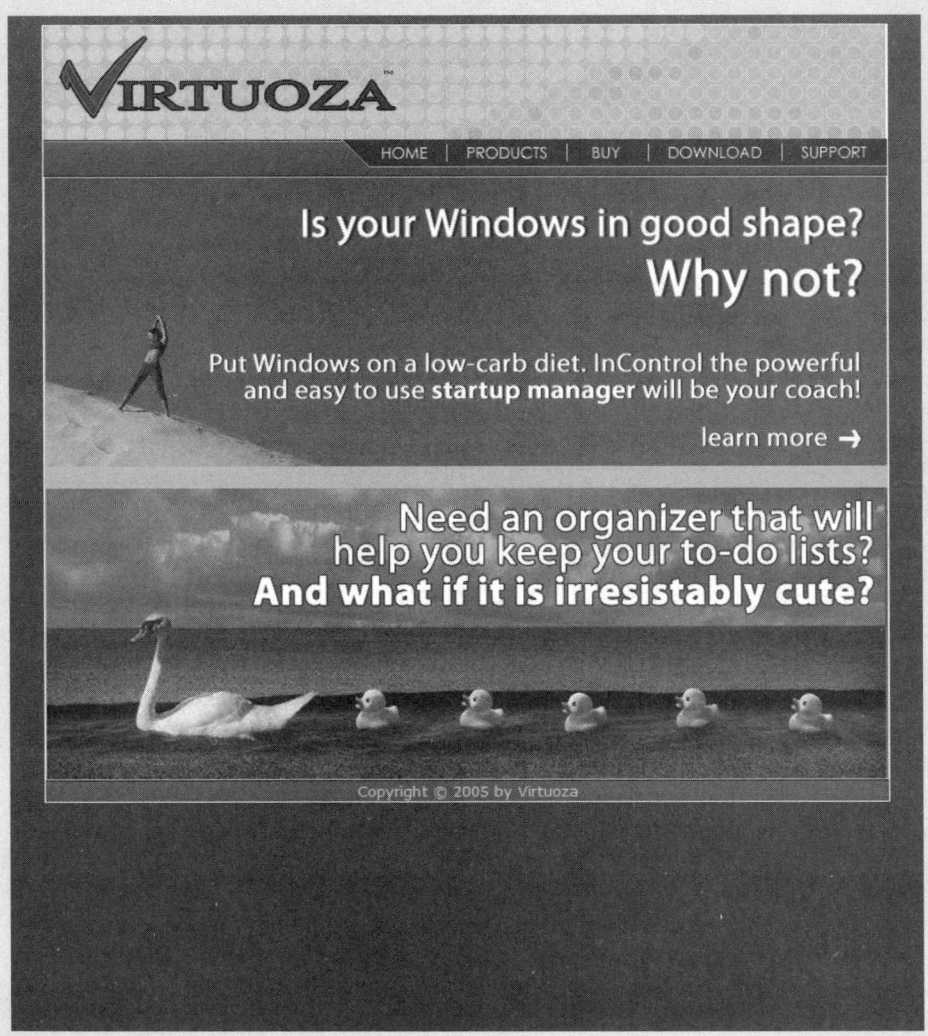

InControl by Virtuoza

Q. When you say, "Finally in March 2005 I began getting more serious," tell me more.

A. The first "serious" thing I did was to give each of my products its own Web site. For a year and a half my main Web site has been unchanged, and I learned a lot about better persuasive techniques. I incorporated them into the new sites (in other words, my previous Web site sucked big in terms of conversion ratios). I also released a version 2 of InControl. This was the time when my orders jumped immediately from the dismal one to two per month to fifteen and began rising.

Q. How do you market your various products?

A. Initially I embraced download sites. I found a long list of these Web sites and submitted to every one of them. Then I thought, "I am ready with my marketing." The problem with this approach is that this will bring you about 50 to 60 not very targeted visitors a day, which will hardly translate to more than a few sales a month. Then comes Search Engine Optimization (SEO). What I preach now is this: learn the basics of SEO so you don't mess things up. Then concentrate on creating a great site with great content.

Then comes Google AdWords. It is great. Conversions are higher than most of the alternatives you have, like advertising on download sites (a bad idea) and advertising on sites related in topic to your software (a better idea).

For my upcoming product, FusionDesk, I will be starting a blog. (FusionDesk will be an advanced task management application. It's somewhat of a competitor to MasterList Professional, but it has a very different philosophy than your app, and the market is huge, so I don't think it will be a problem if I give you more insider details about it.)

Q. Are your ongoing development efforts aimed at new products or new versions of your existing products?

A. I am concentrating on improving my current software. There are people who ask the question, should I develop lots of small apps, or should I concentrate on fewer apps (or even only one)? I strongly suggest keeping the number of products you have to a minimum. A well-done new version of your software can easily bring you two to three times the customers you had with your previous one.

See Joel Spolsky for [an] example. His FogBugz is doing great now; it is in its fourth version. He couldn't achieve this success with ten apps at version 1. He would've been stuck with ten not quite adequate products. He said that good software takes three versions and ten years to complete. And I agree with this.

BRIAN PLEXICO, FOUNDER, CLOUDSHACK AND MICROISV.COM

Micro-ISV: Cloudshack

Web site: `http://microisv.com`

Blog: `http://microisv.com`

Interviewee: Brian Plexico

What it sells: Specialized consumer database applications.

Location: Summerville, South Carolina (near Charleston, South Carolina); United States

Q. Can you tell me a bit about the software or Web services or products your micro-ISV sells?

A. My software was made to help people manage their collections of things such as baseball cards, watches, etc. From that I developed a niche product specifically for model airplane engine collectors.

I have also developed an app to help people keep track of their skeet shooting/sporting clays scores.

Q. Is revenue a) less than what you hoped, b) about what you predicted, c) exceeding expectations, or d) you're going to buy a small Pacific island later this year? Can you share your sales per month?

A. Originally, revenue was what I predicted. I sold my collection software on eBay exclusively for quite a while, but about a year after I started, competition from competing applications and increasing eBay fees brought revenue down to about breakeven. Currently, I am not actively promoting my software, but a few sales still trickle in from people who find the Web site via search engines.

My skeet software was dealt a blow when Google disallowed a lot of my AdWords because they were gun-related. I guess their version of "do no evil" includes anything gun-related even if it is for an established sport.

Q. What has been the biggest surprise in getting your micro-ISV started?

A. The amount of requests that come in for product enhancements and how-to questions. Even if you've designed something that is fairly simple to use and includes comprehensive documentation, people still ask a lot of how-to questions.

The other thing I've learned is that creating a niche product is good, but there needs to be a sufficient market to make it worthwhile. I've created some products that fill niches and had very little competition, but the overall market was limited.

Q. Are you developing any other products?

A. I have a few ideas that are bouncing around my head right now but nothing specific I'm working on. I am doing some research for a new product that may or may not come to fruition. I'm talking to some people who would be potential customers to see whether they would purchase the software if it were available.

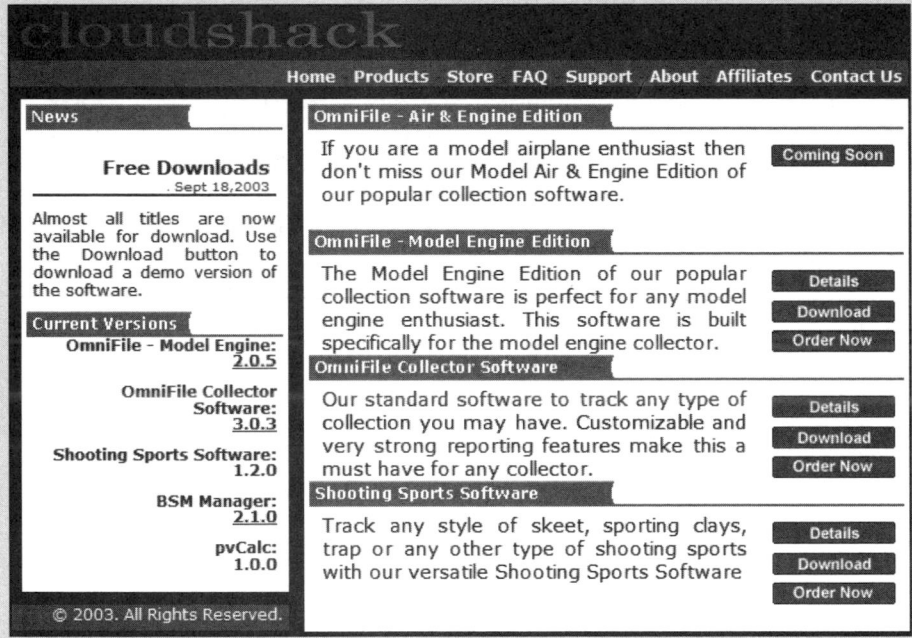

OmniFile by cloudshack

Q. How/why did you start microISV.com?

A. I was reading Eric Sink's original micro-ISV article, and the idea just struck a chord with me since I had developed my first shareware apps not long before the article. I thought it would make a good site to have a place where the micro-ISV crowd could congregate, so I bought the domain name. On a Saturday, a week after I bought the domain name, I downloaded WordPress, made a quick HTML template, and made the first post, which incidentally was one year ago today if I'm not mistaken.

Q. What has been the response to microISV.com?

A. The response has been great! I only wish there was more interaction with comments and the forum. Having more interaction would allow me to take the site in a direction to benefit people even more.

Q. Any advice you'd give to someone starting a micro-ISV today?

A. My advice is to just go ahead and get a product out there. With my first app, the collection software, I spent a year "perfecting" it. I kept coming up with more and more features that I thought would be cool but are probably used only by the most hard-core users. With my shooting software, I conceived the product, coded it, and was selling it within a week.

Getting the software out there so quickly showed me that starting simple is best because you can add the features that are most requested later while starting to make money immediately. It was a pretty cool feeling to go from having an idea for a software app to selling it seven days later for $20 a sale.

GAVIN BOWMAN, DIRECTOR, V4 SOLUTIONS

Micro-ISV: V4 Solutions

Web site: http://www.oriador.com and http://www.webhelperbrowser.com

Blog: http://www.webhelperbrowser.com/blog and http://www.codesnipers.com

Interviewee: Gavin Bowman

What it sells: A staff-scheduling application and an enhanced Web browser.

Location: Cumbria, United Kingdom

Q. Can you tell me a bit about the software or Web services or products your micro-ISV sells?

A. My main product is Oriador Rota. It's a staff scheduling/Rota package. It's been on the market for about 18 months.

Web Helper Browser has been available for about six months, and it's a Web browser with various extras, including features for saving Web pages and fragments.

Q. Is revenue a) less than what you hoped, b) about what you predicted, c) exceeding expectations, or d) you're going to buy a small Pacific island later this year? Can you share your sales per month?

A. It has definitely been *a*, but I feel like it's approaching *b* for revised predictions. If the next year or two go well, it might even make *c*, but I think *d* is a long way off!

Q. What has been the biggest surprise in getting your micro-ISV started?

A. The biggest surprise has been how hard it is to get feedback. I think I thought everyone who used it would take the time to tell us what was lacking or what they'd like to see improved or changed. In retrospect I was very naive, but obviously I didn't know that at the time.

To quickly clarify, so that any "I" or "we" makes sense, there are two people in my company. For the most part I've been the sole developer on both products, but recently my partner took over our latest product so I can focus more clearly on Oriador.

Q. Do you find it easier/harder to market/support two products instead of one?

A. A lot harder. There's no natural connection between the two products, so there's no real crossover between support or marketing. They both need to make it on their own.

Until about a month ago I was developing both products too. It was way too much pressure and way too hard to focus.

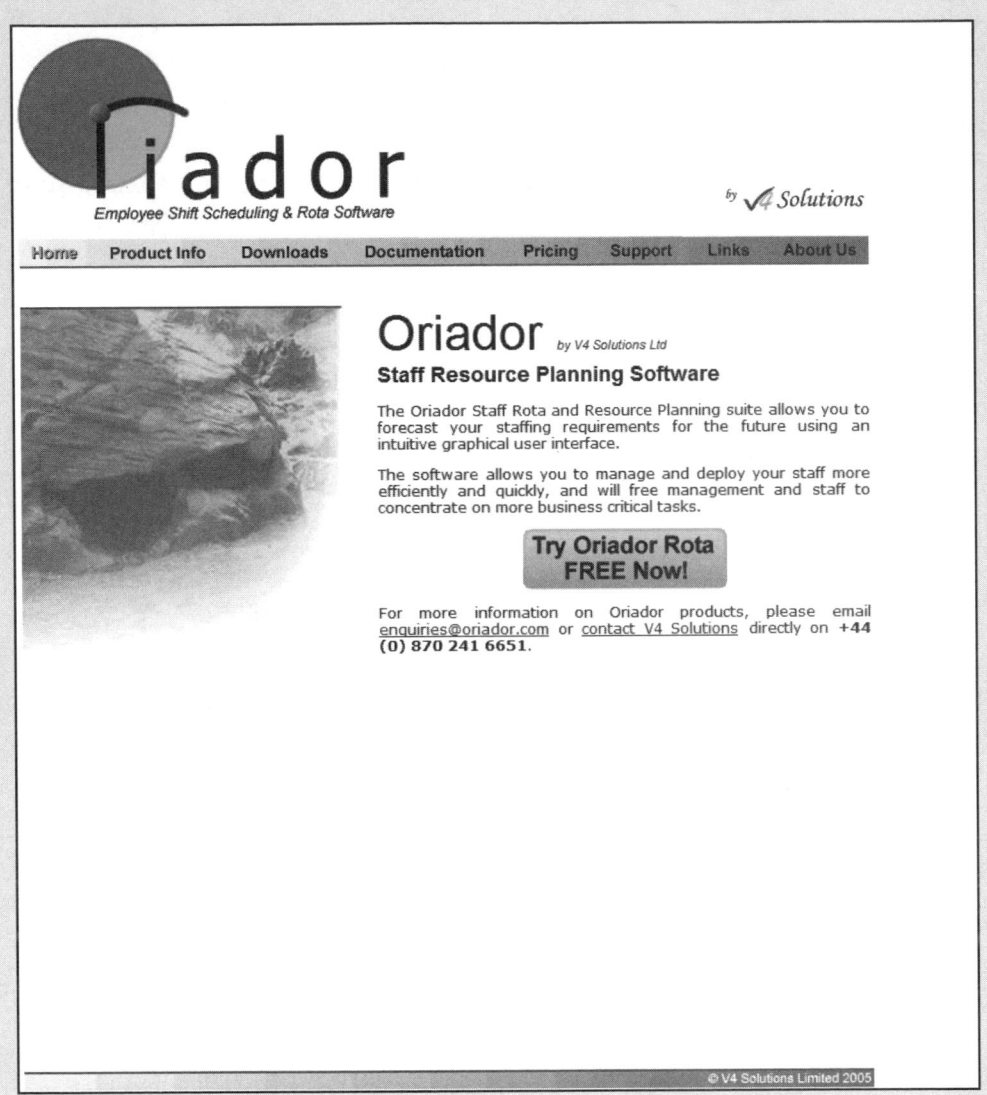

Oriador Rota by V4 Solutions

Q. How do you and your partner make decisions, and how did you decide who gets what?
A. We're very different, but we've known each other a long time. When there's a conflict, the decision seems largely inevitable. It's usually obvious to one how important any idea or suggestion is to the other.

Deciding to divide the products between us was just something that had to happen. With both I was never going to get anywhere, and Neil had reached a place where he wanted to be more involved in the development side of the business. Once we made the decision, I would never have given up Oriador Rota. Fortunately, I think he wanted Web Helper Browser. I'd reached a point with it where I was fairly comfortable with what I'd achieved, so I could take a step back. He's still bursting with ideas to expand on it and take it forward. I've been working on Oriador for a lot longer, and I still have a lot of ideas. I really wouldn't have been able to let it go.

Q. How do you presently market Oriador Rota?

A. At the moment we do it all online, mostly the Web site combined with Google AdWords. The software is listed in some of the software directories, but we don't seem to get a lot of inquiries coming in that way. We tried a little direct mailing and a little cold calling, but we weren't very good at it. We've basically just tried to do as much as we can without overextending our budget.

Q. What has been the response to your blog, especially the micro-ISV mistake postings at CodeSnipers.com (http://codesnipers.com/?q=blog/12)?

A. The response has been great. People seemed to really like the posts and agree with what I was saying. I was a bit worried when I started writing them. I had five mistakes in mind, but I wondered if #6 was going to be telling everyone about all the things I did wrong. [But] if it had turned out to be a mistake, it would have gone against all my previous experience. I've always found that, on a small scale anyway, people like it when you own up to mistakes and accept responsibility. I know I do too. If someone says, "Yeah, sorry, that was my fault," I feel like I can trust them. There's more honesty there than if they try to blame it on someone else. I wasn't sure if it would work like that on a larger scale.

I'd read plenty of advice on what to do and what not to do from successful people but not so much from people still trying to make it. I knew that there were people out there who would make the same mistakes, so I just wanted to tell them what I did, [tell them] how wrong it was, and suggest some alternatives. It had a kind of healing effect on me too, actually accepting some of these things and starting to think about trying to fix them seemed to give me renewed energy.

Overall, blogging has been everything I wanted it to be. I've been able to meet some great people, [I] had some great discussions, and I just generally feel more connected than I did before I started. It probably hasn't been directly responsible for a single software sale, but the change in my motivation and the way I feel about the future seem a lot more valuable.

GRAHAM ASHER, OWNER, CARTOGRAPHY

Micro-ISV: Cartography

Web site: http://www.cartotype.com

Blog: None

Interviewee: Graham Asher

What it sells: Portable mapping library.

Location: Berkhamsted, England (which is a small town about 25 miles northwest of London)

Q. Can you tell me a bit about the software or Web services or products your micro-ISV sells?

A. CartoType is a portable mapping library written in C++. It uses the client's data, via plug-in data accessor interfaces, to draw scalable maps for use in location-based software like navigation programs and city guides.

So far it has been ported to four different OSs: three operating systems for mobile devices (Symbian, Microsoft Pocket PC, and Palm OS) plus Windows.

There's a lot more about it on the Web site if you're interested, and I flatter myself that it's reasonably well-written.

Q. Is revenue a) less than what you hoped, b) about what you predicted, c) exceeding expectations, or d) you're going to buy a small Pacific island later this year? Can you share your sales per month?

A. Less than I hoped. I have sold just one license so far. However, I haven't exactly done much marketing, and I have managed to improve the product a lot lately, so things may change given some extra effort.

Q. What has been the biggest surprise in getting your micro-ISV started?
A. This is very corny, I know, but I've been surprised how easy the bug fixing has been. We used source control, defect tracking, and regression testing from day one, and I was lucky enough to find an excellent fellow programmer who I could trust to do the right thing, so we really haven't had any problems with hard-to-find bugs—well, one, in fact, but that turned out to be a stack overflow in the customer's code.

Oh, one other happy surprise: CartoType uses three open source components, and to my great joy they have been completely reliable and bug-free, as far as I can tell.

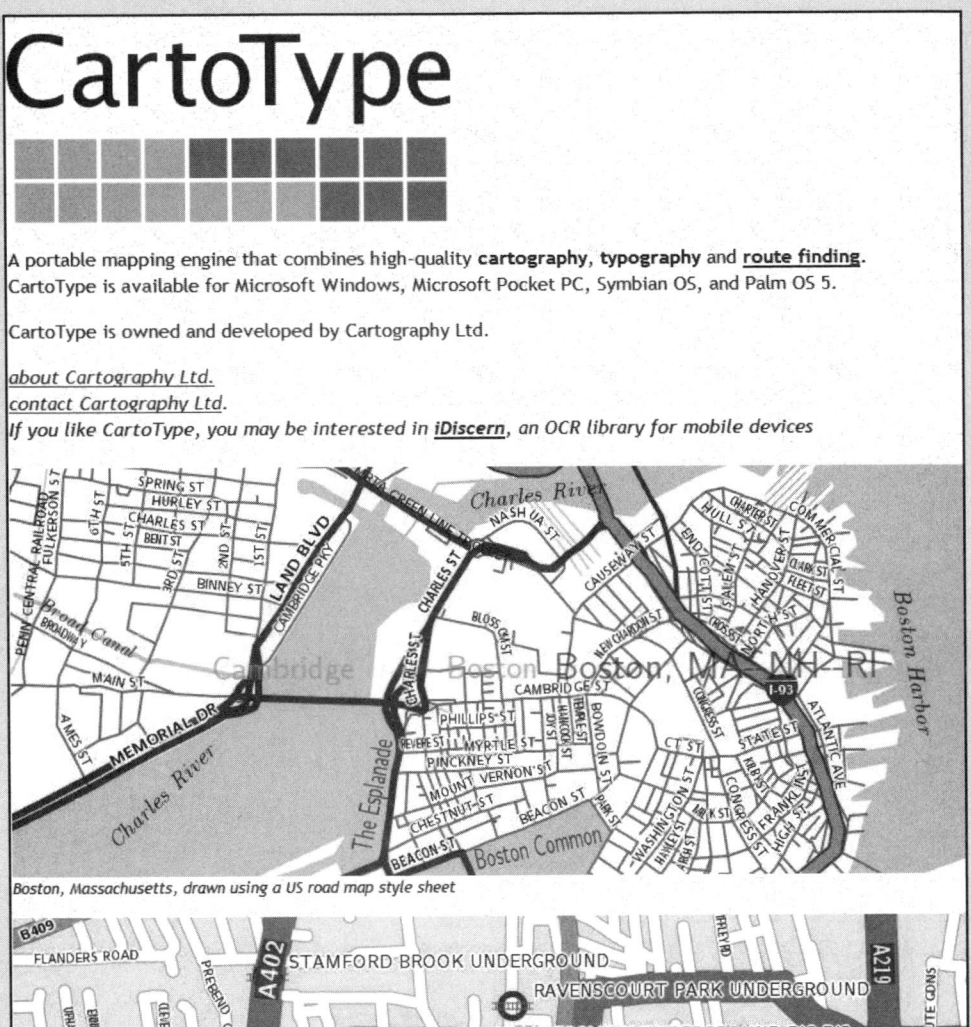

CartoType by Cartography

Q. Would you in general recommend using open source components to other micro-ISVs?

A. Yes, compared to commercial components and with the proviso that I have experience with relatively few open source components. The quality is high, the developers are dedicated and intelligent, and the support from the developers and the user community beats anything I have experienced with commercial components and in-house offerings at large companies I have worked for. These remarks apply mostly to FreeType, our most important open source component.

The three open source components that CartoType uses are FreeType, a font-rendering library; Expat, an XML interpreter; and DImalloc, a heap allocator.

I was very comfortable with FreeType before I started CartoType, because I had used it when I was working for Symbian. (At Symbian I implemented support for scalable fonts in the Symbian OS using FreeType.) I'd seen it develop from a rather messy piece of software to a more professional, understandable, and reliable component, and I'd been in correspondence with some of the FreeType developers (mainly the two founders, David Turner and Werner Lemberg), read their remarks on the FreeType email group, and grown to trust them. I also made a couple of very small contributions of my own to FreeType.

Expat was ported into CartoType by my colleague Lex Warners, who built a C++ wrapper for it and wrote unit tests. I didn't know anything about it before we started, but it has been rock solid.

DImalloc, Doug Lea's heap code, is the basis for Linux's malloc code and widely regarded as the best general-purpose heap allocator around. We use it on the Palm OS port, which has a very slow malloc implementation in its runtime library. The code looks very messy to me, and I can't follow it, but it works perfectly.

I also use two very important open source tools, the Subversion source control system and its Windows client TortoiseSvn. I used Perforce for many years and still use it in my work for a client I do consultancy for. A Perforce license costs several hundred dollars per seat. Subversion does more for me, more conveniently, and is entirely free. (Perforce may of course be more appropriate for large organizations; it may very well be more scalable than Subversion.)

Q. When working with open source components, any special precautions/efforts a developer should make than when working with a commercial component?

A. In a word, no. Open source components and commercial components require exactly the same care in choosing them, testing them, and interfacing them to your code. With commercial components you may not even get the source. But in fact the only commercial components I use in CartoType are the C runtime libraries for the various OSs, and not very much of them.

One obvious point: don't choose an open source project that was started yesterday, unless it's your own, and even then think twice. You need something mature, where the developers have demonstrated continuing commitment.

Q. How long have you been selling CartoType?

A. For just over a year. I sold the first license in January 2005.

Q. What are your current marketing plans?

A. I am going to continue to improve the product, particularly its visual appearance and speed. The appearance is very highly customizable and depends on style sheets written in XML, but users won't understand that or believe it unless I create more sample style sheets that demonstrate well-known mapping styles and display more screen shots on the Web site.

The Web site is very amateurish, although it provides plenty of information in a usable way. I'll have to decide whether to pay somebody to improve it or spend time on it myself.

I am going to find more contacts and potential sales prospects and ask my head of marketing (my wife) to call them and persuade them that CartoType can improve their products. I need to contact companies (like street atlas publishers) who possess cartographic data and are starting to move into location-based applications on mobile devices and need to get to market quickly. We would then point out that they can save a year at least of software development time by licensing CartoType.

IAN LANDSMAN, PRESIDENT, USERSCAPE

Micro-ISV: UserScape

Web site: http://www.userscape.com

Blog: http://www.userscape.com/blog

Interviewee: Ian Landsman

What it sells: HelpSpot, a Web-based help-desk package.

Location: Lagrangeville, New York; United States

Q. Can you tell me a bit about the software or Web services or products your micro-ISV sells?

A. UserScape's first product, HelpSpot, is a Web-based help-desk software package with two major components.

Primarily, HelpSpot was designed to track and manage the workflow for support requests. Requests are created through a manual entry by support staff or automatically from emails or the customer portal form as outlined below. There are a variety of individual support staff workspace tools and global configuration options that allow organizations to effectively manage the request resolution process from initial creation to postresolution reporting.

The second component of HelpSpot is the customer service portal. Designed for organizations seeking to leverage the efficiencies of the self-service support model, the portal includes a robust forum system and knowledge books (similar to a knowledge base). For inquires that require interaction with support staff, there's also a request submission form and a means to check and update current requests.

Q. Is revenue a) less than what you hoped, b) about what you predicted, c) exceeding expectations, or d) you're going to buy a small Pacific island later this year? Can you share your sales per month?

A. HelpSpot is current in beta, so no revenues to report as of yet. I would be happy to share sales information post our mid-October release.

Q. What has been the biggest surprise in getting your micro-ISV started?

A. I'm fortunate to report that this process has largely gone as planned. With respect to budgets and timelines, I began planning and projecting about six months before kickoff, and both have been within my initial estimates.

The most unexpected aspect has been the success in blogging about the process. From the start blogging the process to share my experience starting a company with others was part of my plan, but I had no idea it would be such a huge asset to UserScape and the HelpSpot product. The direct dialogue with my readers has, very often, resulted in a perspective on specific features or overall design I wouldn't have considered without them. Of course, the sheer reach of the blogging community has allowed HelpSpot to capture the attention of over 200 companies, which are currently on our mailing list as well as the over 80 organizations participating in the beta.

Q. Can you describe in detail how you budgeted and planned HelpSpot?

A. Planning for HelpSpot started about a year before the beta launch.

Throughout my career I've worked on technical projects that involved end-user interaction and clearly saw a need for a robust tool to effectively manage incoming issues/requests. My wife is a techie herself so we sat down and talked through the details. After we established the base feature set, I went to work writing up a spec along with several specific user scenarios that served as a way to flesh out much of the workflow and primary screens.

Initially we planned for me to keep the "day job" and leave towards the end of development. However, it quickly became obvious that to finish HelpSpot in anything close to a reasonable amount of time I would have to either scale back our initial vision or leave my job sooner to devote myself full-time to the project. Scaling back the feature set simply wouldn't allow HelpSpot to be the product we envisioned and would result in a product that mirrored the help-desk software on the market, which wasn't our goal.

In agreement that maintaining the scope of initial development would require me to leave my "day job," my wife and I discussed the financial picture. A budget was created, assuming no revenue from HelpSpot, which would allow us to cover home/business expenses for a 12-month period using a combination of her income, our savings, and a short-term contract project I had just taken.

A big part of starting an ISV is bootstrapping what you need, but there are still unavoidable expenses. For us those were design of the Web site and logo, purchase of icon sets, lawyer fees to create the license agreements, an accountant, hardware/software to support development and testing, and a server. We budgeted $12,000 for these expenses and so far have come in at about that number.

UserScape — User Centered Solutions

Help Desk | Workspace · Create Filter · Responses · Email Staff | KB | Forum | Search | Admin | Reports | Portal

▸ **Home**
HelpSpot
• Beta
• Overview
• Pricing
• Preview Article
Support
Founder's Blog
Contact

A new kind of software company

Software for users is what you can create when programmers don't drive design decisions, when software is not developed by a committee, it's what happens when you **leave unnecessary features out.** At UserScape we are dedicated to keeping the software out of your way so you can accomplish your objectives easily and productively.

Our first product, HelpSpot, takes a streamlined, feature-rich approach to traditionally cumbersome help desk software. Quick installation, sensible system configuration, and logical work-flow contribute to a product that is nimble yet robust enough to support a variety of work groups.

HelpSpot

HelpSpot makes it easy to:
© Manage any amount of incoming requests
© Get new team members working productively in minutes not weeks
© Integrate your data no matter where it's located
© Empower your customers to answer questions on their own with built in self service
© Automate many of the more tedious aspects of customer support
© Know exactly how effective your help desk is with advanced reporting
... and a whole lot more.

HelpSpot is designed for:
© Traditional help desk organizations within medium and large corporations
© Small businesses
© Not-for-profits and educational institutions
© E-Learning support
© independent software vendors (ISV's)
... just about anyone who needs to provide effective customer support.

5 Features you're going to love:
© Innovative reporting tags concept lets you get the detailed reporting data you need
© RSS, Email, text page (SMS) notifications mean you're always in the loop
© Unique color coding lets you know instantly if something is urgent, public, and more
© Integrated customer self service knowledge base and forums
© Bayesian SPAM filtering

5 Features your IT staff is going to love:
© Installs in 5 minutes
© Runs on all platforms (Windows, Linux, Unix, Mac)
© Smart design keeps CPU and RAM requirements low
© All data and files are stored in the database making backups ridiculously easy
© Integrates into LDAP single sign on systems

HelpSpot by UserScape

Q. What budgeting and planning advice would you give to other micro-ISVs?

A. I do think budgeting is a key area where some Micro-ISVs go wrong. They aren't realistic. They only budget themselves to the point of release but don't properly plan for the postrelease period. This is critical because you want to give the product ample time to succeed in the market.

Get realistic by committing the numbers to paper! Make sure you get out Excel and really run the numbers on how much it costs you to live, what type of hardware and software you'll need, and how long you can tolerate going until your product catches hold.

While budgeting, also try to build in a "cushion" for those unknown/unexpected expenses. For example, my primary development machine had a serious hard drive crash, and it cost me about $1,000 to get things back up and running.

Q. How do you go from your topmost design to your coding?

A. I guess my style is sort of like an onion. I tend to think in terms of the database first, the core, so that's where I start. With HelpSpot, the core functionality is the creation/tracking of customer requests, so I put a lot of time into thinking about how to optimally store requests. With the database schema in place for requests, I created the framework for things like logging in, creating users, managing categories, and [doing] the other administrative aspects.

Once the foundation was in place, I "layered" on functionality starting with request management and gradually working out to the other self-service features. With the core functions done early in the development process, there's ample time to use that core functionality to make sure it works as well as it can, not just from a code perspective but from a user perspective. Does it really do what I need done? Does the UI work efficiently? Does this layout make the most sense?

In HelpSpot the request management screen is where most users will spend the majority of their time so getting that screen right was extremely important. By building it near the beginning of the process, there was a chance to get lots of feedback on it as well as do a great deal of testing with it.

Q. What developer tools have you found most useful (source code control, automated builds, testing, etc.)?

A. All the development for HelpSpot was done on a Mac, which has provided a great deal of efficiency and flexibility. I'm not a big fan of IDEs, so all the coding was done in BBEdit, a classic Mac text editor. It also integrates with Subversion, which is handy.

I'm a big Subversion fan; it's a great piece of software. It's just so easy to use, at least compared to the other source control systems I've used. I've managed to automate just about everything in the build and development process, which is key to reducing errors. To generate new builds all I need to do is run one shell script, and it gets the source from Subversion, runs it through the Zend Encoder (used to encode the PHP source files), [and] packs it all up in both tar.gz and zip formats, and it's ready to ship.

Another tool critical to my development process is VMware. It's just an amazing product. It allows me to have just one Windows machine in the office [that] can handle all the testing for dozens of platforms and database combinations. It also gives me the ability to easily replicate a customer's exact environment to debug tricky problems that have to do with specific PHP configurations or database setups.

Q. Can you tell me a bit about what you did before starting UserScape?

A. My programming career started at a small start-up called Active Learning Technologies. I started there as a project manager and moved into more of a programming role over time. After three years I went to Marist College where I was the assistant director of Academic Technology and eLearning (it's a mouth full!). In addition to helping run the eLearning program there, my office also had student programmers who did various Web programming projects for the school and community. As the "Web" person there, I also did a lot of internal consulting on various Web initiatives in the school.

KIRBY TURNER, FOUNDER, WHITE PEAK SOFTWARE

Micro-ISV: White Peak Software

Web site: `http://www.whitepeaksoftware.com`

Blog: `http://www.thecave.com`

Interviewee: Kirby Turner

What it sells: Email component and, in 2006, an email client.

Location: Armonk, New York; United States

Q. *Can you tell me a bit about the software or Web services or products your micro-ISV sells?*

A. We sell software that improves online communication specifically around email. The first product, SMTP Diagnostics, helps mail administrators, programmers, and power users troubleshoot problems with outgoing email. It is also useful for testing the configuration of outgoing mail (SMTP) servers.

Our second product is due out around the spring of 2006 and is code-named Vertigo. Vertigo is a new type of email client for the desktop designed specifically for the one- to two-person business that uses a POP3/SMTP mail server. It includes email, contacts, calendar, to-dos, notes, history, and more. Vertigo provides an innovative approach for managing information and addresses the issue of how to manage hundreds of thousands of email messages collected over the years.

Q. *Is revenue a) less than what you hoped, b) about what you predicted, c) exceeding expectations, or d) you're going to buy a small Pacific Island later this year? Can you share your sales per month?*

A. Answer is *b*, about what I predicted.

Sales per month are between $3,000 and $5,000 USD per month. At the moment, the majority of monthly sales revenue comes from professional services, but the plan is to reverse it next year with product sales being the primary source of revenue.

Q. *What has been the biggest surprise in getting your micro-ISV started?*

A. I have had two biggest surprises. The first big surprise was how little I knew about running a company when I started. The second big surprise was how much I enjoy the business side of having a software company. I'm a developer at heart and will always be. But the challenge of running a company [and] learning what makes a product sell, how to market a product, and so on, are all new challenges that get me more excited today than writing code.

Q. *Tell me about your business coach. How did you find them, what did they do for you, how much did it cost, and would you recommend them?*

A. My business coach, Brian Harp of Class IV Solutions (`http://www.class4solutions.com`), is someone I have known for years and who has been a mentor to me in the past. However, it wasn't until I heard him speak at a recent ICCA (Independent Computer Consultants Association) meeting that I realized 1) I needed a coach, and 2) he had started a business around coaching technology companies.

While I'm sure the cost for coaching varies based on the coach and the need, my coach charged me $500 per month. We met face-to-face for one hour each week during the three months of coaching. Also during this time, we talked over the phone and via email. And he continues to check up on my status from time to time.

The primary objective of my coach was to help me obtain focus regarding my company. Prior to this I was trying to be everything to everybody, and I wasn't happy one bit. With his help I was able to put together a plan for my company, and now I have a clear vision of what type of company White Peak Software will be in five years and in ten years.

In addition to my primary objective of becoming more focused, my coach has helped me by reviewing marketing collateral and content on my Web site. He has also provided helpful advice on how to handle various issues that can come up when running a business.

I definitely recommend a business coach to anyone who is looking for help. The experience has turned my company around for the better, and I am much happier now than I've been in a long time.

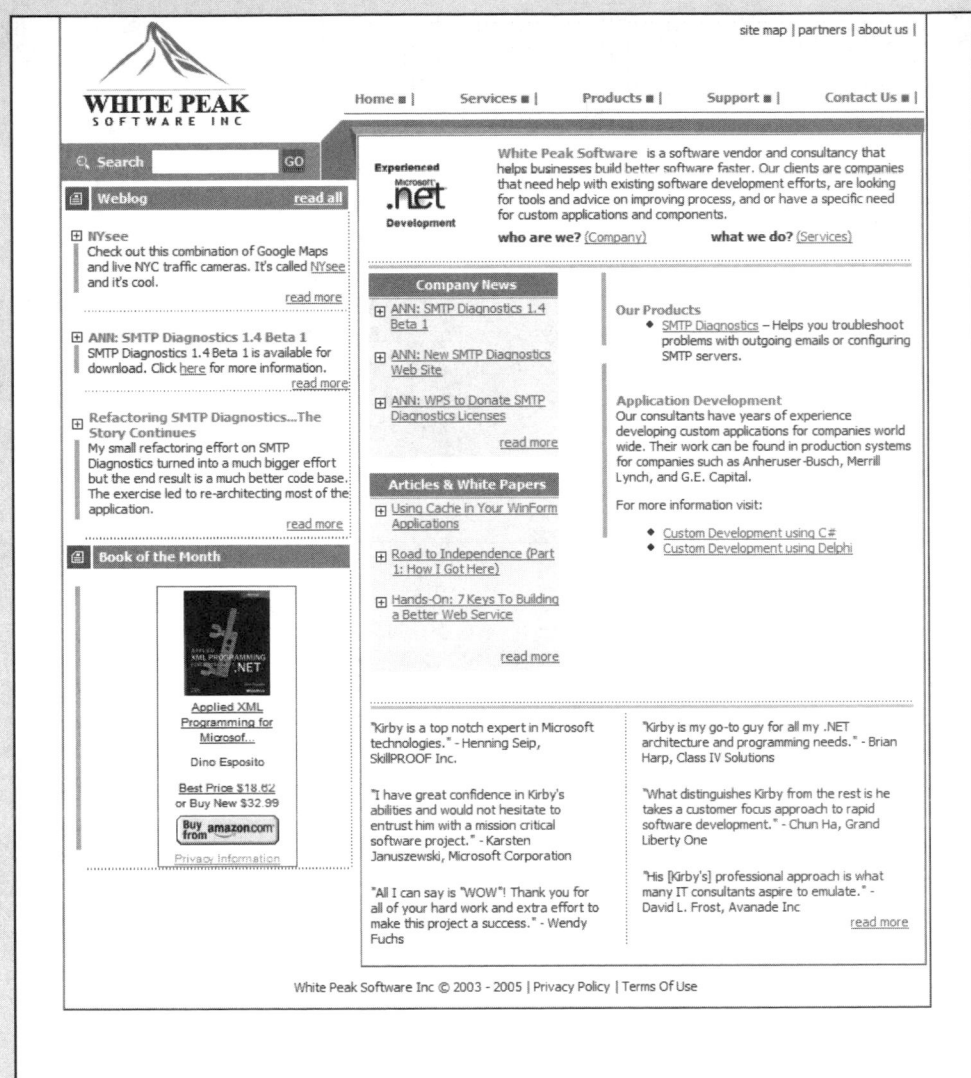

SMTP Diagnostics by White Peak Software

Q. Should micro-ISVs use business coaches in general?
A. No, micro-ISVs should not use a business coach in general. Going to a business coach is like going to a therapist. You have to acknowledge you need help, and you have to have a desire to change. Also, the area that you need help with may be better served by a specialist. For example, someone who specializes in marketing could provide you better help if you need assistance in that one area.

In my case, I realized I did not know how to run a company. Heck, I struggled with describing my company to others. "I run a software company" doesn't say a lot about what you do to prospective customers. I needed a coach to help me work through many small general problems like this. And like a good therapist, my coach was able to pinpoint my problem—the lack of focus—which helped me overcome the problems.

For those micro-ISVs that struggle with the transition from tech person to businessperson, a business coach can be helpful.

Q. How do you like eSellerate, and would you recommend them to other micro-ISVs?

A. My experience with eSellerate has been great, and I highly recommend them to other micro-ISVs. Their SDK and services have saved me countless hours, and the customer service has been top-notch with most of my questions answered within an hour, if not sooner. Setup for a Web store is easy and not time-consuming at all. But one of my favorite services from eSellerate is the integrated eSeller that comes in the SDK.

With an integrated eSeller, customers who are evaluating your software can buy a license from within the program. There is no need to redirect your customers to a Web site. At the moment, almost half of all licenses sold for SMTP Diagnostics came from the integrated eSeller. While I cannot prove it, I believe I have made more sells as a result of having the integrated eSeller.

eSellerate also has a nice reporting system, and all information can be exported should you wish to keep customer information in your database. They also have the ability to post transaction information to your own server using XML, which is useful if you want to automatically update your own database.

Another feature I really like about eSellerate is the generation of Armadillo license keys. This means I can protect my program using Armadillo and still use eSellerate for key generation. And for an added bonus if you use the integrated eSellerate, the license key is sent back to your program after the transaction is complete. You can then programmatically register the Armadillo license key (using the Armadillo API) within your program, eliminating data entry errors from your customers.

There are many other features from eSellerate that I have not yet explored. They have an affiliate program allowing you to cross-sell your products with other products. And you can customize the look of the Web store to your liking. I can ramble on more about features of eSellerate, but I will spare you. However, I will say that I find eSellerate well worth the per-transaction fee they charge.

RUDOLF F. VANEK, FOUNDER AND EXECUTIVE DIRECTOR, QUANTICUS S.A. DE C.V.

Micro-ISV: Quanticus S.A. de C.V.

Web site: `http://www.dbxtra.com`

Blog: None

Interviewee: Rudolf F. Vanek

What it sells: Reporting and query tool.

Location: Querétaro, in the state of Querétaro; México

Q. Can you tell me a bit about the software or Web services or products your micro-ISV sells?

A. DBxtra is a stand-alone reporting and query tool that connects to unlimited databases, including Microsoft Access, Microsoft SQL Server, MySQL, Oracle, DB2, FoxPro, Pervasive, Excel, and any other database through ODBC. No programming or database knowledge is required to explore and report your data with our user-friendly report tool.

Our main market is the United States and Europe, and the product is mainly for database administrators, although we are working on an API right now, which will allow embedding of DBxtra in other software applications. This new version will be released in December 2005.

Q. Is revenue a) less than what you hoped, b) about what you predicted, c) exceeding expectations, or d) you're going to buy a small Pacific island later this year? Can you share your sales per month?

A. *b*, about what I predicted.

Q. What has been the biggest surprise in getting your micro-ISV started?

A. Well, I guess the marketing experience. We sell mostly by the Internet, and we had to learn a lot of online marketing. We experienced almost anything imaginable but now know that the best advertising won't be as effective as, for example, product reviews, press releases, and word of mouth.

Q. Given your main market is database administrators, how do you market to them?

A. Mostly through AdWords campaigns and also advertising on IT sites.

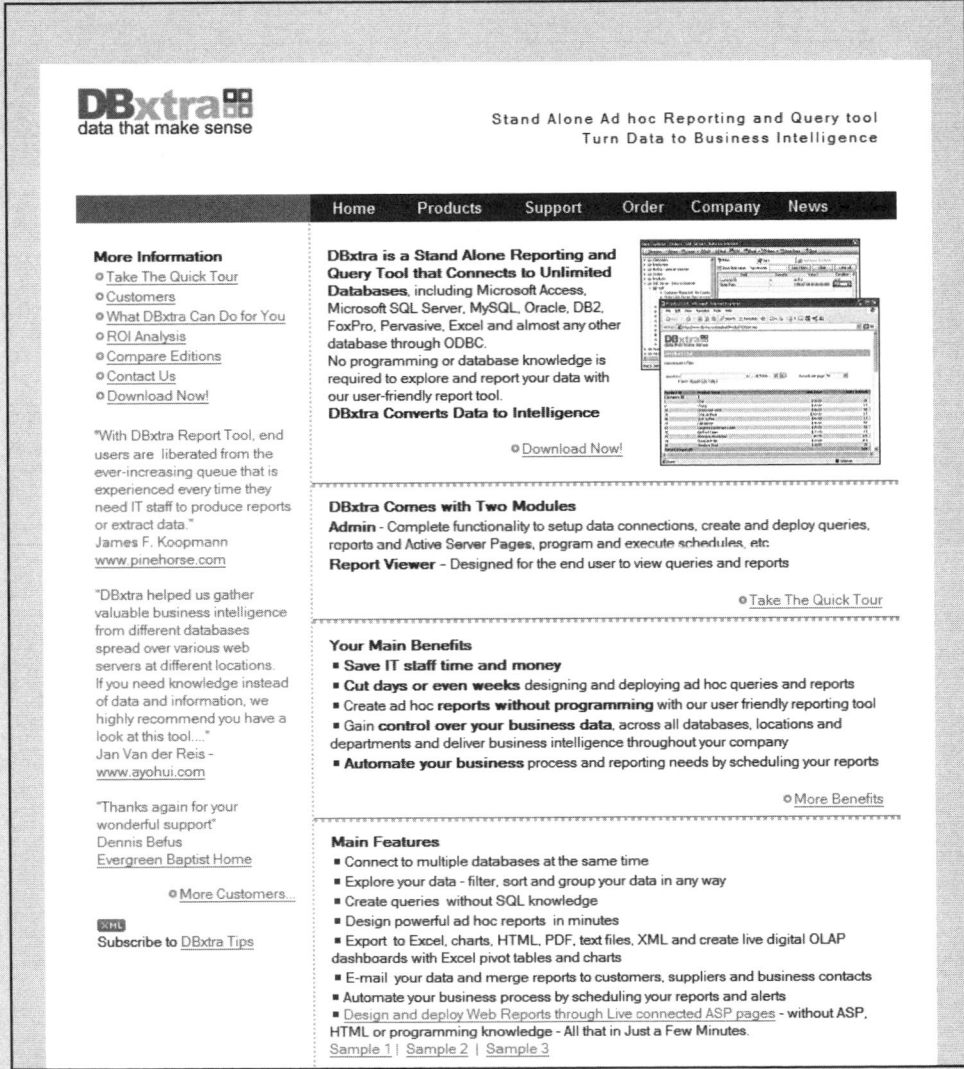

DBxtra by Quanticus S.A. de C.V.

Q. Were database administrators the market you thought DBxtra would appeal to?
A. Yes, absolutely.
Q. How do you deal with tech support?
A. We offer free email support through our help desk, `http://www.dbxtra.com/hd`.

Successful Micro-ISVs

The next group of eleven interviewees are showing solid success and revenue, sometimes because they've put the time and effort into building, nurturing, and growing their customer base and their products and sometimes because they've found a well-defined need and have worked tirelessly to meet it.

Again, certain commonalities come to mind as you read these interviews with successful micro-ISVs:

- Building a successful business is the work of years, not weeks.

- Reputation matters, and reputation is something that needs time to grow.

- Google AdWords, and similar forms of advertising, can work if you have a well-defined market.

Of these interviews, you may be most surprised by two. Yes, Clay Nichols does talk like he's channeling Rodney Dangerfield, but Mr. Analogy, as he's known on the Joel on Software forum, knows how to run a business too. Speaking of business, ever hear of a micro-ISV successfully selling to the biggest of the big banks when it opened for business? Neither had I, which makes Mike Schoeffler's Profitdesk something of a phenomenon and his insights into selling to large enterprises very interesting reading.

ANDY MILLER, OWNER, STRUCTURED SOLUTIONS

Micro-ISV: Structured Solutions
Web site: `http://www.structured-solutions.net`
Blog: `http://www.structured-solutions.net`
Interviewee: Andy Miller
What it sells: Add-ons to two popular e-commerce packages.
Location: Bethany, Pennsylvania; United States
Q. You seem to have several different Web sites. Why?
A. I have several URLs. `http://www.structured-solutions.net` is the main company Web address. Most of the content is a Web log. I also have two stores. Since I sell add-ons for two e-commerce packages (StoreFront and BVC2004), I have created a separate store for each package. StoreFront Add-Ons are sold on `http://www.sfaddons.com`. BVC2004 Add-Ons are sold on `http://www.bvcaddons.com`. Our main site is a blog.
Q. Can you tell me a bit about the software or Web services or products your micro-ISV sells?
A. Both StoreFront and BVC2004 are complete e-commerce packages. They can be installed on a Web site and used as is. However, nearly every merchant wants various tweaks and customizations. Many customizations are so common that they make sense as products. This is the genesis of most of my add-ons.

There are two things wrong with this model: a) add-ons inherently have a low price point (merchants are unwilling to pay very much for what they perceive as a visual or usability feature), and 2) the package vendors will likely incorporate the features into future versions of their base product, rendering my add-ons obsolete.

So, I have shifted most of my effort to a new product called Shipper. This is a stand-alone product that automates shipment processing for the same two e-commerce packages. Shipment processing is a critical and time-consuming task that all merchants face. Shipper significantly reduces the time it takes to process shipments and eliminates errors.

Q. Is revenue a) less than what you hoped, b) about what you predicted, c) exceeding expectations, or d) you're going to buy a small Pacific island later this year? Can you share your sales per month?

A. Revenue is definitely less than I hoped but about what I expected. I am currently running about $2,500/month in sales. I am shooting for $10,000/month.

Q. What has been the biggest surprise in getting your micro-ISV started?

A. The biggest surprise has been how nasty some (luckily few) people are when the relationship is purely over the Internet. I suppose the anonymous aspects of the Internet let some people feel that can behave in ways they never would at home…or perhaps they are just that way.

Several other surprises all fall into the category of "harder than I expected," for example, marketing, answering the phone, and switching hats (related to answering the phone).

Q. What's it like working/partnering with UPS?

A. Right now I am a nonentity to UPS. They have a developer program, but it is geared toward using their Web services. My program (Shipper) works directly with their client application called UPS WorldShip. UPS WorldShip seems to be developed and supported out of an arm of UPS that does not have developer relations.

The next version of Shipper will include support for FedEx Ship Manager (their equivalent client app), and the version after that will include support for Endicia Galaxy (Endicia is a U.S. Postal Service vendor, and Galaxy is their equivalent client app). Both of those companies have contacted me to inquire whether I would support their programs.

Q. Before starting your micro-ISV, what did you do professionally?

A. I was a civil engineer back in the '80s for a paper company headquartered in New York City. That led to an IT position first at the paper company and later for a utility based in New Jersey. We eventually moved (back, for me) to Oregon, where my wife and I both went to work for Intel. The lower cost of living gave me an opportunity to leave the corporate world and play Mr. Mom for a while. Once the kids were in school all day, I started the ISV.

Q. What's your marketing plan currently?

A. When I started the ISV, I was primarily hiring myself out—a fairly typical bootstrapping technique, I think. Eventually I installed an e-commerce site for a customer. It received some attention from other merchants that wanted similar enhancements made. That turned into the first set of add-ons and a lot of custom work. At that time, the only marketing I needed was word of mouth via the platform vendor's newsgroups/forums. I answered every question I could so that my name would appear frequently. That led to more than enough requests for work.

About a year ago I decided that it was too hard to switch back and forth between bidding/working custom jobs and creating packaged products. And I decided that I preferred the packaged products, so I dropped the custom work. It has turned out that answering questions in forums is great advertising for custom work (I still get requests daily that I turn down) but not so good for pitching products. The marketing plan has been slow to change. Eventually I added some advertising (via Google AdWords) and some resellers. But that has not been as effective as I would have hoped. That is where it stands, but it is clear to me that I need to develop a new marketing plan.

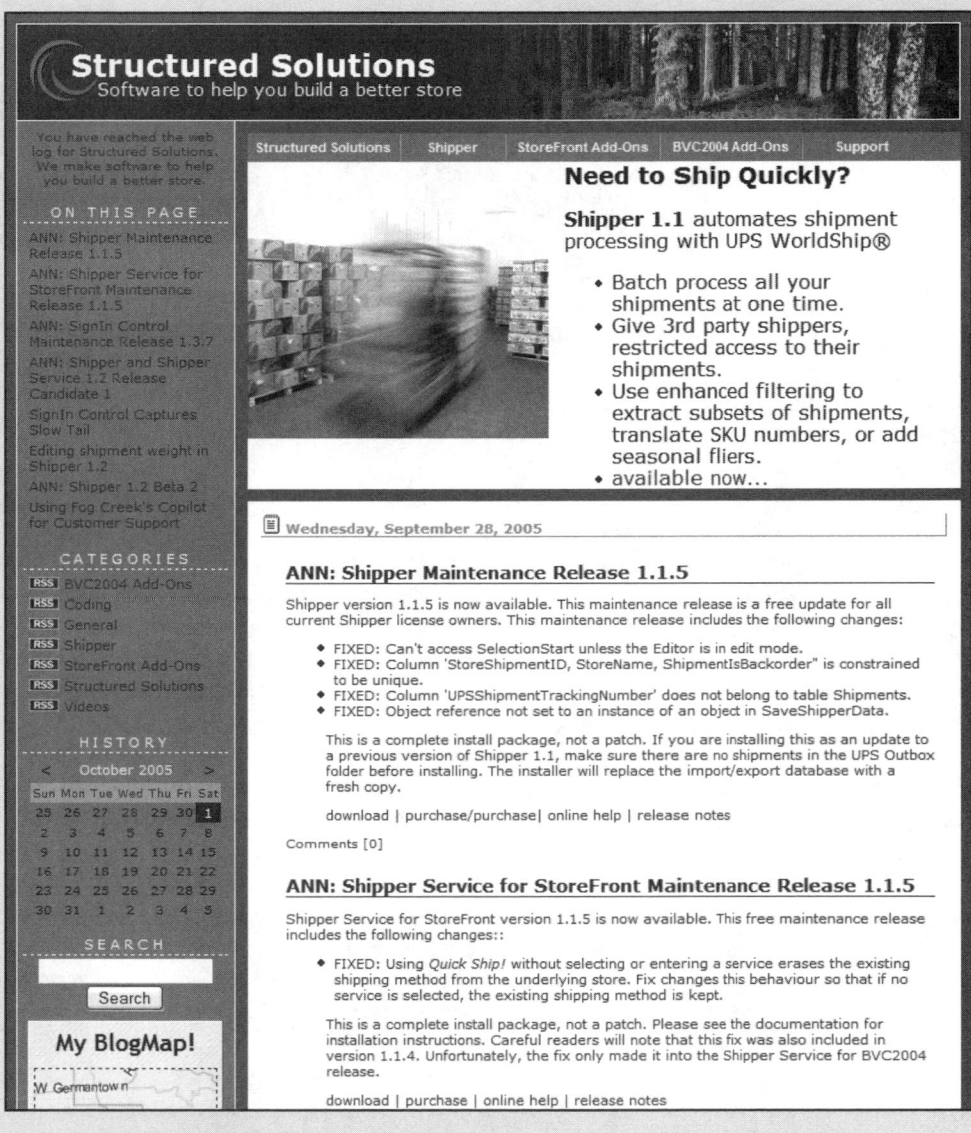

Shipper by Structured Solutions

Q. How do you manage tech support (and nasty customers)?

A. All support is provided free via email or through a Web-based ticket system. This works well for the most part, but some people (perhaps especially merchants) want to talk. I tried accepting phone calls for a while, but it quickly became too expensive both directly (phone charges) and indirectly. Some days I spent literally hours on the phone walking people through simple steps ("click on the Start button..."). So I stopped accepting phone calls. Since I never advertised that I accepted them, this was not a shock to anyone.

Nasty people tend to stay anonymous (which makes me think they know they are behaving badly), so it is fairly easy to ignore them...although it can still be frustrating (see "Arrgh!" at `http://www.structured-solutions.net/ArrghShouldIKeepTheErrorReportInShipper.aspx`).

My vision of the future is headlined by more income, but it also includes a well-designed marketing plan that is being executed and a well-rounded support plan that includes phone support. I suspect there will also be a subscription component that will affect both income and support.

BRIAN NOTTINGHAM, VICE PRESIDENT, INTERAPPTIVE

Micro-ISV: Interapptive

Web site: `http://www.interapptive.com`

Blog: Not at this time

Interviewee: Brian Nottingham

What it sells: ShipWorks, a shipping management system for online sellers.

Location: St. Louis, Missouri; United States

Q. Can you tell me a bit about the software or Web services or products your micro-ISV sells?

A. We sell a single software product called ShipWorks. ShipWorks is a desktop application, written in C#, that connects to online shopping carts and selling platforms to download a merchant's orders. Our focus is on helping people ship their orders as quickly as possible. Through our relationships with UPS, FedEx, the U.S. Postal Service, and online postage services such as Endicia and Stamps.com, ShipWorks is able to connect directly to these services to get rates, download labels, and track shipments.

ShipWorks automates many tasks, such as emailing tracking numbers after a shipment is processed and printing "pick lists" for pulling inventory when new orders are downloaded. Sellers using ShipWorks are able to print reports, compose email, [and] manage their customers, and it can be used across multiple computers on a network.

Q. Is revenue a) less than what you hoped, b) about what you predicted, c) exceeding expectations, or d) you're going to buy a small Pacific island later this year? Can you share your sales per month?

A. Our revenue is what we expected it to be at this time. Our goal has always been to "grow big slowly," and that's exactly what we are doing. We have recently switched from a one-time fee to a recurring price model, and we expect that to have a great impact on our future growth.

Q. What has been the biggest surprise in getting your micro-ISV started?

A. It's a lot of work! During the first months, the excitement of starting a new project is plenty to keep you going. Everything is fresh, you're feeling good, and it's just a great time. Then at some point between working long hours, losing sleep, and sacrificing time with family and friends, you do start to wonder if it's worthwhile— if you're really going to make it. It's that feeling that surprised me, that feeling of "Is this worth it?" that would seem to just sneak up on me.

But, with plenty of encouragement from each other and support from those around us, we just keep pushing on. And each day we get a little bit closer.

Q. How should a micro-ISV maximize its relationship/partnership with "big companies" like FedEx and UPS?

A. I think a big part of being successful is leveraging others that are already successful. We leverage "graduated" micro-ISVs, such as the articles written by Joel Spolsky and Eric Sink. We leverage local small-business groups, college professors, and business advisors provided as a free service by the Chamber of Commerce. And we definitely leverage our partnerships with companies such as UPS, FedEx, Endicia, Marketworks, and the like.

The integration of their services into ShipWorks is obviously a key part of our product, but to leave it at that would be really missing out. We do joint marketing, promotional offers, [and] case studies, and [we] listen to any advice they are willing to give. And to have our name associated with companies that already have customer mind share is a big deal.

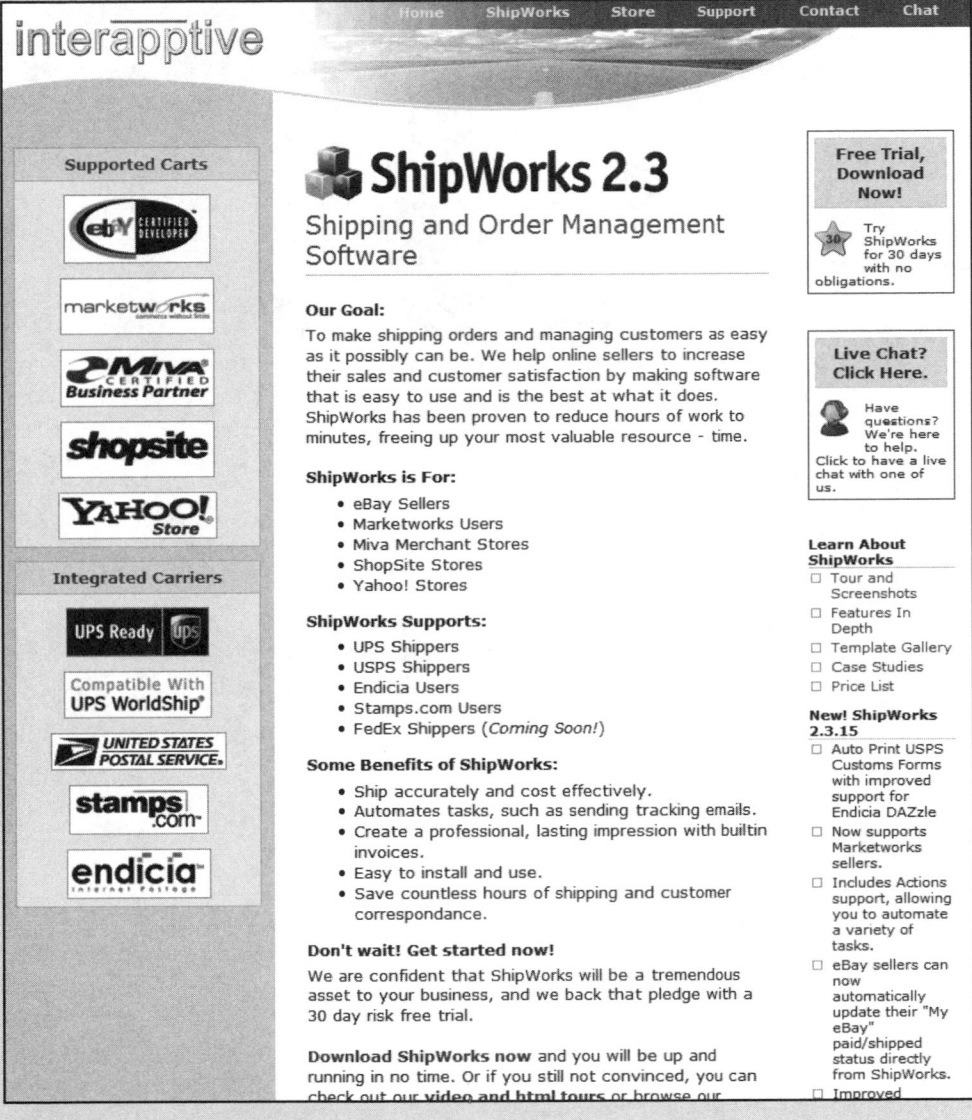

ShipWorks by Interapptive

Q. How did you find/start/create these relationships?

A. ShipWorks [was] called ShopInvoice, and basically all it did was use HTML-based templates to print invoices and packing slips. Based on feedback from the few customers we had, their biggest pain point was printing address and shipping labels. So we started to contact shipping carriers and postage services. Some companies such as the U.S. Postal Service and Endicia have freely available APIs that we integrated right away.

Other companies such as eBay have developer programs that we became apart of. UPS and FedEx had forms on their Web sites to request information about doing third-party integration. We pursued UPS quite heavily for a few months just to get our foot in the door. And FedEx didn't show interest until almost three years later.

Q. It sounds like you have a partner or partners…. If so, how did you work out who does what and who gets what?

A. Wes and I met our first year in college. He was in the business school and doing Web sites for small businesses in the St. Louis area, and I was in the math and computer science program. Several years later, he knowing my software background, asked me to put together a small application for one of his Web site clients. It turned out well, and we wanted to see if we could start selling it as a product.

Wes worked up the contract between us, and we both played a big part in revising it. Since he had initially started the Web site business, we agreed that officially he would be president and I the vice president. More important, we agreed that each of us brought something unique and critical to the company—he on the business side and myself on the technical—and that all decisions, profits, and aspects of the company would be shared equally between us. Four years later, and that is still working well for us. I do all of the product development and technical parts of our Web site; he manages our relationships, finances, and customer support; and we each play an equal role in spending, branding, and business decisions.

Incidentally, the product we initially started our company on didn't even make it off the ground.

CLAY NICHOLS, PRESIDENT, BUNGALOW SOFTWARE

Micro-ISV: Bungalow Software

Web site: `http://www.StrokeSoftware.com`

Blog: None

Interviewee: Clay Nichols

What it sells: Software for speech and language therapy.

Location: Blacksburg, Virginia; United States

Q. Can you tell me a bit about the software or Web services or products your micro-ISV sells?

A. Software for speech and language therapy. Our programs are interactive educational software that helps (primarily adult) stroke survivors regain speech, language, and cognitive skills impaired due to brain trauma (commonly due to a stroke).

Q. Is revenue a) less than what you hoped, b) about what you predicted, c) exceeding expectations, or d) you're going to buy a small Pacific island later this year? Can you share your sales per month?

A. Does anyone share their monthly sales? Maybe I should approach this like Enron: our reported revenue depends on who is asking. Enron told the IRS they were losing money (thus paying little or no tax) and told shareholders they were making it hand over fist.

And, please don't lean over and tell me to whisper it in your ear and it'll be "our little secret." They didn't do much for Connie Chung. But, seriously…sales are *now* where we thought they'd be in the very beginning. We were naive in the beginning to think we'd get to this point that fast. I didn't understand that you had to *market* to your customers. I thought they'd all be looking for us. I think it was Arthur C. Clarke who said that humans extrapolate linearly but development happens exponentially, so in the *short run* humans overestimate progress and in the long run they underestimate it. (That anecdote works much better with a simple graph visual.) But it's also how most growth processes happen, especially marketing.

By the way, that's why I believe so strongly that you better *love* what you're doing as an ISV because the money may take a while to develop.

Q. What has been the biggest surprise in getting your micro-ISV started?

A. That I'm very good at sales. I never even considered a career in sales. Always [I] kind of looked down on it, for the same reason I think most people do: most salespeople we experience are lousy salespeople. They do it all wrong. They try to coerce you into a sale. A good salesman *facilitates* the sale. And that was quite by accident. In the beginning, we were very concerned with "Is our software working well? Does it really help people?" So, I naturally approached sales as "OK, what's your difficulty? Do you think XYZ would help you? Did it help you?" I stumbled onto the right way to do sales, which leads to the second thing I learned, but I'll get back to that in a minute.

Looking back, sales should have been an obvious career path for me. I spent about six years on the speech and debate team in high school and college. I had a debate team scholarship for college, which I got by selling myself (figuratively) to the college's debate coach, who I met at the national finals in Baltimore, which illustrates the point I made earlier: do what you love. I was lousy at debate my first year. We didn't win a single round. My second year I went to the national finals. I'd have never stuck with it if I'd not loved doing it. I've always thought educational software could do more, loved education (I taught for a few years), enjoyed language, and [enjoyed] programming. I guess my subconscious was working overtime to guide me to what is very nearly my perfect career. (Next is a career in usability engineering, but that's another interview.)

I've also discovered that I really need a lot of independence in my work environment. My daughter, Claire (four years old), is very shy. If you bring her to a party, she clings to you. But the other day she was playing with some friends and telling a story. And she did the most amazing thing: when she forgot part of the story, she'd ask the other kids, "And what do you think the princess found?" and then incorporate that into the story. She was fantastic, quite by accident and quite naturally. If we tried to help her, she wouldn't have been able to hear her own quiet internal voice whispering that ingenious improvisation.

I'm kind of the same way. Throw me in the water, and I swim just fine. If you give me a chance to think about what might happen (or give me a crutch to hang onto), I'll flounder.

This is silly, but there's a great line from *The Incredibles* (hey, I have a four year old and a two year old) where the supermom, pursued by the villian's henchmen, tells her doubting superdaughter, "Doubt is a luxury we cannot afford now."

Q. How do you market your extensive line of speech therapy products?

A. Lots of different ways. Print ads, which you have to be frugal about; Internet advertising (AdWords, etc.); and of course people just find us on the Internet.

Q. You sell to both consumers and speech therapy medical professionals. What's that like?

A. It means you're selling to two distinct market niches at the same time. We have to be very careful about our use of jargon. I think it's very difficult to have two different Web pages (one for therapists, one for patients), and you don't always control what page the customer gets to.

Q. Few non-health-care programmers know that much about the health-care industry. I don't! Do you think there are opportunities now there for micro-ISVs?

A. That depends. There are two distinct market segments (maybe more) in health care: software for the system itself and software that a clinician would use as a tool. We fall into the latter category. The first category has higher risk and higher reward—things like Electronic Medical Records (EMR). It's an enormous market but also hard to sell to because it has to satisfy more different use cases, [satisfy] more different customers, [satisfy] more political issues, and interface to more systems. And it's mission-critical.

Products   Success Stories   Benefits   Buy   Trial   FAQ   About Us

Speech & language recovery after stroke, aphasia or brain injury

Proven, effective speech therapy programs. Use them *independently* or with a speech therapist for aphasia therapy or language difficulties.

Thousands of patients and speech therapists have used the Bungalow therapy programs since 1995. Marie Ritchie's story (below) is typical of the underline success stories we receive. These therapy programs are specially designed by speech pathologists to allow patients to work independently, at their own pace, for as long as they like.

"Between the speech therapists and the Bungalow Software, my husband John is doing so well that he is able to communicate his wants and needs by speech. The speech therapists said that your aphasia therapy software has helped John progress to this level of speech."

-Marie Ritchie, caregiver & wife [more success stories]

Start Here

Therapy Advisor
helps you find programs that can help the patient.

View online catalog

Request printed catalog

Risk-free trial

Stroke and other brain injuries are devastating.
Unfortunately, few survivors receive the enormous amount of speech therapy needed for recovery. Bungalow Software provides extra therapy practice to recover speech, reading, and writing, and cognitive skills.

How it helps...

in home therapy   in the clinic

Speech and language recovery products by Bungalow Software

DAVID MICHAEL, OWNER, DAVIDRM SOFTWARE

Micro-ISV: DavidRM Software
Web site: http://www.davidrm.com/thejournal
Blog: http://www.joeindie.com/blog
Interviewee: David Michael
What it sells: Journaling or diary software for Windows.
Location: Tulsa, Oklahoma; United States
Q. Can you tell me a bit about the software or Web services or products your micro-ISV sells?
A. The Journal is journaling or diary software for Windows. Originally released in 1996, The Journal 4 is the most recent version. The Journal has evolved from a simple daily entry journaling program to be a robust personal organizer where people can store just about any information in just about any digital form—text, images, [and] objects of all types. Throughout the growth of the software, though, I've worked to keep it simple to use.

Q. Is revenue a) less than what you hoped, b) about what you predicted, c) exceeding expectations, or d) you're going to buy a small Pacific island later this year? Can you share your sales per month?

A. For 2005, revenue has been about what I expected. Of course, I always strive to exceed my expectations. Summer was a bit sluggish, as it has tended to be over the past eight years, but sales always pick up again in fall and build towards January, historically our best month of the year.

Revenue for 2005 has averaged over $7,500 per month. Comparing the first eight months of 2005 to the same period in 2004, 2005 has seen a 32 percent increase in new sales. 2004 had a 41 percent increase in new sales over 2003.

Q. What has been the biggest surprise in getting your micro-ISV started?

A. Well...the *first* surprise came in 1996 when I realized my "learn Delphi" project interested other people, who found the software as useful as I did. Then there was the whole "people will pay me for this" period of amazement and wonder.

On the "nasty surprise" side of the aisle, there was the effect of this new income on my taxes. First while I was still working for another company full-time, and again when I went full-time working for myself. FICA (the so-called self-employment tax) can be painful if you don't plan for it properly.

As sales began to trickle in, as I tried to be as professional as I could with this sudden new business venture, I realized that my computer science degree (of which I am still immensely proud) had been deficient in several areas, specifically, business management, accounting practices, marketing, and sales.

Q. Where are you based, and where did you get your degree from?

A. I live in Tulsa, Oklahoma. I received my computer science degree from a local, private university (Oral Roberts University). I've been in Tulsa since 1996 and for 19 of the last 20 years.

Q. How have you marketed, and did you/do you have a marketing plan?

A. In the early days, the extent of my marketing was getting listed on Delphi pages and on shareware pages like ZDNet and Download.com (remember when they were separate sites?).

Over the years, though, I've tried to improve my marketing in a number of ways:

- Targeting a specific segment of the market (people who want to do traditional journaling on their computers).

- Building a Web site that has an ever-growing selection of articles about journaling, about how different people use the software, and about tips and tricks for using the software.

- I continue to pursue listings on software pages, though not so much as I did. Now the goal is more to have incoming links that get exposure. The growth of PAD has made this aspect much easier.

- Bidding on search phrases at Google and Yahoo.

I don't have a single, cohesive marketing plan that I follow. Mostly [I have] a collection of things I want to achieve, and when a chance to achieve one of those comes up, I act on it (or try to).

My plan is like what I mentioned for the Web page: try to accumulate good stuff and good decisions over time.

Q. What do you attribute both the success and the longevity of The Journal to?

A. I think that a big reason for the growth of The Journal over the years is that I listen to my users. This takes a few different forms:

- I make a point of responding to all customer support emails in less than 24 hours.

- I try to notice when a particular customer service question is becoming common. I use these to help direct new development and revisions and, of course, bug fixes.

- I take all user requests seriously and try to see how the request would fit into the software and how it could be used for more than what the user initially intends.

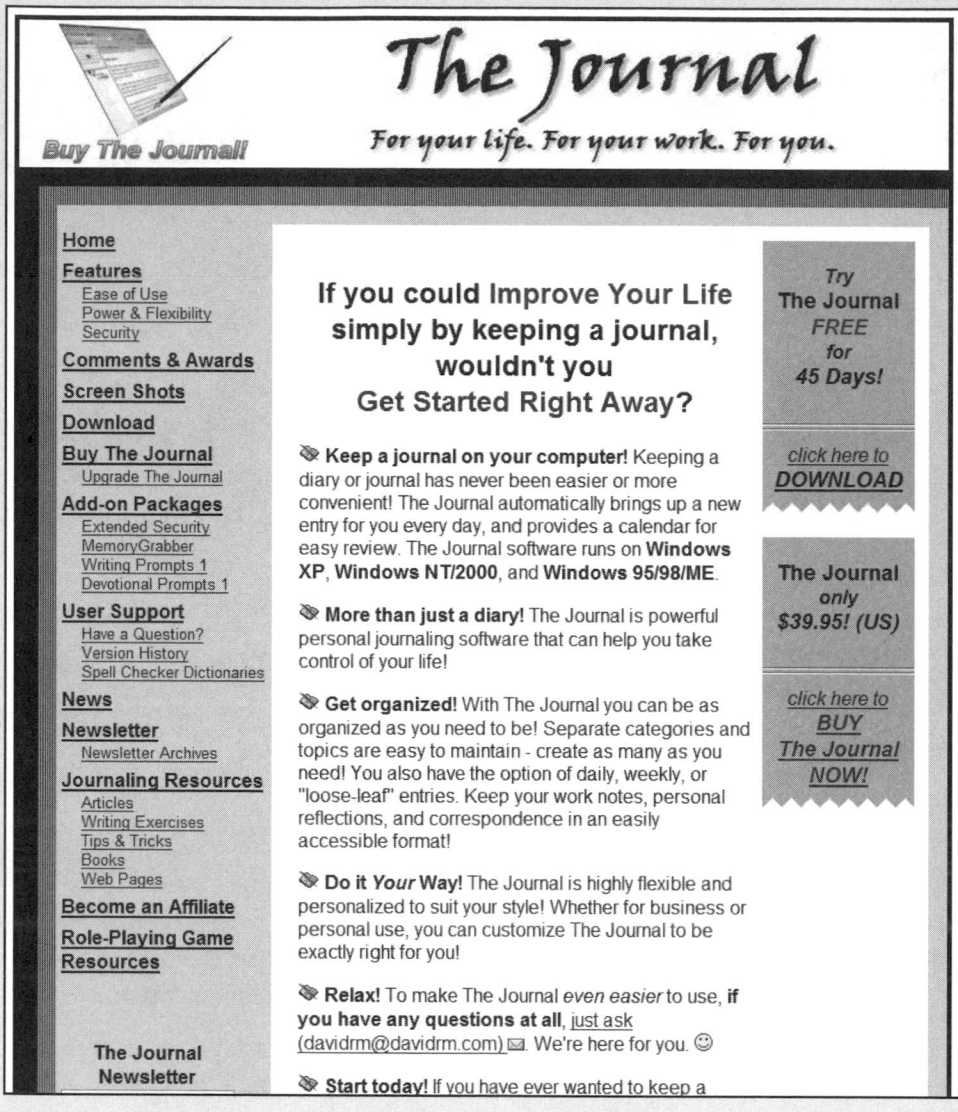

The Journal by davidrm Software

The Journal started out as a more convenient daily journal for myself. I had been using Microsoft Word for Windows since 1993. While Word provided an adequate solution to my main computer journaling goal (copy and paste; I'm not kidding; I *hate* having to retype *anything*), it was too general-purpose to be an easy journaling tool. Because I made it a point to listen to my users from the beginning, though, that very personal design goal has been expanded into something I could never have created on my own.

In other words, The Journal is not just *my* vision of what journaling software should be. It's the combined vision of over 7,000 people, accumulated over 9 years. I take a lot of the credit, of course, but I acknowledge my influences.

Another reason The Journal has been around so long is that I've never grown tired of working on it. That's probably related to my using the software daily. I *live* in this software, tracking progress on my development projects, planning my week, writing articles for blogs, planning projects, writing books…*everything*. (I'm not the only one, either; I hear from users who say much the same thing.) As I use The Journal, I find new ways to extend it and sometimes recognize in a user's suggestion something that has been bugging me, as well, and even see a possible solution.

Yes, I can talk on and on about The Journal.

BEN RICHARDSON, COFOUNDER, SWITCH I.T. PTY

Micro-ISV: Switch I.T. Pty
Web site: `http://www.campaignmonitor.com`
Blog: `http://www.campaignmonitor.com/blog`
Interviewee: Ben Richardson
What it sells: Email newsletter software.
Location: Sydney, Australia

Q. Can you tell me a bit about the software or Web services or products your micro-ISV sells?

A. Sure, we offer email newsletter software as an ASP solution. We're a little bit different [from] the masses of other email newsletter software in that our tool is designed to meet the requirements of one specific group of people, Web designers.

Q. Is revenue a) less than what you hoped, b) about what you predicted, c) exceeding expectations, or d) you're going to buy a small Pacific island later this year? Can you share your sales per month?

A. *b*, about what we predicted, and our revenues are currently growing at about 15 to 20 percent a month, which we're pleased with. One good thing about having a steady growth rate is that it makes it much easier for us to scale with the increase in customers, which is pretty important for an ASP.

Q. What has been the biggest surprise in getting your micro-ISV started?

A. By far the biggest surprise for us was how long it took us to get to version 1 of the software. We'd already built something very similar for our internal use, so we figured we were almost there. We realized pretty quickly that converting something that's built just for your needs to software that any company can start using in a couple of minutes isn't easy!

I still remember how depressing it was sitting down with a customer and watching them try to use an early beta; before the run-through we figured, we [had] a few weeks for launch. Five minutes in, and a few months was looking more realistic.

Q. Has your blog helped your marketing?

A. Definitely, and in a couple of different ways. Firstly, it's helped us become more transparent, which means our customers realize there are actual people behind the product. I even remember someone recommending our product on a forum (`http://discuss.joelonsoftware.com/default.asp?joel.3.85147.13#discussTopic85240`), and they mentioned we had a blog, which made them think we would be more reachable for any presales questions (which is true).

Secondly, we try to post content that's of interest to our target market, Web designers, which means they'll link to it from their blog, add comments to ours, and keep coming back to check for updates. We also try to use our blog as an unobtrusive way of keeping our customers in the loop about any new features and the future of our software.

Campaign Monitor by Switch I.T. Pty

Q. You have a very attractive Web site (naturally enough). Do you think micro-ISVs pay enough attention to how their Web sites look?

A. Thanks, Bob! We're lucky in that we have designers in our team, but I definitely think a lot of micro-ISVs could benefit from getting some outside design help for their Web sites. I know how much more confidence I have when buying a product from a professional-looking, easy-to-use Web site, and I don't think I'm alone there. Yet there are a heap of ISVs trying to sell great software from terrible-looking sites.

I guess with most ISVs it's a cost issue, and since they can whack a half-decent site together themselves, it seems like a no-brainer to keep it in-house and save the money. But this is your one and only chance to impress the customer before they move onto the next result from their Google search—maybe it's worth a few extra bucks?

Q. How do you track/manage your tech support?

A. We currently handle tech support through email but are looking to move to something more sophisticated soon—probably HelpSpot by UserScape. We also use support requests to keep any eye on any areas of the application or help documentation that can be tweaked so users aren't put in a position where they have to contact support.

Q. Are there other products in the works (you can share as much or as little as you want…)?

A. We're currently working on a something similar to Campaign Monitor, which we know a few of our customers are keen to get their hands on. But getting to version 1 is a long road, and the end is still a while off, so we'll be revealing more when the launch date is a little closer.

Q. How many people now work at your company?

A. We've a small team of four full-time staff, which was only two when we first started developing Campaign Monitor. We still do quite a bit of Web site development for clients, so between developing new features for Campaign Monitor, support, marketing, working for clients, and developing a new product, we're all kept pretty busy.

KEITH CASEY, CEO, CASEYSOFTWARE

Micro-ISV: CaseySoftware

Web site: `http://CaseySoftware.com`

Blog: `http://blogs.CaseySoftware.com`, `http://CodeSnipers.com`, and `http://ProjectManagementBlog.com`

Interviewee: Keith Casey

What it sells: dotProject hosting, customized open source applications.

Location: Virginia, United States

Q. It looks like you have a main Web site and several blogs?

A. My company Web site is `http://CaseySoftware.com`, which has been online since July 2004. On the blogging front, there are actually three efforts with which I am involved:

- First, there is my company blog at `http://blogs.CaseySoftware.com`, which has been online since December 2004. I focus on general development principles, business issues, and experiences with customers and projects.

- Next, in order to give something back to the open source community, I started CodeSnipers at `http://CodeSnipers.com`. It is a group blog with approximately 10 to 12 developers posting at least once/week discussing a wide swath of development issues. This site has been very successful so far and has begun to sprout a community around it after only six weeks of being online.

- Finally, my third blogging effort is the Project Management Blog at `http://ProjectManagementBlog.com`. It is based on a group blog model similar to CodeSnipers but is only two weeks old and is therefore in embryonic.

Q. Can you tell me a bit about the software or Web services or products your micro-ISV sells?

A. We have three major areas of development that are going on at any given time:

- First, we have our custom software applications. These we build from a minimal code base and/or from a customers' existing code base. We retain no rights to these in any way.

- Second, we provide customization support for a multitude of open source projects. These projects include dotProject, SugarCRM, Drupal, Mambo, and ZenCart. We build many reusable components, which have steadily increased our libraries.

- Third and finally, we provide dotProject hosting and support packages. Two of the three developers with CaseySoftware are core members of dotProject, so we don't believe there's anyone better to handle hosting needs.

Q. Is revenue a) less than what you hoped, b) about what you predicted, c) exceeding expectations, or d) you're going to buy a small Pacific island later this year? Can you share your sales per month?

A. *c*, with a caveat. Sales started above what I initially hoped but have grown significantly slower than hoped and projected. When I quit my full-time job, I had enough of a customer base with enough revenue on contract to completely replace my income. Within a month, I had enough work and revenue to bring on someone part-time. It took another three months to bring a second person on part-time. Now, after five months, it looks like a third person may be needed part-time.

Q. What has been the biggest surprise in getting your micro-ISV started?

A. What surprised me more than anything else was how little software development I'm doing. When I started out by myself, I was putting in a steady 60 hours/week every week. Now that I have two additional people on staff, I've found that I spend 35 to 40 actively doing development while the rest of the time is used writing specifications, talking with current and potential customers, building connections with like-minded ISVs, and generally learning and studying trends, competitors, and potential partners.

Q. How/why three blogs? (Put more nicely, "Do you see blogs as being a major part of your marketing efforts?")

A. Yes, blogging is a major part of our marketing efforts. From the evaluation of our opportunities at any given point, approximately 60 percent of our business consists of repeat/ongoing customers, but the next biggest segment (30 percent) consists of people who have found CaseySoftware through our blogging efforts. As one of my customers noted last evening, "Your blogging has been note-perfect. I'm an easygoing geek who gets it. And can write. I love it."

I think blogging on a variety of technical and business topics serves as a résumé for myself and my team. When I'm speaking with a potential customer, I make a point of letting them know if I've written something that may be of interest or applicable to their situation. If I can demonstrate to a customer that I a) understand their problem already, b) have dealt with a similar situation, or c) have skills above and beyond the competition, the one to two hours I spend each week writing becomes a business development activity.

Q. Do you find managing your part-time development staff hard when you're the owner and any advice to other micro-ISV about hiring, finding good people, or managing?

A. I believe one of the fundamental strengths of the open source community is the code repositories. It allows you as a recruiter with a technical background to actually investigate a candidate's claims and contributions. In addition, you can most likely browse whatever help forums, mailing lists, etc., to see how the person interacts with others and their general attitude. A candidate who has worked exclusively for private organizations does not have the walking, talking résumé that involvement with an open source project provides.

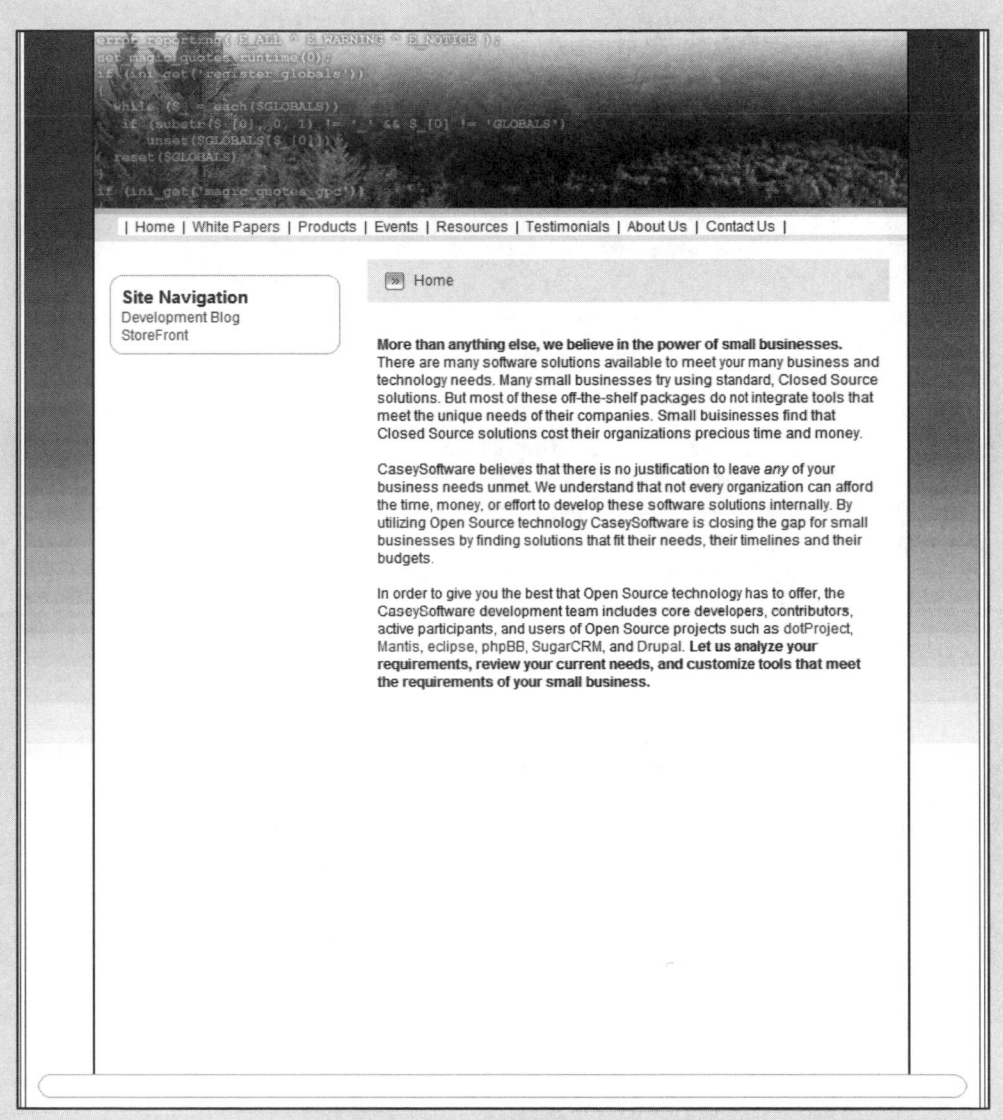

Open source implementations by CaseySoftware

MIKE SCHOEFFLER, PRESIDENT, PROFITDESK

Micro-ISV: Profitdesk

Web site: http://www.profitdesk.com

Blog: No blog

Interviewee: Mike Schoeffler

What it sells: Bank deposit pricing software.

Location: Piscataway, New Jersey; United States

Q. Can you tell me a bit about the software or Web services or products your micro-ISV sells?

A. We make SmartRate deposit pricing software. It statistically analyzes historical bank depositor behavior to help the bank optimize deposit rates. This is a big deal because no one in the industry has the right tools to do this job—they are forced to rely solely on their experience in a very complex arena. Underpaying customers can drive them to the competition. Overpaying depositors is even worse; it restricts a bank's ability to provide what customers really want—more branches and better service. There are trillions on deposit in America, and banks can make a lot more money by optimizing their rates.

Q. Is revenue a) less than what you hoped, b) about what you predicted, c) exceeding expectations, or d) you're going to buy a small Pacific island later this year? Can you share your sales per month?

A. About what I predicted. Initial sales are minimal as we work with our first beta customers. Once the kinks are worked out, we're primed to roll out to the rest of the industry. We have developed a deep pipeline of customers who want the final product.

Q. What has been the biggest surprise in getting your micro-ISV started?

A. I originally figured, I'm a banker who knows how to make software, not a salesman. Marketing to billion-dollar institutions will be the hardest part of my job. [It] turns out to be pretty simple.

I had the most amazing salespeople working for me when I was a banker. I used one, Steve Janaszak, as a role model, partly because he is successful at sales but also because he rises above what I used to think of as "sales."

When I first met Steve, my boss had bought $2 billion in CMOs (Collateralized Mortgage Obligations) from Wall Street. I had no idea how to model them! Steve had sold only some of the CMOs, but he was happy to help me get better at my job—even though it took away from his time focusing on selling more bonds. He saw an opportunity to help and ran with it. Eventually, my boss moved on and so did Steve's major relationship at the bank. When I had the chance to repay the favor by relating Steve's hard work, I was glad to do so.

I remembered how good it felt to work with someone helpful, and I've focused our company's marketing on the principle of good karma. For example, there are no good sources on our field of expertise (deposit pricing). So, we write articles in *American Banker*, *US Banker*, etc., on arcane topics in deposit pricing, and I speak at industry events. Sure, these articles help future competition learn the ropes. But the chance to be useful to the industry is too good to pass up. Likewise, I'm always telling bankers about resources that can help them with odd problems or telling vendors about bankers with odd problems.

The end result? No advertising, no cold-calls. We're too busy working with the banks [that] call us up or come to our booth at trade shows.

I can't see this approach working too well if you sell french fries. But I think it applies broadly to software, even beyond vertical niches like banking. Whether it's Google's amazing free tools, Fog Creek Software's great articles about making better software, or Microsoft's terrific books like *Code Complete*, the companies I admire try hard to move past the quick buck and be helpful.

It only occurred to me afterwards, but there's a rational reason for using "Do Unto Others" beyond making your mom happy. We've all bought software (or signed up for a bank account) and felt jerked around afterwards. Maybe it's the $24.95 you paid to find out how to get around a simple bug in your checkbook software or the time your bank charged you extra to see a teller. All of these experiences left a bad taste in your mouth and subconsciously make you seek out products that you can trust.

Software is an extreme example of this effect because so much of the total value is visible only after you work with the program for a while. Will the user interface be easy to master? Will the company help me use the software as effectively as possible? Is the software tested well for bugs? Will the company improve the software when customers point out the inevitable flaws?

Help people out. Help out your customers. Lend a hand to potential customers. Assist other vendors. Even help your competition. Not only will you have more fun, but it's your best shot to let the market taste how good your total product is.

Q. You sell a "big-ticket" item to a market famed for its conservative nature. How do you get them to try your product?

A. Everyone likes a free taste. But for our software, a trial period is pretty expensive to set up; you need to train the customer, work with the IT department to set up data feeds, etc. We're thinking about it, but for the moment, we give other "tastes." The articles in trade journals help people understand what we are doing and give some free advice to apply without buying the software.

We also sell with a 100 percent money-back guarantee, which is unusual in big-ticket software. We're pretty confident in our product and are happy to absorb as much risk as possible. We are even investigating moving to "zero-cost pricing," where we charge nothing for software or maintenance but take a cut of realized profits. This is complicated to measure accurately and audit, but I think it will be a real winner. Banks like reducing their risk and like buying from companies that stand strongly behind their products.

Finally, it's important to be able to back up your promises with some financial muscle. It looks increasingly unlikely that we will need more funding than our angel round; good software is strongly profitable. But there's a certain comfort in having relationships with the VCs. If we ever needed to, we could get a much bigger round of financing.

Q. Would Profitdesk.com succeed as well as it has if you'd not established credibility and "karma points" with your market?

A. We're young and loathe to give categorical statements on limited experience, but I strongly believe "no." Credibility is just that important.

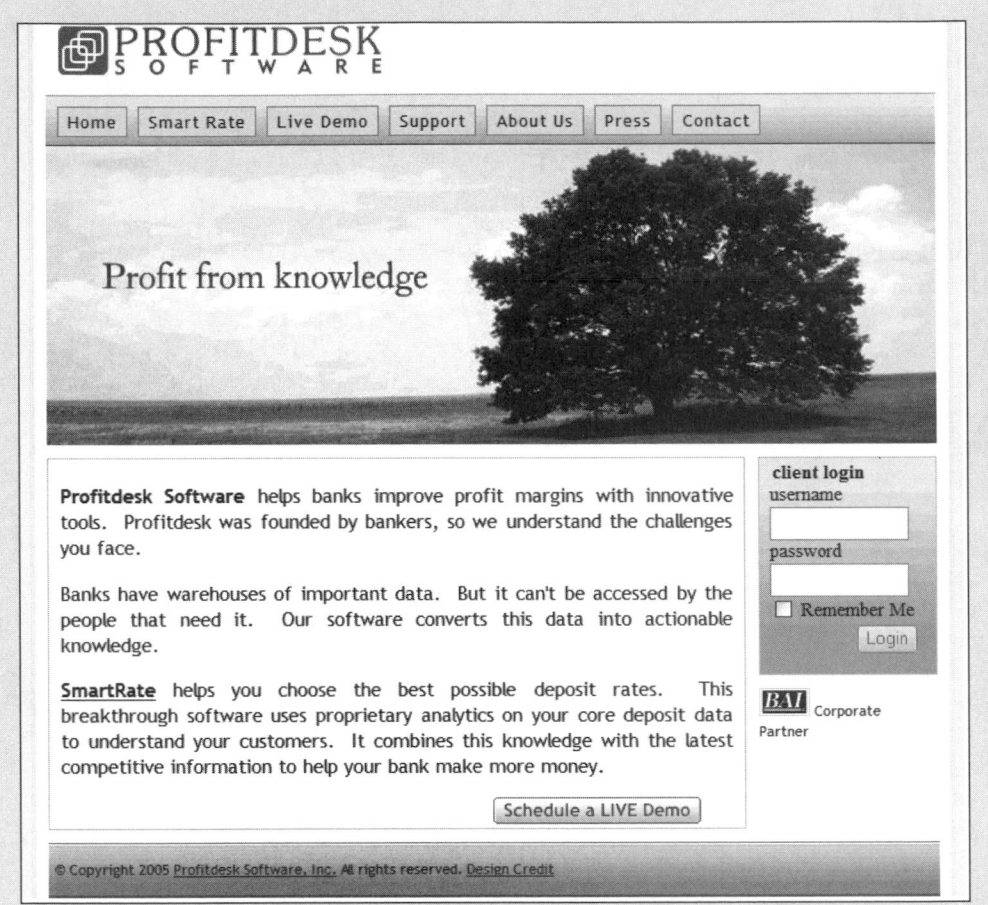

SmartRate by Profitdesk

Q. How do you market to billion-dollar companies?
A. In some ways, marketing to large companies is easier than marketing to smaller companies or consumers. If I want to drive demand for an iPod, I better have the marketing smarts of a Steve Jobs. It takes genius to break through the constant surf of companies shouting to the general market. And let's face it, there are plenty of interesting products for the mass market.

However, there are many small niches within any large company. For example, banks have experts that know all the technicalities behind escheatment (turning over dormant accounts to the state), the Graham-Leach-Bliley Act (protecting consumer data), and a thousand other specialties. Only a few people in the corporation know much about each niche. The flip side is that there are only a few products vying for their attention. The product that hits their needs can easily get noticed.

Otherwise, big companies are like any other small companies or consumers—only more so. You have to do everything extremely well, or the decision makers wonder about the risk in working with you.

I believe every detail is important, from professional artwork in logos and brochures to a short, meaningful URL to toll-free phones, answered by live people. These are all important signals that you care about being easy to work with. By implication, your actual product is at the same level (or will quickly get there if problems are found).

This perfectionism can mean that marketing projects take a while to go live (for example, we've been rolling around blog ideas for six months), but sometimes it's better to offer less. You're forced to plan better and sometimes even decide that a project is not worth the effort of doing well.

A perfectionist attitude is especially tricky in the software world, where the best is truly the enemy of the good. Many software projects have gone south because they could not be released until everything, including the kitchen sink, was thrown in. The best software is built through evolution. Figure out minimum functionality to make the customer happy, find out what they really want once they use it, and put it in the next release. So, while an eye on quality is very important, shipping is the only way to eventually get truly great quality. You almost need to be schizophrenic to market and build with these somewhat conflicting attitudes.

PHIL WRIGHT, FOUNDER, CROWNWOOD SOFTWARE

Micro-ISV: Crownwood Software
Web site: `http://www.dotnetmagic.com`
Blog: None
Interviewee: Phil Wright
What it sells: DotNetMagic, a .NET component.
Location: Berkshire, United Kingdom

Q. Can you tell me a bit about the software or Web services or products your micro-ISV sells?

A. My micro-ISV consists of selling a single product called DotNetMagic. This is a library of user interface components for .NET developers and is written in C#. It contains easy-to-use gadgets such as menus, toolbars, docking windows, and other controls that are not present in the base .NET Framework. It actually started as a spare time project in order to learn all about .NET and C# when the technology was first released. I gave it away for free during the first two years, but as I started receiving requests from companies to include it in commercial projects, I decided it was time to start charging for it.

Q. Is revenue a) less than what you hoped, b) about what you predicted, c) exceeding expectations, or d) you're going to buy a small Pacific island later this year? Can you share your sales per month?

A. I only ever expected a small revenue for a few months. It has exceeded this by generating consistent sales of around $12,000 per month.

Q. What has been the biggest surprise in getting your micro-ISV started?

A. It is actually much easier than you ever realize. I always imagined that only a few entrepreneurs actually start a company or try to create products to sell. With the advent of the Internet just about any programmer can create a product and sell it through a simple Web site. My big fear is that the mass of programmers out there will also realize this, and suddenly the competition will become much more intense.

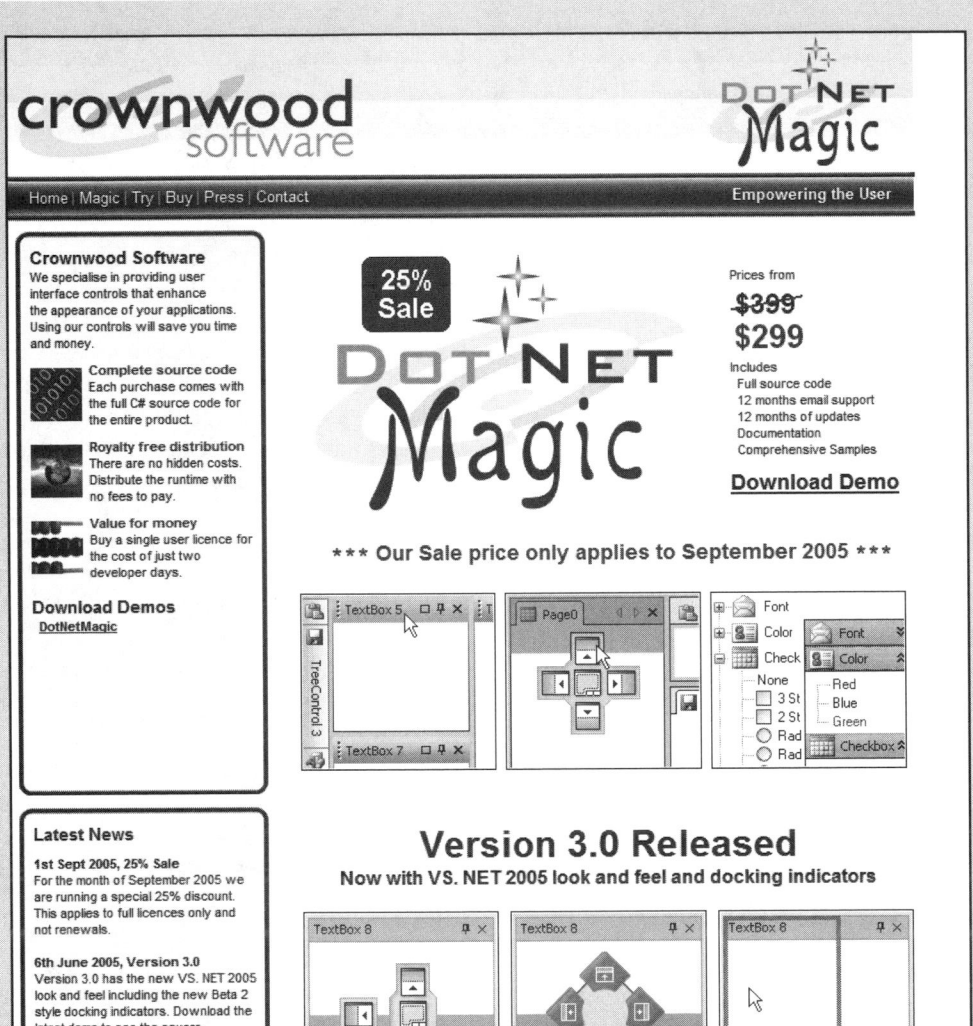

DotNetMagic by Crownwood Software

SANJAY BHATIA, FOUNDER, IZENDA

Micro-ISV: Izenda

Web site: `http://www.izenda.com`

Blog: None

Interviewee: Sanjay Bhatia

What it sells: Data engine and development framework.

Location: Atlanta, Georgia; United States

Q. *Can you tell me a bit about the software or Web services or products your micro-ISV sells?*

A. Through our partnerships, we have done nearly a hundred projects in the past three years. Our original focus was content management and e-commerce. Over the past 18 months, we have made an aggressive transition to business intelligence and reporting, and most of our business is now in that area. Our strategic focus has also shifted from small add-on projects to solutions that critical parts of an entire company or department depend on that are highly visible to decision makers. Our focus on business intelligence has also allowed us to create value by developing reusable components that can be used by multiple clients. We are now in the process of selling our platform on the open market to developers.

You can find a customer list here: `http://www.izenda.com/iws/Company/Customers/tabid/91/Default.aspx`.

Q. *Is revenue a) less than what you hoped, b) about what you predicted, c) exceeding expectations, or d) you're going to buy a small Pacific island later this year? Can you share your sales per month?*

A. Revenue has certainly exceeded expectations. I'm not heading to an island quite yet but will be doing trips abroad every year for the foreseeable future. The great challenge has been revenue stability. While this month will be the first unprofitable month we've had since the company's birth (due to a project being delayed because of Katrina), revenue has been very volatile with good months bringing in five times as much revenue as bad ones. Cash flow has also been a challenge. We've aggressively financed our customers, which has been great in the long run and on paper but has caused some crunches when it comes to the bank balance.

Q. *What has been the biggest surprise in getting your micro-ISV started?*

A. The biggest surprise on the positive side has been learning the power of using networks of partners. I've gone from spending 100 hours a week keeping the business running to 20 hours (and spending the rest of the time growing it). I never would have imagined that you could get so much accomplished by spending the entire day doing emails and going to meetings. These were things that used to feel like a waste of time. I come from a coding culture where progress was measured in lines of code and features implemented. Instead of delivering as much code and as many features as possible, I now think in terms of delivering the smallest set of features that would create the most value and keeping the customer satisfied with as little code as possible.

On the negative side, it has really surprised me how quickly other small business that I've worked with have gone out of business or had serious cash flow problems. It seems a lot of entrepreneurs don't understand basic accounting and finance on a strategic level. I've had a number of customers as well as partners who have run out of money. I am a believer in erring on the side of caution and setting up capital and lines of credit that you don't intend to use but are there in emergencies. I know my HELOC (Home Equity Line of Credit) has certainly saved us more than once when a customer doesn't pay a bill on time.

Q. *How many people work/own Izenda?*

A. I own 100 percent of it. I have one part-time intern. We work with about a dozen people on different projects. In a way the model is that of a virtual corporation that utilizes networks of partners to function as a larger firm.

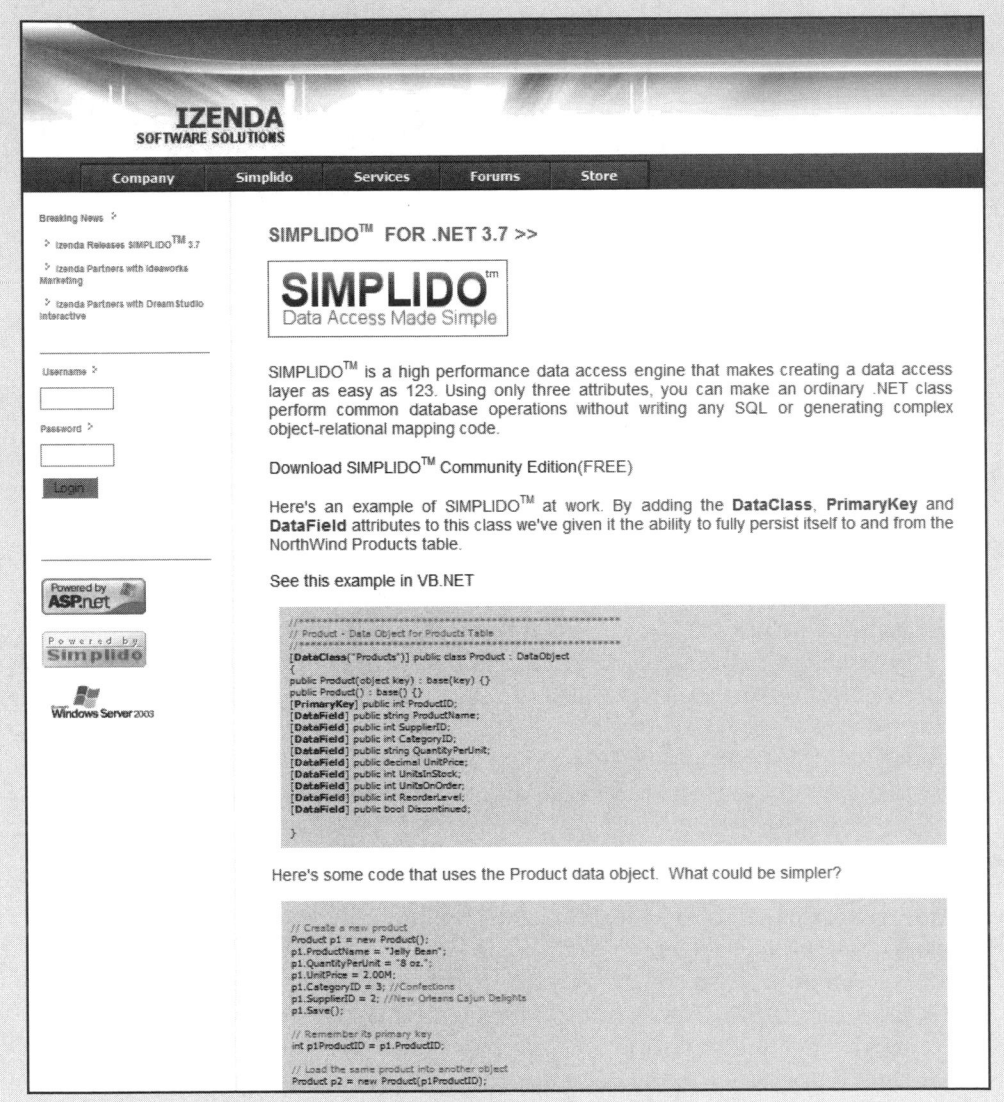

Simplido by Izenda

Q. When you say "Through our partnerships, we have done nearly a hundred projects in the past three years," can you tell me a little more about your partnerships?

A. Mainly we've partnered with companies like DreamStudio and MediumBlue and let them focus on their core competencies while we've focused on the back-end software. We've also worked with other one-person companies.

Q. How do you develop/nurture these partnerships?

A. I meet people over the Internet and at networking events. I just met somebody at a TAG (Technology Association of Georgia) event [who is] developing an application builder that complements our Ad Hoc technology well. I'm meeting him next week to brainstorm ways to do business together. It's a lot like dating; you just have to put yourself out there and play the numbers game and not waste too much time with connection that will be unprofitable. If there is a system to it, I've never discovered it.

Q. How do you market Simplido?

A. In truth, we have abandoned Simplido and are just now bringing it back as a part of our grand strategy of a software development methodology that allows for model-driven architecture based on relational metadata. Simplido was the first piece. It did not really make business sense as an independent product because Microsoft had announced ObjectSpaces, which would render it obsolete. As it turned out, ObjectSpaces somehow got lumped in with the Longhorn stack and is therefore not shipping with Whidbey. If I had known this two years ago, we would have invested in and marketed in Simplido more aggressively. It's really interesting how powerful an announcement from Microsoft is. I used to work there and wish that I had investigated what was on the back burner better, but that was a different life.

We used to market it with Google AdWords and sites like ASP.NET.

Ad Hoc is what's next for us. The product makes sense on its own, and IT people (business people, that is) buy into the concept within seconds of seeing it in action. You don't have to sell the concept. People are getting accustomed to editing their own Web content without needing IT; we are tying to empower the user in the reporting space.

Our marketing plan includes bloggers, articles, AdWords, SEO, and potential partnerships with other component vendors. It depends on how the organic growth works. Really, that's the part we are figuring out.

We have some Ajax-based forms technology that is in the pipeline. These three pillars will make possible what I consider the Holy Grail of software flexibility. Essentially this means that if the client needs a new field added, you add a new field to the database (possibly with additional metadata), and the application detects this and adapts without a recompile or reconfiguration. While purists and *n*-tier folks may cringe at this concept and big consulting firms will fear the lost billable hours, it is really what small enterprises need. You want to add a field, do one thing (maybe even from the browser), and poof!—you have fields, validators, [and] report fields, and it's all laid out cleanly and just works a second later. We have this working for one of our main customers, but it needs a lot of work before it can become a reusable technology. We believe we can extend the VS/SQL 2005 generation of technologies to make this a reality.

While we have a long-term vision, each component of that vision makes sense on its own and [needs to] be a useful concept. Every decision I make takes the future into consideration but solves an immediate client need today. I think that's where a lot of software entrepreneurs fail. They let their vision blind them from taking care of immediate customer pain. It's a challenging balancing act indeed.

TONY EDGECOMBE, FOUNDER, FROGMORE COMPUTER SERVICES

Micro-ISV: Frogmore Computer Services

Web site: `http://www.frogmorecs.com`

Blog: `http://www.pdf-software.com`

Interviewee: Tony Edgecombe

What it sells: Network printing software.

Location: Faringdon, Oxford (a small market town about 15 miles from Oxford); England

Q. Can you tell me a bit about the software or Web services or products your micro-ISV sells?

A. I sell software [that] helps businesses improve their network printing.

This ranges from keeping archives of all printed documents through to applying rules to printing, for instance, blocking big documents from going to small printers and sending them to a larger centralized printer instead.

Q. Is revenue a) less than what you hoped, b) about what you predicted, c) exceeding expectations, or d) you're going to buy a small Pacific island later this year? Can you share your sales per month?

A. It took longer than I originally hoped to reach a level [that] would support me and my family. I started at the beginning of 2002, and my first orders arrived in the middle of that year. It was another 18 months before I could drop the contract work I was doing and focus on my own products full-time. This wasn't a get-rich-quick scheme for me, though; I saw it as an opportunity to get some balance back into my life so was quite happy to plug away for as long as it took to succeed.

The Pacific island is still some time away yet!

Q. What has been the biggest surprise in getting your micro-ISV started?

A. The biggest surprise is the community support I have found; groups like the ASP or AISIP have newsgroups with valuable discussions and regular conferences. Just by following these groups and going to the conferences I have picked up useful knowledge [that] has increased my sales volume.

Q. How do you market your products?

A. The most successful method for me is Google AdWords. Because my software is fairly specialized, most of the keywords aren't that competitive, and so I get a really good return on my investment. The second biggest source comes through some articles I wrote [that] are related to the features in my software; these have been picked up by the search engines and drive a lot of traffic to the Web sites. After that it's a mixture of press releases, posting to download sites, and some activity in forums and newsgroups. I'm also planning some very targeted direct mail in the near future.

Q. Do you find that many of your customers buy more than one product over time?

A. Not very often. They usually have an immediate requirement or problem [that] needs to be solved. Once they have bought the software, that problem is out of the way. Most of my software is installed on servers so it doesn't get rolled out in the same way a client tool like some zip software would.

Q. How has PayPal worked for you in the United Kingdom?

A. Most of my orders come from businesses, and they don't use PayPal very often.

Q. What type of business entity are you (sole trader, etc.), and how is that working out?

A. The business is a UK limited company. There are some small tax advantages to structuring it that way in the UK, and it does mean you have limited liability. My house isn't on the line in the way it could be if I was a sole trader.

Manage printing for better productivity

Products | Download | Purchase | Screen shots | Support | Newsletter | About Us

Print Distributor

Use Print Distributor to distribute, archive, route and control your printed output. Aimed at small to medium sized organisations Print Distributor will enhance your printing environment.

Try Print Distributor free for 30 days, download our fully functional demonstration version without obligation now.

> Buy on-line now from $149 / €119 by credit card, wire, check or PayPal.
>
> [Buy Now]

✓ Print to file with a flexible naming system which allows you to include date, user and document information in the path.

✓ Virtual printers created by Print Distributor look exactly like a normal printer to your user's making the whole system very reliable and support free.

✓ Load balancing improves the reliability of your printing by distributing prints across a group of printers.

✓ Scripting support lets you write your own rules for controlling the routing and processing of documents using simple snippets of VBScript code.

✓ An easy to use manager application means you don't need a technical background to install and configure Print Distributor.

✓ Flexible actions allow you to send copies of prints to as many locations as you require.

✓ Print to email to deliver your documents where they are required.

Print Distributor

Print Distributor by Frogmore Computer Services

Q. Did you find it manageable to deal with the various government bits of red tape?

A. I do moan when I'm dealing with the paperwork, but in reality it's not that bad in the UK; a lot of the tax forms can be handled online now, which makes things a little easier. I deal with most of the financial work myself because I think it's important to understand just how much money is coming into and going out of the business. You do need to be quite thorough to do this, though. If you are the sort of person who never keeps the tickets from the cash machine, then you need to get an accountant doing it for you.

VLADISLAV UKHOV, FOUNDER, CETERA

Micro-ISV: Cetera

Web site: http://www.cetera.ru/ and http://www.cetera.ru/english

Blog: http://www.ageofWeb.ru/blogs/users/svyatoslav

Interviewee: Vladislav Ukhov

What it sells: E-commerce software.

Location: Yaroslavl, Russia

Q. Can you tell me a bit about the software or Web services or products your micro-ISV sells?

A. We develop Cetera e-commerce software, a small e-commerce product for SMB that's written on PHP+MySQL. It's very simple to use and well-documented. It costs $450 USD with a lifelong guarantee and updates.

We also provide development, integration, and support services for this product.

Q. Is revenue a) less than what you hoped, b) about what you predicted, c) exceeding expectations, or d) you're going to buy a small Pacific island later this year? Can you share your sales per month?

A. Licenses: less. Services: exceeding expectations.

Q. What has been the biggest surprise in getting your micro-ISV started?

A. First year: We need to think more about sales and marketing about less about development. Second year: Support is the key! Development waits.

Q. It sounds like the services customizing and installing your product are exceeding your revenue expectations.

A. Yes. A fact.

Q. Would you recommend this approach to other micro-ISV, or do they need to be selling a server-based app to make it work?

A. In our market (Russia, CMS products), revenue is in Consulting > Projects > Products > Support. As I see [it], customers in other countries also value projects more than products.

Q. How do you market Cetera?

A. • Word of mouth

- Products advertising in search engines (Yandex-Direct is a local Google AdWords analog) with a budget near $100 to $150 USD/month

- Two blogs (15 to 20 posts per month)

- Cold calls (near 30 to 40/month)

Nothing more. We don't have any printed materials and so on. This doesn't help in our market. Our Web site is not a sales channel, only a sales support instrument.

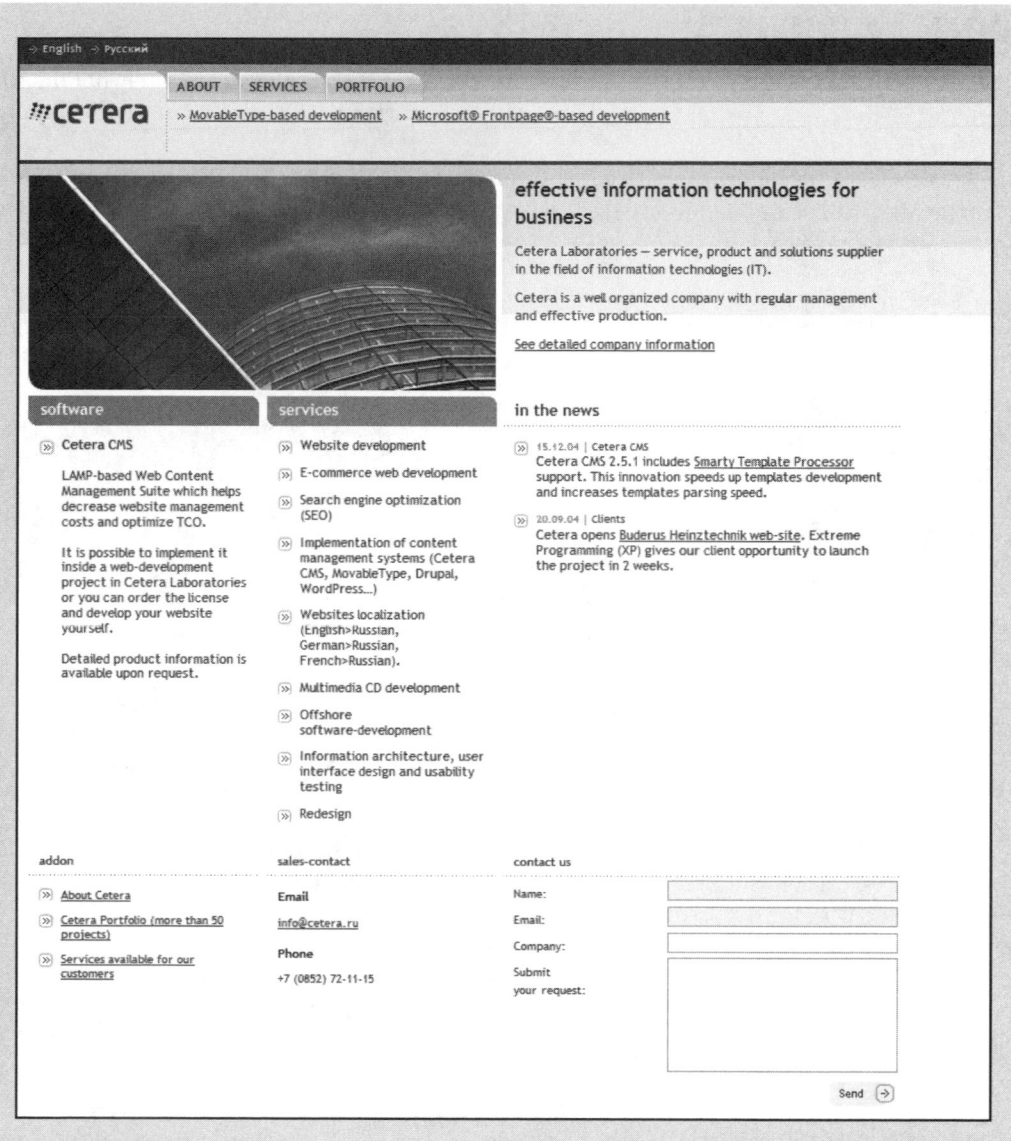

→ English → Русский

///cerera

ABOUT   SERVICES   PORTFOLIO

» MovableType-based development   » Microsoft® Frontpage®-based development

effective information technologies for business

Cetera Laboratories — service, product and solutions supplier in the field of information technologies (IT).

Cetera is a well organized company with regular management and effective production.

See detailed company information

software

» **Cetera CMS**

LAMP-based Web Content Management Suite which helps decrease website management costs and optimize TCO.

It is possible to implement it inside a web-development project in Cetera Laboratories or you can order the license and develop your website yourself.

Detailed product information is available upon request.

services

» Website development

» E-commerce web development

» Search engine optimization (SEO)

» Implementation of content management systems (Cetera CMS, MovableType, Drupal, WordPress...)

» Websites localization (English>Russian, German>Russian, French>Russian).

» Multimedia CD development

» Offshore software-development

» Information architecture, user interface design and usability testing

» Redesign

in the news

» 15.12.04 | Cetera CMS
Cetera CMS 2.5.1 includes Smarty Template Processor support. This innovation speeds up templates development and increases templates parsing speed.

» 20.09.04 | Clients
Cetera opens Buderus Heinztechnik web-site. Extreme Programming (XP) gives our client opportunity to launch the project in 2 weeks.

addon

» About Cetera

» Cetera Portfolio (more than 50 projects)

» Services available for our customers

sales-contact

Email

info@cetera.ru

Phone

+7 (0852) 72-11-15

contact us

Name:

Email:

Company:

Submit your request:

Send →

Cetera CMS by Cetera

Very Successful Micro-ISVs

The final group of five micro-ISVs have achieved a level of success that is definitely not micro. Some have grown out of what you could call micro; some have realized their hard-won equity and been sold.

At this level, it's harder to make generalizations about what works and what doesn't. One clear fact from all these interviews is, as Joel Spolsky puts it, you have to find a little bit of magic to make it to this level.

DHARMESH SHAH, FOUNDER, HUBSPOT

Micro-ISV: HubSpot
Web site: `http://www.hubspot.com`
Blog: None
Interviewee: Dharmesh Shah
What it sells: Platform for solo entrepreneur Web portals.
Location: Boston, Massachusetts; United States

Q. Your Web site seems a bit vague right now. How come?
A. My site's URL is `http://www.hubspot.com`. The information there is intentionally broad and vague (as the product has not been launched yet). This is my third micro-ISV start-up. [The other two are]

- Pyramid Digital Solutions (recently sold to SunGard): `http://www.pyramidonline.com`.

- Captivo (was in the small-business CRM space): Merged with Pyramid, but most intellectual property retained as part of SunGard deal.

Q. Can you tell me a bit about the software or Web services or products your micro-ISV sells?
A. The company is building a platform to allow for the efficient creation of powerful Web portals for solo entrepreneurs (and other micro businesses). The idea is to do what Salesforce.com did for mid-market CRM but broaden the functionality and focus on the micro-business market (fewer than ten employees).

Q. Is revenue a) less than what you hoped, b) about what you predicted, c) exceeding expectations, or d) you're going to buy a small Pacific island later this year? Can you share your sales per month?
A. Revenue has not kicked in yet but will begin to do so in November (when the product goes through a "soft launch" to our alpha/beta customers). The pricing will be done on a per-user subscription model. We also have some creative ideas for marketing the product (given the challenges of distributing to the small-business community).

The first product (SoloPortal) will likely also be submitted to the MIT $50,000 Business Plan competition this year (which will help further refine the idea and get some additional visibility). I'm a graduate student at MIT, and my thesis work will be focusing on the solo entrepreneur community and its economics.

From a personal perspective, I have recently sold my enterprise software company (which has given me the luxury to go back to school and focus on "doing it right" for HubSpot). In this vein, my goal is to focus intensely on creating the right solution (something I would be proud to put my friends and colleagues on) and later worry about the revenue, earnings, and other details.

Q. What has been the biggest surprise in getting your micro-ISV started?

A. The biggest surprise I've found in getting the company kicked off is the difficulty in "narrowing the focus" of the product offering. I think it is a major temptation to create as broad a solution as possible (i.e., build something that millions of people could use), but my business experience tells me a narrow, focused solution on a specific segment of the market is much more likely to succeed. However, it's hard to figure out which customers to focus on first (example: lawyers, software companies, graphics design firms, CPAs, etc.) I'm still not there yet in terms of picking an early vertical.

Q. Why focus on the micro-business market when it seems most attention is on enterprise?

A. I'm currently a graduate student at MIT. One of the courses I'm currently taking is "The Software Business," taught by Michael Cusumano, who (literally) has written a book on the topic (called, *The Software Business*). Having started, grown, and sold a company in the enterprise space, I understand the pros and cons of such a model. The big issue is that competing for enterprise customers is a difficult challenge. Strategically, the customers have too much "power" (since likely, in this space, the customers can to a large degree dictate their terms). As such, it makes it difficult to create a revolutionary product. You start out innovating, but ultimately, your largest customers (from which most of your revenue is coming) have an inherent need to request "incremental" features and improvements. They are not looking for a revolution. And, more often than not, small businesses with large customers must listen (if they are to survive).

On the other hand, the micro-businesses present a completely different set of challenges (which is often very conducive to technology founders/CEOs). In this market, success is largely driven by one's ability to first narrow the focus and create a solution that is compelling for some discrete set of clients (in most cases, you are not replacing an existing solution but creating an entirely new "market"). After that, the challenge is being able to "generalize" the solution so that you can shift to "adjacent" markets over time. This particular model has major, major risks—but also a very large upside.

Though the small-business market has historically been impenetrable (even by the largest of software companies), I think a number of things have now changed the landscape:

- Platforms are constantly changing and creating new "demand" for software. For example, Salesforce.com was able to grab 13,000+ customers simply by taking advance of the software as service model and providing a simpler solution than what Siebel or others had.

- The Internet makes word of mouth and referral marketing possible (not easy, but at least possible). This allows a micro-ISV to organically grow with a small set of customers and build from there.

- There is an entirely new set of customers with new needs that these small businesses now have to address. For example, today, not many one-person law firms have a Web portal where their clients can review contracts (at any time of day/night), provide comments, etc. I would posit that in the next five to ten years as the current generation of Internet-savvy users grows up, they will demand a higher level of transparency and Internet capability than what is currently the benchmark. Just like we saw in the late 1990s with big businesses (companies like Vignette, Plumtree, etc., addressing the Web needs of large customers), there will be a series of software companies that try to fill this new gap for the small businesses that now have new challenges.

HubSpot platform, HubSpot

Q. *What do you see as the challenges of distributing to the small-business market?*
A. The biggest challenge in distributing to the small-business market is that the clients are highly "fragmented." For example, in my enterprise software company, it was easy to reach 90 percent of my target market simply by going to two trade shows a year. That is simply not possible in the small-business market. As such, this market takes a lot more creativity to reach efficiently.

The fact that price points are very, very low (by necessity) makes it imperative that the cost to acquire customers is maintained at the lowest levels possible. This precludes "in-person" meetings (at least one-on-one meetings) and many other forms of traditional sales/marketing.

Q. What would you advise other micro-ISV (in school or out)?
A. My biggest advice to micro-ISVs [is]

- Focus on defining your initial customers and target market. The narrower, the better. This is a paradox; the *smaller* your market (especially initially), the higher your chances of success.

- Don't get drawn into the allure of raising VC money. This is very hard to do; the odds are way against you, and you'll end up spending a lot of time and energy trying to rewrite your business plan and pitch investors (instead of actually solving the problem you're out to solve). Even if you succeed in raising money, your battle is not over (it's only started).

- Read, read, read. One can learn at least 25 percent of the hard lessons out there through the experience of others. Not all mistakes need to be made in order to get internalized.

- Try to find a "nonbinary" business model. This means stay away from businesses where you are in "product development" for one to two years before you have a product that you can sell and your first dollar of revenue comes in. The same model that works in development (iterate, iterate, *iterate!*) applies to business as well. Get *something* out there that *someone* is willing to pay you for. Then, refine *ad nauseum* by listening to the customers. If nobody is willing to buy your partial solution, that's often a sign that they wouldn't buy your full solution (even if you had one).

JAMES SHAW, FOUNDER, DOZING DOGS

Micro-ISV: Dozing Dogs
Web site: http://www.dozingdogs.com
Blog: http://www.dozingdogs.com/news/blog and http://www.coveryourasp.net
Interviewee: James Shaw
What it sells: Content management system.
Location: Roswell, Georgia; United States
Q. Can you tell me a bit about the software or Web services or products your micro-ISV sells?
A. Dozing Dogs sells a content management system written in ASP.NET. Source code is available, and our Enterprise Edition sells for $999. Our Personal Edition sells for $249.
Q. Is revenue a) less than what you hoped, b) about what you predicted, c) exceeding expectations, or d) you're going to buy a small Pacific island later this year? Can you share your sales per month?
A. *a* and *b*. Less than what I hoped but about what I predicted. I'd sooner not share actual sales, for reasons discussed next.
Q. What has been the biggest surprise in getting your micro-ISV started?
A. The biggest surprise was recently accepting an offer to sell the company. I never thought I'd do that, but the right offer came along at the right time. Although all rights are being sold, I will continue to work on the code to integrate it with their product. So, I get a big wad of cash plus the ability to work on my product full-time without the sales/marketing/support pain. It has just been me doing the whole thing (with some independent contractor help here and there), so this next phase is great.

Q. I see you have both a company and a personal blog. Which came first, and how has it worked out for you and where do you get the artwork for your personal blog?

A. The personal blog came first. I wanted to blog about the creation of the product and company. It has been great and gave a place for the old fans of Coveryourasp.com (my classic ASP site) to go to catch up. I heard from many people from the "old days of CYA" (i.e., 2001–2002), and it was great to get to know them again. As for artwork, I just made something up, probably loosely based on `http://www.ourroswell.net`, which is the city network that my CMS evolved from.

CMS V2 by Dozing Dogs

Q. Can you tell me more in general terms about the sale—did they find you, were you recommended, etc.?

A. I have always worked full-time as a C++/C# programmer/manager throughout my ISV time. However, my employer moved to Denver from Atlanta, and I didn't want to move. I worked from home for a few years, which was a huge benefit for running an ISV, but then management changed and I was out of a job. No worries— being an ASP Insider has made me many friends, and they put the word into their companies for me. I ended up at Telligent because I knew all the principals there quite well.

Q. How did you determine what a fair price was for your micro-ISV (not so much numbers, but method)?

A. As for the sale, it came from necessity. There was too much possibility of conflict of interest with Telligent's Community Server product and my CMS. They wanted a CMS for CS, so as soon as I got used to the idea of giving up my baby, it all went smoothly. Fair price? LOL, I simply picked a number that would be enough for me to give up my dream. We worked from there, and Rob came up with a formula that fitted it. In the end, we both wanted the deal so it was easy for both sides to compromise a little. It was all over in a few emails—the hardest part was the week I spent wondering if I wanted to do it at all.

Q. Can you explain this a little more? It sounds like they forced you to sell!

A. There was no forcing involved, but it was obvious that working at Telligent was going to create a conflict as their road map (`http://communityserver.org/i/roadmap.aspx`) showed them having CMS in v2.0. I had to choose: continue with Dozing Dogs and another "normal" job or a great job with people I knew and respected (mostly fellow MVPs and ASP Insiders, `http://www.aspinsiders.com`) and sell my CMS product to them for a very good price. It wasn't a hard decision in hindsight, but you'll probably understand how it can be difficult to give up "your baby." I had to really step back from Dozing Dogs and look at it objectively. I pretended I was advising a friend about his business, and in fact I did get advice from other ISVs, notably good friend Dave Wanta at Advanced Intellect. It took a weekend probably to realize which was the better route.

MARK HOFFMAN, CHIEF TECHNICAL OFFICER, AUTOREVO

Micro-ISV: AutoRevo

Web site: `http://www.autorevo.com`

Blog: None

Interviewee: Mark Hoffman

What it sells: Web-based auto dealer inventory system

Location: Plano, Texas; United States

Q. Can you tell me a bit about the software or Web services or products your micro-ISV sells?

A. Our product offering is a Web-based tool, billed as a monthly service, that allows auto dealers to manage their inventory. With AutoRevo, a car dealer enters a vehicle's VIN and its description, and that vehicle can then be sent to eBay Motors; classified Web sites such as AutoTrader.com, Vehix, [and] Cars.com; and their own Web site. The benefit to the dealer is we provide one place for them to manage their inventory and Internet sales.

Q. Is revenue a) less than what you hoped, b) about what you predicted, c) exceeding expectations, or d) you're going to buy a small Pacific island later this year? Can you share your sales per month?

A. Revenue is about what we anticipated.

Q. What has been the biggest surprise in getting your micro-ISV started?

A. Biggest surprise so far is the difficulty in finding qualified developers. I've recently sifted through over 60 résumés, and only a handful was worth further consideration. I've interviewed people who claimed to be senior-level .NET developers who couldn't answer even the most basic technical questions. I've spoken to people who claimed on their résumés to be "great communicators" [who] could barely construct a single sentence in English. With all of the "doom and gloom" you hear from developers about the job market, I was surprised to learn that the truly talented developers are just as hard to find as they were in the late '90s during the boom. I really expected to be able to find people fairly quickly, but I soon learned about the true state of the job market.

Q. What has your background before launching your micro-ISV?

A. There were three of us who started the company. Myself and another partner worked as consultants at an IT consulting firm as developers for the same client. He had a friend [who] owned a car dealership, and the three of us started the company.

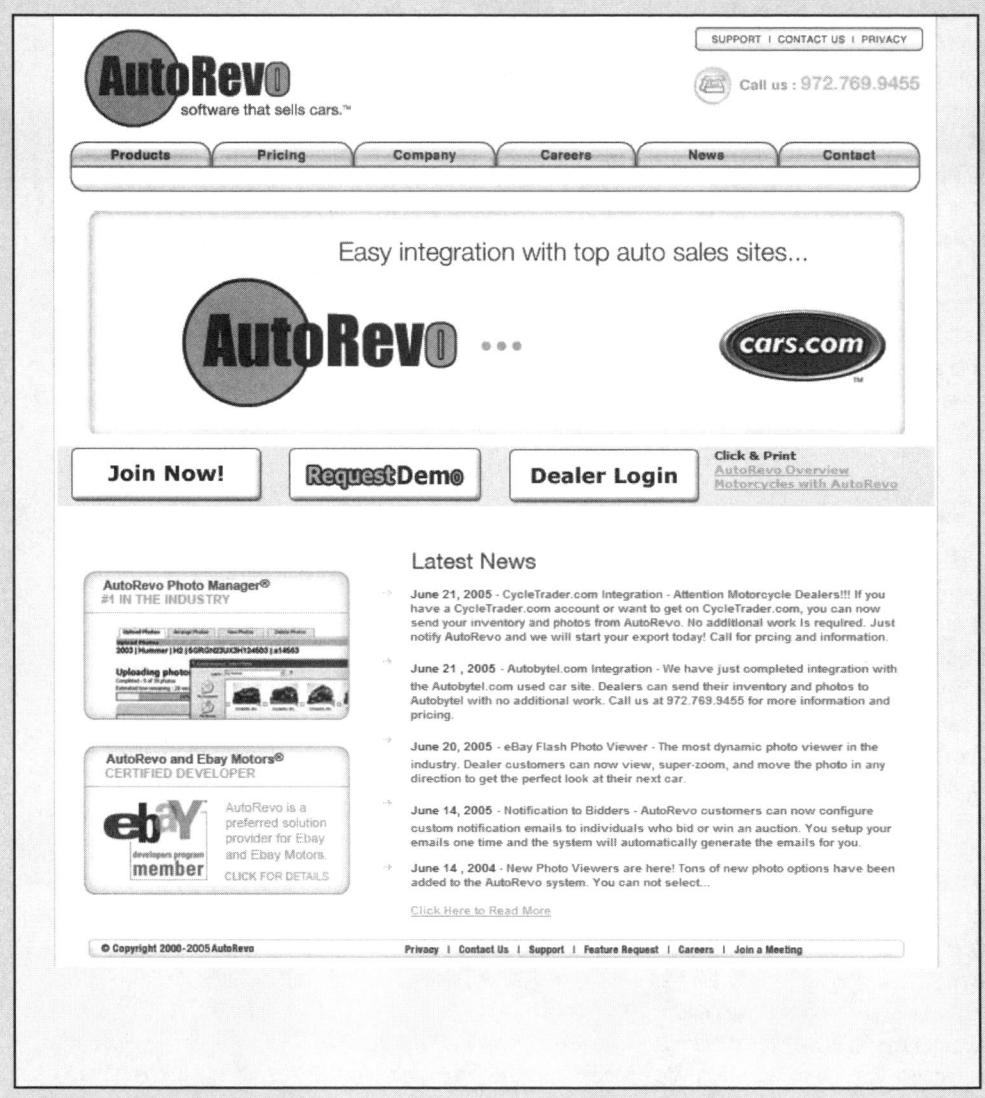

AutoRevo by AutoRevo

Q. Do you think that focusing on a very specific market made it easier or harder to get your revenue numbers where they are?

A. The fact that we focused on independent car dealerships was crucial to us getting traction quickly. We were also very fortunate in our timing. For years, small dealerships (think used-car lots) could compete only locally. Along comes the Internet and eBay Motors, and suddenly they can get national exposure. The problem was, car dealers are *very* nontechnical, and they didn't want to have the ability to create their own Web site or auto-mate pushing their inventory to eBay or to the major classified sites. Large dealerships, such as your giant local Chevy dealerships, have the money and the expertise to do this themselves. The little guys can't. That's where we stepped in.

Q. How do you market to that market?

A. Our primary marketing method is direct sales via the phone. It's anything but high-tech, but it's effective for this market. You can always get a car dealer on the phone, unlike most other decision makers. We have a customer referral program that is quite effective because car dealers interact with each other quite a bit, and it's an easy sale when another dealer recommends us. We're also featured on eBay Motors Products and Services page, and that generates quite a bit of traffic.

Q. How many people besides yourself are there at your micro-ISV?

A. Today, there are four other people here besides myself. (The partner [who] owns the dealership is basically a "silent" partner and continues to run his dealership and isn't directly involved in the day-to-day operations.) We have a salesperson, administrative assistant, a developer, and my other partner. My partner and I work together on the business decision making, marketing strategies, the direction of the product, etc. He primarily focuses on the day-to-day operations while I focus on the development of the product.

BYRON MATHESON, FOUNDER AND CEO, CLEARNOVA

Micro-ISV: ClearNova
Web site: http://www.clearnova.com
Blog: None
Interviewee: Byron Matheson
What it sells: RAD platform for Web 2.0 applications.
Location: Alpharetta, Georgia; United States

Q. Can you tell me a bit about the software or Web services or products your micro-ISV sells?

A. ClearNova sells a Rapid Application Development (RAD) platform for building Rich Internet Applications (RIAs) called ThinkCAP. With that statement full of techno-babble and acronyms, ThinkCAP is a development tool for quickly building Java applications that utilize the hottest Internet technology: Ajax. Think of client/server-type applications but Web-based. Google has been at the forefront of the Ajax movement with the Google Maps project. (We have a demo of an Ajax-enabled application on our Web site…pretty cool stuff, even if I say so myself!)

Q. Is revenue a) less than what you hoped, b) about what you predicted, c) exceeding expectations, or d) you're going to buy a small Pacific island later this year? Can you share your sales per month?

A. Revenue is about what we expect this stage of our growth. We sell both our product ThinkCAP and profes-sional services using ThinkCAP.

Q. What has been the biggest surprise in getting your micro-ISV started?
A. How much of a "herd" mentality there is in the software development space—Ajax being a great example.
How much indecision there is in corporate America. When we can deliver a proof of concept in two days that has a four-week timeline by the customer development team, and we can't get management to make a decision to buy…amazing! We have done this on several occasions but find that IT managers are afraid to take chances on a small company with a superior product!
Q. How many people work at ClearNova?
A. Thirty people and growing!

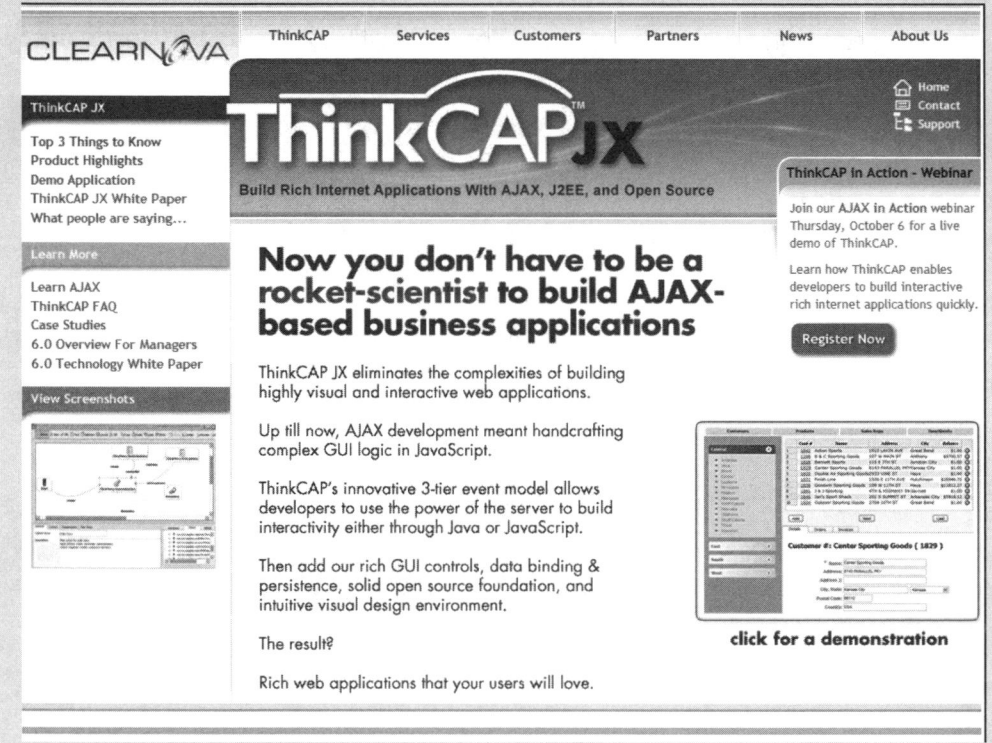

ThinkCAP by ClearNova

Q. Given your company's focus and success, would I be wrong in thinking you think desktop apps are obsolete?
A. Desktop apps will be around awhile, but Web technologies are moving closer to client/server usability. Apps that used to require desktop app productivity are beginning to be delivered via the Web. What I think is obsolete is the current page-based Web-based applications. Once users begin to experience Ajax-enabled Web applications, they will shun those applications delivered under the current page-based format. I believe that we are going to see a major push to rewrite our current Web-based applications; obviously we believe we have the product to assist in that effort!

Q. How do you market ThinkCAP?

A. Currently, our marketing exists of Google ads, speaking engagements, and great PR campaigns. I am shamelessly including a recent article headlining ClearNova with Microsoft. It has had an incredible impact on inquiries. The article is at `http://www.infoworld.com/article/05/09/15/HNajax_1.html`.

Q. What's it like marketing to developers?

A. I have always said that developers are like painters: there are a lot of developers [who] can "paint" but few "artists." (I used to be a developer, so I can say this!) Unfortunately, everyone is an artist in their own mind! So where am I going with this...most Java developers have a "not invented here" mentality. The reason we are as successful as we are is because most Java shops are failing to deliver. To be honest with you, we have had an uphill battle convincing the Java development community to adopt a product like ThinkCAP. They have a herd mentality, which is good if you're leading the herd and hard if your not. Fortunately for us, Ajax is on fire right now, and we are actually leading the herd right now. ([Let's hope] we won't get stampeded.)

JOEL SPOLSKY, COFOUNDER, FOG CREEK SOFTWARE

Micro-ISV: Fog Creek Software

Web site: `http://fogcreek.com`

Blog: `http://fogcreek.com`

Interviewee: Joel Spolsky

What it sells: FogBugz, a Web-based bug-tracking application; Copilot, a remote desktop control service; CityDesk, a desktop Web site manager.

Location: New York, New York; United States

Q. Fog Creek Software started as a consulting company first, right?

A. Right. In fact, everybody told me, "No! You should be product!" We always wanted it to be a product company in the long run, but consulting seemed to generate a lot of money, and the margins were huge. And our thought was a consulting firm would throw off enough spare cash so we could develop products and thus sort of build a software company in the background.

Q. Do you think that's a good approach in general?

A. I have to say that I still do, despite the fact that it really didn't work. It makes a ton of sense. Here's the theory: the story you tell yourself is, I get a group of friends. We're all great at computers and computer stuff, but we don't know what to do. So we'll bill ourselves as computer consultants; we'll charge whatever the going rate is—$100–$200 an hour to develop [and] $300 to $400 an hour for top-notch software developers. And that will generate some cash and give us some business, and as we do consulting work, we'll start to discover common themes and problems our clients are having. At some point a lot of clients will say we all need X, and we'll tell them all, "Listen, why don't you let us develop X for you, and instead of charging our full rate, we'll charge you our discounted rate. And in exchange for the discounted rate, you'll allow us to keep the rights to productize the source code we developed for you."

It's a way of finding a business—of developing a product on somebody else's dime and bootstrapping. And as that evolves, you have this big product that your consulting firm exists to implement and customize and enhance. Theoretically, you want to get into a situation where you have a bunch of developers who develop the product and a bunch of developers who customize, install, and sell it and do consulting. And that's a good way to build what I call a consultingware company.

Q. OK, but that's not the same as a product company?

A. Well, if you're disciplined about it, a product does kind of emerge. Now realistically? I say I haven't seen that succeed, but the average start-up—the average venture-funded enterprise start-up—is doing this. They just don't admit it. They think they're developing a product.

So they have their idea: "We're going to make a security widget." So they go around and talk to people, and in order to make their business plan work, they're in the $100,000 and above per installation ticket price for their product market. And at those prices, there's a long sales cycle, and the customer demands all kinds of things, and half of the customers don't really need the product. They really kind of need to have some developers working on this problem they have, and they're going to pretend to buy the product in exchange for having basically put your developers on retainer.

Q. A commonality of wrong expectations I guess?

A. Kind of. And they deserve each other. But this happens a lot. There's a lot of companies out there with very specific software needs and just no ability to get the program no matter how much they're willing to pay. They can't find good programmers to develop it. Somebody walks in the door and says, "We're starting a software company. And we're going to make a product that kind of does this, and we have no customers yet. And we want you to be our first customer, and it's $500,000 plus $400 an hour for developer time to get it to work for you."

And then they say, "OK, how much developer time can I get?"

Q. Now does this actually really happen?

A. That's what usually happens with these companies.

Q. So Fog Creek Software is a product company. How much are you making?

A. Well, we're under $5 million a year in sales.

Q. And how many customers do you have?

A. These days, we're getting about 1,500 a month. But the point I wanted to make is that we're a company that sells to about 1,500 people, but these companies sell to about one person a month, if they're lucky, and they make $200,000 doing that.

For us, it's nice and stable and easy, and we don't have to do anything for anybody to get that money. But for them, in order to make a $200,000 sale to one customer, or a $400,000 sale to one customer every two months, it's a big rigmarole. and it's very dependent on it. And they really need that money, the customer asks for all sorts of extra things, and they promise them. And they wind up developing one-off versions for each customer.

Q. And at that point, you really are talking consultingware....

A. Yes, and they think of themselves as a product company, but they're slipping down the slippery slope of not having a product. It's the typical VC-enterprise software model. I don't know why it's so common or how they get out of that cycle. They have a ton of customers they are losing money on because they have to customize their product so much, and you have customers who are so good at negotiating that [the software company] is seriously losing money on the deal, but they convince themselves that they will be a good reference customer or something.

Q. They'll make it up on the next one—famous last words....

A. And they never do.

Q. What about your software? You're selling to about 1,500 people a month; that's kind of the midpoint. Do you think midpoint to lowpoint—the under $80 piece of software—works? Or is it only at the midpoint can you see the type of growth that Fog Creek has experienced, doubling revenue every year?

A. If we were doing shareware at the 20 to 30 buck level, it would take forever to build that kind of volume. I think we have a relatively low-priced product, but it's not consumer priced really. I'll give you another example, and numbers for it, but the numbers are completely meaningless since it has been out only a month.

We have the Copilot project—remote desktop software (`http://www.copilot.com`). And it's about ten dollars a day. This is a consumer kind of $10 product. And right now, we're getting about eight users a day. It sounds low; it's significantly up from five users a day. And if you look at the trend, it's a really significant statistical growth. Although the number of users is tiny, the trend line is surprisingly clear, and the number of users we get per day is surprisingly constant.

Copilot by Fog Creek Software

Q. Let me ask you about Copilot—in a way it's a micro-ISV product.
A. It's a classic micro-ISV product, and I'm happy to talk about the numbers because anybody can figure them out. The total cost to me to develop Copilot was $80,000. That $80,000 included computers for four programmers (top-of-the-line Dell PCs with two CPUs, 2GB of memory, RAID drives, and dual 20-inch monitors, costing about $5,000 each), salary for four interns, [and] the housing for the four interns, which basically brought the cost of these interns up to that of full-time employees, and we paid an undisclosed amount of money to buy the domain name, Copilot.com, and that was about it.

So, total cost was about $80,000.
Q. It's going to take a long time to pay that off if you're talking eight sales a day....
A. Basically we figured if we get to about ten sales a day, we break even in about two years. That's not an unreasonable amount of time to make your money back; everything after that is profit. And we've already about hit that with organic marketing [and] no marketing except our blog. [This is] insignificant amounts of marketing, so we're getting insignificant sales, but we are getting organic growth. People are elated when they use Copilot, and it solves their problem in a brilliant way. It saves them $150 to call a tech support person or one of those "Geek Squad" kinds of people or to spend two hours on the phone trying to explain something that they can do in two minutes with Copilot. And these people tell their friends.

Q. So when you say organic growth, you mean there is no marketing?

A. Right. Just word of mouth. So, I already absolutely convinced we're going to make our money back. And the rate at which we've been growing in just the first month or two we've been live convinces me we're going to do a heck of lot better than just make our money back.

Q. That's a good thing. Are you going to stick with word of mouth, or are you going to actually start marketing it?

A. I think I'll stick with the word of mouth.

Q. OK, but you already have the advantage that you have an established company, you have other products, and you have a very influential blog. That's lots of presence. Let's say you're living in the sixth-floor walk-up and you've just come out with this product through the dint of working after your day job for six months, would you go word of mouth, or what would you do at that point?

A. No, that wouldn't work. Let's put it this way. The things that the geeks don't understand about sales, marketing and business, etc….the first thing they don't understand is that there's three components here: there's PR, there's marketing, and there's sales. And they confuse those things.

PR is generating free or low-cost awareness that your product exists, through publicity. And the distinction between PR and marketing is that PR is on the editorial side; it's not on the advertising side of the page. When you look at a newspaper, any child can take a newspaper and show you want the ads are and what the editorial is, and if your story is on the editorial side of the newspaper, that's PR. And there's an editorial side of the Internet too.

Q. Do blogs fit there?

A. Tell me whose blog. On my blog, I don't attempt to blog for the purpose of marketing.

Q. So PR is free and low price. It may be your blog, or it may not be.

A. I don't think a blog can do marketing.

Q. OK, how come?

A. Because who's going to read it? How are they going to find out about it? Who's going to come to your blog?

Q. Well, what would you say about Joel on Software then?

A. Ah! You see this is sort of different. Joel on Software is editorial not on the subject of my business. It's editorial about software development. It's valuable editorial; it has an audience. So, you could tell somebody I've done this little software that does digital photo albums, and you could make a blog and people will hear about it. Well, if you make one of those blogs about your cat, you're going to get the same audience as the average blog about your cat, which is zero or fifty of your friends.

There's nothing wrong with that, and it's a beautiful way to keep in touch with your friends and family. It's just not marketing.

Q. OK, so instead, let's say you are a photo whiz maven, and you put out a blog about photography and all that stuff?

A. If you can make that work for you, that's a great model. And that's my model. But a lot of people can't pull that off, and they have an ersatz-like blog. By ersatz-like blog, I mean they are doing one of two things wrong. One, they are using their blogs in a very pure marketing way, when all they do is talk about their products. They're never even going to get an audience. Usually companies do that.

And then there's that the average programmer doesn't understand the distinction between marketing and sales. Marketing is creating demand; sales is fulfilling it. Marketing is any kind of process that you follow, usually some derivative of advertising or trade shows or Web sites or any of that kind of stuff that exists for the purpose of getting people to want to buy your product. And sales is whatever processes that you have in place that exist for a person once they want to buy your product.

November 8: New York, NY
LispNYC
March 8-9: San Diego, CA
O'Reilly Emerging Technology
March 12: Austin, TX
SXSW Interactive (panelist)
March 20: Santa Clara, CA
Eclipsecon (keynote)
May 23: Wellington, NZ
Webstock

Search: [   ]

I'm your host, Joel Spolsky, a software developer in New York City. Since 2000, I've been writing about software development, management, business, and the Internet on this site. More about me.

There's a complete archive of everything going back to 2000. The home page is reserved for minor, ephemeral thoughts, but occasionally I write a longer article. You can sign up to receive email whenever this happens at the bottom of this page. We also have one of those RSS thingamajiggies. If you don't know what that is, consider yourself lucky.

This site has been translated by volunteers around the world into more than thirty languages.

Have feedback? There are several popular discussion boards on this site:

  Joel on Software
  Business of Software
  Design of Software
  Jobs
  .NET Questions
  TechInterview.org
  CityDesk
  FogBugz
  Fog Creek Copilot

You can also email me directly, although my mailbox is an official disaster area.

For my day job, I'm the CEO of Fog Creek Software, a bootstrapped software company in New York, NY.

We make FogBugz, a bug tracking system that actually works and can be used to manage everything your development does, from bug tracking to customer email to feature management

Aardvark'd DVD Goes on Sale

Monday, November 07, 2005   Link

Last March, when we were starting to plan our summer internships, I was disappointed by the massive bogusness of the so-called "business challenges" on the TV show *The Apprentice*. From the posts over on the discussion groups, it was apparent to me that people were really excited to see each new episode, and then consistently disappointed when the management challenge turned out to consist of two hours of inspecting chocolate bars in a factory, or hawking on street corners to get people to go into a restaurant. Management challenge, indeed! Those are two of the lowest-paying jobs in New York City. Most of the people on the streets handing out flyers are homeless and working for minimum wage.

At the same time, I noticed that there were very few decent documentaries about the software development process. Since the idea of our summer internship was to build a new product, from beginning to end, during the course of one summer, I thought it would be a great opportunity to have a filmmaker come into our offices and film the whole thing. And I thought that the audience that's excited to see inside the business world would be just as enthusiastic to get a view of the software development process at Fog Creek.

So I put out a call for a documentary filmmaker. We got a half-dozen serious applications and picked Lerone Wilson, a recent NYU grad, to invade our office for the summer and make a movie. Instead of paying for the production ourselves, we

Joel on Software

Going Back to the Sixth-Floor Walk-Up

Q. Going back to that sixth-floor walk-up for a second, this is their first product. It's a company of one. What would you suggest they do?

A. Let's cross off things here. They're not going to be able to do an advertising campaign. An advertising campaign doesn't work that well either. Advertising is very questionable, and I think if you ask people out in the field, they have no idea why they're advertising. Print ads/banner ads don't work.

Google AdWords will actually work, and they'll work very well, depending on how specific your product is. If your product is "nichey" enough and has keywords associated with it, Google AdWords might be a brilliant way to get your product out there.

Q. So the more of a niche product you have, the better Google AdWords work?

A. Right. So if you have a product that keeps track of the genealogy of your dairy herd, Google is going to be the best way in the world to advertise that particular thing. If you want to have an online photo album, forget it.

Q. OK, so on generic or horizontal products Google is less effective?

A. Because there's so much noise for those keywords. And actually, I think that's the best bet for a micro-ISV that wants to bootstrap. Figure out how to narrow your audience. I always make fun of the micro-ISV or the person in the sixth-floor walk-up that's doing a photo album start-up, because that's what it seems they're all doing. Programmers look at these things, and they say, that's easy. If other people are doing it, they must be making money. I can do that. But it doesn't work.

What I've told countless people who've come to me about this online photo organizer (and not one of them has taken my advice, and they should because then they would make a lot of money) is don't make the online photo organizer; make the online photo organizer for professional wedding photographers. It is shocking how much money is involved in that particular industry. So, they have money to spend. It's a much easier marketing target—all you've got to reach is the professional wedding photographers. Where are they? They're all in B&H (a very large professional photography store in New York), in the lights section.

My point being, how do you market to people having digital cameras? That's everybody! There's nothing to grab onto there. But wedding photographers? They talk to each other, they know each other, and you can look in the Yellow Pages and get the 12 wedding photographers in your city and call them up. They spend money on this kind of stuff—they have money to spend on this kind of stuff.

Now you've taken a product you know perfectly well can be used by anybody, and you've narrowed down to a very specific field. And all the sudden you'll start to discover that there are very specific problems that wedding photographers have. I could go on and on about this, but when you take a generic or horizontal product and narrow it, you almost always increase your opportunities as a micro-ISV.

Q. That's one of the best points I've heard yet.

A. It's also probably one of the most nonintuitive. And we made that mistake—that's why I know this. We made CityDesk, and it's horizontal, and lo and behold, FogBugz sold a lot better, and it's a vertical application. And if I had taken my own advice, I would have changed CityDesk, and instead of making it a content management system, I would have made it a real estate listing system for realtors who want to put pictures of their current properties up on the Web. And instead of saying *headline*, I would say *address*. And instead of saying *author*, I would say *price range*. And I would add a field for bedrooms and bathrooms. And it would be the same product, but first of all I would know how to market it [and] who my audience was, and I could charge a lot more money for it and serve their needs.

And I'm never going to be Microsoft with the content management system for realtors, but again, we're talking about micro-ISVs, and we are talking about bootstrapping. And that's the way you do it.

Q. So, going back, we were talking about the three things that geeks don't get: PR, marketing, and sales.

A. And we don't get them either. Let me talk about them in the context of Fog Creek Software. PR we had—Joel on Software was very successful PR, and that drives awareness and a lot of turnover basically. A blog is a good cheap way to get PR, but there are other ways—you can do things in your community; there's lots of books about guerilla marketing…about getting awareness for your product by doing stunts that cause the local media to show up. Although Joel on Software generated traffic, it took four or five years before we got the interest of Crain's *New York Business* that now is consistently running stories about us.

Q. It's one of the things you have to work at for a while….

A. Whether by luck or whatever, we're strong in that area because of Joel on Software. Marketing? We are an absolute zero. We've never tried to do it. We don't know how to do it. We don't know if works. We don't believe it works most of the time. A bootstrapping company never had money to pay for ads, so we didn't do it.

Q. So do you run Google AdWords?

A. Nope. No advertising, zilch.

Q. So for purposes of Fog Creek, marketing just isn't a factor?

A. Right. Traditional marketing and advertising and that kind of stuff—we've never had a marketing person; it's never been done here. Now the third part is sales, which traditionally has been a weakness of ours. Only a few weeks ago did we hire a person to figure out the sales thing. And his job is to figure out what procedures we are going to start following and who we are going to hire so we follow up more reliably with people and actually make more sales. That's one of the things we've been bad at, and I hope we're going to improve.

Q. Let's say you had to do it all over again, right now, in 2005. Things have moved along. Where do you see this whole desktop versus software as a Web service thing going?

A. I wouldn't touch the desktop anymore, but that's just me.

Q. So the whole Ajax, Web 2.0, smart client thing is the end of the story for desktop software?

A. I think so. It's kind of weird. Copilot is software as a service, and it's something that just cannot be done on the Web, i.e., remote-controlling somebody else's desktop. Copilot essentially downloads a little app that makes the service possible. That's the core of the service, but it's wrapped in this Web site you go to. And that's what makes it so easy and simple. It makes it so easy for us to upgrade, and every time we find a bug we fix it and get out there the next day, because nobody keeps these little apps on their desktops; they delete them as soon as they're done using them.

So even though it's something that just cannot be done on the Web, we do it on the Web.

Q. Maybe the question isn't desktop versus Web, but service versus product?

A. You know, there are still people with mainframes. And there are still people who go to movies even though we have DVDs; it takes a while for the world to change. And the world does change. I really feel like we had the mainframes, then we had the microcomputers, and then we had the Windows GUI Macintosh generation, and then we had the Web generation. But the Web didn't completely take over from the Windows GUI thing because we really didn't have Ajax, and now we're starting to have Ajax, and I'm really starting to think, a couple more versions of the Web browsers and some clever work, and that will be where the bulk of development is going to be done.

I would say at this point any kind of database in-house development anyone does, it's just nuts to do that any other way than on the Web.

Q. Based on going from you and your partner in 2000 to seven staff now, what should a micro-ISV founder be looking for from that first hire?

A. Well, gee, I'm really good at telling people who not to hire. If you have any kind of doubt, then no. With your first few hires, the more well-rounded they are, the happier you're going to be and the more different holes they can fill. When you're a micro-ISV, you're doing what would be at General Motors 370 different jobs. You're a specialist in all 370. And so, if you're good in only 216 of those, then obviously you want to hire someone who can do at least 100. And that's really what it is—trying to get things covered.

It's sort of a hard problem as a micro-ISV. Chances are the average micro-ISV that doesn't want to do consulting to pay the bills is going to have to hire people before they really have the ability to pay them. They might think they have the ability to pay them based on incoming revenues, but there's no sort of stability there yet. That means you're probably going to have to hire somebody who is willing to take equity and has an entrepreneurial spirit. And that's a whole different type of people than those who answer the Help Wanted ads on Craigslist.

Q. How do you with a small staff of owners and employees maintain who's in charge?

A. That one I can't really give good advice on because it depends so much on the situation and the particular personalities.

Q. What about outsourcing and offshoring? I've read what you've written that a software company that outsources development has given away why they exist.

A. Kind of, yeah.

Q. On the other hand, there's a report out today that one-half of the start-up companies in Silicon Valley outsource....

A. Wow. That's great! It's good to know I'm competing against idiots who have no control of their software—that has an employee pool that has no stake whatsoever in their success. That's great, for me; suicide for them. The only company I can think of that was a successful start-up with employees not in the same country, or wherever, is Skype. They had their employees in Estonia, and they were in the Netherlands. But you know what? They were employees, and they had stock.

Q. So any start-up that goes with outsourcing development is doomed?

A. They have a huge hurdle to overcome because they're working with one hand tied behind their backs. That's really what I feel.

Q. How about the typical way software gets written; you know the "eat pizza and sleep under the desk and work every hour until it's done" approach? Do you think that's the way micro-ISV should develop? Or is there a better way?

A. We did it the nine-to-five, professional way. We took off weekends; we didn't work very hard on weekends kind of stuff. But I think the "sleep under the desk" approach does have a lot to be said for it for the version 1.0 launch. There's something to be said for both ways. The truth is, if I saw a company like Fog Creek, that's starting a company, and they say, "We're not going to work ourselves too hard. We're very strictly nine-to-five company. We believe in the 40-hour thing, etc.," you sort of question the dedication a little bit. Maybe.

I can give you an example. There was a start-up called Westside. It was a start-up created by about 45 ex-Microsoft employees, mostly from the Visual Basic and Access teams. These guys idea was to make something like Access but entirely on the Web. The whole software as a service idea, way before its time, in 1998. They were all ex-Microsoft employees with tons of stock options, so they could afford to go an awfully long time without getting any kind of revenue.

One of the things I remember about them is that they built a company that was operationally almost like Microsoft, in the sense that they gave everybody private offices with doors and windows, and they gave everybody excellent benefits, vacations, and stuff like that. And these people were not like young Microsoft people; these people we kind of like Microsoft middle-age people who don't quite work as hard as the people right out of college who don't have friends.

There's sort of two demographics at Microsoft. There's the people who just got out college [and] don't know anyone in Seattle, and they have nothing else to do but just work around the clock.

Q. You make it sound like a cult!

A. It kind of is. And they love that kind of stuff. And there's a good reason people love to work at Microsoft—they love to program. So they do that for a while. And eventually they find a girlfriend somehow, and they get married, and they have kids, and now suddenly they're all in their Saabs going home at exactly 5:05 p.m., choking up the highways around Redmond, Washington. And that's sort of a second category of people, and those people sort of move into middle management and don't really get as much done as they used to in their golden days. And those are the people who created Westside to a large extent; they were already past the energy stage.

They did build a product, but it took them quite a while. They had all the trappings of success—the very expensive offices. But their product wasn't that good; I don't think they ever had any revenue.

Q. OK, [a couple] more questions. How old are you?

A. 40.

Q. Well, you're past the "don't have any friends/sleeping under the desk" stage. So here's the question: are we too old to do this? I'm 48 by the way. There are people out there who argue that starting companies should be done by adolescents, if not pre-adolescents. Where do you stand on that?

A. I look at these people…very smart people like Aaron Swartz who is starting companies with Paul Graham, who is pre-adolescent, whom I consider to be very smart, but he doesn't know shit. I think my summer interns who are Aaron's age were able to build a whole product and get it selling and shipping (and it's going to break even pretty soon) in one summer because they had a 20-page spec that I wrote for them. All I did was point them in the right direction and say "Go." And if they started to veer off-course, I'd say, "Let me tell you a little story about something that happened to me 16 years ago." And they went back on course.

Paul's young crew, with all power to them, there's something to be said for very young people, because they don't know what they don't know, so they extrapolate like crazy. They can't interpolate like me. And when you're dealing with technology that's changing all the time, it causes them not to be blind to certain things that I'm blind to. So, for example, they would have made a Web content management system while I was still trying to make a Windows content management system, because I'm too old. Because I'm interpolating and they're extrapolating.

Q. Well, you're saying two things at once. Or is there is something to be said for the young person model because they don't know what they don't know?

A. So they invent the future often.

Q. OK, so how about us older folk. Give us some reason not to be whining in to our tank of oxygen over here!

A. Well, let me tell you about how I feel personally. Which is this: what keeps me interested in Fog Creek is the fact that every year it grows, and therefore the problems we have to face on a daily basis change and evolve. And the numbers grow. To the same extent I'm no longer impressed by *"Woo-hoo, I made $100,000. That's OK, I made $200,000."* To some extent, you might be desensitized by doing the same thing again and again, but the great thing about having a growing company is that the growth itself means that it changes all the time so that your job is different everyday. And you evolve in your job.

Last year, everything for me was about recruiting [and] finding the next generation of people. And then there was the whole summer of Copilot, figuring out how to get interns all excited about launching a quick, fast product in a new business. And right now, for the next few weeks, I am going to be obsessing over reducing the amount of work it takes to process purchase orders and checks. So, the business as it grows creates new challenges for you.

Developing at the Bleeding Edge

Q. On a different subject, should micro-ISVs focus on the latest hot technologies? Should they go where the cutting edge is being cut?

A. Probably not. It probably means you're talking with people at conferences instead of your customers. Your customers probably couldn't care less. Let's say you're doing the photo album software thing. Can you imagine talking to a wedding photographer and having them say, "It would be cool if you had some Ajax here"? They're going to say, "I need a way to convert a color photo to a black-and-white photo at the click of a button." Those are going to be the terms they use.

There is one slight exception: if you're first with some exciting new trend, you do have an opportunity to be talked about or passed around. So you've got this one minute to do something, to catch some PR, if you do something that happens to catch on really fast and draw some attention. But that's not a strong or sustainable advantage.

Q. So your customers aren't interested in the latest and greatest, and it may not give you much of an advantage unless you're first?

A. Right. There are ways of using the latest and greatest building tools to build something cool, but everybody has the same tools too, so it doesn't necessarily get you a competitive advantage.

Q. So how as a developer do you keep up with all the new technology?

A. You don't and nobody is, and that's actually a serious threat to Microsoft at this point. It's something I've said again and again. They are turning out new developer technologies faster than developers can pay attention to them. And they really need to calm down. They are adding features to C# [that] are completely unnecessary, that nobody has time to even read about, so they can give Microsoft the feedback to say, "These features are unnecessary and just clutter your language, and we don't need them."

Q. So what should a micro-ISV developer do?

A. Pick one tool and know it obsessively well, and you're going to get stuck with it for five or ten years. The thing about being an ISV and using technology is that you just can't use the latest and greatest. We're stuck using VBScript because we're not going to port our application. It's not worth it. There's no monetary value in porting to new tools. And so we're using very, very old technology here and it works fine, but it's not the greatest and there are advantages to moving, but there are even bigger disadvantages. So we're sort of stuck with this tool, but that's OK.

When you're an ISV because of the cost of porting [and] because your application is going to go for ten or twenty years, you are almost inevitably going to be using what appears to be crappy old technology at any given time. But that's OK—that's the life you choose. If you want to use the latest and greatest at all times, go do in-house development for an insurance company, because they are always doing a new projects, and you can probably convince your boss who's probably not a programmer that porting to C# 3.0 is the most important thing you can do. He'll probably fall for it.

Q. Any advice on anything for a micro-ISV or somebody who wants to be a micro-ISV?

A. Don't do it, you're crazy!

Q. OK, why?

A. I don't really know how to put it. You have to know some advantage you have. If your idea of why your business is going to succeed doesn't have a little bit of magic in there somewhere, that you're sure is going to work, it's not really going to succeed.

Q. By magic, you mean...?

A. Let me see if I can try to explain this. The reason that I knew that Fog Creek was going to work was that we had the following piece of magic: we were going to do consulting, and that would generate cash that would keep us in business long enough to be able to become a software company. We could fail 27 times at making a software product, and if we succeeded on the 28th time, that would be great. The only possible way that Fog Creek could have closed down is if we didn't have enough consulting revenue to keep even one person fed, which is a pretty low barrier. So that was our piece of magic.

The Skype's piece of magic was that people have to pay per minute for phone calls and yet they have unlimited access Internet, and nobody had made a tool for them to actually make phone calls for free. The Kazaa piece of magic—pulled off by the same people—was you could steal records, and you wouldn't have to pay for your records. And they were successful because of that piece of magic.

The PayPal piece of magic was that when you sign up for the account, you get ten free dollars, which you could then take out. The other piece of magic was that you didn't have to wait for the check to arrive for your eBay purchase.

One more example: the Copilot piece of magic was that most of the code we needed to do the remote desktop feature that's the core of Copilot was available in a GPL [General Public License] open source piece of source code we could use as a starting point. And without actually violating their license in any way, we were able to launch a service with very little effort, and we knew that we had searched the world high and low, every possible Web page, to accomplish this particular feature without complicated setup, and we knew we could make a faster, easier setup.

Just by making the setup easier we knew that we could make something that would solve a known problem in a way we couldn't find that anybody else had solved. So that was the magic there.

The other magic that's going on obviously for Fog Creek Software is Joel on Software—a built-in audience that doesn't cost us anything. It's some extra thing that gives us a competitive advantage that has enabled us to be successful. But if you can't tell me what the piece of magic is your micro-ISV is going to have, it probably won't really get there.

You've Reached the Bottom Line

My editor, Jonathan Hassell, rightfully pointed out the first time I submitted this chapter that I had neglected to come to a conclusion in this book. He's absolutely right. As a micro-ISV myself in the "emerging" category, I don't know how the story ends.

But I do know, thanks to all the people who kindly gave of their time for this chapter and all of the other people interviewed for this book, that most likely, the ending is going to be a pretty good one.

Micro-ISVs aren't a business fad that will run its course in a year and disappear. Micro-ISVs are a real alternative to the venture capital companies that come and often go. About one billion people are sharing the same connection called the Internet now, and if you can find a problem just a tiny part of that one billion have, and solve it, you too can succeed.

But you have to try.

Walt Disney, a man who knew a considerable amount about making something out of nothing with some imagination and a lot of hard work, is cited as the person who first said, "Better to have tried and failed than never tried at all."[2]

Maybe so: of course, it's best not to believe everything you read on the Internet! But one thing is for sure: if you've got the drive and the need and the perseverance, you too can go from vision to reality.

I wish you the best of luck; drop me a line at bobw@safarisoftware.com, and let me know how things have worked out for you.

-30-

(That's old reporter-speak for "You've come to the end of the story; now get out there, and do something!")

---

2. http://www.inventionshow.com/17_inv_community/200303/04_entrepreneur_tips.shtml

Appendix

Writing an appendix for a book so intimately tied to the Internet is something of an exercise in frustration. If you'd like to save yourself the typing, visit `http://safarisoftware.com/mivr.htm` where you'll find a clickable version of this appendix.

Chapter 1: "Having a Vision"

Books

- Bolles, Richard Nelson. *What Color Is Your Parachute? 2005: A Practical Manual for Job-Hunters and Career-Changers*. Berkeley, CA: Ten Speed Press, 2004.

Web Sites

Industries and Markets

- `http://www.jobhuntersbible.com/`

- `http://www.labormarketinfo.edd.ca.gov/cgi/career/?PageID=3&SubID=139`

- `http://www.virtualpet.com/industry/howto/search.htm#identify`

- `http://www.hoovers.com/free/ind/dir.xhtml`

- `http://library.geneseo.edu/info/sirind.shtm`

Chapter 2: "Developing the Micro-ISV Way"

Books

User Interface

- Cooper, Allen, and Robert Reimann. *About Face 2.0: The Essentials of Interactive Design*. Hoboken, NJ: Wiley, 2003.

- Gunderloy, Mike. *Developer to Designer: GUI Design for the Busy Developer*. Alameda, CA: Sybex, 2005.

- Snyder, Carolyn. *Paper Prototyping: The Fast and Easy Way to Design and Refine User Interfaces*. San Francisco, CA: Morgan Kaufmann, 2003.

- Spolsky, Joel. *User Interface Design for Programmers*. Berkeley, CA: Apress, 2001.

Programming

- Gunderloy, Mike. *Coder to Developer: Tools and Strategies for Delivering Your Software*. Alameda, CA: Sybex, 2004.

- Hunt, Andrew, and David Thomas. *The Pragmatic Programmer*. Boston, MA: Addison Wesley, 2000.

- McCarthy, Jim. *Dynamics of Software Development*. Redmond, WA: Microsoft Press, 1995.

- McConnell, Steve. *Code Complete, Second Edition*. Redmond, WA: Microsoft Press, 2004.

NUnit

- Hamilton, Bill. *NUnit Pocket Reference*. Sebastopol, CA: O'Reilly, 2004.

Test Driven Development (TDD)

- Newkirk, James W., and Alexei A. Vorontsov. *Test-Driven Development in Microsoft .NET*. Redmond, WA: Microsoft Press, 2004.

Web Sites

Paper Prototyping

- http://www.paperprototyping.com/download.html

- http://www.useit.com/alertbox/20030414.html

Development Infrastructure

- http://sourcegear.com

- http://www.perforce.com/perforce/products.html

- http://www.automatedqa.com

- http://www.vmware.com

The Beta Advantage

- http://www.infacta.com/asp/common/groupmail.asp

- http://www.mailermailer.com

NUnit

- http://www.nunit.org

- http://www.15seconds.com/issue/040922.htm

- http://www.methodsandtools.com/archive/archive.php?id=20

Test Driven Development (TDD)

- http://www.testdriven.com/modules/news/

- http://www.codeproject.com/dotnet/tdd_in_dotnet.asp

- http://www.methodsandtools.com/archive/archive.php?id=20

Chapter 3: "Presenting the Product"

Books

Internet Marketing

- Godin, Seth. *Permission Marketing*. New York, NY: Simon & Schuster, 1999.

- Godin, Seth. *Unleashing the Ideavirus*. New York, NY: Simon & Schuster, 2000.

- Locke, Christopher, Rick Levine, Doc Searls, and David Weinberger. *The Cluetrain Manifesto*. New York, NY: Perseus, 2000.

Marketing (and Business) Plans

- Bangs Jr., David. *The Market Planning Guide, Sixth Edition*. Chicago, IL: Dearborn, 2002.

- Hiam, Alexander. *Marketing Kit for Dummies, Second Edition*. Hoboken, NJ: Wiley, 2005.

- Kennedy, Dan S. *The Ultimate Marketing Plan*. Cincinnati, OH: Adams Media, 2000.

- Peterson, Steven, and Peter Jaret. *Business Plans Kit for Dummies*. Hoboken, NJ: Wiley, 2001.

- Wilson, Ralph F. *Planning Your Internet Marketing Strategy*. Hoboken, NJ: Wiley, 2002.

Payment Processing

- Sofield, Shannon, Dave Nielsen, and Dave Burchell. *PayPal Hacks*. Sebastopol, CA: O'Reilly, 2004.

Web Sites

Internet Marketing

- http://www.cluetrain.com

How to Define Your Micro-ISV

- http://www.ahundredmonkeys.com

- http://www.igorinternational.com/process/naming-guide-product-company-
  names.php

Graphics and Micro-ISVs

- http://www.userscape.com/blog/2005/01/31/creating-a-business-logo/

- http://www.makalumedia.com/

- http://www.flickr.com/

- http://www.flickr.com/creativecommons/

- http://creativecommons.org/

- http://www.techsmith.com/products/snagit/default.asp

- http://www.yessoftware.com/products/product.php?product_id=19

- http://www.pixelmill.com

- http://oswd.org/

How to Register Your Micro-ISV's Internet Domain

- http://godaddy.com

Payment Processors

- http://www.digitalriver.com/corporate/solutions00.shtml

- http://paypal.com

- http://2checkout.com

Recommended Hosting Companies

- http://alentus.com

- http://www.serverintellect.com

All About Blogging

- http://www.technorati.com/

- http://blogger.com

- http://spaces.msn.com/

- http://typepad.com

- http://wordpress.org/

- http://www.sixapart.com/movabletype/

Chapter 4: "Business Is Business"

Books

Legal and Business Guides

- Daily, Frederick W. *Tax Savvy for Small Business, Eighth Edition*. Berkeley, CA: Nolo, 2004.

- Elias, Stephen. *Trademark: Legal Care for Your Business & Product Name, Sixth Edition*. Berkeley, CA: Nolo, 2003.

- Fishman, Stephen. *Copyright Your Software, Third Edition*. Berkeley, CA: Nolo, 2001.

- Fishman, Stephen. *Web & Software Development, Third Edition*. Berkeley, CA: Nolo, 2002.

- Mancuso, Anthony. *The Corporate Minutes Book, Second Edition*. Berkeley, CA: Nolo, 2002.

- Mancuso, Anthony. *Nolo's Quick LLC: All You Need To Know About Limited Liability Companies*. Berkeley, CA: Nolo, 2004.

- Stim, Richard, and Stephen Fishman. *Nondisclosure Agreements*. Berkeley, CA: Nolo, 2001.

Time Management, Productivity, Task Management, and Getting Things Done (GTD)

- Allen, David. *Getting Things Done: The Art of Stress-Free Productivity*. East Rutherford, NJ: Viking Penguin, 2001.

- Allen, David. *Ready For Anything*. East Rutherford, NJ: Viking Penguin, 2003.

- Csikszentmihalyi, Mihaly. *Finding Flow*. New York, NY: Basic Books, 1997.

- Kennedy, Dan. *No B.S. Time Management for Entrepreneurs*. Irvine, CA: Entrepreneur Press, 2004.

- Koch, Richard. *The 80/20 Principle*. New York, NY: Doubleday, 1998.

- Morgenstern, Julie. *Organizing from the Inside Out*. New York, NY: Henry Holt & Co., 1998.

- Morgenstern, Julie. *Time Management from the Inside Out.* New York, NY: Henry Holt & Co., 2000.

Web Sites

Small Business Administration (SBA) Resources

- http://www.sba.gov/starting_business/startup/entrepreneurialtest.html
- http://marriottschool.byu.edu/cfe/startingout/test.cfm

U.S. Legal Entities

- http://dbaform.com
- http://kepler.ss.ca.gov/list.html

How to Set Up a Business in the United Kingdom

- http://startups.co.uk
- http://www.mybusiness.co.uk
- http://www.businesslink.gov.uk
- http://www.hmrc.gov.uk

How to Set Up a Business in Australia

- http://www.search.asic.gov.au/gns001.html
- http://www.business.gov.au
- http://abr.gov.au
- http://www.business.gov.au
- http://www.ato.gov.au/content/downloads/NAT3014-07-2005.pdf
- http://www.bus.vic.gov.au
- http://www.sbcs.org.au/
- http://www.smallbiz.nsw.gov.au

Getting Things Done

- http://www.davidco.com/products.php
- http://livemeeting.com/archive
- http://www.davidco.com/productDetail.php?id=63&IDoption=20

- http://safarisoftware.com

- http://www.davidco.com/tips_tools/tip16.html

- http://mindjet.com

- http://www.actioneer.com

- http://wiki.osafoundation.org/bin/view/Projects/ChandlerHome

End User License Agreements (EULAs)

- http://en.wikipedia.org/wiki/Open_source_licenses

- http://www.eff.org/wp/eula.php

- http://www.soft14.com/upload/software_000039.htm

- http://www.megadox.com/documents.php/589?a_id=74

How to Legally Protect Your Software

- http://www.uspto.gov/tcas/

- http://legalzoom.com

- http://www.nolo.com/index.cfm

- http://asbdc-us.org/

Chapter 5: "Focusing on the Customer"

Books

Bug/Project Management

- Gunderloy, Mike. *Painless Project Management with FogBugz*. Berkeley, CA: Apress, 2005

Google AdWords

- Goodman, Andrew. *Winning Results with Google AdWords*. Emeryville, CA: Osborne, 2005.

- Hill, Brad. *Building Your Business with Google for Dummies*. Hoboken, NJ: Wiley, 2004.

Web Sites

Specific Internet Marketing Segment (SIMS) Planner and Market Action Planner (MAP)

- http://mymicroisv.com

Email

- http://www.ftc.gov/bcp/conline/pubs/buspubs/canspam.htm

- http://emailmarketingmetrics.com

Micro-ISV Discussion Board Software

- http://www.fogcreek.com

- http://www.phpbb.com/support/

- http://www.phpbb.com/downloads.php

- http://www.invision.com

Search Engines and Directories

- http://dir.yahoo.com/Computers_and_Internet/Internet/World_Wide_Web/
  Searching_the_Web/Search_Engines_and_Directories/Submit_a_Site/

- http://dir.yahoo.com/Business_and_Economy/Business_to_Business/
  Marketing_and_Advertising/Internet/Promotion/

- http://dir.yahoo.com/Computers_and_Internet/Internet/World_Wide_Web/
  Searching_the_Web/Search_Engines_and_Directories/Submit_a_Site/

- http://dir.yahoo.com/business_and_economy/business_to_business/
  marketing_and_advertising/internet/promotion/Software/

- http://dir.yahoo.com/computers_and_internet/internet/world_wide_web/
  Site_Announcement_and_Promotion/

How to Submit Your Site

- http://www.submitexpress.com/submit2500.html

- http://www.axandra-web-site-promotion-software-tool.com/index.htm

- http://www.prioritysubmit.com

- http://www.trellian.com/swolf/index.html

Google AdWords

- http://adwords.google.com

- http://www.google.com/adwords/learningcenter/

Download Sites

- http://download.com

- http://office.microsoft.com/en-us/marketplace/default.aspx

Chapter 6: "Welcome to Your Industry"

Books

I can't recommend any books for this category firsthand.

Web Sites

Microsoft

- http://msdn.microsoft.com/

- http://msdn.microsoft.com/isv/isvbuddy/default.aspx

- http://www.windowsmarketplacelabs.com

- http://www.microsoft-watch.com/

- http://minimsft.blogspot.com/

Business Intelligence

- http://pubsub.com

- http://technorati.com

- http://blogsearch.google.com/

Micro-ISV Communities

- http://discuss.joelonsoftware.com/?biz

- http://aisip.com/index.php

- http://www.asp-shareware.org/

- http://www.edu-soft.org

Index

forums.apress.com

JOIN THE APRESS FORUMS AND BE PART OF OUR COMMUNITY. You'll find discussions that cover topics of interest to IT professionals, programmers, and enthusiasts just like you. If you post a query to one of our forums, you can expect that some of the best minds in the business—especially Apress authors, who all write with *The Expert's Voice*™—will chime in to help you. Why not aim to become one of our most valuable participants (MVPs) and win cool stuff? Here's a sampling of what you'll find:

DATABASES
Data drives everything.

Share information, exchange ideas, and discuss any database programming or administration issues.

INTERNET TECHNOLOGIES AND NETWORKING
Try living without plumbing (and eventually IPv6).

Talk about networking topics including protocols, design, administration, wireless, wired, storage, backup, certifications, trends, and new technologies.

JAVA
We've come a long way from the old Oak tree.

Hang out and discuss Java in whatever flavor you choose: J2SE, J2EE, J2ME, Jakarta, and so on.

MAC OS X
All about the Zen of OS X.

OS X is both the present and the future for Mac apps. Make suggestions, offer up ideas, or boast about your new hardware.

OPEN SOURCE
Source code is good; understanding (open) source is better.

Discuss open source technologies and related topics such as PHP, MySQL, Linux, Perl, Apache, Python, and more.

PROGRAMMING/BUSINESS
Unfortunately, it is.

Talk about the Apress line of books that cover software methodology, best practices, and how programmers interact with the "suits."

WEB DEVELOPMENT/DESIGN
Ugly doesn't cut it anymore, and CGI is absurd.

Help is in sight for your site. Find design solutions for your projects and get ideas for building an interactive Web site.

SECURITY
Lots of bad guys out there—the good guys need help.

Discuss computer and network security issues here. Just don't let anyone else know the answers!

TECHNOLOGY IN ACTION
Cool things. Fun things.

It's after hours. It's time to play. Whether you're into LEGO® MINDSTORMS™ or turning an old PC into a DVR, this is where technology turns into fun.

WINDOWS
No defenestration here.

Ask questions about all aspects of Windows programming, get help on Microsoft technologies covered in Apress books, or provide feedback on any Apress Windows book.

HOW TO PARTICIPATE:
Go to the Apress Forums site at **http://forums.apress.com/**.
Click the New User link.